INTELLIGENCE ANALYSIS AS DISCOVERY OF EVIDENCE, HYPOTHESES, AND ARGUMENTS: CONNECTING THE DOTS

This unique book on intelligence analysis covers several vital but often overlooked topics. It teaches the evidential and inferential issues involved in "connecting the dots" to draw defensible and persuasive conclusions from masses of evidence: from observations we make, or questions we ask, we generate alternative hypotheses as explanations or answers; we make use of our hypotheses to generate new lines of inquiry and discover new evidence; and we test the hypotheses with the discovered evidence.

To facilitate understanding of these issues and enable the performance of complex analyses, the book introduces an intelligent analytical tool, called Disciple-CD. Readers will practice with Disciple-CD and learn how to formulate hypotheses; develop arguments that reduce complex hypotheses to simpler ones; collect evidence to evaluate the simplest hypotheses; and assess the relevance and the believability of evidence, which combine in complex ways to determine its inferential force and the probabilities of the hypotheses.

Gheorghe Tecuci (Ph.D., University of Paris-South, July 1988, and Polytechnic Institute of Bucharest, December 1988) is Professor of Computer Science and Director of the Learning Agents Center in the Volgenau School of Engineering of George Mason University, Member of the Romanian Academy, and former Chair of Artificial Intelligence in the Center for Strategic Leadership of the U.S. Army War College.

David A. Schum (Ph.D., Ohio State University, 1964) is Emeritus Professor of Systems Engineering, Operations Research, and Law, as well as Chief Scientist of the Learning Agents Center at George Mason University. He is also Honorary Professor of Evidence Science at University College London.

Dorin Marcu (Ph.D., George Mason University, 2009) is Research Assistant Professor, as well as Senior Software and Knowledge Engineer in the Learning Agents Center, Volgenau School of Engineering, George Mason University.

Mihai Boicu (Ph.D., George Mason University, 2003) is Associate Professor of Information Sciences and Technology and Associate Director of the Learning Agents Center in the Volgenau School of Engineering of George Mason University.

Intelligence Analysis as Discovery of Evidence, Hypotheses, and Arguments

Connecting the Dots

GHEORGHE TECUCI

George Mason University

DAVID A. SCHUM

George Mason University

DORIN MARCU

George Mason University

MIHAI BOICU

George Mason University

CAMBRIDGE
UNIVERSITY PRESS

CAMBRIDGE
UNIVERSITY PRESS

One Liberty Plaza, 20th Floor, New York, NY 10006, USA

Cambridge University Press is part of the University of Cambridge.

It furthers the University's mission by disseminating knowledge in the pursuit of
education, learning, and research at the highest international levels of excellence.

www.cambridge.org
Information on this title: www.cambridge.org/9781107122604

First published 2016

Printed in the United States of America by Sheridan Books, Inc.

A catalog record for this publication is available from the British Library.

Library of Congress Cataloging in Publication Data
Names: Tecuci, Gheorghe, author. | Schum, David A., author. | Marcu, Dorin, author. | Boicu, Mihai, author.
Title: Intelligence analysis as discovery of evidence, hypotheses, and arguments : connecting the dots /
Gheorghe Tecuci, David A. Schum, Dorin Marcu, Mihai Boicu.
Description: New York NY : Cambridge University Press, [2016] | Includes bibliographical references and index.
Identifiers: LCCN 2015042657 | ISBN 9781107122604 (Hardback : alk. paper)
Subjects: LCSH: Intelligence service–Methodology. | Evidence. | Inference. | Reasoning–Data processing.
Classification: LCC JF1525.I6 T44 2016 | DDC 327.12–dc23 LC record available at http://lccn.loc.gov/2015042657

ISBN 978-1-107-12260-4 Hardback

Contents

Contents

Preface

BOOK PURPOSE

This textbook has been written for those studying the process of drawing conclusions from masses of evidence resulting from extensive investigations in a variety of contexts, including intelligence analysis, cybersecurity, criminal investigations, and military and business inferences and decisions. Many universities now offer undergraduate and graduate courses concerning these activities. These courses are offered in order to provide introductory preparation for persons contemplating future work in these contexts. These courses have also been of interest to persons having various levels of past experience in these activities, but who are seeking additional knowledge concerning matters their current work requires.

As you see, our book's subtitle is a frequently used metaphor: *Connecting the Dots*. This metaphor seems appropriate in characterizing the evidential and inferential matters discussed in our book. The metaphor may have gained its current popularity following the terrorist attacks in New York City and Washington, D.C., on September 11, 2001. It was frequently said that the intelligence services did not connect the dots appropriately in order to have possibly prevented the catastrophes that occurred. Since then, we have seen and heard this metaphor applied in the news media to inferences in a very wide array of contexts in addition to the aforementioned intelligence, legal, military, and business contexts. For example, we have seen it applied to allegedly faulty medical diagnoses; to allegedly faulty conclusions in historical studies; to allegedly faulty or unpopular governmental decisions; and in discussions involving the conclusions reached by competing politicians. What is also true is that the commentators on television and radio, or the sources of written accounts of inferential failures, never tell us what they mean by the phrase "connecting the dots." A natural explanation is that they have never even considered what this phrase means and what it might involve.

Our major objective in this book is to provide accurate, useful, and extensive information about the evidential and inferential issues encountered by persons whose tasks require them to "connect the dots" to draw conclusions from masses of different kinds of evidence that come from a variety of different sources. Our book covers several absolutely vital topics that are either slighted or overlooked completely in other works concerning these tasks.

As you will see from this textbook, we have made a detailed study of what "connecting the dots" entails. We have found this metaphor very useful, and quite intuitive, in illustrating the extraordinary complexity of the evidential and inferential reasoning required to draw *defensible and persuasive conclusions* from *masses of evidence* of all kinds from a variety of different sources. The conclusions drawn in these contexts, as well as in many others, must rest on arguments that are *defensible* and *persuasive*. As we all know from experience, not all defensible arguments are persuasive and not all persuasive arguments are defensible. These conclusions, which rest on evidence, are necessarily probabilistic in nature because our evidence is always *incomplete* (we can look for more, if we have time), usually *inconclusive* (it is consistent with the truth of more than one hypothesis or possible explanation), frequently *ambiguous* (we cannot always determine exactly what the evidence is telling us), commonly *dissonant* (some of it favors one hypothesis or possible explanation but other evidence favors other hypotheses), and with various degrees of *believability* shy of perfection.

Thus one thing necessary in the study of argument construction is substantial information concerning the evidential foundations of arguments. Careful study of these evidential foundations requires consideration of the properties, uses, discovery, and marshaling of evidence. Our book covers these foundations in detail and presents a scientific approach to "connecting the dots," where imaginative and critical reasoning are used to establish and defend the three major credentials of evidence: its *relevance*, *believability or credibility*, and *inferential force or weight*. This distinguishes our work from the many other works on the related topic of *critical reasoning* in which these foundations are either slighted or ignored.

But training in the evidential reasoning tasks required to "connect the dots" cannot be learned effectively just by listening to someone discuss his or her own analyses or just by giving students lectures and assigned readings on the topics. What is absolutely necessary is *regular practice involving analyses of evidence* using either hypothetical situations or examples drawn from actual situations. In short, evidential analysis is mastered best by performing analysis contrived to illustrate the wide variety of subtleties or complexities so often encountered in actual evidential analysis. Moreover, complex analysis cannot easily be performed by hand, but requires the use of advanced analytic tools. Thus this book also introduces an intelligent analytic tool, called Disciple-CD (Disciple cognitive assistant for Connecting the Dots).

Disciple-CD is a knowledge-based software system that incorporates a significant amount of knowledge about evidence and its properties, uses, and discovery to help you acquire the knowledge, skills, and abilities involved in discovering and processing of evidence and in drawing defensible and persuasive conclusions from it, by employing an effective learning-by-doing approach. You will practice and learn how to link evidence to hypotheses through abductive, deductive, and inductive reasoning that establish the basic credentials of evidence: its relevance, believability or credibility, and inferential force or weight. You will experiment with "what-if" scenarios and study the influence of various assumptions on the final result of analysis. So, your learning experience will be a joint venture involving this book together with your interaction with Disciple-CD.

You will have access to the Disciple-CD system as you read this book. As you will see in the following chapters of this book, a variety of vital information about evidential reasoning in intelligence analysis is presented. As we present this information, you will be asked to use Disciple-CD at various points to study and construct specific examples of matters and procedures described in the book. Here you encounter the reasoning and tutoring capabilities of Disciple-CD. This system is truly a "smart" system since it has itself already "learned" many of the evidential and inferential elements required in complex intelligence analysis. This allows Disciple-CD to be a valuable tutor since it knows what questions to ask you, and that you should answer, as you confront the various problems you and Disciple-CD will address. Therefore, Disciple-CD will be a most valuable guide along the route to your "hands-on" learning experience concerning some truly complex matters encountered in intelligence analysis.

To support further the learning by doing of intelligence analysis, each chapter contains a list of review questions. Answers to these questions are provided to the instructors using the book in their courses.

This textbook is written in a style congenial to the interests of student analysts regardless of their prior background and training. It will teach you basic knowledge about the properties, uses, discovery, and marshaling of evidence to show you what is involved in assessing the relevance, believability, and inferential force credentials of evidence. It includes a wide array of examples of the use of the Disciple-CD system and hands-on exercises involving both real and hypothetical cases chosen to help you recognize and evaluate many of the complex elements of the analyses you are learning to perform.

BOOK CONTENTS

Here is a route or map we will follow in the learning venture you will have with the assistance of Disciple-CD. Chapter 1 is introductory in nature and includes discussion of the problems we all face in forming defensible and persuasive conclusions about events in a nonstationary world that keeps changing all the while we are trying to understand events that we have observed. In the process, we will also provide an account of the process of "connecting the dots" and what this process actually entails. As you well know, critics of our intelligence services abound in the media. A very frequent charge made by these critics is that intelligence analysts are deficient in the task of connecting the dots. A major problem is that these critics have almost no awareness themselves of what is actually involved in connecting the dots. When examined carefully, the task of connecting dots is astonishingly difficult, even under the best of conditions. Careful study of the topics included in this joint learning venture involving Disciple-CD should, among other things, assist intelligence analysts to respond more effectively to their critics.

Chapter 2 addresses one of the most difficult phases in "connecting the dots": Marshaling thoughts and evidence for imaginative analysis. It presents seven heuristics that take the form of conceptual magnets that attract interesting and useful combinations of details or *trifles*, as Sherlock Holmes called them. Taken together, these trifles may allow us to generate a new possibility or hypothesis, ask a new and important question, or generate some new potential evidence. If you need only a general understanding of the material presented in this book, you may limit yourself to Chapters 1 and 2. If you are also interested in understanding how an intelligent analytic tool may help you with hypotheses analyses, you should also read Chapter 3, which presents an overview of Disciple-CD and some of its basic operations.

The rest of the chapters are for the readers who are interested in a deeper understanding of the theory and practice of intelligence analysis. At the beginning of each of the following chapters, we will present basic information about some important matters. Then we will ask you to make use of Disciple-CD to observe, by way of examples, how this system can incorporate these matters. In some cases, you will be asked to provide Disciple-CD with information required to solve an analytic problem. Disciple-CD will assist you in this process since it will know generally the kinds of information that are required. The instruction in the use of Disciple-CD is structured in two parts, the first containing basic operations, and the second advanced operations. You may skip the second part altogether or return to it after finishing the rest of the book. This is the "hands-on" capability of the approach we are taking to help you learn more about the complexities of evidential reasoning.

Chapter 4 contains basic information about evidence, and its three basic properties or credentials: *relevance, believability or credibility*, and *inferential force or weight*. These credentials are not inherent properties of evidence – analysts must establish them through defensible and persuasive arguments. The development of these arguments is discussed in Chapter 5. It involves an approach that can be termed *divide and conquer*, or *task decomposition*, in which we break some complex hypothesis into simpler elements and then reassemble these elements in forming a final conclusion.

Chapter 6 discusses various types of evidence. It also presents an automatic approach of evaluating the believability of evidence by considering lower-level believability credentials that depend on the type of evidence, such as competence and credibility, or veracity, objectivity, and observational sensitivity, in the case of testimonial evidence. This is followed, in Chapter 7, with a discussion of the believability of evidence that went through a chain of custody, where different intermediary persons or devices may have altered what an original source provided. Chapter 7 may also be skipped during a first reading of the book.

Chapter 8 discusses the recurrent combination of evidence: harmonious, dissonant, and redundant. Then Chapter 9 discusses the five major sources of uncertainty in masses of evidence: incompleteness, inconclusiveness, ambiguity, dissonance, and imperfect believability. This prepares the discussion, in Chapter 10, of four uncertainty methods that are used to assess and report the uncertainty. This is necessary because each such method captures some important elements of probabilistic reasoning, but no single method captures all of them.

Chapter 11 discusses different biases that have been identified in intelligence analysis and how Disciple-CD can help recognize and partially counter them. They include analysts' biases in the evaluation of evidence, in the perception of cause and effect, in the estimation of probabilities, and in the retrospective evaluation of intelligence reports. This chapter also introduces three other types of bias that are rarely discussed: biases of the sources of testimonial evidence, biases in the chain of custody of evidence, and biases of the consumers of intelligence, which can also be recognized and countered with Disciple-CD.

Finally, Chapter 12 addresses the learning and reuse of analytic expertise. Disciple-CD is a very general cognitive assistant for an end-user analyst who has no knowledge engineering experience and no access to or support from a knowledge engineer. If, however, an organization can (occasionally) provide some knowledge engineering support to its analysts, then it can use Disciple-EBR, which can acquire deeper expertise from its expert analysts. Such a trained Disciple-EBR system will both reduce the analysis time and improve its quality by reusing the learned analytic expertise. The use of Disciple-EBR is presented in a complementary book, *Knowledge Engineering: Building Cognitive Assistants for Evidence-Based Reasoning* (Tecuci et al., 2016).

The book also includes a glossary of terms and several appendixes that summarize important aspects from the previous chapters (the list of methodological guidelines, the list of the hands-on exercises, and the list of the operations of Disciple-CD).

HOW TO USE THE BOOK

As already indicated in the previous section, we have structured this book to be used by a wide variety of users with different prior backgrounds, training, and interests. This allows the book to be used either as the main textbook for an entire course in intelligence analysis or as a textbook for a part of the course. In the following, we summarize several possible uses, based on the desired coverage of intelligence analysis topics (general introduction, basic topics, comprehensive discussion) and the desired level of use of Disciple-CD (no use, demonstration of use, use of basic operations, use of all operations).

> *General Introduction to Intelligence Analysis* (without Disciple-CD)
>
> Chapters 1, 2
>
> *Intelligence Analysis* (without Disciple-CD)
>
> Chapters 1, 2, Sections 4.1–4.3, 4.6, 5.1–5.6, 5.10, 6.1–6.8, 6.10
>
> *Advanced Intelligence Analysis* (with demonstration of Disciple-CD)
>
> Chapters 1, 2, Sections 3.1, 3.5.1, 4.1–4.3, 4.6, 5.1–5.6, 5.10, 6.1–6.8, 6.10, Chapter 7, Sections 8.1–8.4, 8.6, 9.1–9.5, 9.7, 10.1–10.9, 10.11, Chapter 11
>
> *General Introduction to Intelligence Analysis* (with an introduction to Disciple-CD)
>
> Chapters 1, 2, Sections 3.1, 3.5.1
>
> *Intelligence Analysis* (with basic use of Disciple-CD)

Chapters 1–3, Sections 4.1–4.4, 4.6, 5.1–5.7, 5.9, 5.10, 6.1–6.8, 6.10

Advanced Intelligence Analysis (with basic use of Disciple-CD)

Chapters 1–3, Sections 4.1–4.4, 4.6, 5.1–5.7, 5.9, 5.10, 6.1–6.8, 6.10,
    Chapters 7–12

Intelligence Analysis (with advanced use of Disciple-CD)

Chapters 1–6

Advanced Intelligence Analysis (with advanced use of Disciple-CD)

Chapters 1–12

Naturally, we hope that your learning venture with or without the assistance of Disciple-CD will be a most valuable experience in which you will discover many very important elements of intelligence analysis, some of which you might not have heard anything about before. We also hope that this venture will be directly relevant to tasks you face, or will face, every day in your analytic careers. Finally, we hope that it will be as enjoyable as it will be informative. So, as you begin this learning venture, we wish you *bon voyage!*

Acknowledgments

We are very grateful to the many individuals who, in various ways, supported our research, including Kelcy Allwein, Keith Anthony, Cindy Ayers, John Donelan, Susan Durham, Keri Eustis, Michael Fletcher, Erin Gibbens, John Greer, Lloyd Griffiths, Ben Hamilton, Sharon Hamilton, Jim Homer, Phillip Hwang, Donald Kerr, James Kindig, Joan McIntyre, Jean-Michel Pomarede, William Nolte, Michelle Quirk, George Stemler, Kimberly Urban, Joan Vallancewhitacre, and Benjamin Wible.

We also want to thank Lauren Cowles, Cambridge University Press senior editor, who is an outstanding professional, and a great pleasure to work with.

About the Authors

Gheorghe Tecuci (Ph.D., University of Paris-South, July 1988, and Polytechnic Institute of Bucharest, December 1988) is Professor of Computer Science and Director of the Learning Agents Center in the Volgenau School of Engineering of George Mason University, Member of the Romanian Academy, and former Chair of Artificial Intelligence in the Center for Strategic Leadership of the U.S. Army War College. He has followed a career-long interest in the development of a computational theory and technology allowing non–computer scientists to develop cognitive agents that incorporate their problem-solving expertise and can act as cognitive assistants to experts, as expert consultants to nonexperts, and as intelligent tutors to students. He has published around 200 papers, including 11 books, with contributions to artificial intelligence, knowledge engineering, cognitive assistants, machine learning, evidence-based reasoning, and intelligence analysis. He has received the U.S. Army Outstanding Civilian Service Medal (for "groundbreaking contributions to the application of artificial intelligence to center of gravity determination") and the Innovative Application Award from the American Association for Artificial Intelligence.

David A. Schum (Ph.D., Ohio State University, 1964) is Emeritus Professor of Systems Engineering, Operations Research, and Law, as well as Chief Scientist of the Learning Agents Center at George Mason University, and Honorary Professor of Evidence Science at University College London. He has followed a career-long interest in the study of the properties, uses, discovery, and marshaling of evidence in probabilistic reasoning. His major lines of research have involved the tracking of evidential and inferential subtleties in complex inference; the design of various strategies for assisting persons in the performance of complex inference tasks; the study of the task of assessing the inferential force of various forms and combinations of evidence; and study of ways to enhance the process of discovery of new ideas and their relevant evidential tests. Dr. Schum has published more than one hundred papers in a variety of journals and eight books, including *The Evidential Foundations of Probabilistic Reasoning, Analysis of Evidence, Evidence and Inference for the Intelligence Analyst,* and *Probabilistic Analysis of the Sacco and Vanzetti Evidence,* and is recognized as one of the founding fathers of the Science of Evidence.

Dorin Marcu (Ph.D., George Mason University, 2009) is Research Assistant Professor, as well as Senior Software and Knowledge Engineer in the

Learning Agents Center, Volgenau School of Engineering, George Mason University. He has published over forty papers, including five books, with contributions to intelligent user interfaces, mixed-initiative interaction, abstraction of reasoning, and cognitive assistants. He has received the Innovative Application Award from the American Association for Artificial Intelligence.

Mihai Boicu (Ph.D., George Mason University, 2002) is Associate Professor of Information Sciences and Technology and Associate Director of the Learning Agents Center in the Volgenau School of Engineering of George Mason University. He has published over ninety papers, including five books, with contributions to problem solving and multistrategy learning in dynamic and evolving representation spaces, mixed-initiative interaction, multi-agent systems architecture, collaboration and coordination, abstraction-based reasoning, knowledge representation, and knowledge acquisition. He has received the Innovative Application Award from the American Association for Artificial Intelligence.

1 Intelligence Analysis: "Connecting the Dots"

We have included a frequently used metaphor in our book's title: "Connecting the Dots." This metaphor seems appropriate in characterizing the evidential and inferential matters discussed in this book. The metaphor may have gained its current popularity following the terrorist attacks in New York City and Washington, D.C., on September 11, 2001. It was frequently said that the intelligence services did not connect the dots appropriately in order to have possibly prevented the catastrophes that occurred. Since then, we have seen and heard this metaphor applied in the news media to inferences in a very wide array of contexts, in addition to intelligence, including legal, military, and business contexts. For example, we have seen it applied to allegedly faulty medical diagnoses; to allegedly faulty conclusions in historical studies; to allegedly faulty or unpopular governmental decisions; and in discussions involving the conclusions reached by competing politicians. What is also true is that the commentators on television and radio, or the sources of written accounts of inferential failures, never tell us what they mean by the phrase "connecting the dots." A natural explanation is that they have never even considered what this phrase means and what it might involve.

But we have made a detailed study of what "connecting the dots" entails. We have found this metaphor very useful, and quite intuitive, in illustrating the extraordinary complexity of the evidential and inferential reasoning required in the contexts we have mentioned. Listening or seeing some media accounts of this process may lead one to believe that it resembles the simple tasks we performed as children when, if we connected some collection of *numbered* dots correctly, a figure of Santa Claus, or some other familiar figure, would emerge. Our belief is that critics employing this metaphor in criticizing intelligence analysts have very little awareness of how astonishingly difficult the process of connecting the (unnumbered) dots can be in so many contexts, especially in intelligence analysis.

A natural place to begin our examination is by trying to define what is meant by the metaphor "connecting the dots," when it is applied to evidence-based reasoning tasks performed by intelligence analysts and others.

"Connecting the dots" refers to the task of marshaling thoughts and evidence in the generation or discovery of productive hypotheses and new evidence, and in the construction of defensible and persuasive arguments on hypotheses we believe to be most favored by the evidence we have gathered and evaluated.

The following represents an account of seven complexities in the process of "connecting the dots."

1.1.1 How Many Kinds of Dots Are There?

It is so easy to assume that the only kind of dot to be connected concerns details in the observable information or data we collect that may eventually be considered as evidence in some analysis. We might refer to these dots as being *evidential dots*. Sherlock Holmes had another term for the details in observations he made, calling them *trifles*. As he told Dr. Watson, "You know my method, it is based on the observance of trifles." A related problem here is that most items of intelligence evidence may contain many details, dots, or trifles, some of which are interesting and others not. What this means is that incoming intelligence information must be carefully parsed in order to observe its significant evidential dots. In Chapter 4, we give special attention to the problem of what qualifies as an evidential dot. *Not all data or items of information we have will ever become evidence in an analysis task.*

Example 1.1.

Consider the bombing during the Boston Marathon that took place on April 15, 2013. Many images have been taken during this event. One is a widely televised videotape of two young men, one walking closely behind the other, both carrying black backpacks. This is the evidential dot shown in the bottom left of Figure 1.1. Why should we be interested in this evidence dot? Because it suggests to us ideas or hypotheses of what might have actually happened. Consider our ideas or thoughts concerning the relevance of the backpack dot just described. We have other evidence that the two bombs that were set off were small enough to be carried in backpacks. This allows the inference that the backpacks carried by the two young men might have contained explosive devices and that they should be considered as suspects in the bombing. A further inference is that these two men were the ones who actually detonated the two bombs.

Thus, the second type of dot concerns ideas we have about how some evidential dot, or a collection of evidential dots, is connected to matters we are trying to prove or disprove.

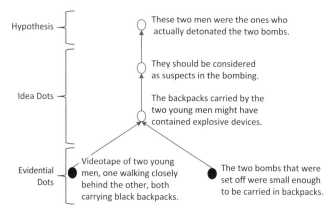

Figure 1.1. Types of dots to be connected: evidence, ideas, and hypotheses.

We commonly refer to the matters to be proved or disproved as *hypotheses*. Hypotheses commonly refer to possible alternative conclusions we could entertain about matters of interest in an analysis. These other dots, which we call *idea dots*, come in the form of links in chains of reasoning or arguments we construct to link evidential dots to hypotheses. Of course, hypotheses are also ideas. Each of these idea dots refers to sources of uncertainty or doubt we believe to be interposed between our evidence and our hypotheses. This is precisely where imaginative reasoning is involved. The essential task for the analyst is to *imagine* what evidential dots mean as far as hypotheses or possible conclusions are concerned. Careful *critical reasoning* is then required to check on the logical coherence of sequences of idea dots in our arguments or chains of reasoning. In other words, does the meaning we have attached to sequences of idea dots make logical sense?

1.1.2 Which Evidential Dots Can Be Believed?

The next problem we discuss is one of the most important, challenging, and interesting problems raised in any area of intelligence analysis. From some source, a sensor of some sort, or from a person, we obtain an evidential dot saying that a certain event has occurred. Just because this source says that this event occurred does not entail that it did occur. *So what is vitally necessary is to distinguish between evidence of an event and the event itself.* We adopt the following notational device to make this distinction:

- E represents the actual occurrence of event E.
- E^*_i represents the reported occurrence of event E from source I.

So, a basic inference we encounter is whether or not E did occur based on our evidence E^*_i. Clearly, this inference rests upon what we know about the *believability* of source I. There are some real challenges here in discussing the believability of source I. Chapter 6 of this book is devoted to the task of assessing the believability of our sources of intelligence evidence. As we will see, the Disciple-CD system already knows much about this crucial task.

But there are even distinctions to be made in what we have called *evidential dots*. Some of these dots arise from objects we obtain or from sensors that supply us with records or images of various sorts. So one major kind of evidential dot involves what we can call *tangible evidence* that we can observe for ourselves to see what events it may reveal. In many other cases, we have no such tangible evidence but must rely upon the reports of human sources who allegedly have made observations of events of interest to us. Their reports to us come in the form of *testimonial evidence* or assertions about what they have observed. Therefore, an evidential dot E^*_i can be one of the following types:

- *Tangible evidence* such as objects of various kinds, or sensor records like those obtained by signals intelligence (SIGINT), imagery intelligence (IMINT), measurement and signature intelligence (MASINT), and other possible sources.
- *Testimonial evidence* obtained from human sources, or human intelligence (HUMINT).

The origin of one of the greatest challenges in assessing the *believability* of evidence is that we must ask different questions about the sources of tangible evidence than those we ask about the sources of testimonial evidence. Stated another way, the believability attributes of tangible evidence are different from the believability attributes of testimonial evidence.

Example 1.2.

Consider again the evidential dot concerning the two men carrying backpacks. This is an example of *tangible evidence*. We can all examine this videotape to our heart's content to see what events it might reveal. The most important attribute of tangible evidence is its *authenticity*: is this evidential dot what it is claimed to be? The FBI claims that this videotape was recorded on April 15, 2013, on Boyleston Street in Boston, Massachusetts, where the bombings occurred, and recorded before the bombings occurred. Our imaginations are excited by this claim and lead to questions such as those that would certainly arise in the minds of defense attorneys during the trial. Was this videotape actually recorded on April 15, 2013? Maybe it was recorded on a different date. If it was recorded on April 15, 2013, was it recorded before the bombings occurred? Perhaps it was recorded after the bombings occurred. And, was this videotape actually recorded on Boyleston Street in Boston, Massachusetts? It may have been recorded on a different street in Boston, or perhaps on a street in a different city.

But there is another difficulty that is not always recognized that can cause endless trouble. While, in the case of tangible evidence, believability and credibility may be considered as equivalent terms, human sources of evidence have another characteristic apart from credibility; this characteristic involves their *competence*. As we discuss in Section 6.4, the credibility and competence characteristics of human sources must not be confused; to do so invites *inferential catastrophes*, as we will illustrate. The questions required to assess human source competence are different from those required to assess human source credibility. Competence requires answers to questions concerning the source's actual *access* to, and *understanding* of, the evidence he or she reports. Credibility assessment for a testimonial source requires answers to questions concerning the *veracity*, *objectivity*, and *observational sensitivity or accuracy* of the source. The Disciple-CD system knows what credibility-related questions to ask of tangible evidence and the competence and credibility-related questions to ask of HUMINT sources. We have much more to say about the forms and combinations of evidence in Chapters 6, 7, and 8 of this book.

There is no better way of illustrating the importance of evidence believability assessments than to show how such assessments form the very foundation for all arguments we make from evidence to possible conclusions. In many situations, people will mistakenly base inferences on the assumption that an event E has occurred just because we have evidence E^*_i from source I. This amounts to the suppression of any uncertainty we have about the believability of source I (whatever this source might be). In Figure 1.2 is a simple

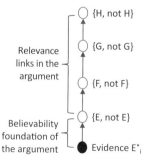

Figure 1.2. The believability foundation for an argument.

example illustrating this believability foundation; it will also allow us to introduce the next problem in connecting the dots.

What this figure shows is an argument from evidence E^*_i to whether or not hypothesis H is true. As shown, the very first stage in this argument concerns an inference about whether or not event E actually occurred. This is precisely where we consider whatever evidence we may have about the believability of source I. We may have considerable uncertainty about whether or not event E occurred. All subsequent links in this argument concern the *relevance* of event E to hypothesis H. As we noted in Figure 1.1, these relevance links connect the *idea dots* we discussed. As Figure 1.2 shows, each idea dot is a source of uncertainty associated with the logical connection between whether or not event E did occur and whether or not H is true.

1.1.3 Which Evidential Dots Should Be Considered?

In all of the contexts we have considered, there is usually no shortage of potential evidential dots. In fact, in many of these contexts, persons drawing conclusions about matters of importance are swamped with information or data. This situation is currently being called the "big data" problem. Here we begin to consider vital matters concerning the discovery-related or investigative tasks and the imaginative or creative reasoning these tasks involve. Unfortunately, in many situations people or organizations try to collect *everything* in the hope of finding *something* useful in an inference task. This wasteful practice is one reason why the big data problem exists, since only a minute fraction of the information collected will be relevant in any inference of concern. In our work, we have paid great attention to the process of discovery that necessarily takes place in a world that keeps changing all the while we are trying to understand parts of it of interest to us in our inference tasks. As will be discussed in Section 1.3, this is an ongoing seamless activity in which we have evidence in search of hypotheses, hypotheses in search of evidence, and the testing of hypotheses *all going on at the same time*. Hypotheses you entertain, questions you ask, particular evidence items, and your accumulated experience all allow you to examine which evidential dots to consider. Part of our objectives here is to make the process of discovery more efficient. As we will also discuss, these discovery tasks involve mixtures of three different forms of reasoning: *abduction* (imaginative, creative, or insightful reasoning), *deduction*, and *induction* (probabilistic reasoning). These forms of reasoning provide the bases for our idea dots.

1.1.4 Which Evidential Dots Should We Try to Connect?

Here comes a matter of great complexity. It usually happens that hypotheses we entertain are generated from observations we have made involving potential evidential dots. On limited occasions, we can generate a hypothesis from a single evidential dot. For example, in a criminal investigation, finding a fingerprint will suggest a possible suspect in the case. But in most cases, it takes consideration of *combinations of evidential dots* in order to generate plausible and useful hypotheses, as illustrated in the following example based on accounts given in *Time* magazine and the *Washington Post*.

Example 1.3.

From European sources came word that terrorists of Middle Eastern origin would make new attempts to destroy the World Trade Center, this time using airliners. Many threats are received every day, most of which come to nothing. However, from several civilian flying schools in the United States came word (to the FBI) that persons from the Middle East were taking flying lessons, paying for them in cash, and wanting to learn only how to steer and navigate heavy aircraft but not how to make takeoffs and landings in these aircraft. By itself, this information, though admittedly strange, may not have seemed very important. But, *taken together*, these two items of information might have caused even an Inspector Lestrade (the rather incompetent police investigator in Sherlock Holmes stories) to generate the hypothesis that there would be attacks on the World Trade Center using hijacked airliners. The hijackers would not need to learn how to make takeoffs; the aircrafts' regular pilots would do this. There would be no need for the hijackers to know how to land aircraft, since no landings were intended, only crashes into the World Trade Center and the Pentagon. Why were these two crucial items of information *not considered together*? The answer seems to be that they were not *shared* among relevant agencies. Information not shared cannot be considered jointly, with the result that their joint inferential impact could never have been assessed. For all time, this may become the best (worst) example of failure to consider evidence items together. This is just one reason why we will so strongly emphasize the importance of evidence-marshaling strategies in this volume. Even Sherlock Holmes would perhaps not have inferred what happened on September 11, 2001, if he had not been given these two items of information together.

The problem, however, is that here we encounter a *combinatorial explosion*, since the number of possible combinations of two or more evidential dots is *exponentially* related to the number of evidential dots we are considering. Suppose we consider having some number N of evidential dots. We ask the question: How many combinations C of two or more evidential dots are there when we have N evidential dots? The answer is given by the following expression: $C = 2^N - (N + 1)$. This expression by itself does not reveal how quickly this combinatorial explosion takes place. Here are a few examples showing how quickly C mounts up with increases in N:

- For $N = 10$, $C = 1013$
- For $N = 25$, $C = 33,554,406$
- For $N = 50$, $C = 1.13 \times 10^{15}$
- For $N = 100$, $C = 1.27 \times 10^{30}$

There are several important messages in this combinatorial analysis for intelligence analysis. The first concerns the size of N, the number of potential evidential dots that might be connected. Given the array of sensing devices and human observers available to our intelligence services, the number N of potential evidential dots is as large as you wish to make it. In most analyses, N would certainly be greater than one hundred and would increase as time passes. Remember that we live in a nonstationary world in which things change and we find out about new things all the time. So, in most cases, even if we had access to the world's fastest computer, *we could not possibly examine all possible evidential dot combinations* even when N is quite small.

Second, *trying to examine all possible evidential dot combinations would be the act of looking through everything with the hope of finding something.* This would be a silly thing to do, even if it were possible. The reason of course is that most of the dot combinations would tell us nothing at all. What we are looking for are combinations of evidential dots that interact or are dependent in ways that suggest new hypotheses or possible conclusions. If we examined these dots separately or independently, we would not perceive these new possibilities. Figure 1.3 is an abstract example; a tragic real-life example is what happened on September 11, 2001.

In Figure 1.3, there are four numbered evidential dots. The numbers might indicate the order in which we obtained them. In part (a) of the figure, we show an instance where these four dots have been examined separately or independently, in which case they tell us nothing interesting. Then someone notices that, taken together, these four dots combine to suggest a new hypothesis H_k that no one has thought about before, as shown in part (b) of the figure. What we have here is a case of *evidential synergism* in which two or more evidence items mean something quite different when they are examined jointly than they would mean if examined separately or independently. *Here we come to one of the most interesting and crucial evidence subtleties or complexities that have, quite frankly, led to intelligence failures in the past: failure to identify and exploit evidential synergisms.* We will address this matter in other problems we mention concerning connecting the dots.

It might be said that the act of looking through everything in the hope of finding something is the equivalent of giving yourself a prefrontal lobotomy, meaning that you are ignoring any imaginative capability you naturally have concerning which evidential dot combinations to look for in your analytic problem area. What is absolutely crucial in selecting dot combinations to examine is an analyst's experience and imaginative reasoning capabilities. What we should like to have is a conceptual "magnet" that we could direct at a base of evidential dots that would "attract" interesting and important dot combinations, as discussed in Section 2.3.

1.1.5   How to Connect Evidential Dots to Hypotheses?

As discussed in Section 4.2, all evidence has three major credentials or properties: *relevance, believability* or *credibility*, and *inferential force* or *weight*. No evidence ever comes to us with these three credentials already attached; they must be established by defensible and persuasive arguments linking the evidence to the hypotheses we are considering. As we will see, *relevance* answers the question, "So what? How is this datum or information item linked to something we are trying to prove or disprove?" If such relevance linkage cannot be established, this datum is irrelevant or useless. As discussed

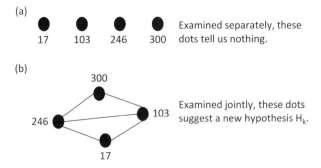

Figure 1.3. Evidential synergism.

previously, *believability* answers the question, "Can we believe what this evidence is telling us?" The force or weight credential asks, "How strong is this evidence in favoring or disfavoring the hypothesis?" This is where probability enters our picture, since, for very good reasons, the force or weight of evidence is always graded in probabilistic terms.

A relevance argument is precisely where the *idea dots* become so important. Considering an item of information, an analyst must imagine how this item could be linked to some hypothesis being considered before it could become an item of evidence. These idea dots forming this linkage come in the form of propositions or statements indicating possible sources of doubt or uncertainty in the imagined linkage between the item of information and hypotheses being considered. For a simple example, look again at Figure 1.2, where we show a connection between evidence E^*_i and hypothesis H. An analyst has an item of information from source *I* concerning the occurrence of event E that sounds very interesting. This analyst attempts to show how event E, if it did occur, would be relevant in an inference about whether hypothesis H is true or not. So the analyst forms the following chain of reasoning involving idea dots. The analyst says, "If event E were true, this would allow us to infer that event F might be true, and if F were true, this would allow us to infer that event G might be true. Finally, if event G were true, this would make hypothesis H more probable." If this chain of reasoning is defensible, the analyst has established the *relevance* of evidence E^*_i to hypothesis H.

In forming this argument, the analyst wisely begins with the believability foundation for this whole argument: Did event E really occur just because source *I* says it did? Also notice in Figure 1.2 that we have indicated the uncertainty associated with each idea dot in this argument. For example, the analyst only infers from E that F might have occurred, and so we note that we must consider F and notF as possibilities. The same is true for the other idea dots G and H.

There are several important things to note about relevance arguments; the first concerns their defense. Suppose the argument in Figure 1.2 was constructed by analyst *A*. *A* shows this argument to analyst *B*, who can have an assortment of quibbles about this argument. Suppose *B* says, "You cannot infer F directly from E; you need another step here involving event K. From E you can infer that K occurred, and then if K occurred, then you can infer F." Now comes analyst *C*, who also listens to *A*'s argument. *C* says, "I think your whole argument is wrong. I see a different reasoning route from E to hypothesis H. From E, we can infer event R, and from R, we can infer event S, and from S, we can infer T, which will show that hypothesis H is less probable." Whether or not there is any final agreement about the relevance of evidence E^*_i, analyst *A* has performed a valuable service by making the argument openly and available for discourse and criticism by colleagues. There are several important messages here.

First, there is no such thing as a uniquely correct argument from evidence to hypotheses. What we all try to avoid are disconnects or non sequiturs in the arguments we construct. But even when we have an argument that has no disconnects, someone may be able to come up with a better argument. Second, we have considered only the simplest possible situation, in which we used just a single item of potential evidence. But intelligence analyses are based on masses of evidence of many different kinds and that come from an array of different sources. In this case, we are obliged to consider multiple lines of argument that can be connected in different ways. It is customary to call these complex arguments *inference networks*.

From years of experience teaching law students to construct defensible and persuasive arguments from evidence, we have found that most of them often experience difficulty in constructing arguments from single items of evidence; they quickly become overwhelmed when they are confronted with argument construction involving masses of evidence. But they gain much assistance in such tasks by learning about argument construction methods devised nearly a hundred years ago by a world-class evidence scholar named John H. Wigmore (1863–1943). Wigmore (1913; 1937) was the very first person to carefully study what today we call inference networks. We will encounter Wigmore's work in several places in our discussions, and you will see that the Disciple-CD system employs elements of Wigmore's methods of argument construction.

There is also a message here for critics such as news writers and the taking heads on television. These critics always have an advantage never available to practicing intelligence analysts. Namely, they know how things turned out or what actually happened in some previously investigated matter affecting the nation's security. In the absence of clairvoyance, analysts studying a problem will never know for sure, or be able to predict with absolute certainty, what will happen in the future. A natural question to ask these critics is, "What arguments would you have constructed if all you knew was what the analysts had when they made their assessments? " This would be a very difficult question for them to answer fairly, even if they were given access to the classified evidence the analysts may have known at the time.

1.1.6　What Do Our Dot Connections Mean?

The previous item concerns efforts designed to establish the *defensibility* of complex arguments. But what do these arguments mean to persons for whom these arguments are being constructed? This question raises matters concerning how *persuasive* are our arguments when they are taken all together. Our view is that the persuasiveness of an argument structure depends, in large part, upon the nature of the probabilities we assess and combine in our arguments and in stating our major conclusions.

Here we consider the *direction* and *force* of our arguments based on the combined evidence we have considered. *Direction* refers to the hypothesis we believe our evidence favors most. *Force* means how strongly we believe the evidence favors this hypothesis over alternative hypotheses we have considered. There are two uncontroversial statements we can make about the force or weight of evidence. The first is that the force or weight of evidence has *vector-like* properties. What this means is that evidence points us in the direction of certain hypotheses or possible conclusions with varying degrees of strength. The second is that the force or weight of evidence is always graded in *probabilistic terms* indicating our uncertainties or doubts about what the evidence means in terms of its inferential direction and force. But beyond these two statements, controversies begin to arise.

Before we consider assorted controversies, it is advisable to consider where our uncertainties or doubts come from in the conclusions we reach from evidence. Have a look once again at Figure 1.2 involving a simple example based on a single item of evidence. Our evidence here was E^*_i, from source I, saying that event E occurred. We ask the question, "How strongly does this evidence E^*_i favor hypothesis H over not-H?" As we discussed, this argument was indicated by what we termed *idea dots*, each one indicating what the analyst constructing this argument believed to be sources of doubt or uncertainty associated with the argument from the evidence to the hypothesis. As you see, there are two major origins of uncertainty: those associated with the *believability* of source I, and those associated with links in the analyst's *relevance* argument. So, the force of evidence E^*_i on hypotheses H and not-H depends on how much uncertainty exists in this entire argument involving each one of its believability and relevance links. The interesting message here is that the evidence force or weight credential depends on its other two credentials: believability and relevance.

In the simple example just discussed, there are four major origins of uncertainty, one associated with believability and three associated with relevance. But this is the easiest possible situation since it involves only one item of evidence. Think of how many sources of uncertainty there might be when we have a mass of evidence together with multiple complex and possibly interrelated arguments. The mind boggles at the enormity of the task of assessing the force or weight of a mass of evidence commonly encountered in intelligence analysis when we have some untold numbers of sources of believability and relevance uncertainties to assess and combine. We are certain that critics of intelligence analysts have never considered how many evidential and idea dots there would be to connect.

So, the question remains: How do we assess and combine the assorted uncertainties in complex arguments in intelligence analysis, and in any other context in which we have the task of trying to make sense out of masses of evidence? Here is where controversies arise. The problem is that there are several quite different views among probabilists about what the force or weight of evidence means and how it should be assessed and combined across evidence in either simple or complex arguments. Each of these views has something interesting to say, but no one view says it all. As you will see in Chapter 10, we consider four systems of probability in our work. We do consider the conventional or *Bayesian* system that involves numerical probability judgments, but there are some severe limitations to this approach. Therefore, we also consider the *Belief Functions*, the *Baconian*, and the *Fuzzy* probability systems. But we devote considerable attention to a combination of the Baconian and the Fuzzy systems that require probabilities to be expressed in words rather than in numbers. The Baconian system, resting upon the view of Sir Francis Bacon, is especially relevant in the contexts we have mentioned. It is the *only* system of probability that concerns the completeness, as well as the strength, of the evidential coverage we can claim in the conclusions we reach from our evidential dots.

Later in this book, we will discuss how the Disciple-CD system allows you to assess and combine probabilistic judgments in situations in which many such judgments are required. There is further difficulty as far as judgments of the weight or force of evidence are concerned. Analysts, or teams of analysts, may agree about the construction of an argument but disagree, often vigorously, about the extent and direction of the force or weight this argument reveals. There may be strong disagreements about the believability of sources of evidence or about the strength of relevance linkages. These disagreements can be resolved only when arguments are made carefully and are openly revealed so that they can be tested by colleagues. A major mission of the Disciple-CD system is to allow you to construct arguments carefully and critically and encourage you to share them with colleagues so that they can be critically examined.

There is one final matter of interest in making sense out of masses of evidence and complex arguments. Careful and detailed argument construction might seem a very laborious task, no matter how necessary it is. Now consider the task of revealing the conclusions resulting from an analysis to some policy-making "customer" who has decisions to make that rest in no small part on the results of an intelligence analysis. What this "customer" will probably not wish to see is a detailed inference network analysis that displays all of the dots that have been connected and the uncertainties that have been assessed and combined in the process. A fair guess is that this "customer" will wish to have a narrative account or a story about what the analysis predicts or explains. In some cases, "customers" will require only short and not extensive narratives. This person may say, "Just tell me the conclusions you have reached and briefly why you have reached them." So the question may be asked, "Why go to all the trouble to construct defensible and persuasive arguments when our 'customers' may not wish to see their details?"

There is a very good answer to the question just raised. *Your narrative account of an analysis must be appropriately anchored on the evidence you have.* What you wish to be able to tell is a story that you believe contains some truth; that is, it is not just a good story. The virtue of careful and critical argument construction is that it will allow you to anchor your narrative not only on your imagination, but also on the care you have taken to subject your analysis to critical examination. There is no telling what questions you might be asked about your analysis. Rigor in constructing your arguments from your evidence is the best protection you have in dealing with "customers" and other critics who might have entirely different views regarding the conclusions you have reached. The Disciple-CD system is designed to allow you and others to evaluate critically the arguments you have constructed.

1.1.7 Whose Evidential Dots Should Be Connected?

There are several very easy answers to this question. One obvious answer is that all the potential evidential dots collected by any intelligence service that bear upon a problem involving our nation's security should be shared or brought together. Since September 11, 2001, so many examples of potential relevant evidence, gathered by different intelligence services, were never shared across agencies and offices. The basic problem this creates is that the extremely important *evidential synergisms* we discussed previously can never be detected and exploited in reaching analytic conclusions. In some cases, this has resulted in our failure to reach any conclusion at all in some important matter. This forms the basis for one of the major criticisms of our intelligence services in their failure to "connect the dots." In some instances in the past, potential evidence may have been viewed as a "proprietary" commodity to be shared only at the discretion of the agency or person who collected it. In other cases, there have been various statutory rules preventing sharing of evidence across intelligence-related services. Whatever the causes for this lack of sharing of intelligence information, this problem has been of great concern in the past few years.

But there is one way that the Disciple-CD process can assist in the detection and inferential exploitation of possible evidential synergisms, and it is something that rests on analysts, and analyst teams, at work on an intelligence problem. Careful argument construction will help reveal the *incompleteness of available evidence*. The analysts might easily observe that not all questions that should be asked about the problem at hand have in fact been answered. So, this forms the basis for asking questions such as:

- Have any other agencies or offices attempted to answer these questions that we believe have gone unanswered?
- If these other agencies have gathered such evidence, how can we best justify or be able to have ready access to it?
- What collection efforts should be mounted to gather evidence necessary in order to provide more complete assessments of evidence necessary to form more productive conclusions?

In many cases, such evidence may have never been collected. In these cases, analysts can play very important roles in directing effective and productive evidence collection efforts. In so many instances, it seems that we try to collect everything with the hope of finding something. This is one reason why we often correctly believe that we are drowning in information. More imaginative efforts are required in order to collect potential evidential dots of actual relevance in inference problems faced by intelligence analysts. This is another area in which the imagination of analysts becomes so important.

1.2   IMAGINATIVE REASONING IN INTELLIGENCE ANALYSIS

1.2.1   Imaginative Reasoning

We often hear it claimed that some people have imaginative reasoning capabilities and others don't. If you don't have it, you are out of luck. The truth of the matter is that nature has endowed *all of us* with imaginative reasoning capabilities (Howe, 1999). The trouble is that we are not always given the opportunity or encouragement to be imaginative or creative in our thinking. Our work on Disciple-CD is based on the idea that you are naturally required to exercise your imaginations in the act of trying to make sense out of the masses of evidence you will encounter. Our role in this process is to assist you in various ways. What *you* think about the evidence you will encounter is all-important. *You* may be able to assign possible meanings to evidence that others do not perceive. Another very important matter concerns how *productive* are the exercises of our imaginations. We all encounter persons who seem to be imaginative in the new ideas they generate. However, many of these same persons do not always generate new ideas that are helpful in the analytic tasks at hand. So, what needs to be encouraged in intelligence analysis is *productively imaginative thought*. But there are other ingredients necessary in efforts to help you become more like Sherlock or Mycroft Holmes than Inspector Lestrade.

The Disciple-CD system we have developed can only assist you in various ways, and so much depends on you and your analytic capabilities. You will be able to exercise your imaginative reasoning capabilities to the fullest only when you are *driven by curiosity or wonder* to find solutions to the analytic problems you encounter. If you don't care whether anyone finds a solution to these problems, you stand very little chance of generating a productively imaginative solution. Experience in many areas has shown that the most productively imaginative persons are also those who have the greatest degree of commitment to find solutions to problems that confront them.

The final ingredient we mention here concerns the *diligence* with which you approach each new analytic problem you face. There is an old saying that fortune favors the prepared mind. Unless you have done your homework in the particular substantive areas your analytic problems involve, you also stand little chance of generating productively imaginative new ideas. Your brain requires something to work with; as we all learn, this requires burning the midnight oil. But being well acquainted only with the specifics of the substance of your analytic problems is often not quite enough. Productively imaginative persons usually also have a *breadth* of knowledge and experience to draw upon. Productive new ideas so often spring from the analogies we perceive; these analogies are often stated in the form of metaphors. But the forming of useful metaphors requires knowledge that goes beyond the boundaries of the believed substance of an analytic problem. For example, if you knew a fair amount about the behavior of various animal species, you might be able to generate very useful metaphors for characterizing the behavior of terrorists.

One of the most difficult problems we have faced in our work on Disciple-CD is assisting you to construct defensible and persuasive arguments from a *mass* of evidence supporting or challenging hypotheses being considered. How well we are able to marshal our thoughts and evidence is vitally important in constructing defensible and persuasive arguments. The task of constructing arguments from a mass of different kinds of evidence is inherently difficult; perhaps it is the most difficult element of intelligence analysis. Though methods for performing complex argument construction have been around for a long time, such as the Wigmorean methods we mentioned previously in this chapter, few people have made particular use of them until quite recently. In this volume, we have combined concerns about these argument methods with concerns about thought and evidence marshaling.

Argument construction involves the interplay of imaginative and critical reasoning processes. As a result, different persons will imagine different reasoning routes from the same evidence to the same hypotheses. In addition, different persons may believe that the same body of evidence favors entirely different hypotheses. In short, there is no such thing as a uniquely correct argument from some collection of evidence to hypotheses being entertained. Add to this the fact that our evidence is always incomplete and any conclusion drawn today may have to be revised tomorrow in light of recently discovered evidence.

A final point concerns the argument construction methods themselves. The methods we discuss in connection with Disciple-CD may appear overly compulsive and may seem to require "too much thought." One response here is to remind persons reading our works that careful intelligence analyses always require careful thought, regardless of what methods are being used. Using methods we describe, we construct "pictures" of a complex argument in the form of what today are called *inference networks*. You may have had some exposure to the use of various software systems that now exist for the probabilistic analysis of inference networks. The trouble is that *no* such system tells the user *how to construct* an inference network appropriate in the analysis of some existing mass of evidence. These systems all assume that the imaginative and critical reasoning steps necessary in inference network construction have already been performed by the user. Having experience with the methods we discuss will offer analysts great assistance in seeing what is involved in the construction of defensible and persuasive arguments, regardless of whether you try to apply these methods in every analysis you undertake. Far too many persons are looking for a book entitled *Intelligence Analysis Made Simple*. We do not see any hope for any *serious* works or courses having this title. Intelligence analysis is an inherently difficult task; the methods we describe form one way of coping with the complexity of such tasks. Our Disciple-CD system provides assistance in performing these complex tasks.

1.2.2 What Ingredients of Analysis Are to Be Generated by Imaginative Thought?

If we place such a premium on your imaginative reasoning, we ought to be able to tell you precisely what elements of intelligence analyses need to be generated or discovered and, if possible, how these activities might best be assisted. Figure 1.4 describes the major ingredients of intelligence analysis that result from *imaginative reasoning* coupled with *critical reasoning*.

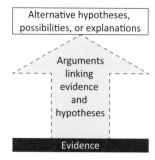

Figure 1.4. Major ingredients of intelligence analysis.

It would be a very rare occurrence if you encountered an analytic task in which all possible hypotheses, all available evidence, and all arguments connecting the evidence and the hypotheses were supplied for you. All these ingredients you will have to generate or discover for yourself. This is where your imaginative reasoning becomes necessary. Now it happens that imaginative reasoning, though necessary, is not sufficient. Suppose you have generated some alternative hypotheses from the evidence you have discovered, or selected from some larger collection of evidence, that seems relevant to these hypotheses. As we will discuss in this volume, you must also establish the relevance, believability, and inferential force "credentials" of the evidence you have. This involves *critical as well as imaginative reasoning* on your part. You must be able to construct arguments from evidence to hypotheses that are both defensible and persuasive; this is where critical reasoning also becomes vitally necessary. You may have generated entirely plausible hypotheses as well as evidence that you believe bears on these hypotheses. But, if your arguments linking your evidence and your hypotheses have non sequiturs, disconnects, or "short circuits" that are recognized by others, your analysis will fail to be defensible or persuasive.

We understand that intelligence analysis is a very complex activity often involving many persons in many locations. It may certainly be the case that potential evidence in your current analytic task is actually generated by other persons. For example, you may have a steady stream of message traffic or regular reports of some kind that arrive at your desk every day. Though you did not yourself generate or discover these items of information, you must decide which items from the mass of items you receive could indeed be evidence relevant in an inference task you presently have. But it is also true that your imaginative reasoning is involved when you request information, and potential evidence, that no one has at present.

1.2.3   Generating Main Hypotheses to Be Defended by Evidence and Argument

In any intelligence analysis, you will have to draw some kind of a conclusion. The *possible conclusions* you might draw can be in the form of *main hypotheses*. In most cases, these hypotheses will arise from observations we make. In this case, we have *evidence in search of hypotheses*, or possible explanations for what we have observed. In some cases, when our evidence is scant, it may even be appropriate to refer to an initial hypothesis as a guess. Generally, our main hypotheses refer to events or situations that we are presently unable to observe directly. These events may have happened in the past, are now possibly happening, or may possibly happen in the future. Here are three examples of hypotheses concerning past, present, or future events:

Example 1.4.

(Hypotheses concerning a past event) A terrorist incident occurred two months ago in which several lives were lost. After an investigation, two suspects, X and Y, have been identified. Here are some hypotheses we could entertain about this past event:

H_1: Person X was the one involved in this incident.

H_2: Person Y was the one involved in this incident.

H_3: Both X and Y were involved in this incident.

H_4: Neither X nor Y were involved in this incident.

Example 1.5.

(Hypotheses concerning an event that may be happening "now") You might have reason to suspect that Country Z is still holding prisoners of war (POWs) taken years ago during a conflict we had with it. Your suspicion here forms one hypothesis:

H_5: Country Z is now holding some of our POWs.

This example illustrates why it is true that we always have more than one hypothesis. Another possibility is "not H_5":

H_6: Country Z is not holding any of our POWs.

Example 1.6.

(Hypotheses concerning a future event or situation) We have been closely monitoring the deteriorating relations between countries A and B that share a common border. We now entertain the possibility that there will be armed conflict between these two countries "in the near future." Thus, we have as major hypothesis:

H_7: There will be armed conflict between A and B in the near future.

Another hypothesis, of course, is "not H_7":

H_8: There will be no armed conflict between A and B in the near future.

This example allows us to see that we will often need to make our hypotheses more specific. The hypothesis that there will be armed conflict between A and B is actually not very informative if it is our final stated conclusion. Decision makers will wish to know such things as who will start the conflict, how will it proceed, how long will it last, and who will win.

All of these examples concern events/situations that *might have happened*, are *now possibly happening*, or *might happen in the future*. We have no certainty about any of these hypotheses. At the moment, they are all simply possibilities. If, at the moment, we reported any of these hypotheses in the form of a conclusion, we would not be taken seriously. We have given no one else any reasons why the hypothesis we have chosen to report as a conclusion should be favored over any of the other hypotheses that are possible. This is where our next two ingredients, evidence and arguments, come in.

1.2.4   Generating the Evidential Grounds for Arguments

The second major ingredient of intelligence analyses is evidence that can be defended as relevant in showing why some hypothesis is true or not. Here is an example of its importance.

Take any of the three situations just mentioned in Section 1.2.3 concerning hypotheses about either past, current, or future events:

H_1:   Person X was the one involved in this incident.
H_5:   Country Z is now holding some of our POWs.
H_7:   There will be armed conflict between A and B in the near future.

All of these situations involve events that are *not now directly observable to us*. We were not at the scene of the terrorist incident; we have no direct observations of the presence of the POWs; and we cannot see into the minds of the leaders in countries A and B in order to read their intentions. But, we can observe other events or things that can serve as *evidence*, *signs*, or *indicators* of any of these hypotheses. So, we might define evidence in the following way:

> *Evidence is any observable sign, indicator, or datum we believe is relevant in deciding upon the extent to which we infer any hypotheses we have entertained as being correct or incorrect.*

Here are some examples of evidence we might find concerning the preceding hypotheses:

For H_1:   We might find evidence showing that X was in the near vicinity of the incident one hour before it happened.
For H_5:   A recent visitor to Country Z shows us a dog-tag he says was given to him by a resident of Z. On this tag is the name of a soldier who has been missing since our conflict with Country Z ended.
For H_7:   We might obtain evidence bearing upon the state of military preparedness of either country.

1.2.5   Generating Arguments Linking Evidence and Hypotheses

The third major ingredient of intelligence analysis concerns the arguments we must construct in defense of the relevance, believability or credibility, and force or weight of our evidence. Again, no item of evidence comes to us with these credentials already established; they must be established by *arguments*. The arguments we make form logical links between the evidence we have and the hypotheses we entertain. One way to look at an argument is to say that it forms a *chain of reasoning* from evidence to hypotheses. Often, there will be many links in a chain of reasoning.

Figure 1.5 shows an argument from the evidence E* (X was in the near vicinity of the incident one hour before it happened) to the hypothesis H_1 (Person X was the one involved in this incident).

Our argument might run as follows: "We have evidence that X was in the near vicinity of the incident one hour before it occurred. Therefore, it is possible that X was indeed in the near vicinity of the incident one hour before it occurred. Then he *might have been* at the scene of the incident when it occurred. Then, if he was at the scene of the incident at the time it occurred, he *might have been* a participant in the incident."

The argument just constructed is one made in defense of the *relevance* of evidence that X was in the near vicinity of the incident an hour before it occurred. Notice that, if you regard this argument as plausible, we have a link between the evidence and our hypothesis.

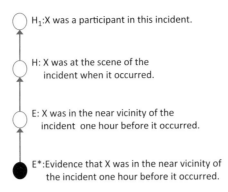

Figure 1.5. Sample argument.

However, all the argument in Figure 1.5 shows is that X *might have been* a participant in the incident. Remember from Section 1.2.3 that we were considering three other hypotheses, in addition to this one. Therefore, what we would like to know is which of the four is most likely. This would require the analysis of all these hypotheses, and not just based on a single item of evidence. It would also require an assessment of how likely each hypothesis is, based on the relevance, the believability, and the inferential force of evidence.

The next section introduces a systematic approach to intelligence analysis that is based on the scientific method and is supported by the Disciple-CD system.

1.3   INTELLIGENCE ANALYSIS AS DISCOVERY OF EVIDENCE, HYPOTHESES, AND ARGUMENTS

1.3.1   Intelligence Analysis in the Framework of the Scientific Method

Within the framework of the scientific method, intelligence analysis can be viewed as ceaseless discovery of evidence, hypotheses, and arguments in a nonstationary world, involving collaborative processes of evidence in search of hypotheses, hypotheses in search of evidence, and evidentiary testing of hypotheses, as represented in Figure 1.6.

Since these processes are generally very complex and involve both imaginative and critical reasoning, they can be best approached through the synergistic integration of the analyst's imaginative reasoning and computer's knowledge-based critical reasoning, as will be illustrated with the use of the Disciple-CD cognitive assistant.

Through *abductive reasoning* (Peirce, 1992 [1898]; 1995 [1901]; Schum, 2001b) (which shows that something is *possibly* true), the analyst and Disciple-CD generate alternative hypotheses that explain their observations (see the left-hand side of Figure 1.6). Through *deductive reasoning* (which shows that something is *necessarily* true), they use these hypotheses to generate new lines of inquiry and discover new evidence (see the middle of Figure 1.6). And through *inductive reasoning* (which shows that something is *probably* true), they test each of these hypotheses with the discovered evidence and select the most likely one (see the right-hand side of Figure 1.6).

The following sections illustrate this systematic approach to intelligence analysis by using a specific example of anticipatory analysis where evidence about a canister of cesium-137 missing from a company leads to anticipating the fact that a dirty bomb will

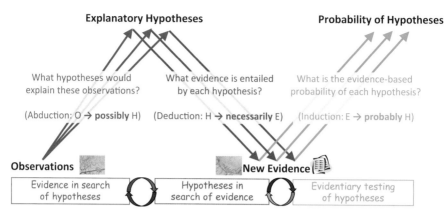

Figure 1.6. Framework of the computational theory of intelligence analysis.

be set off in the Washington, D.C., area. At the same time, this example will introduce the main concepts related to evidence and inference, which will be detailed and experimented throughout the rest of this book.

1.3.2   Evidence in Search of Hypotheses

Consider that you are an intelligence analyst and you read in today's *Washington Post* an article that concerns how safely radioactive materials are stored in this general area. Willard, the investigative reporter and author of this piece, begins by noting how the storage of nuclear and radioactive materials is so frequently haphazard in other countries and wonders how carefully these materials are guarded here in the United States, particularly in this general area. In the process of his investigations, the reporter notes his discovery that a canister containing cesium-137 has gone missing from the XYZ Company in Maryland just three days ago. The XYZ Company manufactures devices for sterilizing medical equipment and uses cesium-137 in these devices along with other radioactive materials. This piece arouses your curiosity because of your concern about terrorists planting dirty bombs in our cities. The question is, "What hypotheses would explain this observation?" You experience a flash of insight that a dirty bomb may be set off in the Washington, D.C., area (see Figure 1.7).

However, no matter how imaginative or important this hypothesis is, no one will take it seriously unless you are able to justify it. So you develop the chain of abductive inferences (Peirce, 1992 [1898]; 1995 [1901]; Schum 2001b) shown in Table 1.1 and in Figure 1.8.

The chain of inferences from Table 1.1 and Figure 1.8 shows clearly the possibility that a dirty bomb will be set off in the Washington, D.C., area. Can you then conclude that this will actually happen? No, because there are many other hypotheses that may explain this evidence, as shown in Figure 1.9 and discussed in the following text.

Just because there is evidence that the cesium-137 canister is missing does not mean that it is indeed missing. At issue here is the believability of Willard, the source of this information. What if Willard is mistaken or deceptive? Thus, an alternative hypothesis is that the cesium-137 canister is not missing.

But let us assume that the cesium-137 canister is indeed missing. Then it is possible that it was stolen. But it is also possible that it was misplaced, or maybe it was used in a project at the XYZ Company without being checked out from the warehouse.

H: A dirty bomb
will be set off in
the Washington,
DC, area

Insight

E*: Article on
cesium-137
canister
missing

What hypotheses would
explain this observation?

Figure 1.7. Hypothesis generation through imaginative reasoning.

Table 1.1 Abductive Reasoning Steps Justifying a Hypothesis

There is evidence that the cesium-137 canister is missing (E*).
Therefore it is possible that the cesium-137 canister is indeed missing (H_1).
Therefore it is possible that the cesium-137 canister was stolen (H_2).
Therefore it is possible that the cesium-137 canister was stolen by someone associated with a terrorist organization (H_3).
Therefore it is possible that the terrorist organization will use the cesium-137 canister to construct a dirty bomb (H_4).
Therefore it is possible that the dirty bomb will be set off in the Washington, D.C., area (H_5).

However, let us assume that the cesium-137 canister was indeed stolen. It is then possible that it might have been stolen by a terrorist organization, but it is also possible that it might have been stolen by a competitor or by an employee, and so on.

This is the process of *evidence in search of hypotheses*, shown in the left-hand side of Figure 1.6. We cannot conclude that a dirty bomb will be set off in the Washington, D.C., area (i.e., hypothesis H_5) until we consider all the alternative hypotheses and show that those on the chain from E* to H_5 are actually the most likely ones. But to analyze all these alternative hypotheses and make such an assessment, we need additional items of evidence. How can we get them? As represented in the middle of Figure 1.6, we put each hypothesis at work to guide us in the collection of additional evidence. This process is discussed in the next section.

1.3.3   Hypotheses in Search of Evidence

Let us first consider the hypothesis "H_1: missing" from near the bottom of Figure 1.9, shown as "H_1: cesium-137 canister is missing from the warehouse" in the top-left of

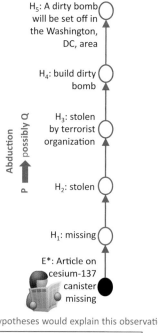

Figure 1.8. Justification of the generated hypothesis.

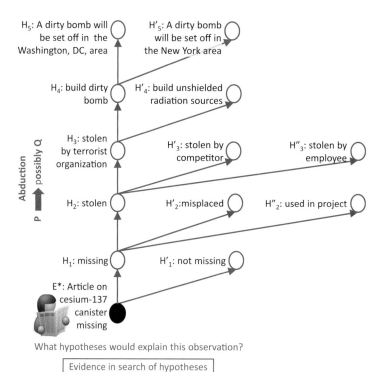

Figure 1.9. Competing hypotheses explaining an item of evidence.

Figure 1.10. The question is, *"Assuming that this hypothesis is true, what other things should be observable?"*

> *What are the necessary conditions for an object to be missing from a warehouse?*
> *It was in the warehouse, it is no longer there, and no one has checked it out.*

This suggests the decomposition of the hypothesis H_1 into three simpler hypotheses, as shown in the left part of Figure 1.10. This clearly indicates that you should look for evidence that indeed the cesium-137 canister was in the warehouse, that it is no longer there, and that no one has checked it out. That is, by putting hypothesis H_1 to work, you were guided to perform the collection tasks from Table 1.2, represented in Figure 1.10 by the gray circles.

Guided by the evidence collection tasks in Table 1.2, you contact Ralph, the supervisor of the XYZ warehouse, who provides the information shown in Table 1.3 and in Figure 1.10.

When we are given testimonial information, or descriptions of tangible items, the information might contain very many details, dots, or trifles. Some of the details might be interesting and relevant evidence, and others not. What we always have to do is to parse the information to extract the information that we believe is relevant in the inference task at hand. Consider, for example, the information provided by Willard in his *Washington*

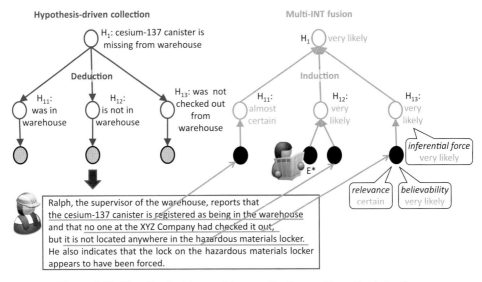

Figure 1.10. Hypothesis-driven evidence collection and hypothesis testing.

Table 1.2 Evidence Collection Tasks Obtained from the Analysis in Figure 1.10

Collection Task1: Look for evidence that the cesium-137 canister was in the XYZ warehouse before being reported as missing.
Collection Task2: Look for evidence that the cesium-137 canister is no longer in the XYZ warehouse.
Collection Task3: Look for evidence that the cesium-137 canister was not checked out from the XYZ warehouse.

Table 1.3 Information Obtained through the Collection Tasks in Table 1.2

INFO-002-Ralph: Ralph, the supervisor of the warehouse, reports that the cesium-137 canister is registered as being in the warehouse and that no one at the XYZ Company had checked it out, but it is not located anywhere in the hazardous materials locker. He also indicates that the lock on the hazardous materials locker appears to have been forced.

Table 1.4. Dots or Items of Evidence Obtained from Willard and Ralph

E001-Willard: Willard's report in the *Washington Post* that a canister containing cesium-137 was missing from the XYZ warehouse in Baltimore, MD.

E002-Ralph: Ralph's testimony that the cesium-137 canister is registered as being in the XYZ warehouse.

E003-Ralph: Ralph's testimony that no one at the XYZ Company had checked out the cesium-137 canister.

E004-Ralph: Ralph's testimony that the canister is not located anywhere in the hazardous materials locker.

E005-Ralph: Ralph's testimony that the lock on the hazardous materials locker appears to have been forced.

Post article. We parse it to extract the relevant information represented as E001-Willard in Table 1.4. Similarly, Ralph's testimony from Table 1.3 provides us with several dots or items of evidence that are relevant to assessing the hypotheses from Figure 1.10. These items of evidence are represented in Table 1.4.

This is the process of *hypothesis in search of evidence* that guides us in collecting new evidence. The next step now is to assess the *probability or likeliness* of hypothesis H_1 based on the collected evidence, as represented in the right-hand side of Figure 1.6 and discussed in the next section.

1.3.4   Evidentiary Testing of Hypotheses

Having identified evidence relevant to the hypotheses in Figure 1.10, the next step is to use it in order to assess these hypotheses. The assessments of the hypotheses will be done by using probabilities that are expressed in words rather than in numbers. In particular, we will use the ordered symbolic probability scale from Table 1.5. This is based on a combination of ideas from the Baconian and Fuzzy probability systems. As in the Baconian system, "no support" for a hypothesis means that we have no basis to consider that the hypothesis might be true. However, we may later find evidence that may make us believe that the hypothesis is "very likely," for instance.

To assess the hypotheses, we first need to attach each item of evidence to the hypothesis to which it is relevant, as shown in the right-hand side of Figure 1.10. Then we need to establish the *relevance* and the *believability* of each item of evidence, which will result in the *inferential force* of that item of evidence on the corresponding hypothesis, as illustrated at the right-hand side of Figure 1.10 and explained in the following.

> **Table 1.5 Ordered Symbolic Probability Scale**
>
> no support < likely < very likely < almost certain < certain

So let us consider the hypothesis "H_{13}: cesium-137 canister was not checked-out from the warehouse" and the item of evidence "E003-Ralph: Ralph's testimony that no one at the XYZ Company had checked out the cesium-137 canister."

Relevance answers the question, "So what? How does E003-Ralph bear on the hypothesis H_{13} that we are trying to prove or disprove?" If we believe what E003-Ralph is telling us, then H_{13} is "certain."

Believability answers the question, "To what extent can we believe what E003-Ralph is telling us?" Let us assume this to be "very likely."

Inferential force or weight answers the question, "How strong is E003-Ralph in favoring H_{13}?" Obviously, an item of evidence that is not relevant to the considered hypothesis will have no inferential force on it and will not convince us that the hypothesis is true. An item of evidence that is not believable will have no inferential force either. Only an item of evidence that is both very relevant and very believable will convince us that the hypothesis is true. In general, the inferential force of an item of evidence (such as E003-Ralph) on a hypothesis (such as H_{13}) is the minimum of its relevance and its believability. We can therefore conclude that, based on E003-Ralph, the probability of the hypothesis H_{13} is "very likely" (i.e., the minimum of "certain" and "very likely"), as shown in Figure 1.10.

Notice in Figure 1.10 that there are two items of evidence that are relevant to the hypothesis H_{12}. In this case, the probability of H_{12} is the result of the combined (maximum) inferential force of these two items of evidence.

Once we have the assessments of the hypotheses H_{11}, H_{12}, and H_{13}, the assessment of the hypothesis H_1 is obtained as their minimum, because these three subhypotheses are necessary and sufficient conditions. Therefore, all need to be true in order for H_1 to be true, and H_1 is as weak as its weakest component.

Thus, as shown at the top-right side of Figure 1.10, we conclude that it is "very likely" that the cesium-137 canister is missing from the warehouse.

Notice that this is a process of *multi-INT fusion* since, in general, the assessment of a hypothesis involves fusing different types of evidence.

Figure 1.11 summarizes the preceding analysis, which is an illustration of the general framework from Figure 1.6.

Now that we have concluded "H_1: missing," we repeat this process for the upper hypotheses (i.e., H_2: stolen; H'_2: misplaced; and H''_2: used in project), as will be discussed in the next section.

1.3.5 Completing the Analysis

Let us first consider the hypothesis "H_2: stolen." We need to put this hypothesis to work to guide us in collecting relevant evidence for its analysis. During our investigation of the security camera of the warehouse, we discover a video segment showing a person loading a container into a U-Haul panel truck. This new item of evidence, together with Ralph's testimony that the lock on the hazardous materials locker appears to have been

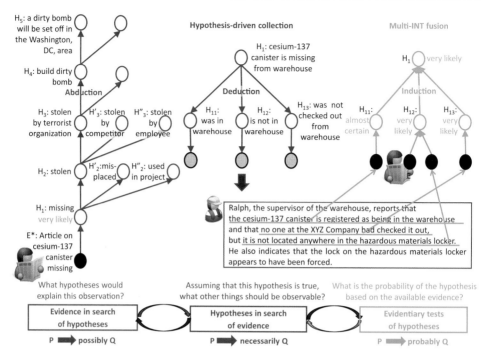

Figure 1.11. An illustration of the general framework from Figure 1.6.

forced (E005-Ralph in Table 1.4), suggests the following scenario of how the cesium-137 might have been stolen (see Figure 1.12): *The truck entered the company, the canister was stolen from the locker, the canister was loaded into the truck, and the truck left with the canister.*

Such scenarios have enormous heuristic value in advancing the investigation because they consist of mixtures of what is taken to be factual and what is conjectural. Conjecture is necessary in order to fill in natural gaps left by the absence of existing evidence. Each such conjecture, however, opens up new avenues of investigation, and the discovery of additional evidence, if the scenario turns out to be true. For instance, the first hypothesized action from the scenario ("Truck entered company") leads us to check the record of the security guard, which shows that a panel truck bearing Maryland license plate number MDC-578 was in the XYZ parking area the day before the discovery that the cesium-137 canister was missing.

The second hypothesized action in the scenario (i.e., "cesium-137 canister stolen from locker") is further decomposed into two hypotheses. The first one was already analyzed, "It is very likely that the cesium-137 canister is missing from the warehouse." The second subhypothesis ("Warehouse locker was forced") is supported both by Ralph's testimony (i.e., E005-Ralph in Table 1.4) and by the professional locksmith, Clyde, who was asked to examine it (E007-Clyde: Professional locksmith Clyde testimony that the lock has been forced, but it was a clumsy job).

Fusing all the discovered evidence, Disciple-CD concludes that it is very likely that the cesium-137 canister was stolen with the MDC-678 truck.

We repeat the same process for the other two competing hypotheses, H′$_2$: misplaced, and H″$_2$: used in project. However, we find no evidence that the cesium-137 canister might have been misplaced. Moreover, we find disfavoring evidence for the second

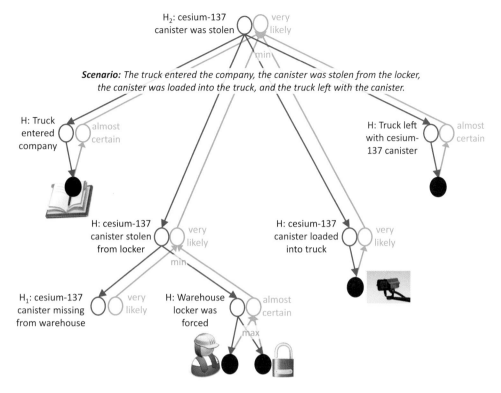

Figure 1.12. Another example of hypothesis-driven evidence collection and hypothesis testing.

competing hypothesis: Grace, the Vice President for Operations at XYZ, tells us that no one at the XYZ Company had checked out the canister for work on any project.

Thus we conclude that the cesium-137 canister was stolen and we continue our analysis with investigating the next level up of competing hypotheses: H_3: stolen by terrorist organization; H'_3: stolen by competitor; and H''_3: stolen by employee. Of course, at any point, the discovery of new information may lead us to refine our hypotheses, add new hypotheses, or eliminate existing hypotheses.

This example is not as simple as it may be inferred from this presentation. It is the methodology that guides you and makes it look simple. Many things can and will indeed go wrong. But the computational theory of intelligence analysis and Disciple-CD provide you the means to deal with any problems. Based on evidence, you come up with some hypotheses, but then you cannot find evidence to support any of them. So you need to come up with other hypotheses, and you should always consider alternative hypotheses. The deduction-based decomposition approach guides you on how to look for evidence, but your knowledge and imagination also play a crucial role. As illustrated here, we imagined a scenario where the cesium-137 canister was stolen with a truck. But let us now assume that we did not find supporting evidence for this scenario. Should we conclude that the cesium-137 canister was not stolen? No, because this was just one scenario. If we can prove it, we have an assessment of our hypothesis. However, if we cannot prove it, there still may be another scenario explaining how the cesium-137 canister might have been stolen. Maybe the cesium canister was stolen by someone working at the XYZ Company. Maybe it was stolen by Ralph, the administrator of the warehouse. The important thing is that each such scenario opens a new line of investigation and a new way to prove the hypothesis.

The next chapters of this book include exercises for completing this analysis that will further illustrate the synergistic integration of an analyst's imagination with a computer's critical reasoning. Having established that cesium-137 canister was stolen, we would further like to determine by whom and for what purpose. If it is for constructing and setting off a dirty bomb, we would like to know who will do this, where in the Washington, D.C., area the bomb will be set off, precisely when this action will happen, what form of dirty bomb will be used, and how powerful it will be. These are very hard questions that the computational theory of intelligence analysis presented in this book (as well as its current implementation in Disciple-CD) will help to answer.

One major challenge in performing such an analysis is the development of argumentation structures. An advantage of using an advanced analytic tool such as Disciple-CD is that it can learn reasoning patterns from the analyst to greatly facilitate and improve the analysis of similar hypotheses, as will be shown in the next chapters of this book.

In conclusion, the computational theory of intelligence analysis presented in this volume, as well as its current implementation in Disciple-CD, provides a framework for integrating the art and science of intelligence analysis to cope with its astonishing complexity.

However, while the computational theory and Disciple-CD guide you through the intelligence analysis steps, and also automates many of them, it requires you to continuously exercise your imagination. Therefore, in Chapter 2, we return to this all-important capability to describe useful heuristics for marshaling your thoughts and evidence. Using such heuristics in conjunction with a cognitive assistant such as Disciple-CD is the approach we advocate for coping with the astonishing complexity of "connecting the dots."

1.4   REVIEW QUESTIONS

1.1.   Two weeks ago in an American city, a terrorist incident occurred involving considerable destruction and some loss of lives. After an investigation, two foreign terrorist groups were identified as possible initiators of this terrorist action: an Al Qaeda Group A from Yemen and a Taliban Group B from Pakistan. Which are some hypotheses we could entertain about this event?

1.2.   You might have reason to suspect that Iran is now supplying improvised explosive devices (IEDs) to a Taliban group in Afghanistan. Since there are other possible sources for these weapons, you will have more than one main hypothesis about possible suppliers of these IEDs. What are some of these other hypotheses?

1.3.   Consider the hypothesis that Iran is now supplying IEDs to a Taliban group in Afghanistan. What evidence we might find concerning this hypotheses?

1.4.   Consider the hypothesis that Al Qaeda Group A from Yemen was the one involved in the terrorist incident. What evidence we might find concerning this hypothesis?

1.5.   Sometimes we have evidence in search of hypotheses or possible explanations. For example, consider the dog-tag containing the name of one of our soldiers who has been missing since the end of our conflict with Country Z. This tag was allegedly given to a recent visitor in Country Z who then gave it to us. One possibility is that this soldier is still being held as a prisoner in Country Z. What are some other possibilities?

1.6.   Sometimes we have hypotheses in search of evidence. Suppose our hypothesis is that Person X was involved in the terrorist incident. So far, all we have is evidence that he was at the scene of the incident an hour before it happened. If this hypothesis were true, what other kinds of evidence might we be able to observe about X?

1.7. Consider the hypothesis that countries A and B are about to engage in armed conflict. Here is a report you have just obtained; it says that there has just been an attempt on the life of the president of Country B by an unknown assailant. Why is this report, if credible, relevant evidence on the hypothesis that countries A and B are about to engage in armed conflict?

1.8. Defendant Dave is accused of shooting a victim, Vic. When Dave was arrested sometime after the shooting, he was carrying a 32-caliber Colt automatic pistol. Let H be the hypothesis that it was Dave who shot Vic. A witness named Frank appears and says he saw Dave fire a pistol at the scene of the crime when it occurred; that's all Frank can tell us. Construct a simple chain of reasoning that connects Frank's report to the hypothesis that it was Dave who shot Vic.

1.9. Consider the situation from Question 1.8. The chain of reasoning that connects Frank's report to the hypothesis that it was Dave who shot Vic shows only the possibility of this hypothesis being true. What are some alternative hypotheses?

1.10. Consider again the situation from Questions 1.8 and 1.9. In order to prove the hypothesis that it was Dave who shot Vic, we need additional evidence. As discussed in Section 1.3.3, we need to put this hypothesis to work to guide us in collecting new evidence. Decompose this hypothesis into simpler hypotheses, as was illustrated by the blue trees in Figures 1.11 and 1.12.

1.11. Our investigation described in Questions 1.8, 1.9, and 1.10, has led to the discovery of additional evidence. By itself, each evidence item is hardly conclusive that Dave was the one who shot Vic. Someone else might have been using Dave's Colt automatic. But Frank's testimony along with the fact that Dave was carrying his weapon, and with the ballistics evidence puts additional heat on Dave. Extend the decomposition tree from Question 1.10 with assessments of the probability of the hypotheses, as was illustrated by the green trees in Figures 1.11 and 1.12. In Section 4.3, we will discuss more rigorous methods for making such probabilistic assessments. In this exercise, just use your common sense.

1.12. A car bomb was set off in front of a power substation in Washington, D.C., on November 25. The building was damaged but, fortunately, no one was injured. From the car's identification plate, which survived, it was learned that the car belonged to Budget Car Rental Agency. From information provided by Budget, it was learned that the car was last rented on November 24 by a man named M. Construct an argument from this evidence to the hypothesis that Person M was involved in this car-bombing incident.

1.13. Consider the situation from Question 1.12 and the corresponding argument. Suppose that we have determined that evidence E* is believable and therefore we think that M indeed rented a car on November 24. We want now to assess F, whether M drove the car on November 25. For this we need additional evidence. As discussed in Section 1.3.3, we need to put this hypothesis to work to guide us in collecting new evidence. Decompose this hypothesis into simpler hypotheses, as was illustrated by the blue trees in Figures 1.11 and 1.12.

2 Marshaling Thoughts and Evidence for Imaginative Analysis

2.1 SHERLOCK HOLMES AND INVESTIGATION OR DISCOVERY

If you have read any Sherlock Holmes mysteries, you know that Holmes had several foils in the form of rather incompetent police investigators such as Inspector Lestrade and Inspector Gregory. Confidently believing that they had a case solved, Lestrade or Gregory had obviously overlooked details that were observed and then imaginatively analyzed by Holmes. In one case, *The Boscombe Valley Mystery* (Baring-Gould, 1967, vol. II, p. 148), Holmes tells his colleague Dr. Watson:

> "By an examination of the ground I gained the trifling details which I gave to that imbecile Lestrade, as to the personality of the criminal." Watson asks: "But how did you gain them?" Holmes replies: "You know my method. It is founded on the observance of trifles."

As an intelligence analyst, you are confronted daily with hundreds, perhaps thousands, of *trifles* or *details*. We could also refer to Sherlock Holmes' observed *trifles* as one form of *dot* that we must try to connect. Taken alone, an individual trifle may mean very little. But some of them, taken in combination, may suggest new and important hypotheses or possibilities that should be taken very seriously. *The trick is to be able to identify which combinations of trifles to examine carefully and which ones to ignore.* This is where alternative schemes for selecting and marshaling trifles, together with our thoughts about them, become all important. As we noted in Section 1.1.4, it would not make any sense to examine all possible combinations of trifles, even if we could do so. Considerable imagination is required, both in deciding which trifle combinations to examine and in generating new and productive hypotheses from the trifle combinations you have identified. Given the extreme perils faced today, we need more Sherlock Holmeses and fewer Inspector Lestrades.

Sherlock Holmes also seemed particularly adept at asking questions as his investigations unfolded. The process of discovery involving the generation of new hypotheses or possibilities rests crucially on the questions we ask. One noted logician claims that Sherlock Holmes' imaginative feats of skill were largely due to his skill at inquiry, the asking of questions (Hintikka, 1983, pp. 170–178). If we do not ask appropriate questions, as our intelligence investigations unfold, we stand little chance, without an abundance of luck, of generating hypotheses that stand some chance of containing truth.

2.2   MYCROFT HOLMES AND EVIDENCE MARSHALING

It is here that we must introduce Sherlock Holmes' older brother Mycroft Holmes. We do not hear much about Mycroft since he appears in only two of the Holmes mystery stories, *The Greek Interpreter* (Baring-Gould, 1967, vol. I, pp. 590–605) and *The Bruce-Partington Plans* (Baring-Gould, 1967, vol. II, pp. 432–452). On first impression, Mycroft appears as a minor civil servant working as an auditor for various British government departments in Whitehall. But Sherlock says that this would be dramatically misleading since, as Sherlock admits, Mycroft's investigative and inferential capabilities are far greater than his own. Mycroft's true role was obviously kept a closely guarded secret. We get the clearest account of Mycroft's capabilities in *The Bruce-Partington Plans*. Sherlock says that Mycroft is in fact the most indispensable man in the country. One reason is that Mycroft has the tidiest and most orderly brain with the greatest capacity for storing facts of anyone living. Further, the conclusions of every governmental department are passed to Mycroft, who serves as a central exchange or a clearinghouse that makes out a balance. In examining these various inputs, Mycroft can focus on them all and say how each input would influence the others. In Mycroft's brain, everything is pigeonholed and can be accessed instantly. Sherlock says that again and again Mycroft's word has decided national policy and that, on occasion, Mycroft has been *the* British government. So, one way to describe Mycroft's major capability is to say that he had superlative skills in marshaling masses of evidence and in generating correct conclusions from this marshaled evidence. Sherlock said of Mycroft, "All other men are specialists, but his specialism is omniscience."

Perhaps the most frequently overlooked element of intelligence analysis concerns the manner in which we marshal or organize our thoughts and our evidence as we proceed with some analytic task. But such oversight causes no end of difficulties since how skillful we are in marshaling our *existing* thoughts and evidence greatly influences how skillful we will be in generating or discovering *new* ideas (in the form of possible hypotheses) and *new* lines of inquiry and evidence. Skillful evidence marshaling is not only necessary during the discovery-related processes of intelligence analysis, it forms the very basis for the later task of constructing defensible and persuasive arguments on hypotheses we entertain. In short, developing useful strategies for marshaling thoughts and evidence during intelligence analysis is absolutely crucial. From experience, we know that intelligence analysts have various personal schemes for organizing or marshaling information they receive. One well-known scheme has, in the past, involved the use of index cards, on which items of information are recorded and then sorted out in shoeboxes. There are, of course, newer schemes that have arisen as a result of common access to computers.

Concern about means for marshaling our thoughts and our evidence arises for two major reasons. The first is the fact that marshaling methods can assist us in being more imaginative during the process of discovery as we are attempting to determine what has happened or what will happen in some situation of interest to us. Appropriate marshaling strategies can assist us in generating productive new hypotheses and new lines of inquiry and evidence. Second, evidence marshaling strategies are key ingredients of the task of determining what our evidence means and in constructing defensible and persuasive arguments on hypotheses we are considering. This is where the marshaling of ideas in addition to evidence becomes so important. We must generate chains of reasoning whose ingredients consist of ideas we have in showing how we believe the evidence we have is linked to, or is relevant to, hypotheses we are considering. This is why we say that what we are marshaling are our *thoughts* and our *evidence*. It is quite obvious that marshaling thoughts and evidence is a major task in the process of "connecting the dots."

Concern about thought and evidence marshaling is not of course limited to intelligence analysis. Many persons in science and mathematics (including several Nobel laureates) have emphasized the importance of combining ideas during the process of discovery in which new ideas and new lines of evidence are being generated. You will find references to the works of some of these persons in an article written by D. A. Schum (1999). All of these noted persons emphasize the fact that new ideas frequently result from particular combinations of evidence and ideas we already have. The trouble is that we could never look through all possible combinations of information that we have. Indeed, this would be the attempt to look through *everything* in the hope of finding *something*. Most combinations of trifles would be meaningless anyway; just a few combinations might lead to startling and productive new ideas. How do we decide which combinations of trifles or details to examine? Here is where the process of imaginative reasoning is so necessary and where evidence marshaling becomes so important. Our imaginative reasoning begins to be applied by the questions we ask *of* and *about* the evidence we already have. Questions we ask *about* our evidence help us to determine the three major credentials of evidence already mentioned: relevance, believability, and inferential force. Questions we ask *of* our existing evidence allow us to generate new hypotheses and new lines of inquiry and evidence. We cannot productively ask these appropriate questions unless we have marshaled or organized our existing thoughts in meaningful ways.

As you recognize, every intelligence analysis is unique; so are the situations and events that form the subject of intelligence analyses. In most intelligence analyses, the events of concern are singular, unique, or one of a kind. What this means is that there are very few if any statistical records available to allow us to predict events that are of concern to the nation's defense. There were no statistics available that would have allowed us to forecast the tragic events that took place on September 11, 2001. In many discussions in the field of artificial intelligence concerning the process of discovery, it is claimed that all discovery amounts to is having sophisticated methods of *search*. In such discussions, something crucial is left out, namely the process of *inquiry*, the asking of questions. *Having productive search methods is necessary but not sufficient during the process of discovery in many fields such as intelligence analysis.* The reason is that, absent any relevant statistical or other prior records, we may have nothing to search as some intelligence analysis task begins. We begin to have relevant evidence to search through only when we begin to ask questions about the situation of concern. No discovery process, in any discipline, can proceed in the absence of someone asking important questions. The issue then is: *How do we become more skillful in forming the questions we ask of and about our existing evidence and about the situation(s) of interest to us?* Answers to this question are supplied in part by the strategies we employ in marshaling our thoughts and our evidence in different ways.

2.3   MARSHALING "MAGNETS" OR ATTRACTORS

Apart from convenience, it probably does not matter very much how we organize the clothes in our closet, the food in our pantry, or the books on our shelves. But in intelligence analysis and other inference tasks it does matter *very much* how we organize our *thoughts* and our *evidence*. How well we organize or marshal our ideas and evidence helps determine what new evidence and hypotheses we will generate and what conclusions we will draw. Different ways of organizing thoughts and evidence may lead us to:

- Ask different questions of and about our evidence
- Discover different evidence and hypotheses
- Draw different conclusions

The processes of discovering evidence and hypotheses, and then using evidence as a basis for drawing conclusions, involve many different mental tasks. It is clear that there is no *single* way of organizing thoughts and evidence that will meet the demands of all of these tasks. We now examine various ways in which evidence you gather might be organized in different ways, each of which serves a useful purpose. Figure 2.1 is a simple picture of what different evidence marshaling strategies should help you accomplish; it involves the metaphor of a "magnet" or an attractor.

What we would like to have are conceptual "magnets" that could attract interesting and useful combinations of "trifles," as Sherlock Holmes called them. In Figure 2.1, the magnet has attracted several trifles that, together, may allow us to generate a new possibility or hypothesis, ask a new and important question, or generate some new potential evidence. It happens that different ways in which we marshal our thoughts and evidence can in fact serve like the "magnet" shown in this figure. On occasion, you may be able to generate a new idea, possibility, or hypothesis from a single trifle. More often, however, new ideas, new questions, and new possible evidence will only emerge in your mind from combinations of two or more trifles. Remember, it makes no sense to try to examine every possible combination of trifles or details you collect. The purpose of the evidence marshaling magnets we will mention is to help you decide which combinations of trifles would be valuable for you to identify and evaluate. Different ways of organizing your thoughts and your evidence may be heuristically valuable in suggesting questions you might ask of your data. *A heuristic is simply a rule of thumb that aids you in any discovery, inference, learning, or decision problem.* You need such heuristics as aids in deciding which combinations of data you might most profitably examine. Discussed in the following paragraphs are some specific marshaling strategies, or "magnets," you might consider. The sequence in which you employ these magnets depends upon the nature of the analysis tasks you will actually encounter.

In an intelligence analysis, you may begin to accumulate trifles or details at a very rapid rate. Some of these details will be provided for you as a matter of course (for example, your daily message traffic). Other details you will obtain in response to questions you ask. Some

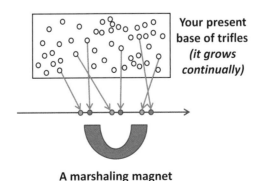

A marshaling magnet

Figure 2.1. Marshaling magnet attracting interesting combinations of "trifles."

of the details will be tangible in nature; others will be items of testimony received from human sources. *Which details should you keep and which should you ignore?* If you could answer this question, your task would be much simpler. However, unless you are clairvoyant you cannot know for sure, at least in the early stages of an analysis, which details will become important, relevant evidence, and which will not. This task may get easier as your analysis proceeds and you begin to form a collection of plausible hypotheses to which certain details can become relevant evidence. Stated in other words, as your analysis proceeds, you may be able to ask better questions and obtain relevant details more efficiently.

Before we consider some specific marshaling operations or "magnets," it seems wise to acknowledge that analysts will already have some schemes for organizing the information they acquire. But these schemes may exist only for the purpose of *archiving* their information in orderly ways. Such archiving, by itself, has little heuristic value, but it may facilitate marshaling operations that do have heuristic value in suggesting new hypotheses and new lines of inquiry and evidence.

2.4   TYPES OF MARSHALING MAGNETS

2.4.1   Believability Magnet

One rather obvious way to archive trifles or details is in terms of the *sources* from which you received them. For example, we could organize evidence by "INTs": HUMINT, SIGINT, IMINT, MASINT, and so on. In some cases, particularly regarding HUMINT, security matters will arise and you may not always be able to precisely identify a human source; you may only have an alias of some sort (such as a code word). It may also be useful to keep separate tracks of tangible evidence and testimonial evidence. If you organize your data in terms of their sources, there are two kinds of information you need to record, if you have them. The first, of course, are the trifles or details you receive *from* a source (whatever it is). In other words, you record what the source tells you. The second are details you have *about* this source. Details *about* a source become important as you begin to assess the believability of what the source has given you. Believability assessment will be discussed in detail in Chapter 6. Suppose a source has provided you with some tangible evidence. You should record whatever information you have about the authenticity and accuracy of this tangible item. If the detail exists in the form of a testimonial assertion from some human source, you should record whatever information you have regarding this source's veracity, objectivity, observational sensitivity, and competence. This forms the basis for the first marshaling magnet we will mention.

Keeping careful accounts of the trifles or details we have *about* our intelligence sources will provide a basis for our decision concerning whether or not to believe what a source is reporting to us. Suppose a source is discovered to be faulty in some way. If you have marshaled together all the trifles you have obtained about this source, you may begin to question the extent to which the items you have received from this source might not be believable. This can often pay huge inferential dividends. For example, suppose we now believe that a source S of HUMINT was lying to us in his report that event E occurred. We ask, "Why did S choose to lie about event E in preference to other lies he might have told us?" Answers to this question may suggest very interesting new possibilities. Second, if we have at hand (that is, marshaled) all the other events source S has reported, we might now begin to question the believability of other reports S has provided. What we know *about* a source of evidence (testimonial or tangible) is often at least as interesting as what this source tells us.

We can characterize this Believability Magnet in the following way:

> *Believability Magnet is a magnet that attracts trifles we have concerning the competence and credibility of our sources of intelligence information.*

Now the issue becomes, "What questions should we be asking about our sources?" We have given much thought to these questions, especially as they concern HUMINT evidence. Some years ago, we proposed a system called MACE (Method for Assessing the Credibility of Evidence). This system rests on more than six hundred years of experience in the Anglo-American judicial system for assessing the competence and credibility of human witnesses. This experience has allowed us to generate a wide array of questions we should be asking about the competence, veracity, objectivity, and observational sensitivity of our HUMINT sources (Schum and Morris, 2007). The MACE idea can easily be extended to questions we should ask about the authenticity, reliability, and accuracy of tangible evidence.

In the design and development of our Disciple-CD system, we have also given attention to an often-overlooked credibility assessment problem. This problem also arises because of the many things that are done to information before it reaches the attention of analysts who will attempt to draw conclusions from this information. It is common to refer to this matter as involving the *chain of custody* through which information is passed before an intelligence analyst receives it. Many things might have been done to this information, including translations, interpretations, editing, processing, and summarizing. A number of persons or automated processes might have been involved. The issue is, "How *authentic* is the information received by an analyst? To what degree is this information an accurate and complete account of what an original source has reported?" We have recorded our thoughts on believability matters involving chains of custody of intelligence information (Schum et al., 2009). They will also be discussed in Chapter 7.

Table 2.1 shows some trifles we have received *from* several sources and examples of the believability information we might have *about* them.

2.4.2   Chronology Magnet

Many of the trifles or data we receive are "time-stamped" in terms of the time at which events in the data are *alleged* to have occurred. We are just as interested in when events have occurred as we are in their occurrence. The timing of events can be a most valuable heuristic source of possible hypotheses and new lines of inquiry and evidence. There is an inference here: Sometimes we are misled about the time some reported event has occurred. An event chronology is simply an ordering of events according to the times at which *we believe them to have occurred* (new evidence might cause us to change our minds about this temporal ordering). Having some idea about the order in which events might have occurred also gives us some basis for establishing causal patterns that may be very important in reaching any final conclusions. Such chronologies can also be very useful in efforts to predict events that may happen in the future. So, our Chronology Magnet has this purpose:

Table 2.1 Illustration of the Application of the Believability Magnet

Trifles from Sources	Trifles about Sources
An extract from a HUMINT report from Source A.	We have not been able to communicate with Source A since he gave us the information in his HUMINT report.
An extract from a copy of a document said to have been obtained by Source B from the files of a potential adversary.	An expert's assessment that there is a 30% chance that the document we received from Source B is a fake.
An extract from a table compiled by Source C showing the range of a certain missile.	Information that Source C has made errors in the past in calculating the range of missiles.
A fragment of the door panel of a car said to contain the explosive device that destroyed an overseas embassy.	Information that there were other cars parked in the vicinity of the explosion that were also destroyed.

Chronology Magnet is a magnet that attracts inferred times at which reported events have occurred and allows inferences about the temporal ordering of these events.

There is nothing new about event chronologies; you may already be naturally constructing them. But there are some difficulties here; event chronologies can get very messy if we have many events to record. One strategy is to form *parallel event chronologies*, each of which records events belonging to a certain class. Figure 2.2 shows an example involving an intelligence analysis in which there may be many "actors." An actor may be either a person or an entire group of persons, such as a terrorist organization or an army battalion.

These parallel chronologies record the times at which we believe the events associated with each actor have occurred. Evidence about the events associated with each actor may have come from the actor or from another source. It is not difficult to observe how event chronologies serve as important "magnets" that can stimulate the process of inquiry. Consider the three events associated with Actor 1: A, B, and C. We might ask, "If Actor 1 did A, and then sometime later did B, what was he doing in the interval?" We might also ask such questions as, "If Actor 2 did D and E between the time Actor 1 did A and B, did Actor 2's actions have any effect on what Actor 1 did during this interval?" By such means, we are stimulated to examine particular combinations of trifles and to try to discover them if they are not now at hand. We add here that Indications and Warnings (I&W) assignments involve the use of evidence chronologies. Such marshaling allows us to provide timely warnings of future events involving matters of national security.

Example 2.1.

Here are three events not in any order:
    Event A = Person P drank three double martinis.
    Event B = Person P left the base parking lot.
    Event C = Person P was involved in a car accident.

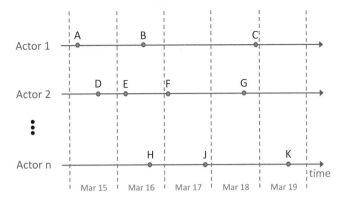

Figure 2.2. Parallel event chronologies.

Consider each possible sequence and see what story it tells. If you were person P, you would rather have the following sequence of events B–C–A than either of the two sequences B–A–C or A–B–C. In these two sequences, P faces a charge of driving while intoxicated, which he does not face in the first sequence B–C–A.

2.4.3   Question Magnet

In the search for hypotheses or possibilities that will account for all of the evidence you believe to be relevant, various specific issues and questions will arise. Here is an example:

Example 2.2.

You are trying to determine whether or not a certain terrorist organization is planning an act of destruction at a certain location in the near future. You now have some evidence that this group is obtaining materials for the construction of explosive devices from a particular source. A variety of questions come to mind, such as:

What type of explosives might be used?
How are they to be detonated?
Where are they to be detonated?
When are they to be detonated?

Questions you ask serve as most important "magnets" for attracting combinations of data from your records. We can define this Question Magnet as follows:

Question Magnet is a magnet that attracts trifles representing possible answers to any question that comes to mind as an intelligence analysis proceeds.

Remember that the process of *inquiry* is a most vital ingredient of productively imaginative intelligence analysis. Each question you ask not only serves as a device for attracting existing trifles, but also serves as a device for generating new trifles you do not presently have. Keeping track of all the trifles attracted by a certain question can be most valuable in generating new hypotheses and new potential evidence.

2.4.4 Hypothesis Magnet

Suppose we now have a large assortment of trifles and we identify ten of them as being evidence we regard as relevant to three hypotheses we are now considering. One obvious method of organizing these ten items of evidence is in terms of the hypothesis each item seems to favor (see Figure 2.3). This marshaling method is closely tied to what is frequently said to be the method of "competing hypotheses" in which we attempt to judge each hypothesis on its merits (Heuer, 1999, pp. 95–110; Heuer, 2008).

In the situation from Figure 2.3, evidence items 6, 8, and 10 are relevant to hypothesis H_1; items 1, 2, and 4 are relevant to hypothesis H_3; and the rest are relevant to hypothesis H_2. Notice that, under each hypothesis, we group the evidence into favoring and disfavoring. This form of marshaling is often useful since it allows us to observe which hypothesis seems to have the most evidence in its favor. We can define this Hypothesis Magnet as follows:

> *Hypothesis Magnet is a magnet that uses generated hypotheses to attract information items that could become relevant evidence in their favor or against.*

Marshaling evidence by hypotheses has another useful feature that concerns the completeness or sufficiency of the evidence we have. Suppose someone says, "Hypothesis H_2 (in Figure 2.3) has the most evidence favoring it, so we should conclude that this hypothesis is the one we ought to advocate." But, another person very wisely says, "Before we decide on Hypothesis H_2, or any other, we ought to ask how many questions there are that remain *unanswered* by all the evidence we have." This question of evidential completeness or sufficiency is so often overlooked and can result in some dramatic inferential miscarriages. Marshaling by hypotheses, as well as marshaling by argument, to be presented next, allows us to survey what we have and we don't have in the way of evidence on every hypothesis we are considering.

In some instances, evidence will say something about one hypothesis but say nothing at all about other hypotheses. For example, evidence E^*_{10} in Figure 2.3 goes against hypothesis H_1, but does not favor or disfavor hypotheses H_2 or H_3. Similarly, E^*_6 favors H_1 but it is not relevant to the other hypotheses. As an example, consider two organizations, A and B, which may now be distributing narcotics in a certain city. We have evidence that A has contacts with foreign suppliers of narcotics. This tends to raise our suspicions about A but it tells us nothing about B.

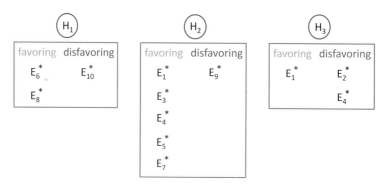

Figure 2.3. Evidence marshaling by hypotheses.

In other instances, evidence may favor more than one hypothesis. For example, E^*_1 in Figure 2.3 favors both H_2 and H_3. As a concrete example, suppose that Person X belongs to two terrorist groups. Evidence that X was at the scene of a terrorist incident might favor hypotheses concerning either or both of these groups being responsible.

We may also encounter evidence we regard as relevant but which is not well explained by any hypotheses we are currently considering. One way to describe this evidence as unexplainable by any existing hypothesis being considered is to say that it is an *anomaly*. *We might consider disregarding this anomalous evidence completely; but to do so would be the height of foolishness.* Perhaps this anomaly means that there is a hypothesis we have not yet considered that could explain this anomaly and, perhaps, better explain all the other evidence we have. This is one frequently observed way in which new hypotheses and new evidence are generated. Pondering an anomaly, we are led to generate a new hypothesis and new evidential tests of all of our hypotheses.

2.4.5 Argument Magnet

Here is an important and useful refinement of marshaling by hypotheses. Consider again the situation in Figure 2.3 showing the generated hypotheses and the collection of relevant evidence bearing upon each of them. Suppose further that you are preparing to argue that H_2 is the most likely hypothesis from among those you have considered. In your defense of hypothesis H_2, you expect to be required to produce specific evidence-based arguments about why you favor hypothesis H_2 over hypotheses H_1 and H_3. You think about this problem carefully and decide that your evidence suggests three major lines of argument on hypothesis H_2; these major lines of argument (or subhypotheses) are A_1, A_2, and A_3. A natural form of evidence marshaling would be to organize your existing evidence under each of these subhypotheses, as shown in Figure 2.4.

In this case, the Marshaling Magnet has the following function:

Argument Magnet is a magnet that attracts trifles that will form relevant evidence on major arguments for some hypothesis being entertained.

This form of marshaling is both useful and necessary in your efforts to construct defensible and persuasive arguments as far as hypothesis H_2 is concerned. Such marshaling helps you to see what additional evidence you will need to construct stronger and more complete arguments in defense of hypothesis H_2. Remember the discussion from the previous section concerning the selection of hypothesis H_2 because it has the most

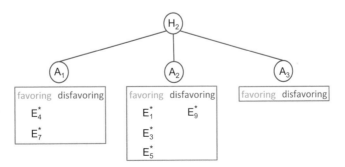

Figure 2.4. Evidence marshaling by arguments.

evidence favoring it (see Figure 2.3)? The advice there was that before we decide on hypothesis H_2, we ought to ask how many questions there are that remain *unanswered* by all the evidence we have. The argument in Figure 2.4 shows that we have no evidence bearing on subhypothesis A_3, and we should not reach any conclusion before we are also able to assess A_3.

As you construct your arguments from this array of marshaled evidence, you can obtain a better idea about how strong and sufficient your arguments favoring H_2 will be at this time. There are specific ways in which you can construct chains of reasoning from the evidence you have to each of these main lines of argument in your analysis. The very first step in the process is a careful marshaling of evidence under each of your main lines of argument. These marshaling efforts may allow you to see that your main lines of argument are not sufficient and that you may need additional lines of evidence. Your hope is that your main lines of argument will be necessary and sufficient or, at least, sufficient to show that hypothesis H_2 is true.

2.4.6   Eliminative Magnet

In many situations, we use evidence not to support hypotheses but to try to eliminate them on the basis of a *variety* of *different* questions we ask and hope to have answered by evidence. This is precisely the method Sherlock Holmes says he used in solving his cases. The hypothesis that survives our best attempts to eliminate all of our hypotheses is the one we should take seriously. Now, one of the most embarrassing things that can happen to an analyst is to eliminate some hypothesis that later proves to be true. Critics will say that this analyst "snatched defeat from the jaws of victory." So, when we say we are eliminating some hypothesis (we should never do so completely), we ought to make sure that we have exhausted all reasons for keeping this hypothesis alive. To do this is to protect ourselves from the "hindsight critic" who will say, post mortem, you had the truth in your grasp and you let it slip away. By implication, this critic is saying that he would have kept it alive. He can make himself look good, of course, since he now knows what did happen. So what we should do is to keep track of all of the questions we asked and all of the evidence obtained, in response to these questions, that *argued against* the hypothesis we have chosen to eliminate. Unless we do this, someone can always later say, "Why did you reject this hypothesis that now seems so obvious?

Suppose you have decided to eliminate hypothesis H_3 from consideration (see Figure 2.3). You will want to have evidence showing why you have chosen not to keep H_3 alive. So the Eliminative Marshaling Magnet has the following interpretation:

> *Eliminative Magnet is a magnet that attracts trifles representing evidence relevant in showing why some hypotheses can be safely eliminated.*

Suppose you have eliminated hypothesis H_3 early in your analysis because someone tells you that it is too improbable for anyone to believe. Though you don't have much evidence yet, you decide to forget about this hypothesis. You gather further evidence and draw a conclusion that hypothesis H_2 is true and you report your conclusion to higher authorities. Later, it turns out that H_3 was true after all and you are reprimanded. You are reminded that you dismissed hypothesis H_3 without attempting to gather other evidence that might have been in its favor. In short, your evidence was not complete enough for you to rule out H_3.

Example 2.3.

As an example, consider that someone has been leaking classified information from your organization. Person Y is presently a suspect. You decide to eliminate Y as a possibility. What general factors should you consider before you decide to rule out Y as a possibility?

It seems you could only rule out Y if:

(1) Y would never have had access to this information, and
(2) Y never attempted to obtain this information from someone who did have access to it, and
(3) Y had no reason to wish or need to obtain this information.

2.4.7 Scenario Magnet

The aforementioned event chronologies simply allow us to list interesting events in the order in which we believe they occurred. *One of the most heuristically valuable exercises is to construct stories or scenarios about what we believe might have happened, might be happening, or might happen in the future.* An example of a scenario is that from Figure 1.12. Like any stories, the ones we construct always consist of a mixture of evidence and fiction or fancy. It is the fanciful elements of stories we tell that are most valuable in generating new hypotheses and new evidence. Such stories also provide yet another heuristic for focusing attention on specific combinations of data we have on file. Figure 2.5 shows a simple picture of a story or scenario constructed for heuristic purposes.

Suppose we have evidence that events A, B, C, and D have occurred at the times indicated in Figure 2.5. But to tell a coherent story or to construct a coherent scenario about what these events mean, we need to fill in the gaps with evidence we do not now have. Suppose that, for example, part of our story involves saying that the occurrence of A led to the occurrence of B, and we have evidence that both of these events occurred. But, we then think that A, by itself, could not have given rise to B unless events E and F had also happened. So, we fill in the gap between A and B by these two hypotheticals or *gap fillers* in order to tell this part of our story. We do the same thing at other points, such as filling in the B–C gap with G and filling in the C–D gap with H. Here is the payoff: Each new gap filler we identify alerts us to examine our existing database to see whether such data exist. If they do not, then we are stimulated to try to discover them. Naturally, we may discover that these hypothesized events did not occur. If this happens on enough occasions, we have to change our story. We may also be led to question the believability of the evidence that suggested this story in the first place. The Story or Scenario Magnet has the following interpretation:

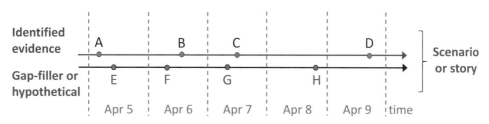

Figure 2.5. Evidence marshaling through the construction of scenarios or stories.

Scenario Magnet is a magnet that attracts a temporally ordered sequence of trifles forming relevant evidence about events that will form the basis for a story or scenario about what has happened in some situation of interest.

Example 2.4.

From any collection of information arranged in chronological order, a virtual infinity of different stories might be told. The smaller the number of evidence items, the more possible stories there are. As an illustration, suppose we now have just the three items of evidence from Figure 2.6 whose temporal ordering we have reason to believe. What possible scenario does this sequence of events suggests?

    The top part of Figure 2.7 shows a possible scenario: Premier X was killed by a member of a group in his own country that regarded his leadership as reckless. The group will argue that its action prevented a war between countries A and B.

    This Scenario 1 suggests the two gap fillers shown below the time line. These gap fillers open new lines of investigations, suggesting that we should look for evidence that:

(1) Members of a certain group in Country A were enraged by what they regarded as a reckless speech by X; and
(2) Members of this group within A determined that X has to go.

But Scenario 1 is not the only scenario consistent with the available sequence of events. Another one is Scenario 2 from the bottom part of Figure 2.7: Hoping that their own interests would be better served by a leadership change in Country A, the leaders of Country B decide to take matters into their own hands.

    Scenario 2 suggests other gap fillers and guides us to look for evidence that:

(1) The leadership in Country B reacts strongly against the leadership in Country A; and
(2) The leadership in B initiates a plot against the life of Premier X in Country A.

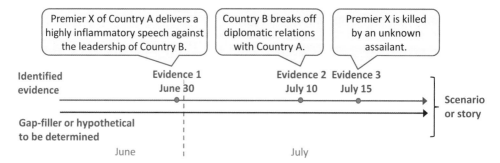

Figure 2.6. Evidence about a sequence of events.

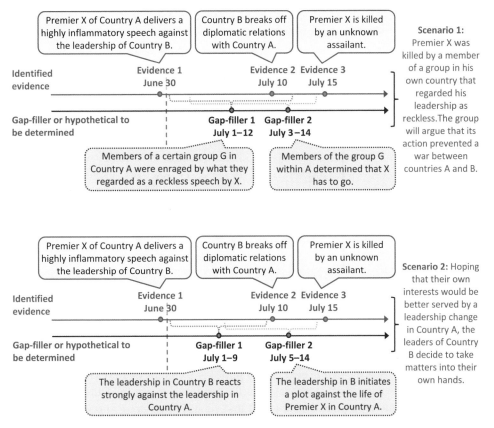

Figure 2.7. Two different scenarios hypothesized from the events in Figure 2.6.

USE OF THE MARSHALING MAGNETS

The seven marshaling magnets we have considered are some of the most important ways in which we might organize our thoughts and our evidence as we work on intelligence analyses. Each of these methods serves as a magnet in attracting combinations of trifles or details from an emerging base of trifles in order to help us generate new possibilities in productively imaginative ways and then construct arguments in defense of hypotheses we believe to contain truth.

Figure 2.8 shows all seven of the marshaling magnets taken together. There is a certain fairly natural, but not a strict, ordering of the operation of these seven marshaling magnets. First, we have shown a trifle base that has been archived in various ways, such as in terms of the "INTs," as we illustrated previously. But analysts could archive a trifle base in any way that suits them. Now notice the "Analysis Progress" arrow to the left of Figure 2.8. What this arrow indicates is an ordering of how these marshaling operations might usually be performed. We have shown these seven operations in three order-related tiers. At the start of an analysis task, we do not have any hypotheses yet, have constructed no arguments, and can tell no stories. The three marshaling operations at Tier 1 serve to get us started in generating hypotheses, new lines of inquiry, and new possible trifles that can become relevant evidence on these hypotheses. Then, at Tier 2, when hypotheses have been generated, we can put them to use to collect new evidence and see how well

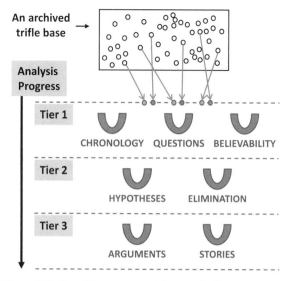

Figure 2.8. Possible ordering of the marshaling magnets.

they can be supported. Also at Tier 2, we can marshal evidence we have supplying reasons why we have eliminated certain hypotheses. But then we are prepared to generate main lines of argument, at Tier 3, to see how well we are supporting hypotheses we have retained. We are then also prepared to begin to tell stories or scenarios we have constructed in part to see what new lines of evidence we need (the gap fillers shown in Figure 2.5).

Now, it will happen at Tiers 2 and 3 that we will often need to revisit Tier 1. We will need to ask new questions, consider new believability matters, and perhaps revise our chronologies. What we must always keep in mind is that our analytic tasks are always dynamic in nature because the world keeps changing all the while we are trying to understand parts of it of interest to us. This is one reason why we have dwelled on the fact that we have evidence in search of hypotheses at the same time we have hypotheses in search of evidence. In addition, there are instances in which we could begin at Tier 2. In some situations, such as in "current intelligence," for example, we may begin with a hypothesis. Suppose you are asked whether or not some event E has occurred. So, you begin by attempting to test the hypothesis H = event E did occur. But this would require you to ask questions encountered at Tier 1. These matters all reinforce our claim that there is no single form of marshaling thoughts and evidence that will be adequate in capturing all the requirements of drawing defensible conclusions from masses of evidence.

All of the thoughts and evidence marshaling examples we have discussed in this chapter bear directly or indirectly on arguments that can be constructed concerning the situations and events we are analyzing. We cannot oversell the importance of having careful methods for marshaling thoughts and evidence in intelligence analysis. Until someone like Mycroft Holmes appears, we must do the best we can.

2.6   REVIEW QUESTIONS

2.1. From any collection of information arranged in chronological order, a virtual infinity of different stories might be told. Suppose we have the following three items of evidence whose temporal ordering we have reason to believe:

- Person Y agreed on March 4 to supply us with information about the military in his country.
- On August 1, Source Y supplied us with a HUMINT report saying that the commanding general of the military was planning to launch a coup attempt against the elected leadership in his country on August 15.
- On August 18, the leadership in this country announced that the commanding general of its military, along with several members of his staff, were being held in prison.

Think of all the different stories that might be told about why the event predicted in Y's HUMINT did not come to pass.

2.2. The use of index cards and shoeboxes to organize incoming intelligence information is old hat. Are there any computer-based methods you have tried? Have they been helpful in allowing you to generate hypotheses for any analysis you have been working on?

2.3. Here is a HUMINT Source S who tells us that a Person P has been assembling explosive devices in his garage. What kind of questions should you be asking *about* and *of* Source S? Have another look at the examples shown in Table 2.1 concerning questions *of* and *about* our sources.

2.4. In Section 2.4.2, we presented an example of the importance of event ordering to Person P, who we assume does not wish to have a certain event ordering happen as he left work today; the event of concern involves his having consumed three double martinis. Can you think of other cases in which event ordering is so important?

2.5. What other questions seem natural to ask about the terrorist organization described in Section 2.4.3?

2.6. Hypotheses become most useful "magnets" for attracting productive combinations of evidence to consider, as we illustrated in Section 2.4.4. Here we consider instances of hypotheses in search of evidence we mentioned earlier. As an example, suppose we form the hypothesis that S is a credible source of information about an important event E. This source might either tell us that event E occurred or it did not occur. What evidence would we need to justify our hypothesis that S is credible?

2.7. Consider the argument "magnet" described in Section 2.4.5. Here we must consider arguments favoring or disfavoring subhypotheses we are considering. Consider again testing your hypothesis that S is a credible source. What arguments should you be prepared to offer in support of this hypothesis?

2.8. Consider the situation shown in Section 2.4.6, in which we are concerned with the leakage of classified information from an intelligence office. You have been charged with investigating the activities of Person Y, who is suspected of being the leaker. As a result of your investigation, you report that Person Y can be eliminated from consideration. At some time later, the classified documents are found on a laptop belonging to Y, and Y admits to having been the leaker. You are then confronted by your boss, who says, "You managed to snatch defeat from the jaws of victory; how could you have been so foolish? You had Y and you let him go. You made all of us look bad and I am considering demoting you." What defense can you offer your boss and perhaps preserve your position?

2.9. We hope you will appreciate the many heuristic virtues of telling yourself stories or constructing scenarios based on evidence you have gathered. From the same collection of available evidence, you may be able to tell an array of different stories depending on the "gap fillers" or hypothetical events you include. Every different story you can tell suggests different hypotheses and new lines of evidence you might consider. Look again at the two different stories we told based on the same evidence as shown in Figure 2.7. What is another different story you could tell?

3 Disciple-CD: A Cognitive Assistant for Connecting the Dots

3.1 SYSTEM OVERVIEW

Disciple-CD (Tecuci et al., 2014) is cognitive assistant for intelligence analysis that implements the computational theory of intelligence analysis presented in Section 1.3. It is a significant improvement of an earlier system, called TIACRITIS (Teaching Intelligence Analysts Critical Thinking Skills), and it subsumes all the reasoning and learning capabilities of TIACRITIS, which have been described in several papers (Tecuci et al., 2010; 2011a; 2011b).

Disciple-CD is an intelligent, knowledge-based analytic tool that incorporates a significant amount of knowledge about evidence and its credentials, and about evidence-based hypotheses analysis, helping the user to formulate alternative hypotheses, collect evidence, and build argumentation structures to determine to most likely hypothesis. It is organized in modules specialized for different analytic functions. They are invoked through the menus shown at the top of the screen capture from Figure 3.1: **Hypothesis**, **Reasoner**, **Evidence**, **Assumption**, and **Description**. They will be introduced in this chapter. You may select a module, such as **Reasoner**, by clicking on the corresponding menu, which will appear with a brown background.

When you start Disciple-CD with a case study, the **Hypothesis** module is automatically invoked, as shown in Figure 3.2. This module allows you to either select a hypothesis from those shown in the upper panel or click on the [NEW] command to define a new hypothesis.

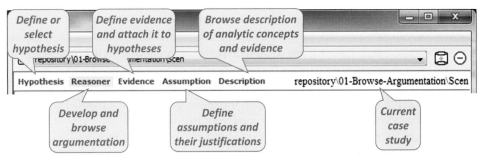

Figure 3.1. The main modules of Disciple-CD.

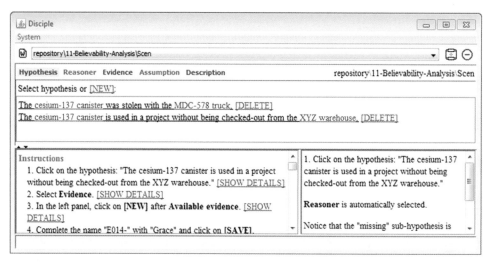

Figure 3.2. The interface of the Hypothesis module.

The bottom panel shows a list of instructions that you have to follow to perform the case study. Clicking on [SHOW DETAILS] following an instruction will provide additional explanations in the bottom-right panel.

Once a hypothesis is selected or defined, the system starts the **Reasoner,** the interface of which is shown in Figure 3.3. The left panel shows an abstraction of the entire argumentation structure consisting of hypotheses and their subhypotheses, together with their assessments.

When you click on a hypothesis and its assessment in the left panel, such as "cesium 137 canister missing from XYZ warehouse: likely," the right panel shows the details of its decomposition, including the complete names of the hypotheses.

To define items of evidence and associate them with elementary hypotheses, the user has to click on the **Evidence** module, the interface of which is shown in Figure 3.4. This module has several modes of operations, which are shown at the top of the left panel.

When the [AVAILABLE EVIDENCE] mode is selected, the left panel lists all the evidence items from the current case study. When the user clicks on one such item (e.g., E001-Willard), the right panel displays its characteristics, as follows: its description, the item of information from which it was extracted (if any), its type and associated information (e.g., its source), the list of elementary hypotheses it favors (if any), and the list of elementary hypotheses it disfavors (if any).

At the bottom of the right panel, under the **Irrelevant to** label, is the list of all the other leaf hypotheses from the analysis tree. The user may indicate that the current item of evidence favors or disfavors any of these hypotheses by clicking on the [FAVORS] or on the [DISFAVORS] command following that hypothesis.

To define a new item of evidence, the user has to click on the [NEW] command following the **Available evidence** label, in the upper part of the left panel. Then the system will guide the user to define the elements from the right panel.

Ideally, each leaf hypothesis in an argumentation is assessed based on evidence. When there is no relevant evidence, you may provide its assessment as an assumption. A simple way to make an assumption is just to right-click on the hypothesis and select the option **New Assumption**. If, however, you also want to provide a justification, you need to invoke the **Assumption** module, the interface of which is shown in Figure 3.5. This module lists a

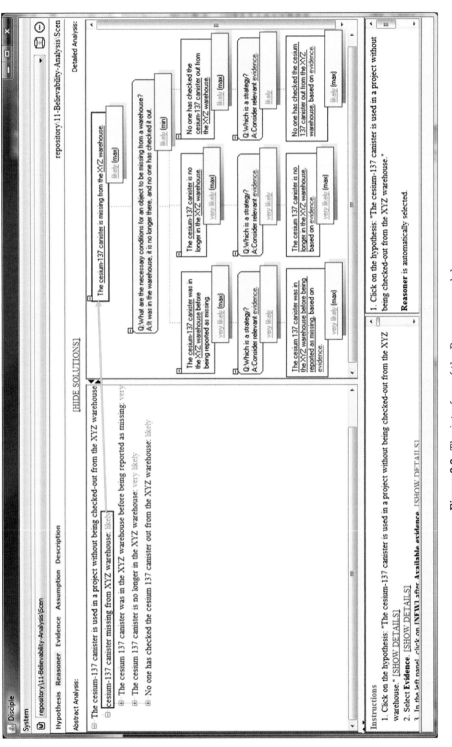

Figure 3.3. The interface of the Reasoner module.

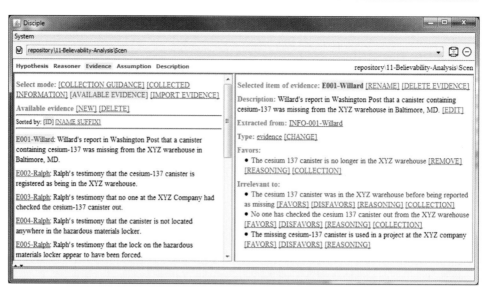

Figure 3.4. The interface of the Evidence module.

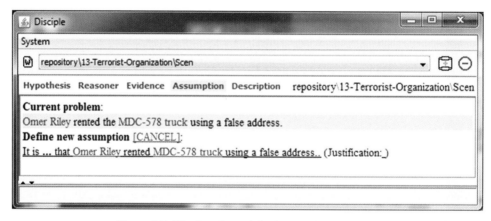

Figure 3.5. The interface of the Assumption module.

pattern for the assumption, which you have to instantiate by selecting a probability value. You will then type a justification after the label "Justification."

The system also includes definitions and short lessons on important evidence concepts, such as the different types of evidence and the corresponding credentials. To view them, you may select the **Description** menu, the interface of which is shown in Figure 3.6. Then, clicking on an item in the left panel causes its description to be displayed in the right panel.

The next section provides instructions for obtaining and installing the Disciple-CD system on your computer. After that, Section 3.3 introduces a hands on exercise to better familiarize you with the aforementioned modules of Disciple-CD.

3.2   OBTAINING DISCIPLE-CD

Disciple-CD is a research prototype implemented in Java and tested on PC. It is a stand-alone system that needs to be installed on the user's computer.

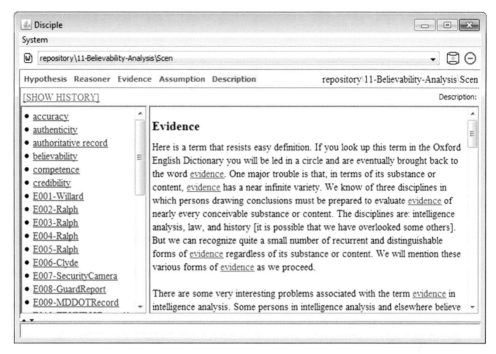

Figure 3.6. The interface of the Description module.

For installation requirements and to download the system, go to lac.gmu.edu/IABook/ Disciple-CD/. At this address, you will also find instructions on how to install and uninstall Disciple-CD, a section with frequently asked questions (FAQs), and a section that allows users to submit error reports to the developers of the system.

3.3   HANDS ON: WORKING WITH KNOWLEDGE BASES

3.3.1   Overview

Disciple-CD is a knowledge-based agent whose reasoning is determined by the knowledge from its knowledge bases. As shown in Figure 3.7, the knowledge bases are located in the repository folder that is inside the installation folder of Disciple-CD. From your point of view, each knowledge base consists of a top-level domain part, such as "01-Browse-Argumentation" (which contains knowledge common to several scenarios in a domain), and one scenario part, such as "01-Browse-Argumentation/Scen" (which inherits the knowledge from "01-Browse-Argumentation" and also contains knowledge specific to a particular scenario). There could be more than one scenario under a domain. In such a case, the domain and each of the scenarios correspond to a different knowledge base. Loading, saving, or closing a scenario will automatically load, save, or close both the scenario part and the corresponding domain part of the knowledge base. However, loading, saving, or closing the domain part will only load, save, or close the domain part of the knowledge base. In general, you will load, save, or close the entire knowledge base by applying these operations to scenarios.

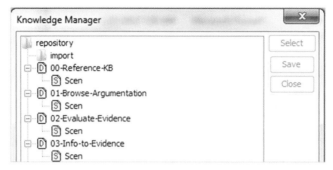

Figure 3.7. The interface of the Knowledge Manager.

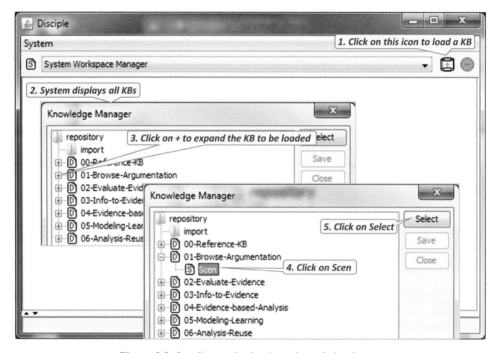

Figure 3.8. Loading and selecting a knowledge base.

3.3.2   Basic Operations

Loading and selecting a knowledge base is described in Operation 3.1 and illustrated in Figure 3.8.

Operation 3.1. Load and select a knowledge base

- In the System Workspace Manager, click on the knowledge base (KB) icon containing the + sign.
- The **Knowledge Manager** window will be opened, showing all the knowledge bases from the repository.
- Click on the + icon of the domain knowledge base to be loaded, to display all its scenario knowledge bases.

- Click on the scenario knowledge base to be loaded.
- Click on the **Select** button. This will both load the scenario and domain KBs and will select them as the current ones to work with. Their names will be shown in bold in the **Knowledge Manager** window.

Once a scenario is selected, the Hypothesis module is invoked, as shown in Figure 3.2. The steps to save all the knowledge bases loaded in memory are described in Operation 3.2 and illustrated in Figure 3.9.

Operation 3.2. Save all the knowledge bases
- Select the **System** menu.
- Select **Save All**.

It is highly recommended to have only one knowledge base loaded in memory. Therefore, before loading a new knowledge base, one should close all the opened KBs by following the instructions described in Operation 3.3 and illustrated in Figure 3.10.

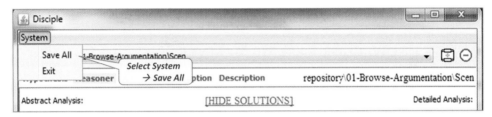

Figure 3.9. Saving all the knowledge bases.

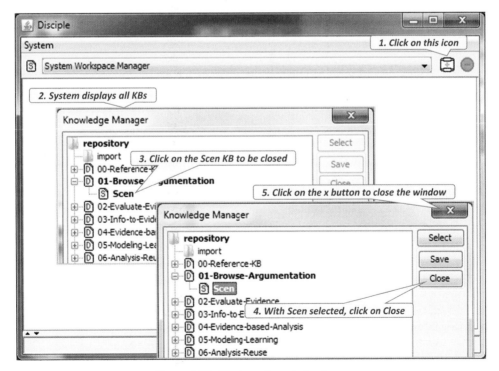

Figure 3.10. Closing a knowledge base.

Operation 3.3. Close a knowledge base

- Click on the knowledge base (KB) icon containing the + sign situated at the right of the workspace selector.
- The **Knowledge Manager** window will be opened, showing all the knowledge bases.
- Click on the scenario knowledge base to be closed.
- Click on the **Close** button in the right side of the window.
- Click on the **X** button to close the **Knowledge Manager** window.

The knowledge base 00-Reference-KB contains general knowledge for evidence-based reasoning, an empty domain, and an empty scenario. Users can create their knowledge bases as renamed copies of 00-Reference-KB, as indicated in Operation 3.4. They should never work with 00-Reference-KB, which should be kept as a reference knowledge base.

Operation 3.4. Create a user knowledge base

- Open the repository folder from the installation directory in **Windows Explorer**.
- Make a copy of the entire 00-Reference-KB folder and give it a new name.
- Use the Disciple-CD modules to develop the newly created knowledge base.

3.4   KNOWLEDGE BASE GUIDELINES

The following are methodological guidelines for knowledge base development.

Guideline 3.1. Work with only one knowledge base loaded in memory.

To maintain the performance of the Disciple-CD modules, work only with one knowledge base loaded in memory. Therefore, close all the knowledge bases before loading a new one.

Guideline 3.2. Create a knowledge base and save successive versions.

Because there is no undo option for knowledge bases, it is a good practice to save successive versions of the knowledge base being developed, in order to be able to return to a previous version.

Create your knowledge base by making a copy of 00-Reference-KB and giving it a new name, for instance WA. From now on, you will work only with WA, but, as you develop it, you will have to save successive copies of it with different names, as explained in the following.

Suppose that you have developed WA to contain part of the analysis of a hypothesis. Save **WA**, make a copy of **WA**, and rename it as **WA-1**. Continue working with WA and expand your analysis. Save and make a copy of **WA**. Then rename the copy as **WA-2** and so forth. Through such a process, you would have saved a sequence of knowledge bases (i.e., WA-1, WA-2, etc.), each corresponding to a given stage in your development of WA. In this way, if your WA knowledge base is damaged for any reason, you may always resume from the most recently saved version, as illustrated in the following scenario:

- WA has errors and the most recently saved version is WA-4.
- Delete **WA**, copy **WA-4**, and rename this copy as **WA**.
- Continue with the development of WA.

HANDS ON: BROWSING AN ARGUMENTATION

3.5.1   Overview

The use of Disciple-CD will consist in running case studies with associated instructions that will provide detailed guidance. We will illustrate this process by running the case study stored in the knowledge base called "01-Browse-Argumentation." This case study concerns the hypothesis "The cesium-137 canister is missing from the XYZ warehouse," which is part of the analysis example discussed in Section 1.3.3. It has three objectives:

- Learning how to run a case study
- Learning how to browse a reasoning tree or argumentation
- Understanding the process of hypothesis assessment through reduction and synthesis

As discussed in Section 3.1, once a hypothesis is selected in the **Hypothesis** module, the **Reasoner** is automatically invoked, showing its current analysis, as illustrated in Figure 3.11. The right panel shows the decomposition of this hypothesis into three simpler hypotheses, including the corresponding question/answer pair that determined this decomposition. Each of the three simpler hypotheses is further reduced to the direct assessment of an elementary hypothesis based on evidence, which is a leaf hypothesis in the displayed argumentation tree.

Notice the assessments of the leaf hypotheses in the right panel: "very likely," "very likely," and "likely." These assessments have been obtained based on evidence, as will be discussed later. Then they have been propagated upward, as the assessments of the three subhypotheses of the top-level hypothesis. After that, these three assessments have been combined, from the bottom up, to obtain the assessment associated with the question/answer pair ("likely"), and then the assessment of the top-level hypothesis ("likely").

The question/answer pair corresponds to one strategy of assessing the top-level hypothesis. The assessment associated with this strategy is computed as the minimum (*min*) of the assessments of the three subhypotheses because all these hypotheses need to be true in order to conclude that the canister is missing. This assessment is then transmitted upward as the assessment of the top-level hypothesis. The *max* function associated with this assessment indicates that, if additional assessment strategies are considered, the assessment of the top-level hypothesis will be the maximum of all the obtained assessments.

The left panel shows an abstraction of the analysis tree from the right panel. It consists of abstractions (or shorter sentences) of the top hypothesis and the three leaf hypotheses, together with their assessments. When you click on an abstract hypothesis in the left panel (such as "The cesium 137 canister was in the XYZ warehouse before being reported as missing: very likely"), the left panel shows its abstract decomposition into simpler hypotheses, while the right panel shows the details of this decomposition, as illustrated in Figure 3.12.

When you right-click on the top-level abstract hypothesis and select **Expand**, the left panel displays the abstraction of the entire reasoning tree or argumentation. If you then click on any abstract hypothesis (such as "E002-Ralph: very likely"), the left panel shows its abstract decomposition and the corresponding assessments, while the right panel shows their detailed descriptions. This is illustrated in Figure 3.13.

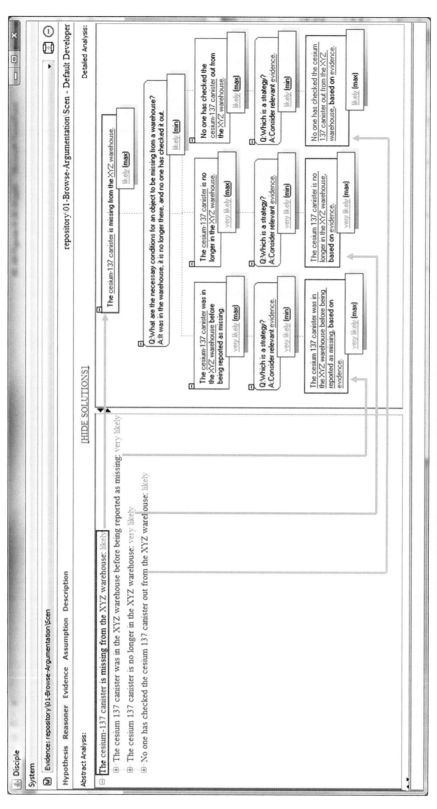

Figure 3.11. Abstract and detailed views of the top part of the analysis.

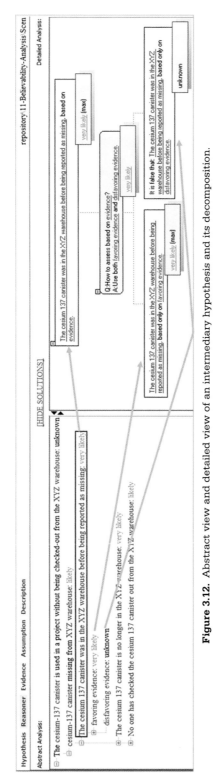

Figure 3.12. Abstract view and detailed view of an intermediary hypothesis and its decomposition.

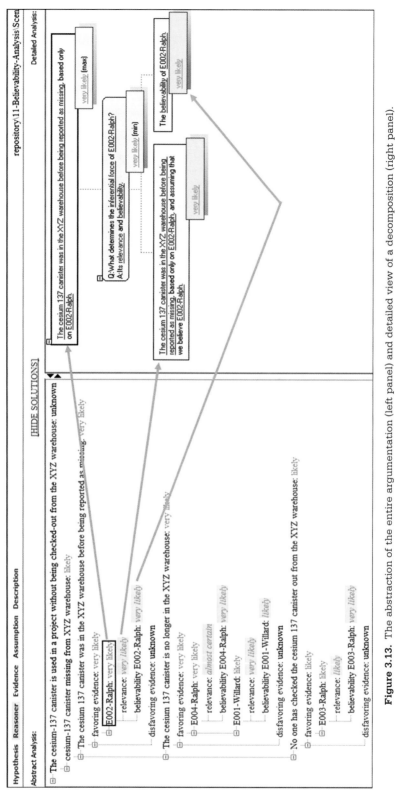

Figure 3.13. The abstraction of the entire argumentation (left panel) and detailed view of a decomposition (right panel).

Notice that the names of the hypotheses in the abstract argumentation have to be interpreted in context. For example, favoring evidence under the hypothesis H: "The cesium 137 canister was in the XYZ warehouse before being reported as missing" refers to the assessment of this hypothesis based only on favoring evidence (which is "very likely").

E002-Ralph under favoring evidence refers to the assessment of the hypothesis H based on this item of evidence (which is also "very likely"). Relevance under E002-Ralph refers to the assessment of the relevance of E002-Ralph with respect to the hypothesis H, and so on.

Thus, assessing the hypothesis "The cesium 137 canister was in the XYZ warehouse before being reported as missing," based on E002-Ralph, is reduced to assessing the relevance and the believability of this item of evidence. The relevance and believability assessments have a yellow background to indicate that they have been made by the analyst.

The phrases in (dark or bright) blue represent specific entities from an application domain (such as cesium-137 canister), items of evidence (such as E002-Ralph), or general concepts (such as relevance). If you click on such a (blue) word *in the right panel*, the Description module is automatically invoked to display the description of that entity (if it exists in the knowledge base of Disciple-CD), as illustrated in Figure 3.14.

3.5.2 Practice

In this case study, you will practice the preceding operations to browse the analysis of the hypothesis "The cesium-137 canister is missing from the XYZ warehouse." You will select this hypothesis and then you will browse its analysis tree to see how it is decomposed into simpler hypotheses and how the assessments of these simpler hypotheses are composed. You will visualize both the detailed descriptions of these decomposition and synthesis operations, as well as the abstract ones, including an abstract view of the entire tree. You will visualize the descriptions of the concepts and instances that are referred in the analysis tree.

Start Disciple-CD, select the knowledge base "01-Browse-Argumentation/Scen," and proceed as indicated in the instructions from the bottom of the opened window.

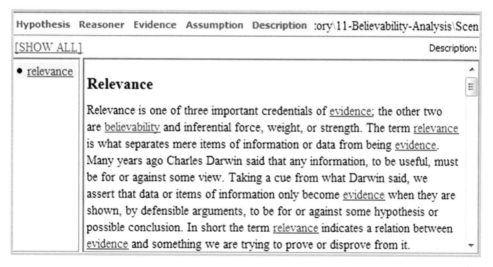

Figure 3.14. The relevance concept in the Description module.

3.5.3   Basic Operations

Operation 3.5. Run a case study

- Start Disciple-CD.
- In the **System Workspace Manager**, click on the knowledge base (KB) icon containing the + sign.
- The **Knowledge Manager** window will be opened, showing all the knowledge bases from the repository.
- Click on the + icon of the case study domain knowledge base to be run. This will display one or several scenario knowledge bases.
- Click on the scenario knowledge base corresponding to the case study to be run.
- Click on the **Select** button. This will both load the case study knowledge bases in memory (i.e., the domain KB and the scenario KB) and select them as the current ones to work with. Because they are loaded in memory, their names will be shown in bold in the **Knowledge Manager** window.
- Follow the instructions at the bottom of the displayed window and run the case study. After running the case study, you have to close the corresponding knowledge base, as instructed in the following steps.
- Close the workspace open on the current knowledge base (case study) by clicking on the – icon to the right of the knowledge base icon containing the + sign.
- Click on the knowledge base icon containing the + sign situated at the right of the workspace selector.
- The **Knowledge Manager** window will be opened, showing all the knowledge bases.
- Click on the **Scen** node corresponded to the case study knowledge base that was run.
- Click on the **Close** button in the right side of the window.
- Click on the **X** button to close the **Knowledge Manager** window.

Operation 3.6. Browse the analysis of a hypothesis

- In the Hypothesis module, select a hypothesis.
- The Reasoner module will be automatically selected, showing the corresponding reasoning tree.
- To browse the entire reasoning tree, step by step, click on the hypotheses in the left panel, or one of the + and – icons preceding them.
- To expand or collapse the entire subtree of a hypothesis, right-click on it, and select the corresponding action.
- To view the detailed description of an abstract decomposition of a hypothesis in the left panel, click on the hypothesis, and the detailed decomposition will be displayed in the right panel.
- To browse a detailed reasoning tree in the right panel, click on the + and – icons.

Operation 3.7. Save and close a case study

- From the **System** menu, select **Save All** to save the knowledge bases.
- Close the workspace open on the current knowledge base (case study) by clicking on the – icon to the right of the knowledge base icon containing the + sign.
- Close the opened knowledge bases corresponding to the case study by following the instructions from Operation 3.3.

4 Evidence

4.1   WHAT IS EVIDENCE?

You might think that a section with this title is silly or unnecessary since everyone knows what evidence is. However, matters are not quite that simple since the term *evidence* is not so easy to define and its use often arouses controversy, especially in the field of intelligence analysis. One problem with definition of evidence is that several other terms are often used synonymously with it, when in fact there are distinctions to be made among these terms that are not always apparent. Quite unnecessary controversy occurs since some believe that the term *evidence* arises and has meaning only in the field of law. We will start with discussing these matters, since evidence is the foundation of all intelligence analyses.

We are actually not assisted very much in defining evidence by consulting a dictionary. For example, look at the *Oxford English Dictionary* under the term *evidence* and you will be led in a circle; *evidence* is ultimately defined as being evidence.

A variety of terms are so often used as synonyms for the term *evidence*: *data, items of information, facts,* and *knowledge*. When examined carefully, there are some valid and important distinctions to be made among these terms. First, consider the terms *data* and *items of information*. There are untold trillions of data or items of information in existence that will almost certainly never become evidence in any intelligence analysis or in most other inferences either. Here's a datum or item of information for you: Professor Schum has a long and steep driveway in front of his house that makes shoveling snow off of it very difficult in the winter. Can you think of any intelligence analysis problem in which this datum could become evidence? About the only matter in which this datum could become interesting evidence involves the question: Why did Schum and his wife, Anne, ever purchase this house in the first place? As we will discuss, *data or items of information only become evidence when their* relevance *is established regarding some matter to be proved or disproved.*

Now consider the term *fact*; there are some real troubles here as far as its relation to the term *evidence* is concerned. How many times have you heard someone say, "I want all the facts before I draw a conclusion or make a decision?" Or, "I want to know the facts in this matter?" The first question is easily answered; we will never have all the facts in any matter of inferential interest. Answers to the second question require a bit of careful thought. Here is an example of what is involved: Suppose we are case officers interviewing a HUMINT asset or informant having the code name "Mouse." Mouse tells us that a person of interest, Amad M., attended an Al Qaeda weapons training class near Madyan in

Northwest Pakistan in October 2013. Now we regard it as fact that Mouse gave us this information; we all just heard him give it to us. But, whether Amad actually did attend an Al Qaeda weapons training class near Madyan in Northwest Pakistan in October 2013 *is only an inference and is not a fact*. This is precisely why, in Section 1.1.2, we carefully distinguished between an event E and evidence for this event E*.

Here is what we have: Mouse has given us evidence E*, saying that event E occurred, where E is the event that Amad attended an Al Qaeda weapons training class near Madyan in Northwest Pakistan in October 2013. Whether this event E did occur or not is open to question and depends on Mouse's competence and credibility.

If we take it as *fact* that event E did occur, just because Mouse said it did, we would be overlooking the believability foundation for any inference we might make from his report E*. Unfortunately, it so often happens that people regard the events reported in evidence as being facts when they are not. Doing this suppresses all uncertainties we may have about the source's credibility and competence if the evidence is testimonial in nature. We have exactly the same concerns about the credibility of tangible evidence. For example, we have been given a tangible object or an image as evidence E* that we believe reveals the occurrence of event E. But we must consider whether this object or image is authentic and it is what we believe it to be. In any case, the events recorded in evidence can be regarded as facts only if provided by perfectly believable (credible) sources, something we almost never have.

The term *knowledge* is as perplexing as it is interesting, particularly when we try to relate it to evidence from our sources, whatever they are. As you know, *the field of epistemology is the study of knowledge and what we believe it may be*. We have heard intelligence analysis described as doing "applied epistemology." Here is an example of why this makes a great deal of sense. Two questions we would normally ask regarding what our source Mouse just told us are as follows:

- Does Mouse really *know* what he just told us regarding Amad attending an Al Qaeda weapons training class near Madyan in Northwest Pakistan in October 2013?
- Do we ourselves then also *know*, based on Mouse's report, that Amad actually attended this Al Qaeda weapons training class near Madyan in Northwest Pakistan in October 2013?

Let's consider the first question regarding our source Mouse. For more than two millennia, some very learned people have troubled over the question: What do we mean when we say that person *A knows* that event B occurred? To apply this question to our source Mouse, let's make an assumption that will simplify our answering this question. Let's assume that Mouse is a *competent* observer in this matter. Suppose we have evidence that Mouse was actually himself at the Al Qaeda weapons training center near Madyan in Northwest Pakistan in October 2013, and suppose Mouse knows Amad by sight. What we can then focus on is Mouse's credibility.

Here is what a standard or conventional account says about whether Mouse knows that Amad was at the Al Qaeda weapons training center near Madyan in Northwest Pakistan in October 2013:

- Amad was in fact at the Al Qaeda weapons training center near Madyan in Northwest Pakistan in October 2013.
- Mouse got nondefective evidence that Amad was at the Al Qaeda weapons training center near Madyan in Northwest Pakistan in October 2013.
- Mouse believed this evidence.

If all of these three things are true, we can state on this standard analysis that Mouse knows that Amad was at the Al Qaeda weapons training center near Madyan in Northwest Pakistan in October 2013.

But now we have several matters to consider in answering the second question: Do we ourselves also *know*, based on Mouse's report, that Amad actually attended this Al Qaeda weapons training class near Madyan in Northwest Pakistan in October 2013? The first and most obvious fact is that we do not know the extent to which any of the three events just described in the standard analysis are true. Starting at the bottom, we do not know for sure that Mouse believes what he just told us about Ahmad being at the Al Qaeda training center. This is a matter of Mouse's *veracity* or *truthfulness*. We would not say that Mouse is being truthful if he told us something he did not believe.

Second, we do not know what sensory evidence Mouse obtained on which to base his belief, and whether he based his belief at all on this evidence. Mouse might have believed that Ahmad was at the Al Qaeda weapons training center either because he expected or desired Ahmad to be there. This involves Mouse's *objectivity* as an observer. We would not say that Mouse was objective in this observation if he did not base his belief on the sensory evidence he obtained in his observation.

Finally, even if we believe that Mouse was an objective observer who based his belief about Ahmad on sensory evidence, we do not know how good this evidence was. *Here we are obliged to consider Mouse's sensory sensitivities or accuracy in the conditions under which Mouse made his observations.* Here we consider such obvious things as Mouse's visual acuity. But there are many other considerations, such as, "Did Mouse only get a fleeting look at the person he identified as Ahmad M.?" "Did he make this observation during a sand storm?" And, "What time of day did he make this observation?" For a variety of such reasons, Mouse might simply have been mistaken in his observation; it was not Ahmad who Mouse observed.

So, what it comes down to is that the extent of our knowledge about whether Ahmad M., was at the Al Qaeda weapons training center, based on Mouse's evidence, depends on these three attributes of Mouse's credibility. We will have much more to say about assessing the credibility of sources of evidence, and how Disciple-CD can assist you in this difficult process, in Chapter 6 of this book. But there is yet another matter concerning the relation between evidence and knowledge; this matter arises when we consider various hypotheses we may entertain to which Mouse's evidence might be relevant. As far as the linkage between Mouse's evidence and these hypotheses, the extent of our knowledge about the relative probability of these hypotheses depends on the defensibility and strength of our relevance arguments and these credibility and competence considerations. The whole point here is that the relation between evidence and knowledge is not a simple one at all.

Finally, we must consider the controversy over the use of the term *evidence* instead of the other terms we just examined. We have read several accounts by intelligence officials saying that intelligence analysis does not involve evidence since intelligence services are not courts of law. The idea expressed here is that evidence concerns only objects, testimony, or other items introduced in a court trial. The same argument often occurs in other areas in addition to intelligence analysis. But this controversy and confusion has been recognized by eminent evidence scholars in the field of law. For example, in his marvelous book *Evidence, Proof, and Facts: A Book of Sources*, Professor Peter Murphy (2003, p. 1) notes the curious fact that the term *evidence* is so commonly associated only with the field of law:

> The word "evidence" is associated more often with lawyers and judicial trials than with any other cross-section of society or form of activity. ... In its simplest sense, evidence may be defined as any factual datum which in some manner assists in drawing conclusions, either favorable or unfavorable, to some hypothesis whose proof or refutation is being attempted.

He notes that this term is appropriate in any field in which conclusions are reached from any relevant datum. Thus, physicians, scientists of any ilk, historians, and persons of any other conceivable discipline, as well as ordinary persons, use evidence every day in order to draw conclusions about matters of interest to them.

We believe there is a very good reason why many persons are so often tempted to associate evidence only with the field of law. It happens that the Anglo-American system of laws has provided us with by far the richest legacy of experience and scholarship on evidence of any field known to us. This legacy has arisen as a result of the development of the adversarial system for settling disputes and the gradual emergence of the jury system, whose members deliberate on evidence provided by external witnesses. This legacy has now been accumulating over at least the past six hundred years. Some of us have tried repeatedly to make persons in a variety of disciplines, including intelligence analysis, aware of this rich legacy, but we have not always been successful. In Chapter 8, we provide an account of how many recurrent and generic forms and combinations of evidence there are. Development of this account was initially stimulated by the rich legacy concerning evidence that the Anglo-American system of laws has provided.

4.2   THE CREDENTIALS OF ALL EVIDENCE

As we have noted on several occasions in the preceding sections of this book, evidence has three major properties or credentials: *relevance, believability or credibility*, and *inferential force or weight*. Let's now make sure that we understand what these three evidence credentials mean and why they are so important.

4.2.1   Relevance

We know of no better definition of the term *relevance*, applied to evidence, than the one provided in the *Federal Rules of Evidence for United States Courts* (Mueller and Kirkpatrick, 2009). These Federal Rules of Evidence (FREs) govern the offering and admissibility of evidence introduced in the U.S. courts, and they are the result of centuries of experience in the Anglo-American system of common law. But these rules are not set in stone and can be revised in light of new experience and insight. One of these numbered rules, FRE-401, defines *relevant evidence* as follows:

> "Relevant evidence" means evidence having any tendency to make the existence of any fact that is of consequence to the determination of the action more probable or less probable than it would be without the evidence (Mueller and Kirkpatrick, 2009).

We need to parse this definition in order to see what it says and how it applies to intelligence analysis. First, consider the words "any tendency." What this allows for is evidence being relevant in more than one way. We can make a distinction between *directly relevant evidence* and *indirectly relevant evidence.* Indirectly relevant evidence is often called *ancillary,* *auxiliary,* or *meta-evidence,* since it is evidence about other evidence. For example, in an inference about whether to believe what some HUMINT source tells us, we make use of whatever ancillary evidence we have about the competence and credibility of this source.

Now consider the phrase "any fact that is of consequence to the determination of the action." This basically refers to the matters to be proved or disproved; that is, it refers to the hypotheses being considered. In law, the hypotheses will involve some charge in a criminal case or a complaint lodged in a civil case. For example, in a murder case the determination of the action would involve such hypotheses as, "The defendant being charged was the one who unlawfully killed the victim." In intelligence analysis, one hypothesis that might be considered is, "At least one terrorist action will be initiated against homeland United States in the next year." In both the law and intelligence examples just mentioned, these would be major or upper-level hypotheses. But in constructing arguments bearing on these major hypotheses, there will be any number of lower-level hypotheses involving the sources of doubt we recognize in our arguments. Thus, evidence is relevant if it bears either directly or indirectly on any of our recognized sources of doubt.

Now consider the phrase "more probable or less probable than it would be without the evidence." What this says is that relevant evidence causes us to change our beliefs, one way or the other, about some hypothesis being tested. But notice that it does not tell us how much we should change our beliefs in these hypotheses. Another way of stating this is to say that relevant evidence has *some inferential force or weight,* but it does not say how much force or weight it should have. One very good reason why FRE-401 does not say how much force or weight evidence should have is that assessing the force or weight of evidence is a very complex matter involving the probabilistic strength of our arguments based on evidence that concern both relevance and believability matters. In law and in intelligence analysis, reasonable people may disagree strongly about how forceful a given item of evidence, or some collection of evidence, is on hypotheses of interest.

Defending the relevance of evidence is no easy task, especially when we have masses of it to consider, as we do in intelligence analysis. There is a problem associated with what we termed *evidential synergism,* which we discussed in Section 1.1.4. Suppose we have an item of information about event A that, by itself, seems irrelevant or useless with respect to an analysis problem we are currently facing, and we contemplate discarding it. But someone notices that we also have other items about events B and C that would make item A seem relevant when we take all these three items together. The point here is that the relevance of an item of information often depends on what other items of information we have. Another way of stating this is to say that items of information interact or are dependent in ways that influence their relevance on hypotheses being considered. As we also emphasized, the detection of these interactions producing evidential synergisms depends on how devoted the analysts are to sharing information across agencies and offices in the intelligence services.

Relevance answers the question: *So what? How is this item linked to any hypothesis or possible conclusion of interest in an intelligence analysis?*

Example 4.1.

Suppose your intelligence analysis involves inferences about possible forms of terrorist actions that could be taken against targets here in the United States. Here are two items of information you have just received:

Item #1: Professor David A. Schum is the owner of a green 2000 Toyota Corolla vehicle carrying Virginia license plate # TSL-782.

The first question you would ask about Item #1 is: "So what? What conceivable bearing does this bit of information have on any possible conclusions I could reach about possible terrorist incidents here in the United States?" Unless David Schum was associated with any terrorist organization, you would be justified in saying that this datum is totally *irrelevant* in your present analysis. The concept of relevance concerns our attempts to answer *"So what?"* questions regarding items of information we have.

Now consider this second datum:

Item #2: The XYZ Company in Baltimore, Maryland, manufactures devices for sterilizing medical equipment. A person named Willard reported in a *Washington Post* article that a canister containing powder, including approximately three thousand curies of cesium-137, had gone missing from the company's warehouse in Baltimore. There were indications that the storage area where this powdered cesium-137 was located showed signs of forcible entry.

Asking the same question, "So what?" an analyst would give a different answer to this second item than the one given to Item #1. Cesium-137 has all sorts of uses in medicine and in industry. It is used to sterilize food and to manufacture thickness and moisture density gauges, and it is used for various diagnostic purposes in medicine in addition to the sterilization purposes just mentioned. Unfortunately, cesium-137 could be put to other uses, including the construction of a dirty bomb. Just a few ounces of this powdered material set off by a conventional explosive in a bomb could contaminate an entire city for decades. Indeed, it is known that the Chechen Mujahidin placed a canister of cesium in a Moscow park in the hopes of spreading radiation throughout the city. Fortunately, this canister was discovered by the police before it was set off. So, Item #2 seems relevant in inferences about what kind of actions terrorist groups may be contemplating here in the United States. In Section 1.3, we have shown arguments justifying the relevance of this item.

The arguments concerning the relevance of evidence involve chains of reasoning. Consider an item of relevant evidence and the argument or chain of reasoning an analyst has constructed that links this item to hypotheses being considered. Here starts the initial root of uncertainty in intelligence analysis. In forming this chain of reasoning, each identified link in a relevance chain of reasoning involves a proposition that might be true or untrue; that is, it is a source of doubt or uncertainty. The argument being constructed thus forms a chain of sources of doubt the analyst believes to be interposed between the evidence and what the analyst is trying to prove or disprove from it. These links or sources of doubt are laid out in a logically consistent order in which one link is inferable from its predecessor.

Where do these links (sources of doubt) come from? They come from the analyst's imagination based upon his or her experience and knowledge of the analytic problem area.

Here we have the roots of disagreements among analysts concerning the relevance of evidence and disagreements about uncertainties in conclusions that may be reached. Different analysts may construct different arguments from the same evidence and thus perceive different sources of uncertainty. Even if they agree about the links in an argument, they may disagree about how strong they are. It is also true, of course, that analysts may generate different possible hypotheses from the same evidence.

Notice, however, that a software agent such as Disciple-CD can learn from the relevance arguments initially defined by the analyst. It can then use this knowledge to help the analyst in the generation of arguments that bear some similarities with previous arguments. This will be illustrated in Section 5.7.3.

A relevance argument having been constructed, it is now time for its evaluation; here is where the necessity for critical reasoning arises. The analyst must ask the questions, "Is the chain of reasoning I have just constructed that shows the relevance of this evidence item logically coherent? Does it contain any disconnects or nonsequiturs?"

An absolutely crucial element in intelligence analysis is the defensibility of arguments constructed by analysts from the evidence available to possible conclusions to be proved or disproved. Should anyone else take an analyst's argument seriously as far as the relevance of this evidence is concerned? As we will see in a moment, this question also involves the extent to which anyone else should take the analyst's assessments of uncertainty seriously. Of course, it is also true that an argument must be persuasive and that not all defensible arguments are persuasive. One fairly certain way of failing to make an argument persuasive is to have it revealed that it is not defensible on logical grounds. But there is an important point here that needs further elaboration.

There is no such thing as a uniquely correct or perfect argument from evidence. Here is a chain of reasoning an analyst has just constructed to establish the relevance as evidence of an item of information. Someone, another analyst or perhaps another critic, will always be able to find what this person believes to be a missing link or a link that is improperly stated. Perhaps this fellow analyst or critic discovers a disconnect in the analyst's initial relevance argument. What no one, be they analyst or critic, can say is that they have the "correct" argument justifying the relevance of this item of evidence. Someone can come along later and discover inadequacies in the revised argument proposed by the other analyst or critic. What can be done is to have someone identify defects in an argument and to improve it. But what no one can do is to say that the argument being proposed is the final or ultimately true argument that anyone could propose. What this says is that someone can correct defects in an argument without ever being able to say that they have the only argument that could ever be made regarding the relevance of evidence. This also accounts for the fact that there will always be some disagreement about the uncertainty that is assessed, combined, and reported among analysts themselves and among persons for whom the analysis was performed. Different persons will construct different arguments from the same bodies of evidence.

The fact that there is no such thing as the ultimately true argument has an important bearing on the many examples we provide of various evidential and inferential issues. We will never say that the arguments we construct in providing examples are the only correct or true ones. You, the reader, may perceive other reasoning routes from the evidence we present and may indeed see other possible conclusions. Our major hope, of course, is that you will not see any disconnects or nonsequiturs in our arguments.

4.2.2   Believability or Credibility

Here is an item of evidence E^*_i, from source I, that all of us believe is relevant on hypotheses we are considering. We strongly believe that we can defend the relevance of event E, as reported in our evidence E^*_i, by the argument we have constructed that we all agree is very strong and free of disconnects or nonsequiturs. But the crucial question remains, "How certain are we that event E did occur just because source I said it did?" Source I's credibility and competence are the major issues here. This is why we have said that source believability considerations form the very foundation for all arguments we make from evidence to our hypotheses. We illustrated this fact in Figure 1.2 in Section 1.1.2 (p. 4). However strong our relevance argument may be, if it rests on a weak believability foundation, it will falter. Perhaps the best example of inferential calamities known to us in the open-source literature concerns the believability (i.e., competence and credibility) of the human source called "Curveball" (Bruce, 2008).

The Federal Rules of Evidence contain many rules associated with testing the believability (i.e., competence and credibility) of witnesses, and the authenticity, reliability, and accuracy of tangible evidence (Mueller and Kirkpatrick, 2009). But there are no rules concerning how we ought to grade believability and how strong it should be. As far as witness credibility is concerned, we have consulted over a hundred works on evidence in law that contain most valuable accumulated strategies for supporting or undermining human testimonial credibility (i.e., HUMINT credibility) and the credibility of various forms of tangible evidence. These strategies have been accumulated in over six hundred years of experience in our courts and concern the veracity, objectivity, and observational sensitivity of witnesses. We also have accounts of strategies for testing the competence of human witnesses. These accounts of credibility and competence matters allow us to generate experience-tested questions to ask about the competence and credibility of HUMINT sources and of the credibility-related attributes of tangible evidence from a variety of sources. These questions are discussed in Chapter 6. We add here that the Disciple-CD system knows what questions you should try to answer regarding the believability of different forms of evidence.

There is another very important believability-related matter to be mentioned. It is true that a major origin of our uncertainty or doubt in an intelligence analysis concerns the believability of our sources of evidence, whatever these sources might be. But there are other origins of doubt we are obliged to consider that are not always noticed and incorporated in our assessments of evidence believability. The truth is that lots of things might be done to an item of incoming intelligence information between the time it is first received and the time it reaches the desk or the computer of an intelligence analyst. Any number of persons or devices may have had access to this information item and may have done various things to it. One result is that the intelligence analyst may not have received either an authentic or a complete account of the actual information received from the source. In law, this fact is recognized and so there are elaborate procedures for dealing with what are called *chains of custody*. Well-qualified persons are designated as *evidence custodians* who make careful records of every person who had access to an evidence item from the time it was received, what they did with this item, how long they held the item, and who next received the item before it was finally introduced at trial. Although we are not privy to the procedures for dealing with chains of custody of information received in intelligence analysis, and whether there are any persons who act as evidence custodians, we have written a paper for intelligence agencies on such matters that also illustrates how Disciple-LTA (Tecuci et al., 2005a; 2007b; 2008a), a forerunner of the Disciple-CD system, can assist analysts to capture doubts associated with chains of custody of intelligence information (Schum et al., 2009). A detailed discussion of the analysis of the chains of custody is provided in Chapter 7.

A final matter here concerns some terms and definitions that have been associated with evidence believability-related matters. One aspect is the *distinction between believability and credibility*. Very often credibility is used instead of believability. While this is fine with respect to tangible evidence, it is not appropriate for testimonial evidence because the credibility is only one aspect of believability, with the other being the competence. That is why, in this book, we use the term *believability* for all types of evidence, noticing that, for tangible evidence, it is the same with credibility. Another aspect is the correct use of the term *reliability*. So often we hear of persons being described as *reliable sources*. There is a difficulty associated with using this term with reference to human sources such as for HUMINT. The trouble is that the term *reliability* is most often used to indicate how *consistent* or *repeatable* some process is. You say your car is reliable to the extent to which it will take you where you wish to go for some period of time in the future. A test of any kind is reliable to the extent that it gives the same result over again if it is repeated. But there is so much more to the believability of a human source than mere consistency; we have discussed how attributes of the credibility of sources of HUMINT concern their veracity, objectivity, and observational sensitivity. We are also concerned about the competence of these persons. What counts most is the *believability* of what these sources tell us. Such judgments rest on all the credibility and competence attributes we have mentioned. The term *reliability* does not capture any of these attributes. Where we use the term *reliability* is with reference only to our sources of tangible evidence, such as sensors of various kinds. In our work, we will use the term *believability* with reference to our sources since, at least with reference to HUMINT sources and other persons involved in the chains of custody we just mentioned, in addition to credibility we have to also be concerned about their competence. What matters in all cases is whether an analyst can believe the information he or she has received.

4.2.3   Force or Weight of Evidence

In a very general sense, the force or weight of evidence indicates how strong the evidence is in favoring or disfavoring hypotheses we are considering. But this is as far as we can go, since there is considerable controversy about what the terms *force* and *weight* mean, and especially how these concepts should be assessed and combined. As we noted in Section 1.1.6, there are only two uncontroversial statements we can make about the force or weight of evidence. First, it has vector-like properties indicating the direction and the strength with which evidence favors or disfavors hypotheses we are considering. Second, the force or weight of evidence is always graded in probabilistic terms. This second statement is actually the greatest source of controversy since a variety of careful scholars in probability, who have given their days and nights to the study of evidence and probability, cannot agree about how force or weight of evidence should be assessed and combined. In Chapter 10, we will review such alternative probability methods.

Probabilistic judgments can be expressed numerically in several ways, and also in terms of words, as will be discussed in Chapter 10. Speaking of numerical judgments of probability, a very wise and devoted scholar, Professor Glenn Shafer (1988, pp. 5–9), has correctly noted:

> Probability is more about structuring arguments than it is about numbers. All probabilities rest upon arguments. If the arguments are faulty, the probabilities, however determined, will make no sense.

We add the same concern about verbal assessments of probability, such as "very probable," "probable," "unlikely," and so on. If these arguments are not defensible, no one will take seriously any numerical or verbal assessments we make concerning the force or weight of our evidence. This is just one reason why we consider the construction and defense of our relevance and believability arguments so carefully in the sections to follow.

So, we have found it much easier to provide definitions and meaning to the relevance and believability credentials of evidence than we have been able to do for the force or weight credential. All we can say at this point is that the force of evidence depends on the strength of our believability and relevance arguments, as shown in Figure 1.2 (p. 4) and in Figure 4.1. But as we proceed, will provide an assortment of examples about assessing the force or weight of evidence that will be useful in intelligence analysis. Remember that all conclusions in intelligence analysis, in common with all other contexts in which conclusions are based on evidence, must always be hedged probabilistically by some means. This is because, as we will again discuss in Chapter 9, our evidence is always incomplete, usually inconclusive, frequently ambiguous, commonly dissonant, and comes to us from sources having any gradation of believability shy of perfection. As we will observe, alternative views of probabilistic reasoning capture some of these important considerations, but no single view captures them all.

4.3   ASSESSING THE RELEVANCE, BELIEVABILITY, AND INFERENTIAL FORCE OF EVIDENCE

Let us consider again the abstract example from Figure 4.1 concerning the evidence E* about the event E, and the hypothesis H. The question is, "How could we evaluate the probability or likeliness of H given the evidence item E*?" There are several judgments to be made.

One is a *believability* judgment, *"How likely is it that E* is true? That is, how likely is it that the event E reported in E* is true?"*

Another one is a *relevance* judgment, *"Assuming that E is true, how likely is it that H is true?"*

Finally, there is the *inferential force or weight* judgment, which, as discussed in the previous section, is based on the previous two judgments, *"How likely is it that H is true, based only on E*?"*

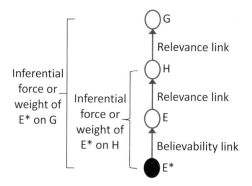

Figure 4.1. Relevance, believability, and inferential force or weight of evidence.

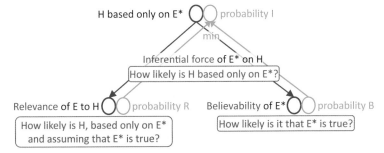

Figure 4.2. Assessing the credentials of evidence with Disciple-CD.

In Disciple-CD, these judgments are represented as shown in Figure 4.2 and explained in the following. This approach combines elements of Baconian and Fuzzy probabilities, which will be discussed in Chapter 10.

We want to assess the probability or likeliness of H based only on evidence E*, that is, the probability P(H|E*). First notice that we call this *likeliness* and not *likelihood* because in classic probability theory, likelihood is P(E*|H), while here we are interested in determining the posterior probability of H given E*, that is, P(H|E*).

Second, notice that, given the use of symbolic probabilities in Disciple-CD, we expect the probability of H to have one of the ordered values shown in Table 1.5, repeated here for convenience:

no support < likely < very likely < almost certain < certain

Of course, the number of probability values can be increased or decreased in various implementations of Disciple-CD.

As discussed previously and illustrated in Figure 4.2, to assess H based *only on* E*, we have three judgments to make by answering three questions:

The *relevance* question is, "How likely is H, based only on E* and assuming that E* is true?" If E* tends to favor H, then our answer should be one of the values from "likely" to "certain." If, however, E* is either not relevant to H, or it tends to disfavor H, then our answer should be "no support," because E* provides no support for the truthfulness of H. As we will discuss later on, E* may provide support for the truthfulness of the negation, or the complement of H, that is, for H^c.

The *believability* question is, "How likely is it that E* is true?" Here the answer should be one of the values from "no support" to "certain." The maximal value, "certain," means that we are sure that the event E reported in E* did indeed happen. The minimal value, "no support," means that E* provides no reason for us to believe that the event E reported in E* did happen.

The *inferential force or weight* question is, "How likely is H based only on E*?" Disciple-CD automatically computes this answer as the minimum of the relevance and believability answers. What is the justification for this? To believe that H is true, based *only on* E*, E* should be both relevant to (i.e., favors) H and believable.

Consider the hypothesis "H: M committed the crime," and the evidence E*, provided by W, who says, "I saw M in the act of committing the crime." Clearly the evidence E* provided by W is completely relevant to H because the event E reported is precisely H (i.e., relevance = certain). If we have complete confidence in the testimony of W (i.e., believability = certain), then we can safely conclude that indeed M committed the crime (i.e., inferential force = certain), which is also the minimum between the relevance and the believability.

But let us now assume that we know for sure that W is lying (e.g., we have absolutely believable evidence that W was at another location when M committed the crime and he could have not seen M). In this case, believability = no support, and inferential force = min (certain, no support) = no support.

In general, neither the relevance nor the believability will have extreme values. Let us consider, for example, that what W says is, "I saw someone who looked like M, in the act of committing the crime." In this case, the relevance may be assessed as "likely." W is not telling us that M committed the crime. He is only telling us that the person who committed the crime *looked like* M. Thus this person might have or might have not been M. Now, if the believability is assessed as being one of the values from "likely" to "certain," then the inferential force is "likely," that is, the minimum between the relevance and the believability.

Figure 4.2 shows that Disciple-CD reduces the problem of assessing H based only on E* to assessing the relevance of E to H, and assessing the believability of E* (the blue tree). Then it determines the inferential force of E* on H by taking the minimum of the two assessments (the green tree).

As an example, consider that we have evidence E_1^* that a Person X was in the near vicinity of an incident one hour before it occurred. We want to assess the hypothesis that X was at the scene of the incident when it occurred. This assessment is represented in the syntax of Disciple-CD, as shown in Figure 4.3.

In general, when we assess a hypothesis, we have several items of evidence, not just one. Let us assume that we have an additional item of evidence E_2^* that X was at the scene of the incident when it occurred. So we have now two items of favoring evidence. They are composed as shown in Figure 4.4. The inferential force of E_2^* is determined to be "almost certain," by employing the procedure discussed previously. Then Disciple-CD determines the inferential force of both E_1^* and E_2^* on the hypothesis "H: X was at the scene of the incident when it occurred," as the maximum of the inferential force of E_1^* and that of E_2^*, which is "almost certain." We take the maximum because it is enough to have one very relevant and believable item of evidence to convince us that the hypothesis is true. Other items of evidence that have lower relevance and/or believability cannot change our assessment of H.

But let us now assume that we receive a third item of evidence E_3^* that X was at another location when the incident occurred. Obviously, E_3^* favors the negation or the

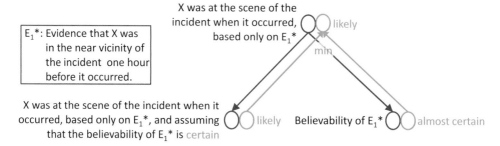

Figure 4.3. Assessing the credentials of evidence, using the syntax of Disciple-CD.

complement hypothesis "H^c: It is false that: X was at the scene of the incident when it occurred." Because the disfavoring evidence for H is favoring evidence for H^c, the assessment process for H^c is similar to the assessment for H. Therefore, Disciple-CD assesses the inferential force of E_3^* on H^c as discussed previously for favoring evidence, and illustrated at the bottom part of Figure 4.5. Thus, based only on E_3^*, H^c is "likely."

E_4^* is another item of disfavoring evidence for H and, based only on E_4^*, H^c is "very likely," as shown in the right-hand side of Figure 4.5. Now, combining the inferential force of E_3^* with that of E_4^* (using the same maximum function as in the case of favoring evidence), Disciple-CD determines the inferential force of the disfavoring evidence on H^c as "very likely."

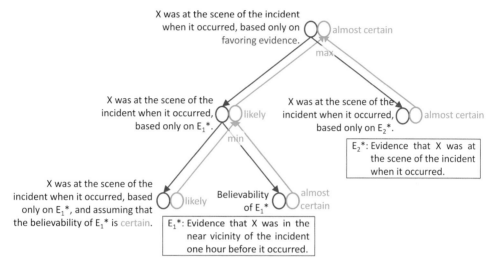

Figure 4.4. Composing the inferential force of several items of favoring evidence.

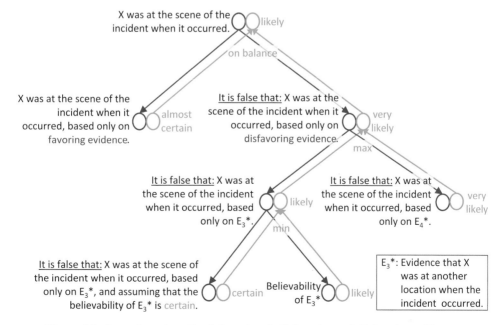

Figure 4.5. Assessing a hypothesis based on both favoring and disfavoring evidence.

So, what is the inferential force of the entire body of evidence on H? Based on the favoring evidence (i.e., E_1^* and E_2^*), it is "almost certain" that X *was* at the scene of the incident when it occurred. But, based on the disfavoring evidence (i.e., E_3^* and E_4^*), it is "very likely" that X *was not* at the scene of the incident when it occurred. In such a case, Disciple-CD uses an *"on-balance"* function to estimate the probability of H. In this particular case, Disciple-CD estimates that, based on all the available evidence, it is "likely" that X *was* at the scene of the incident when it occurred.

The complete specification of the *on-balance* function used by Disciple-CD is shown in Table 4.1. In general, as indicated in the right and upper side of Table 4.1, if the assessment of H^c based on disfavoring evidence (for H) is higher than or equal to the assessment of H based on favoring evidence, then we conclude that, based on all the available evidence, there is no support for H. If, on the other hand, the assessment of H is strictly greater than the assessment of H^c, then the assessment of H is decreased to a lower symbolic value, depending on the actual assessment of H^c (see the left and lower side of Table 4.1).

An important aspect to notice is that the direct assessment of hypotheses based on favoring and disfavoring evidence is done automatically by Disciple-CD, once the relevance and the believability of each item of evidence are assessed by the analyst.

A more complex hypothesis is assessed by first reducing it to (or decomposing it into) several subhypotheses that are directly assessed based on evidence. This is illustrated in Figure 4.6, where the hypothesis **K** is decomposed into three subhypotheses: **G**, **H**, and **I**. Then, each of **G**, **H**, and **I** is directly assessed based on evidence, as discussed previously. For example, we use the favoring evidence to assess the probability of **H**, and the disfavoring evidence to assess the probability of the negation or complement of **H** (i.e., **H^c**). These two assessments are then composed using the on-balance function from Table 4.1. This process results in assessments for **G**, **H**, and **I** (e.g., "almost certain," "very likely," and "likely"). These assessments are then combined in the assessment of **K** by using a user-defined composition function. What function to use depends on whether **G**, **H**, and **I** represent a sufficient condition for **K** or just an indicator, and what type of indicator. This process will be discussed in Chapter 5.

Table 4.1. On-Balance Function in Disciple-CD.

H based on all evidence	H^c based only on disfavoring evidence				
	no support	likely	very likely	almost certain	certain
no support	no support	no support	no support	no support	no support
likely	likely	no support	no support	no support	no support
very likely	very likely	likely	no support	no support	no support
almost certain	almost certain	very likely	likely	no support	no support
certain	certain	almost certain	very likely	likely	no support

(Left vertical axis label: H based only on favoring evidence)

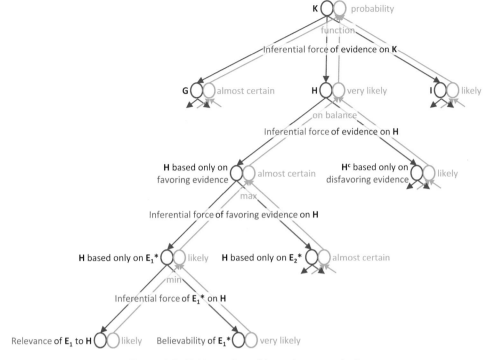

Figure 4.6. Evidence-based hypotheses analysis.

Before we conclude this section, let us mention that this process of assessing the probability of a hypothesis is based on a combination of ideas from the Baconian and Fuzzy probability systems that will be discussed in Chapter 10. In particular, Disciple-CD uses fuzzy qualifiers (such as "likely" and "almost certain") to express the probability of a hypothesis. But these qualifiers are only symbolic and are organized according to an ordered Baconian scale, as shown in Table 1.5. In this scale, the lowest value is "no support." A hypothesis may initially be assessed as having "no support" in evidence. However, future evidence may change this assessment to other values (such as "very likely"). The *min* and *max* composition functions of Disciple-CD correspond to the min-max rules used in both the Baconian system and the Fuzzy system to treat the conjunctions and the disjunctions of hypotheses.

In the next sections, you will use Disciple-CD to define and evaluate evidence.

4.4 BASIC OPERATIONS WITH DISCIPLE-CD

4.4.1 Hands On: Define and Evaluate Evidence

4.4.1.1 Overview

The objectives of this case study are the following:

- Learning how to define items of evidence
- Learning how to associate an item of evidence to a hypothesis
- Learning how to assess the relevance and the believability of an item of evidence

It concerns the analysis of the familiar hypothesis "the cesium-137 canister is missing from XYZ warehouse." You will select this hypothesis and notice that its current analysis does not include any item of evidence. You will then define the items of evidence from Table 1.4 in Section 1.3.3 (p. 22), associate them to the hypotheses to which they are relevant, and evaluate their relevance and believability.

The items of evidence are defined in the **Evidence** module, the interface of which is shown in Figure 4.7. This module has four modes of operation, shown at the top of the left panel. To define new items of evidence, you have to select the [AVAILABLE EVIDENCE] mode.

To define an item of evidence, you have to click on the [NEW] command. As a result, the right panel displays a partial name for the evidence, E001-, to be completed by you. You then have to click on the [EDIT] button, which will open an editor where you can write or copy the description of this item of evidence from a document. The result is shown in the right panel of Figure 4.8.

The bottom part of the right panel shows all the leaf hypotheses in the current argumentation structure under the label **Irrelevant to** because you have not yet indicated that E001-Willard is relevant to any of these hypotheses. To indicate that the current item of evidence favors or disfavors any hypothesis under the **Irrelevant to** label, you have to click on the [FAVORS] or the [DISFAVORS] command following that hypothesis. As a result, the agent automatically generates the analysis tree shown in Figure 4.9. In particular, it generated the hypothesis reduction shown at the bottom of the right panel, where the hypothesis "The cesium-137 canister cannot be found in the

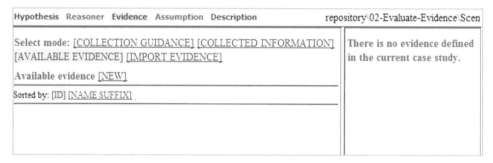

Figure 4.7. Interface of the Evidence module when no item of evidence is defined.

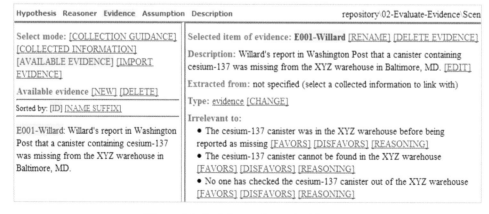

Figure 4.8. Defining an item of evidence.

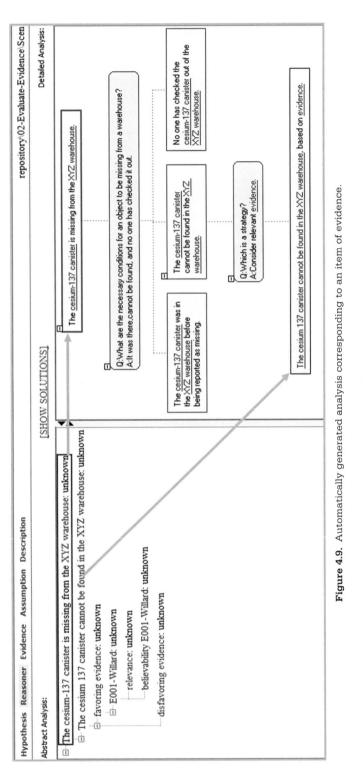

Figure 4.9. Automatically generated analysis corresponding to an item of evidence.

XYZ warehouse" was reduced to "The cesium-137 canister cannot be found in the XYZ warehouse, based on evidence."

What happened is that the agent generated the elementary hypothesis "The cesium-137 canister cannot be found in the XYZ warehouse," to be directly assessed based on evidence, and added it in the abstract tree, shown in the left side of Figure 4.9. Although this elementary hypothesis and its parent hypothesis are composed of the same words, internally they are different, the former being a hypothesis instance introduced in the agent's ontology. This elementary hypothesis corresponds to the hypothesis **H** in Figure 4.6. The agent automatically decomposes this hypothesis as shown in the left panel of Figure 4.9.

Now you can assess the relevance and the believability of E001-Willard. You click on E001-Willard in the left panel, and the agent will display in the right panel the hypotheses corresponding to its relevance and believability. Then you right-click on each of these nodes and select **New Assumption**, as illustrated in the right panel of Figure 4.10. The agent will generate a default assessment of "certain," which you may change by clicking on it and selecting a different value from the displayed list.

Evidence assessments are displayed with a yellow background, indicating that they have been made by you. The left side of Figure 4.11 shows the final assessments of the relevance and believability of E001-Willard and how they are combined to produce the assessment of the hypothesis "The cesium canister is no longer in the XYZ warehouse." The right panel shows the decomposition of this hypothesis into two subhypotheses, corresponding to its favoring and disfavoring evidence.

4.4.1.2 Practice

In this case study, you will learn to perform the aforementioned operations. Start Disciple-CD, select the knowledge base "02-Evaluate-Evidence/Scen" and proceed as indicated in the instructions from the bottom of the opened window.

4.4.1.3 Basic Operations

This case study illustrated the following basic operations:

Operation 4.1. Define an item of evidence

- Click on the **Evidence** menu at the top of the window.
- Notice the four modes of operations from the top part of the left panel. Because the selected one is [AVAILABLE EVIDENCE], the left panel shows the current evidence (if any) from the knowledge base.
- In the left panel, click on [NEW]. As a result, the right panel shows a partially defined item of evidence, such as E002-. You will complete the definition of this item of evidence.
- Complete the name E. . .- at the top of the right panel and click on [SAVE].
- Click on [EDIT] for **Description**, click inside the pane, and type the description of the item of evidence.
- Click on [SAVE].
- This concludes the basic definition. You may now provide additional information about the item of evidence (as indicated in Operation 6.1), or define additional items of evidence (by repeating this operation).

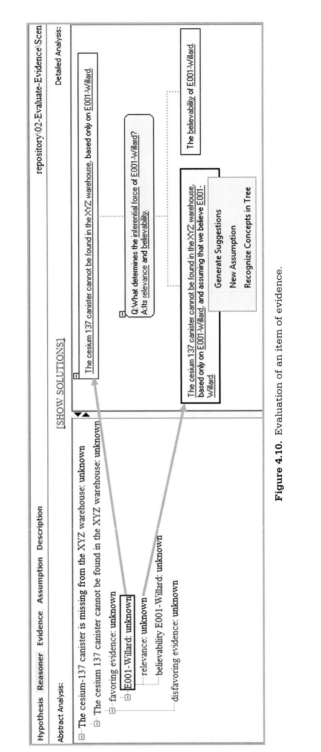

Figure 4.10. Evaluation of an item of evidence.

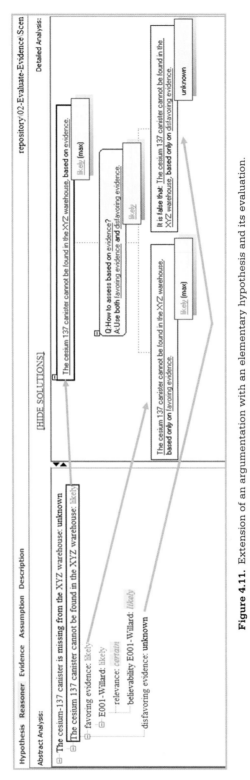

Figure 4.11. Extension of an argumentation with an elementary hypothesis and its evaluation.

Operation 4.2. Associate evidence to hypotheses

- Click on the **Evidence** menu at the top of the window.
- Notice the four modes of operations from the top part of the left panel. Because the selected one is [AVAILABLE EVIDENCE], the left panel shows the current evidence from the knowledge base.
- In the left panel, click on the item of evidence you would like to associate with a leaf hypothesis from the current argumentation. As a result, the upper part of the right panel shows the main characteristics of this item of evidence, followed by all the leaf hypotheses in the analysis tree. You will have to decide whether the selected item of evidence favors or disfavors any of the hypotheses under the **Irrelevant to** label, and indicate this by clicking on [FAVORS] or [DISFAVORS] following that hypothesis.
- Clicking on [FAVORS] or [DISFAVORS] automatically creates an elementary hypothesis to be assessed based on evidence, and moves it under the **Favors** (or **Disfavors**) label. Clicking on [REMOVE] will move the leaf hypothesis under the **Irrelevant to** label.
- To return to the **Reasoner** module, click on [REASONING] following the hypothesis.
- To associate another evidence item to a hypothesis, click on it in the left panel and repeat the preceding steps.

Operation 4.3. Assess evidence

- In the left panel of the **Reasoner** module, click on the name of the item of evidence to assess. You may need to right-click on the top hypothesis and select **Expand** to make the evidence item visible. As a result, the right panel shows the decomposition of evidence assessment into a relevance assessment (the left leaf) and a believability assessment (the right leaf).
- If the right panel does not show the solutions of the hypotheses, then click on [SHOW SOLUTIONS] at the top of the panel.
- In the right panel, right-click on the left (relevance) leaf and select **New Assumption**. As a result, the agent proposes the default assumption (for example, certain).
- If necessary, click on the default assumption (the underlined text) and, from the displayed list, select (double-click) the appropriate value.
- In the right panel, right-click on the right (believability) leaf and select **New Assumption**. As a result, the agent proposes the default assumption.
- If necessary, click on the default assumption and, from the displayed list, select the appropriate value. The agent automatically determines the inferential force of the item of evidence.

4.5 ADVANCED OPERATIONS WITH DISCIPLE-CD

4.5.1 Hands On: From Information to Evidence

4.5.1.1 Overview

When you are given testimonial information or descriptions of tangible items, or you find a document on the Internet, the information might contain very many details, dots, or trifles. Some of the details might be interesting and relevant evidence, and others not. What you always have to do is to parse the information to extract the information that you believe is relevant to the inference task at hand. We have encountered this situation in

Section 1.3.3, where Ralph's testimony from Table 1.3 (p. 22) provided us with several dots or items of evidence that are relevant to assessing the hypotheses from the Figure 1.10 (p. 21). These items of evidence are represented in Table 1.4 (p. 22).

This case study has the following objectives:

- Learning how to represent an item of information in Disciple-CD (which is very similar to how to represent an item of evidence)
- Learning how to define more directly items of evidence that are extracted from an item of information

4.5.1.2 Practice

We will consider again the analysis of the hypothesis "the cesium-137 canister is missing from XYZ warehouse." You will start the **Evidence** module, define the item of information from Table 1.3, and then define the enclosed items of evidence shown in Table 1.4.

Start Disciple-CD, select the knowledge base "03-Info-to-Evidence/Scen" and proceed as indicated in the instructions from the bottom of the opened window.

4.5.1.3 Advanced Operations

This case study illustrated the following advanced operation:

Operation 4.4. Define an item of information
- Click on the **Evidence** menu at the top of the window.
- After **Select mode**, click on [COLLECTED INFORMATION].
- In the left panel, click on [NEW]. As a result, the right panel shows a partially defined item of information, such as INFO-002-. You will complete the definition of this item of information.
- Complete the name INFO-. . .- at the top of the right panel and click on [SAVE].
- Click on [EDIT] for **Description**, click inside the pane, and type the description of the item of information or copy it from a document.
- Click on [SAVE].

Yet another operation is defining an item of evidence from a previously defined item of information.

Operation 4.5. Define an item of evidence from an item of information
- Click on the **Evidence** menu at the top of the window.
- After **Select mode**, click on [COLLECTED INFORMATION].
- In the left panel, click on an item of information (e.g., INFO-002-Ralph).
- In the right panel, after **Description**, select the text corresponding to the item of evidence to be defined and click on [DEFINE EVIDENCE].
- Finalize the definition of the item of evidence partially created by the system.

4.6   REVIEW QUESTIONS

4.1. Evidence, especially testimonial evidence, often relates the occurrence of several events. For example, here is an item of evidence coming from a human source where the source tells us several things. The source says: "I observed Person P in company with a known Al Qaeda operative in Vienna, Austria, on August 21, 2002. During their conversation, I observed the Al Qaeda operative taking a stack of $100 bills and a document from Person P. The document looked like a flight manual." This report, carefully parsed, contains several events. Can you identify them?

4.2. We have emphasized the fact that evidence about some event is not the same as knowledge that this event actually occurred. Suppose we have some evidence E* that event E occurred. We gave an example involving HUMINT evidence E* from a source named Mouse that event E occurred, where E is the event that Amad M., attended an Al Qaeda weapons training class near Madyan in Northwest Pakistan in October 2013. There we had the task of inferring E based on evidence E*. Can you think of another example in which we infer an event E, based on evidence E*?

4.3. In discussing the relevance of evidence, we noted that this credential of evidence answers the question, "So what? How is this evidence linked to hypotheses we are trying to prove or disprove?" Suppose we have IMINT evidence E* in the form of a photograph concerning event E, where E is the event that Person P was running from a car just before a bomb in the car exploded at 10 AM yesterday in Kabul, Afghanistan. Then consider the hypothesis "H: Person P was acting on behalf of Al Qaeda in this car bombing incident." How would you defend the relevance of this evidence E* on hypothesis H?

4.4. Consider your answer to Question 4.3, in which you proposed a chain of reasoning between evidence E* and hypothesis H. The links you considered in this relevance argument consisted of events, such as E, A, B, C, and H. All these links are sources of doubt or uncertainty. In other words, any of these events might not be true. Provide some reasons why these events might not be true.

4.5. As we also noted, there is no such thing as a perfect argument or one that is absolutely correct and complete. For example, someone can always find one or more missing links in an argument that should be considered. Can you find any missing links in your argument shown in the answer to Question 4.3?

4.6. Here's an interesting and important question for you to consider. If you have a weak link in an argument from evidence to some major hypothesis, is it worse to have this weak link at the top or at the bottom of your argument?

4.7. Why are believability questions different for different forms of evidence and its sources?

4.8. The third credential of evidence, its force or weight, depends upon our beliefs about the other two credentials: relevance and believability. Give some examples of this relationship. You can do this in words and without any equations.

5 Divide and Conquer: A Necessary Approach to Complex Analysis

HOLISTIC APPROACH TO ANALYSIS

In our work, and in our personal affairs, we can address inference and decision problems at various levels of detail. As an introductory example, we describe a situation in which we do not decompose a problem at all and consider some of the consequences of failure to do any decomposition. Faced with the task of drawing a conclusion about some matter of interest, we may gather some information that seems relevant and believable, think about it for a while, and eventually draw at least a tentative conclusion. We do this all in our own heads without recording any of the stages and details in our analysis. Furthermore, there is usually no orderly structure to our trains of thought in this analysis. This approach has a name: It is called a *holistic approach* to emphasize the fact that we deal with some problem in its perceived entirety all at once and without any kind of outside assistance or interference. In simple problems involving our own personal affairs, we may do this very frequently. But there are some natural hazards involved in a completely holistic approach to inference and decision problems. The following is a very simple example of what can happen as a result of an entirely holistic approach.

Example 5.1.

Suppose, in discussing with your spouse an upcoming political election, you say that you have reached the conclusion that Person X will be the best candidate. Here are just a few of the questions your spouse might raise while listening to your conclusion:

Your spouse first says, "Tell me what evidence you used to reach the conclusion that X would be the best candidate?" Suppose you say, "Well, I believe I considered evidence A, B, C, and D, that I thought on balance favored X." Your spouse listens to your account and has further questions.

Your spouse says, "Why did you believe that evidence B was relevant at all? And why did you believe that the source of evidence D deserved to be believed?" You search for answers to these questions and have difficulty deciding what you had previously thought about these matters, if you thought about them at all.

Your spouse asks a related question, saying, "I would have thought that evidence E, F, and G should also be taken into consideration. Why did you not consider these items?" You say, "Well, I might have considered E, but I don't believe I considered F and G."

Then your spouse asks, "You say that this evidence 'on balance' favors candidate X. This means that you considered some other candidates; which ones did you consider?" You say, "Well, I did consider another candidate, Y," to which your spouse replies, "Two weeks ago, Z announced her candidacy. Why did you not consider her as well?" Here you draw a complete blank since you did not consider Z.

Finally, your spouse asks, "As far as the evidence items you did consider, which ones were the strongest in favoring candidate X?" Here, unfortunately, you say that you considered evidence items B and D to be the strongest in favoring candidate X. But they are the two items your spouse challenged as far as their relevance and believability are concerned. One trouble you have is your inability to say why you believed these two items to be relevant and believable.

Let's leave aside any consideration of the extent to which your spouse's penetrating analysis of your holistic conclusion affects your subsequent marital harmony. You could have several possible defenses to your inability to answer your spouse's questions. First, you could say that it is all a matter of memory; who can remember all of the details in one's trains of thought? You say you did not tape record all the ideas you considered while thinking about this election candidate problem and note that almost no one would ever do so. But there is another problem you may or may not have recognized: It concerns your likely failure to consider the *structure* of your inferential problem and to consider all the factors or elements it requires. Your only defense here is to say that you are not a logician, a probabilist, or an attorney, but only an ordinary person who draws conclusions every day without being an expert in evidence and inference.

5.2   DIVIDE AND CONQUER

Reading about the problems with holistic assessments in the example discussed in the previous section, you might believe that they have very little relevance to intelligence analysis. You might say that complex intelligence analysis requires *teams of analysts* working together to address some problem; it rarely involves just a single analyst thinking alone in some secluded office. You might easily give an example involving counterterrorism. In this situation, we would have weapons experts, existing terrorist group experts, geopolitical experts, cultural affairs experts, and a whole host of other experts at work trying to predict the next occurrence of a terrorist incident. But this is actually the very first stage of a problem we now address concerning the structure of an intelligence problem and its specific ingredients. All we have done so far is to note the obvious multidimensional nature of so many intelligence problems. We have just begun the process called *divide and conquer.*

Within any of the areas of expertise just noted, there are questions raised that require answers, there are masses of evidence to be considered, and there are many dots to be connected. And there are further dots to be connected when conclusions from the experts in each area are brought together in order to draw any conclusion. Now consider any of the experts such as in the counterterrorism example just mentioned. Each one of these experts faces the problems just discussed in Chapter 1 concerning the task of connecting the dots. We have no way of knowing about the extent to which intelligence experts employ holistic approaches to some degree such as that described in the preceding example. But we strongly suspect that most analysts take great care to be able to defend their conclusions more extensively than in the example involving the dialogue with your spouse. One well-established key to being more easily able to defend the conclusions in some inferential or decision problem you face is to decompose this problem into smaller elements; this is the basic strategy of divide and conquer.

It has been recognized for many years that decomposing a problem into smaller elements seems an obvious way of simplifying difficult problems. Task decomposition has been an object of study by psychologists and others for a long time. As obvious as the benefits of divide-and-conquer approaches are, there are some difficulties that are not always recognized. First, it is not always recognized how many pieces or smaller elements there are in some problem being decomposed. This is of course related to the issue, "How deep do we wish to decompose a problem?" There could be any number of levels or gradations of any problem decomposition. If we do not make our decomposition fine enough, or detailed enough, we may fail to make important distinctions that should be made and that will affect the accuracy of our conclusions. On the other hand, when we decompose a problem into too many smaller elements, we may easily be overcome by their number and never reach any conclusion at all. We have all heard the expression "paralysis by analysis." Too detailed an analysis is one reason for this paralysis. So, an abiding issue is, "How detailed should task decomposition be and how many of the complexities of an evidential reasoning problem should we try to capture and analyze?" Another way of stating this problem is to ask, "How many sources of doubt should we try to expose in our intelligence analysis?"

But there is a second problem often associated with task decomposition. It is often alleged that the smaller elements into which a complex problem is decomposed are easier to deal with. Unfortunately, this is not always the case. In making holistic or even partially decomposed judgments, we may so often fail to recognize how many of these judgments there actually are and how difficult it is to make them.

Analysts face different requirements in their efforts to serve their policy- and decision-making "customers." In some cases, they are required to answer questions that are of immediate interest and that do not allow time for extensive research and deliberation of available evidence. In other cases, teams of analysts participate in more lengthy finished intelligence that combines evidence from every available source. Sometimes finished intelligence can refer to long-term assessments on matters of current and abiding interest. Each such requirement will have a direct influence on the depth of the problem decompositions performed by the analysts. That is, the analysts may decompose problems at various levels of detail (depending on the available time and evidence), evaluating the problems at those levels, as will be discussed in the following sections.

5.3   ASSESSING COMPLEX HYPOTHESES THROUGH ANALYSIS AND SYNTHESIS

We have already illustrated the process of assessing a hypothesis through analysis and synthesis in the previous sections. What we do in this section is provide a more detailed, precise, and formal description of it. This approach is grounded in the problem-reduction representations developed in artificial intelligence (Nilsson, 1971; Tecuci 1988; 1998) and in the argument construction methods provided by the noted jurist John H. Wigmore

(1937), the philosopher of science Stephen Toulmin (1963), and the evidence professor David Schum (1987; 2001a).

> *Analysis comes from the Greek word* analyein, *which means "to break up." It is a reasoning operation by which we break down a system or problem into parts or components to better understand or solve it.*
>
> *Synthesis also comes from a Greek word,* syntithenai, *which means "to put together." It is a complementary reasoning operation by which we combine system or solution components to form a coherent system or solution.*

Assessing the probability of a complex hypothesis involves both analysis and synthesis. We break down the hypothesis into simpler hypotheses, we assess the probabilities of the simpler hypotheses, and then we combine the assessments of these simpler hypotheses into the assessment of the complex hypothesis. One such analysis and synthesis step is shown in Figure 5.1. The complex hypothesis H is reduced to (or decomposed into) n simpler hypotheses $H_1, H_2, \ldots, H_n$. If we can then find the probabilities $P_1, P_2, \ldots, P_n$ of these subhypotheses, then these probabilities can be combined into the probability P of the hypothesis H.

If any of the subhypotheses is still very complex, it can be approached in a similar way, successively reducing it to simpler hypotheses, as illustrated in Figure 5.2.

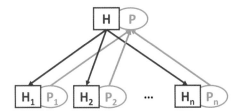

Figure 5.1. Hypothesis reduction (decomposition) and solution synthesis (composition).

A complex hypothesis H is assessed by:

- Successively reducing it, from top-down, to simpler and simpler hypotheses;

- Assessing the simplest hypotheses;

- Successively combining, from bottom-up, the assessments of the simpler hypotheses, until the assessment of the top-level hypothesis is obtained.

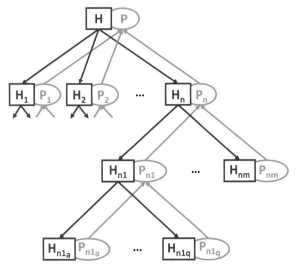

Figure 5.2. Hypothesis assessment through analysis and synthesis.

5.4   INQUIRY-DRIVEN ANALYSIS AND SYNTHESIS

Cognitive assistants, such as Disciple-CD, require the use of problem-solving paradigms that are both natural enough for their human users and formal enough to be automatically executed by the agents. Inquiry-driven analysis and synthesis is such a problem-solving paradigm where the reduction operations are guided by corresponding questions and answers, each representing a different strategy of assessing a hypothesis, as illustrated by the abstract example from Figure 5.3. Thus, to assess Hypothesis, one asks Question 1, which has Answer 1 and leads to the reduction of Hypothesis to two simpler hypotheses, Hypothesis 1 and Hypothesis 2. However, one may also ask Question 2 with Answer 2, which leads to the reduction of Hypothesis to Hypothesis 3 and Hypothesis 4.

Here we have two strategies to assess Hypothesis. We are investigating both of them and we obtain the probabilities of the corresponding subhypotheses, as shown in Figure 5.4. How do we combine these probabilities to obtain the probability of Hypothesis?

The approach is similar to how we assess a hypothesis by considering multiple items of evidence (see Section 4.3). In that case, we assess the hypothesis based on each individual item of evidence, and then we combine the results of these assessments. Thus, we combine the probabilities of Hypothesis 1 and Hypothesis 2 to obtain Probability 1 of Hypothesis corresponding to Answer 1. We also combine the probabilities of Hypothesis 3 and Hypothesis 4 to obtain Probability 2 of Hypothesis corresponding to Answer 2. Each of these two synthesis operations is called a *reduction-level synthesis* because it corresponds to a specific *reduction* of a hypothesis.

Now we need to combine Probability 1 with Probability 2 into the Probability of Hypothesis that takes both strategies into account. This synthesis operation is called a *hypothesis-level synthesis* because it corresponds to all the considered reductions of a *hypothesis.*

An example of inquiry-driven analysis and synthesis is shown in Figure 5.5. Notice that, in this case, there is a single question ("Which is an item of favoring evidence?"), which has as many answers as favoring items identified. We assess the hypothesis based on each favoring item of evidence, and then we compose the obtained probabilities.

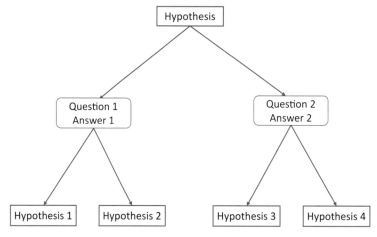

Figure 5.3. Two strategies for assessing a hypothesis.

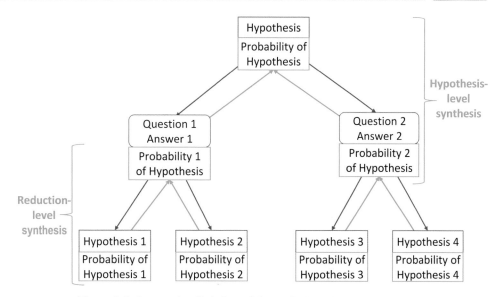

Figure 5.4. A more detailed view of the analysis and synthesis process.

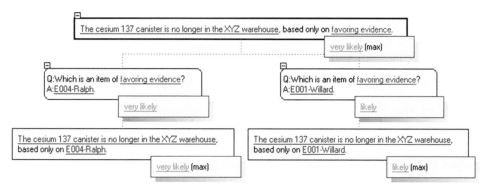

Figure 5.5. An example of inquiry-driven analysis and synthesis.

5.5   TYPES OF REDUCTIONS AND CORRESPONDING SYNTHESES

In the previous section, we have discussed the general process of inquiry-driven analysis and synthesis, but we have not explained what composition functions are to be used. The composition function depends on the type of reduction strategy used. In the following section, we will consider different types of reduction strategies and the corresponding synthesis functions.

5.5.1   Necessary and Sufficient Conditions

Ideally, a hypothesis would be reduced to several subhypotheses that would represent a necessary and sufficient condition. An example is the one from Figure 1.10 in Section 1.3.3 (p. 21), reproduced in more detail in Figure 5.6. In this case, the top hypothesis is

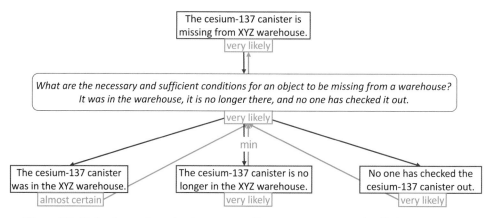

Figure 5.6. Reduction and synthesis corresponding to a necessary and sufficient condition.

equivalent to the conjunction of the three subhypotheses. That is, if the top hypothesis is true, then all the subhypotheses are also true. And, conversely, if all the subhypotheses are true, then the top hypothesis is true. Therefore, in accordance with the Baconian and the Fuzzy probability systems, the probability of the top hypothesis is the minimum of the probabilities of the subhypotheses.

5.5.2   Sufficient Conditions and Scenarios

Most of the time, because of the complexity of the real world, it will not be possible to identify necessary and sufficient conditions to reduce a hypothesis. In such a case, a second best reduction would be a sufficient condition. A scenario, such as the one illustrated in Figure 1.12 from Section 1.3.5 (p. 25), represents such a sufficient condition. If the scenario is true, then the hypothesis is true. But, as we have discussed in Section 1.3.5 and Section 2.4.7, there may be multiple alternative scenarios. For example, in Figure 5.7, there are two alternative scenarios. Scenario 1 consists of Hypothesis 1 and Hypothesis 2. For this scenario to be true, both these hypotheses need to be true. Therefore, we combine their corresponding probabilities with a minimum function, as shown at the bottom-left of Figure 5.7.

The top hypothesis, however, would be true if either of the two scenarios is true. Therefore, we combine the probabilities corresponding to the two scenarios through a maximum function.

5.5.3   Indicators

Many times when we are assessing a hypothesis, we only have indicators. An indicator is, however, weaker than a sufficient condition. If we determine that a sufficient condition is satisfied (e.g., a scenario has actually happened), we may conclude that the hypothesis is true. But we cannot draw such a conclusion just because we have discovered an indicator. However, we may be more or less inclined to conclude that the hypothesis is true, based on the strength of the indicator. Therefore, Disciple-CD distinguishes between three types of indicators, of different strengths: "likely indicator," "very likely indicator," and "almost certain indicator."

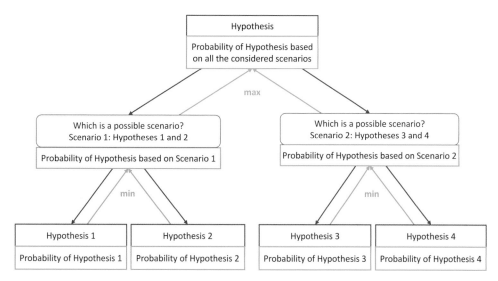

Figure 5.7. Reductions and syntheses corresponding to two sufficient conditions.

A "likely indicator" is one that, if discovered to be true, would lead Disciple-CD to conclude that the considered hypothesis is "likely." Similarly, a "very likely indicator" would lead to the conclusion that the hypothesis is "very likely," and an "almost certain indicator" would lead to the conclusion that the hypothesis is "almost certain."

Thus if I is a "likely" indicator of H and the probability of I is assessed to be "almost certain," then Disciple-CD concludes that the probability of H is "likely," the minimum between "likely" and "almost certain."

In general, *the probability of a hypothesis H based on an indicator I is the minimum between the probability of the indicator and the strength of the indicator* (which could be "likely," "very likely," or "almost certain").

Why do we not consider the type "certain indicator"? Because this would be a sufficient condition, not an indicator.

What about "no support indicator"? If it does not provide any support to the hypothesis, then it is not an indicator of that hypothesis.

Thus, although there are five probabilities in the scale used by Disciple-CD, there are only three indicators.

As an abstract example, Figure 5.8 shows a hypothesis that has two likely indicators, A and B, if only one of them is observed. However, if both of them are observed, they synergize to become an almost certain indicator. We assess A as being "almost certain." Therefore, the assessment of Hypothesis, based only on indicator A, is minimum(almost certain, likely) = likely. We assess B as being very likely. Thus, the assessment of Hypothesis, based only on indicator B, is minimum(very likely, likely) = likely. Similarly, the assessment of Hypothesis, based on the combined indicator "A and B," is minimum (almost certain, very likely, almost certain) = very likely. Now the assessment of Hypothesis based on all the indicators is the maximum of all the individual assessments, that is, "very likely."

Example 5.2.

As a more concrete example, consider Person Y, who has been under surveillance in connection with terrorist activities. We suspect that Y will attempt to

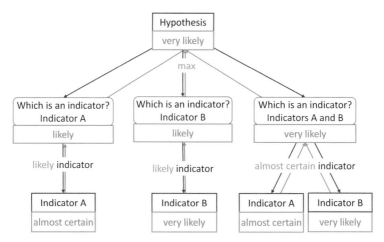

Figure 5.8. Hypothesis assessment based on indicators.

leave the country in a short while. Three days ago, we received information that Y sold his car. Today, we received information that he closed his account at his bank. Each of these is only a likely indicator of the hypothesis that Y plans to leave the country. He could be planning to buy a new car, or he could be dissatisfied with his bank. But, taken together, these two indicators are almost certainly suggesting that Y is planning to leave the country.

Example 5.3.

Figure 5.9 shows a possible analysis of the hypothesis that Country X has nuclear weapons. The analysis includes different types of reductions. At the top level there is a necessary and sufficient condition, at the middle level there are two sufficient conditions, and at the bottom level there is an indicator. The figure shows also possible synthesis functions. Notice that, when there is only one question/answer node, it is advisable to use a max function. This is because Disciple-CD learns the function indicated by the user and will automatically apply it, no matter how many questions answer nodes are in a particular analysis.

We will illustrate the use of indicators in the case study in Section 5.7.1

5.6   PROBLEMS WITH ARGUMENT CONSTRUCTION

We began this book by dwelling upon attributes of the very complex process of "connecting the dots" in intelligence analysis, which we defined as the process of marshaling our thoughts and our evidence in order to generate productive hypotheses and then to form defensible and persuasive arguments on hypotheses that seem most favored by the evidence we have.

As we noted, generating hypotheses as well as arguments rests on *imaginative* as well as *critical* reasoning. Further, the arguments we generate rest on evidence having the three credentials: *relevance, believability or credibility,* and *inferential force or weight.* No

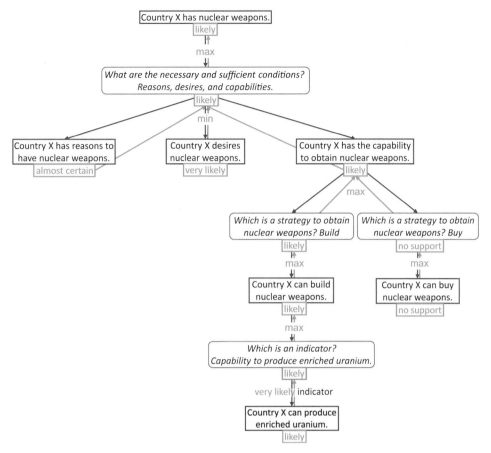

Figure 5.9. An example of different types of reductions and corresponding synthesis functions.

evidence ever comes to us with these three credentials already attached; they must be established by the defensible arguments we construct. One thing this means is that the process of *intelligence analysis* rests on the careful *structuring of defensible arguments*. How *persuasive* these arguments will be depends, in large part, on how we assess the inferential force or weight of the evidence we have. As we will discuss in Chapter 10, there are various ways in which this can be done.

We began discussion in Chapter 5 on the importance and necessity of *decomposing* evidential reasoning problems by giving you an example of how failure to do so invites all manner of analysis failures. We provided an example of how your own undecomposed and unstructured analysis, based on your "off the top of your head" or holistic analysis, was demolished by your spouse's penetrating and critical questions that you could not answer. The same thing can and will happen to intelligence analysts facing criticism, not from their spouses, but from policy-making customers or members of the press, who are often eager to demolish an analysis whose results are made public. The best protection an intelligence analyst has against these critics is carefully structured arguments bearing on the conclusions that were reached in an analysis. Such careful structuring, of course, requires the decomposition of a problem in as much detail as is possible. But there are some obvious problems here that we will always have to consider.

The first problem is that there are bound to be disagreements among analysts themselves about which argument patterns are best and, of course, about which conclusions should be reached. Two or more analysts may construct different arguments or chains of reasoning from the same evidence; the result can be that these analysts will draw different conclusions from the same evidence patterns. Remember that argument construction rests in large part on the imaginations of the persons doing the construction. What analyst $\mathcal{A}$ imagines an argument to be may be quite different from what analyst $\mathcal{B}$ imagines. In many cases, different analysts may consider different patterns of potential evidence to begin with. In other words, their arguments begin from different possible evidential foundations. What analyst $\mathcal{A}$ takes to be the essential dots to be connected may be quite different from the dots that analyst $\mathcal{B}$ considers. We cannot assess the relative merits of $\mathcal{A}$'s and $\mathcal{B}$'s arguments unless we know what patterns of dots they have each tried to connect. But this requires that they have decomposed their evidential reasoning problems in enough detail so that they can tell us which patterns of dots they have tried to connect.

The second problem endemic in argument construction is that arguments are subject to criticism in various ways. *The major issue here is the defensibility of an argument.* Here are some examples of how arguments can be criticized.

Suppose an analyst $\mathcal{A}$ constructs the following chain of reasoning from evidence E* to hypothesis H. He says, "From evidence E* we can infer that event E did probably occur; from event E we can infer that event F probably occurred; from event F we can infer that event G probably occurred; and finally, if event G occurred, we can infer that hypothesis H is probably true."

Now along comes a critic, analyst $\mathcal{B}$, who listens to this argument. She says, "You have a disconnect in your argument. I claim that your inference of G from F is a nonsequitur; G does not follow from F. This makes your whole argument bearing on the relevance of evidence E* to hypothesis H incoherent and indefensible." All it takes is showing that one of the links in a chain of reasoning breaks. This is enough to uncouple the relevance linkage from E* to H.

But another critic, analyst C, hears this dialogue between analysts $\mathcal{A}$ and $\mathcal{B}$. She says, "I agree with $\mathcal{B}$ that event G in $\mathcal{A}$'s argument does not follow from event F. But there may be a way of rescuing $\mathcal{A}$'s original argument. If $\mathcal{A}$ inserts event J between events F and G, and says event J follows from event F, and G follows from event J, then the rest of the argument would make sense to me." This whole defensibility dialogue between analysts $\mathcal{A}$, $\mathcal{B}$, and C was possible only because $\mathcal{A}$ decomposed his argument from evidence E* to hypothesis H. If $\mathcal{A}$ had only said (holistically), "Evidence E* is obviously and strongly relevant to hypothesis H," as one would do when using Heuer's ACH method (Heuer, 1999; 2008), critics who disagree would not know where to begin their criticism of $\mathcal{A}$'s argument. *The message here is that assessing the defensibility of an argument requires that it can be decomposed.*

The third problem we always face in argument construction is that there is never any "true" or "uniquely correct" argument available in any evidential reasoning task. Stated in other words, there is never any "answer key" or "gold standard" against which we can assess the adequacy of any argument. Any argument can be criticized on a number of grounds. No person or system – including Disciple-CD – can supply you with uniquely correct arguments. A related fact is that intelligence analysts, faced with the task of constructing arguments in defense of the relevance, believability, and force or weight of evidence, will never have any reference sources or persons who can tell them what any argument should be. This may come as a source of comfort to analysts who do not take argument construction seriously. But it is no source of comfort at all because an analyst will always encounter critics who will offer alternative arguments and conclusions at variance with what this analyst believes to be the ones that should be taken most seriously.

There are other grounds for criticizing conclusions reached in an analysis, even by the most carefully constructed arguments. These are criticisms concerning the inferential strength of arguments and the evidence on which they are based. To illustrate, let's return to the analysts $\mathcal{A}$, $\mathcal{B}$, and $\mathcal{C}$, who quibbled about the argument or chain of reasoning $\mathcal{A}$ constructed originally from evidence E* to hypothesis H. Suppose these three analysts now agree that the revised argument from E* to E, then from E to F, then from F to J, then from J to G, and finally from G to H makes sense. Analyst $\mathcal{A}$ is now asked by analysts $\mathcal{B}$ and $\mathcal{C}$ if he still believes that E* offers strong support for hypothesis H. One thing true is that the force or weight of evidence depends on the strength of each of the believability and relevance links in chains of reasoning, which connect the evidence to the hypotheses. Analyst $\mathcal{A}$ now says that he still believes that E* offers strong support for believing that hypothesis H is true. Asked by $\mathcal{B}$ and $\mathcal{C}$ why he still believes this, $\mathcal{A}$ says, "Thanks to your help, we now have a strong argument regarding the relevance of event E on hypothesis H. Since my belief is that the source of evidence E* is very believable, this justifies my belief since we have a strong argument that rests upon a strong believability foundation." In reply, both $\mathcal{B}$ and $\mathcal{C}$ say, "We cannot agree with the strength of your conclusion since we strongly believe that you have too strongly assessed the believability of the source of evidence E*. On the evidence we have, the believability of this source is not nearly as strong as you believe it to be." But analysts $\mathcal{B}$ and $\mathcal{C}$ could just as well have challenged the strength of any link in their relevance argument. If analyst $\mathcal{A}$ had decomposed the link between evidence E* and event E (e.g., by considering the competence and the credibility of the source), analysts $\mathcal{B}$ and $\mathcal{C}$ could have challenged these specific attributes of the believability of the evidence.

The following sections will guide you to use Disciple-CD to construct arguments to assess hypotheses based on evidence.

5.7   BASIC OPERATIONS WITH DISCIPLE-CD

5.7.1   Hands On: Was the Cesium Canister Stolen?

5.7.1.1 Hypothesis in Search of Evidence: Illustration

To illustrate the divide-and-conquer approach to hypothesis analysis, let us continue with the cesium example, where we have already established that the cesium-137 canister is missing (see Figure 1.11 on p. 24). The next step is to consider the competing hypotheses:

H_2:   The cesium-137 canister was stolen.
H_2':   The cesium-137 canister was misplaced.
H_2'':   The cesium-137 canister is used in a project without being checked out from the XYZ warehouse.

We have to put each of these hypotheses to work, to guide the collection of relevant evidence. One general strategy to guide the collection of evidence relevant to a given hypothesis H is to look for indicators that the hypothesis H is true. An example of such an indicators-based reasoning tree is provided in Figure 5.10.

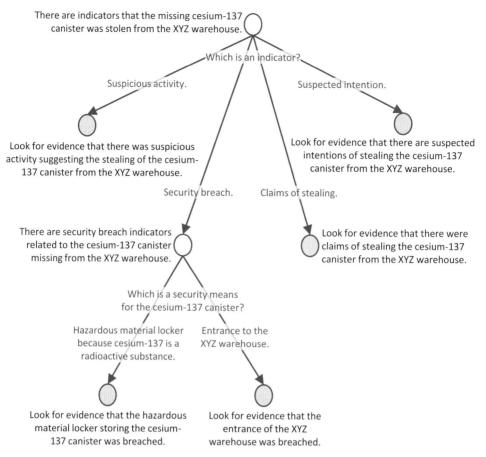

Figure 5.10. Evidence collection guided by indicators of stealing.

In looking for evidence that the hazardous material locker storing the cesium-137 canister was breached, we talk to a professional locksmith named Clyde, who says that the lock had been forced, but that it was a clumsy job (see INFO-003-Clyde in Table 5.1).

In looking for evidence of suspicious activity, we investigate the security camera of the warehouse and discover a video segment showing a person loading a container into a U-Haul panel truck (see INFO-004-SecurityCamera in Table 5.1).

In looking for evidence that the entrance of the XYZ warehouse was breached, we investigate its security procedures and obtain the information labeled INFO-005-Guard in Table 5.1, concerning the panel truck having Maryland license plate MDC-578, which was inside the XYZ warehouse on the day before Willard's discovery of the missing cesium-137 canister. This leads us to the identification of the renting company owning the truck, as well as the name and the address of the person who rented the truck (see INFO-006-TRUXINC). Further investigation of the person and the truck reveal the information in INFO-007-SilverSpring and INFO-008-InvestigativeRecord.

In searching for evidence concerning the hypothesis that someone at the XYZ Company had removed this canister and was using the cesium-137 in current work for an XYZ customer, we have contacted Grace, the Vice President for Operations at XYZ. She tells us that no one at the XYZ Company had checked out the canister for work on any project the XYZ Company was working on at the time. She says that the XYZ Company had other

---

Table 5.1. Additional Information on the Missing Cesium-137 Canister

INFO-003-Clyde: We talked to a professional locksmith named Clyde, who said that the lock had been forced, but it was a clumsy job.

INFO-004-SecurityCamera: The security camera of the XYZ warehouse contains a video segment showing a person loading a container into a U-Haul panel truck.

INFO-005-Guard: There is a security perimeter around the XYZ warehouse and employee parking area having just one gate that is controlled by a guard. On the day before the missing canister was observed, the security guard, Sam, recorded that a panel truck having Maryland license plate MDC-578 was granted entry at 4:45 pm just before the XYZ closing hour at 5:00 pm. The driver of this vehicle showed the guard a manifest containing items being delivered to the XYZ warehouse. This manifest contained a list of packing materials allegedly ordered by the XYZ Company. The vehicle was allowed to enter the parking area. At 8:30 pm, this same vehicle was allowed to exit the parking area. A different guard was on duty in the evenings and noticed that his records showed that this vehicle had been permitted entry, so he allowed the vehicle to exit the parking area.

INFO-006-TRUXINC: The Maryland Department of Transportation (DOT)'s records indicate that the panel truck carrying the license plate number MDC-578 is registered in the name of a truck-rental company called TRUXINC, located in Silver Spring, MD. The manager of this agency showed records indicating that this truck was rented to a person who gave his name as Omer Riley, having as his listed address 6176 Williams Ave. in Silver Spring. The truck was rented on the day before Willard's discovery of the missing cesium-137, and it was returned the day after he made the discovery.

INFO-007-SilverSpring: Silver Spring city records indicate that there is no residence at 6176 Williams Ave. in Silver Spring, MD.

INFO-008-InvestigativeRecord: A Geiger counter examination of the panel truck rented by Omer Riley revealed minute traces of cesium-137.

INFO-009-Grace: Grace, the Vice President for Operations at XYZ, tells us that no one at the XYZ Company had checked out the canister for work on any project the XYZ Company was working on at the time. She says that the XYZ Company had other projects involving hazardous materials, but none that involved the use of cesium-137.

---

projects involving hazardous materials but none that involved the use of cesium-137 (see INFO-009-Grace in Table 5.1).

The collected information from Table 5.1 suggests that the cesium-137 canister was stolen with the panel truck having Maryland license MDC-578. This leads to the development of the analysis tree in Figure 5.11.

We have to identify the "dots" in the text from Table 5.1, which are fragments representing relevant items of evidence for the leaf hypotheses in Figure 5.11. These dots are presented in Table 5.2.

5.7.1.2 Hands-On Overview

This hands on exercise has the following objectives:

- Practicing with associating evidence items to the hypotheses they are relevant to, and with evaluating the evidence
- Learning how to define assumptions

Table 5.2. Dots from Table 5.1.

E006-Clyde: Locksmith Clyde's report that the lock was forced.
E007-SecurityCamera: Video segment on the security camera of the XYZ warehouse showing a person loading a container into a U-Haul panel truck.
E008-GuardReport: The record, made by Sam, security guard at the XYZ Company, that a panel truck bearing Maryland license plate number MDC-578 was in the XYZ parking area on the day before Willard's discovery of the missing cesium-137 canister.
E009-MDDOTRecord: Maryland DOT's record that the truck bearing license plate number MDC-578 is registered in the name of the TRUXINC Company in Silver Spring, MD.
E010-TRUXINCRecord1: TRUXINC's record that the truck bearing MD license plate number MDC-578 was rented to a man who gave his name as Omer Riley on the day before Willard's discovery of the missing cesium-137 canister.
E011-TRUXINCRecord2: TRUXINC's record that Omer Riley gave his address as 6176 Williams Ave.
E012-SilverSpringRecord: Silver Spring city record according to which there is no residence at 6176 Williams Ave. in Silver Spring, MD.
E013-InvestigativeRecord: Investigative record that traces of cesium-137 were found in the truck bearing license plate number MDC-578.
E014-Grace: Grace, the Vice President for Operations at XYZ, tells us that no one at the XYZ Company had checked out the canister for work on any project.

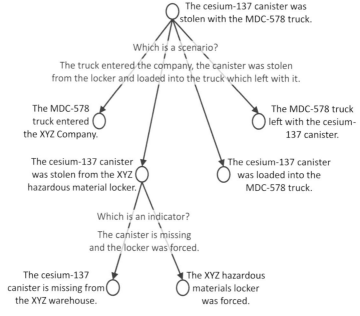

Figure 5.11. Analysis of the hypothesis that the cesium-137 canister was stolen with the MDC-578 truck.

- Learning to select synthesis functions
- Better understanding the process of evaluating the probability of a hypothesis based on the available evidence

Figure 5.12 illustrates the selection of a synthesis function indicating how to evaluate the probability of a node (a question/answer node in this case) based on the probabilities of its children. You have to right-click on the node (but not on any word in blue), select "New Solution with," and then select the function from the displayed list.

5.7.1.3 Practice

Now you can actually perform the case study. Start Disciple-CD, select the case study knowledge base "04-Evidence-based-Analysis/Scen," and proceed as indicated in the instructions from the bottom of the opened window.

5.7.1.4 Basic Operations

This case study illustrated the operation of selecting a synthesis function that is described in Operation 5.1 and Figure 5.13. It also illustrated the operation of defining an assumption for a hypothesis that is described in Operation 5.2 and Figure 5.14.

Operation 5.1. Select synthesis function

- In the **Reasoner** module, in the right panel, right-click on the node for which you have to select the synthesis function, select **New Solution with**, and then select the function from the displayed list.
- To select a synthesis function for a node, all its children must have solutions.

Operation 5.2. Define assumption

- Click on the **Reasoner** menu at the top of the window.
- If the right panel does not show the solutions of the hypotheses, then click on [SHOW SOLUTIONS] at the top of the panel.

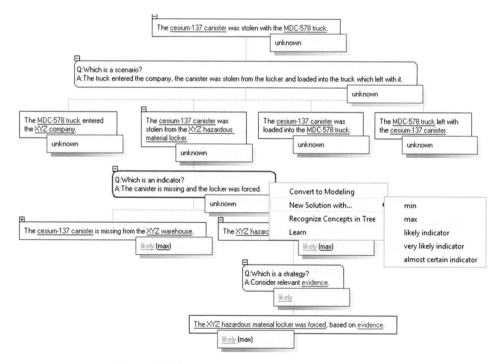

Figure 5.12. Selecting the synthesis function for a node.

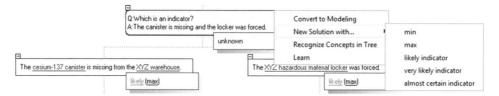

Figure 5.13. Selecting a synthesis function.

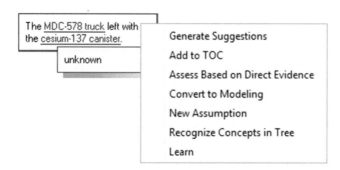

Figure 5.14. Defining an assumption.

- Browse the analysis tree until the (formalized or learned) hypothesis for which you wish to define an assumption is displayed in the right panel.
- Right-click on that hypothesis node and select **New Assumption**.
- If several assumption patterns are available, select the desired one from the displayed list.
- If necessary, change the automatically selected probability value by clicking on it and selecting another value from the displayed list.

Operation 5.3. Delete assumption

- In the right panel of the **Reasoner** module, right-click on the hypothesis node with the assumption to be deleted and select **Delete Assumption**.

5.7.2   Hands On: Development and Evaluation of an Argument

5.7.2.1 Overview

The objective of this case study is to learn how to use Disciple-CD to model the analysis of a hypothesis. More specifically, you will learn how to:

- Specify a new hypothesis
- Specify a question/answer pair that suggests how the hypothesis can be reduced to simpler hypotheses
- Specify the subhypotheses suggested by the question/answer pair
- Select ontology names to be used in hypotheses, questions, and answers

- Convert a hypothesis to an elementary solution
- Formalize a reasoning tree or a part of it to learn reduction patterns
- Convert formalized nodes back to modeling, to update them further

This case study will guide you through the process of defining the hypothesis "CS580 is a potential course for Mike Rice," and decomposing it, as shown in Figure 5.15.

5.7.2.2 Practice

You will first specify the hypothesis "CS580 is a potential course for Mike Rice." Then you will develop the argumentation structure from Figure 5.15 that reduces it to simpler hypotheses and solutions. You will make an assumption with respect to one of the leaf hypotheses. Finally, you will successively compose the assessments of the lower-level hypotheses into the assessment of the top hypothesis. As a side effect of this process, Disciple-CD will learn analysis patterns that will enable you to analyze more quickly similar hypotheses, as illustrated in Section 5.7.3.

Start Disciple-CD, select the case study knowledge base "05-Modeling-Learning/ Scen," and proceed as indicated in the instructions from the bottom of the opened window.

5.7.2.3 Basic Operations

The above practice exercise has illustrated several important operations described in the following.

Operation 5.4. Specify a new hypothesis

- Click on the **Hypothesis** menu at the top of the window.
- Click on [NEW].
- At the top of the window, click on [NEW EXAMPLE]. The **Reasoner** module is automatically selected.

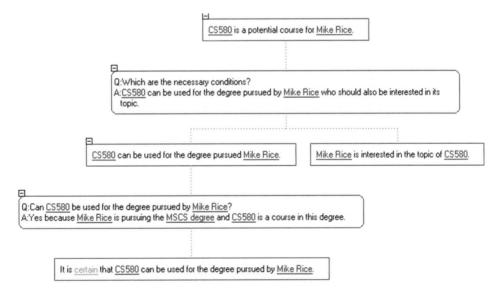

Figure 5.15. Hypothesis reduction tree.

- Double-click on the red-border box and define the hypothesis (for example, "CS580 is a potential course for Mike Rice").
- Define instances and concepts as indicated in Operation 5.5.
- Click outside the editing box when finished.

Operation 5.5. Define instances and constants

- In the Reasoner module, while editing a node in the reasoning tree, select the text representing the instance or constant, right-click on it, and select the corresponding type, as illustrated in Figure 5.16.

Operation 5.6. Specify question/answer nodes, subhypotheses, and solutions

- In right panel of the Reasoner module, right-click on the node under which the new node will be defined and select **Generate Suggestions**.
- If only a generic suggestion is made, double-click on that node and write the desired text.
- If several suggestions are made, right-click on one of them and select **Accept Suggestion**.

Operation 5.7. Delete question/answer nodes, subhypotheses, and solutions

- When a node is deleted, the entire subtree under it is also deleted.
- In the right panel of the Reasoner module, right-click on the node to be deleted and select **Remove Node**.

Operation 5.8. Convert between modeled and formalized hypotheses and solutions

- In the right panel of the Reasoner module, right-click on the node to be converted and select the desired and applicable conversion option, for example, **Convert to Modeling** (to convert a formalized node), **Learn Hypothesis Pattern** (to formalize a modeled hypothesis and learn a hypothesis pattern), **Learn Tree Patterns** (to formalize the entire tree under a hypothesis and learn reduction patterns), **Change to Assessment** (to convert a hypothesis into an assessment), or **Change to Hypothesis** (to convert an assessment into a hypothesis to be assessed).

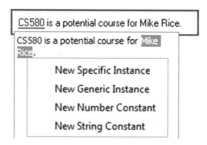

Figure 5.16. Defining Mike Rice as a specific instance.

5.7.3   Hands On: Analysis Based on Previously Learned Patterns and Synthesis Functions

5.7.3.1 Overview

The objective of this exercise is to learn how to use Disciple-CD to model the analysis of a hypothesis by reusing learned patterns. More specifically, you will learn how to:

- Specify a new hypothesis by instantiating a learned hypothesis pattern
- Specify the reduction of a hypothesis by reusing a learned reduction pattern
- Instantiate variables in a reduction
- Understand how the solution composition functions from the employed patterns are automatically applied

5.7.3.2 Practice

You will first define the hypothesis by selecting an existing pattern and instantiating it to: "CS681 is a potential course for Dan Bolt." Then you will successively reduce it to simpler hypotheses by reusing learned patterns. This will include the instantiation of variables from the learned patterns.

Start Disciple-CD, select the case study knowledge base "06-Analysis-Reuse/Scen," and proceed as indicated in the instructions from the bottom of the opened window.

5.7.3.3 Basic Operations

This case study has illustrated several important operations described in the following.

Operation 5.9. Specify a new hypothesis by instantiating a pattern
- Click on the **Hypothesis** menu at the top of the window.
- Click on [NEW].
- Click on the pattern to instantiate and notice that each pattern variable is replaced with "…"
- Click on each "…" and, in the text field that appears under it, write the desired value and press the **Enter** key.
- Select an answer from those proposed by the system.
- After all the values have been defined, click on [CREATE].

Operation 5.10. Specify the reduction of a hypothesis by reusing a learned pattern
- In the right panel of the **Reasoner** module, right-click on a formalized hypothesis node and select **Generate suggestions**.
- If the knowledge base has applicable learned patterns, it will propose them together with a generic suggestion.
- If a generated pattern to be selected contains variables, click on each of them and select the desired values.
- When the pattern to be selected is completely instantiated, right-click on its Q/A node and select **Accept Suggestion**.

5.8   ADVANCED OPERATIONS WITH DISCIPLE-CD

5.8.1   Hands On: Abstraction of Analysis

5.8.1.1 Overview

The objective of this case study is to learn how to use Disciple-CD to abstract a reasoning tree. More specifically, you will learn how to:

- Introduce a hypothesis into the abstract reasoning tree
- Define the abstraction of a hypothesis
- Modify the abstraction of a hypothesis
- Remove a hypothesis from the abstract tree

You have already worked with the abstract view of a reasoning tree, which is always shown in the left panel. However, when you model the analysis of a hypothesis, such as the one from Figure 5.15, you specify the detailed view of the reasoning tree. You will now learn how to define and update the abstract view of the reasoning tree. By abstraction of a hypothesis, we simply mean a shorter hypothesis summarizing its meaning, in the context of its upper-level hypotheses.

Consider, for example, the following hypothesis:

"The US Republican Party desires United States to become a global leader in wind power within the next decade."

This hypothesis could be abstracted to shorter hypotheses, such as:

"US Republican Party desires United States to become a leader in wind power"
"US Republican Party desires United States to become a leader"
"US Republican Party"
"US Republican Party supports wind power leadership"

You need to decide which abstraction is short enough to simplify the display of the tree while still conveying the meaning of the hypothesis. One abstraction technique is just to eliminate some of the words, as illustrated by the first three abstractions. Additionally, one may abstract phrases by using new words, as illustrated by the last example.

As indicated, the abstractions have to be considered in context. Let us consider the abstract analysis tree from the left panel in Figure 5.17. In this case, by considering its ancestor hypotheses, the abstract hypothesis "US Republican Party" is understood as one of the "major political parties" that has as a "desire" "United States global leader in wind power." This is indeed consistent with the fact that "US Republican Party" is the abstraction of "The US Republican Party desires United States to become a global leader in wind power within the next decade."

To define the abstraction of a hypothesis, you simply right-click on that hypothesis in the right panel and select **Add to TOC**. This will add the hypothesis in the left panel containing the abstract tree. Then you may update (shorten) the hypothesis in the left panel by right-clicking on it and selecting **Modify**.

When abstracting a hypothesis, make sure to properly select the words recognized by the agent, such as US Republican Party, which have to appear in blue. This is because the

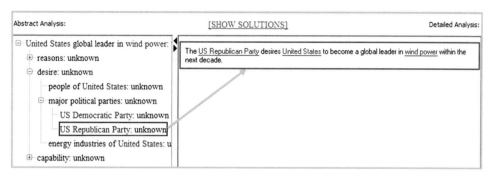

Figure 5.17. Understanding the meaning of an abstracted hypothesis in the context of its upper-level hypotheses.

agent learns abstraction patterns and will automatically apply them to similar hypotheses. For example, when you abstract the hypothesis "The US Republican Party desires United States to become a global leader in wind power within the next decade" to "US Republican Party," the agent learns that the pattern "?O1" is an abstraction of the pattern "The ?O1 desires ?O2 to become a global leader in ?O3 within the next decade." Therefore, the hypothesis "The US Democratic Party desires United States to become a global leader in wind power within the next decade" is automatically abstracted to "US Democratic Party."

Since a hypothesis may have only one abstraction at a time, when we change the abstraction of a specific hypothesis, the abstraction of all the similar hypotheses will automatically be updated to the new abstraction.

Finally, notice that the agent automatically abstracts the probabilistic assessments of the hypotheses to the actual probabilities. Thus, the assessment "It is almost certain that the US Republican Party desires United States to become a global leader in wind power within the next decade" is automatically abstracted to "almost certain."

5.8.1.2 Practice

You will first select the hypothesis "United States will be a global leader in wind power within the next decade." Then you will browse the predefined argumentation and abstract it with the goal of creating the abstract analysis tree from Figure 5.18.

Start Disciple-CD, select the case study knowledge base "07-Abstraction/Scen," and proceed as indicated in the instructions from the bottom of the opened window.

5.8.1.3 Advanced Operations

This case study has illustrated the following operations for the abstraction of reasoning:

Operation 5.11. Introduce a hypothesis into the abstract reasoning tree

- In the right panel of the **Reasoner** module, right-click on the (formalized) hypothesis to be abstracted and select **Add to TOC**.
- Notice that the hypothesis is now displayed in the left panel, while the right panel no longer displays its reasoning subtree.
- If you click on the hypothesis in the left panel, you will see its subtree in the right panel.

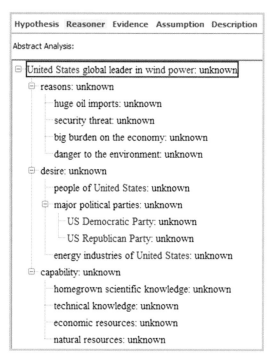

Figure 5.18. Abstract analysis tree.

Operation 5.12. Modify the abstraction of a hypothesis

- In the left panel of the **Reasoner** module, right-click on the hypothesis to be abstracted and select **Modify**.
- In the opened editor, edit the hypothesis to abstract it, making sure that all the remaining instances and constants are recognized (i.e., appear in blue or green). Then click outside the editor.

Operation 5.13. Remove a hypothesis from the abstract reasoning tree

- In the left panel of the **Reasoner** module, right-click on the hypothesis to be deleted and select **Remove from TOC**.
- Notice that the hypothesis is no longer displayed in the left panel, while the right panel now displays its reasoning subtree.

5.8.2   Hands On: Hypothesis Analysis and Evidence Search

5.8.2.1 Overview

The objective of this case study is to learn how to use Disciple-CD to analyze hypotheses based on evidence retrieved from the Internet. More specifically, you will learn how to:

- Associate search criteria with elementary hypotheses
- Invoke various search engines (such as Google, Yahoo!, or Bing) to identify relevant documents
- Define evidence based on the retrieved documents

The case study concerns the following hypothesis: "United States will be a global leader in wind power within the next decade."

To search for evidence that is relevant to a leaf hypothesis, the agent guides you to associate search criteria with it and to invoke various search engines on the Internet. Figure 5.19 shows the corresponding interface of the **Evidence** module. Because the [COLLECTION GUIDANCE] mode is selected in the left panel, it shows all the leaf hypotheses and their current evidential support. Clicking on one of these hypotheses, such as "United States imports huge quantities of oil," displays it in the right panel, enabling you to define search criteria for it. You just need to click on the [NEW] button following the **Search criterion** label and the agent will open an editor you can use to enter the search criterion.

Figure 5.20 shows two defined search criteria: "top oil importing countries" and "oil import by United States." We can now invoke Bing, Google, or Yahoo! with any one of these criteria to search for relevant evidence on the Internet. This will open a new window with the results of the search, as shown in Figure 5.21.

You have to browse the retrieved documents shown in Figure 5.21 and determine whether any of them contains information that is relevant to the hypothesis that the

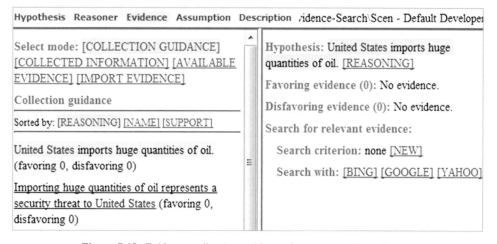

Figure 5.19. Evidence collection guidance for a selected hypothesis.

Hypothesis: United States imports huge quantities of oil. [REASONING]

Favoring evidence (0): No evidence.

Disfavoring evidence (0): No evidence.

Search for relevant evidence:

    Search criterion: oil import by United States [EDIT] [DELETE] [NEW]
- top oil importing countries
- oil import by United States

    Search with: [BING] [GOOGLE] [YAHOO]

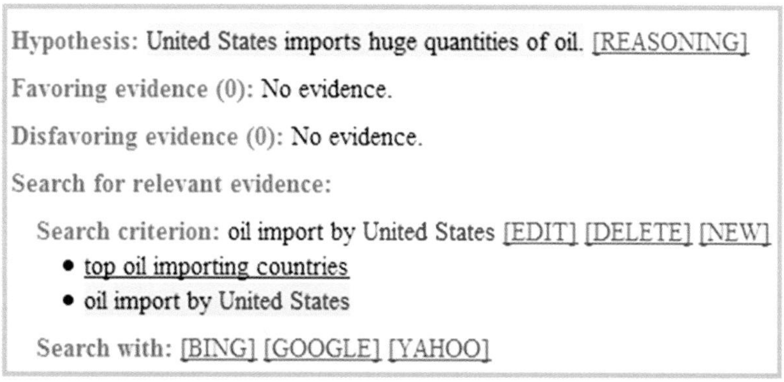

Figure 5.20. Defined search criteria for a selected hypothesis.

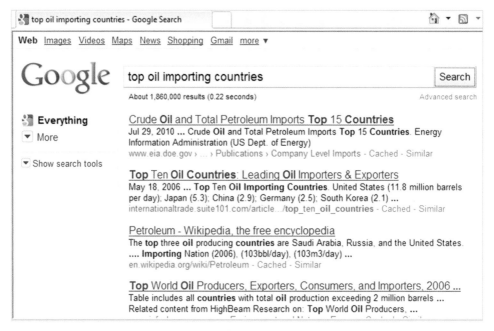

Figure 5.21. Searching relevant evidence on the Internet.

Figure 5.22. Selected document providing relevant information.

United States imports huge quantities of oil. Such a document is the second one whose content is shown in Figure 5.22.

You can now define one or several items of evidence with information copied from the retrieved document, as illustrated in Figure 5.23. In the left panel of the **Evidence** module, you switch the selection mode to [AVAILABLE EVIDENCE] and then click on [NEW]. As a result, the right panel displays a partial name for the evidence E001- to be completed by you. You then have to click on the [EDIT] button, which will open an editor where you can

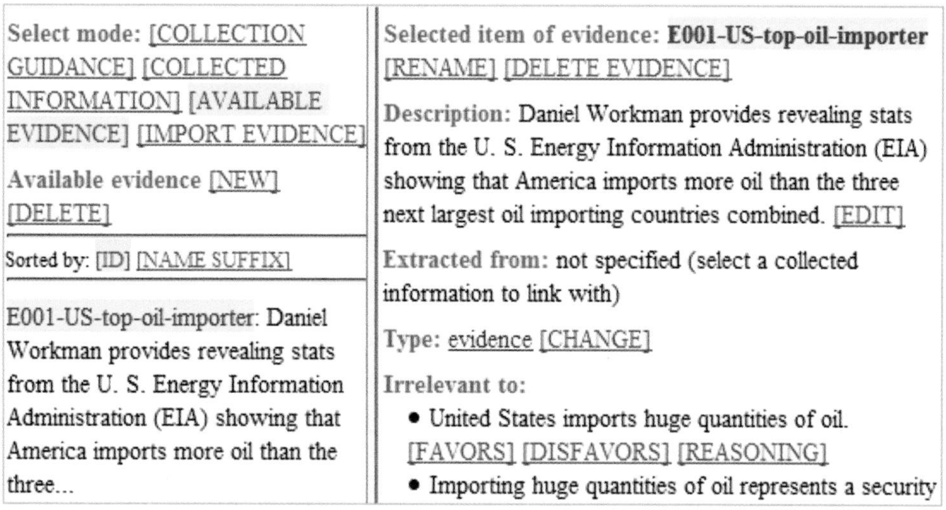

Select mode: [COLLECTION GUIDANCE] [COLLECTED INFORMATION] [AVAILABLE EVIDENCE] [IMPORT EVIDENCE] Available evidence [NEW] [DELETE]	Selected item of evidence: **E001-US-top-oil-importer** [RENAME] [DELETE EVIDENCE] Description: Daniel Workman provides revealing stats from the U. S. Energy Information Administration (EIA) showing that America imports more oil than the three next largest oil importing countries combined. [EDIT]
Sorted by: [ID] [NAME SUFFIX] E001-US-top-oil-importer: Daniel Workman provides revealing stats from the U. S. Energy Information Administration (EIA) showing that America imports more oil than the three...	Extracted from: not specified (select a collected information to link with) Type: evidence [CHANGE] Irrelevant to: • United States imports huge quantities of oil. [FAVORS] [DISFAVORS] [REASONING] • Importing huge quantities of oil represents a security

Figure 5.23. Defining an item of evidence.

copy the description of this item of evidence from the retrieved document. The result is shown in the right panel of Figure 5.23.

You can define additional characteristics of this item of evidence, such as its type (as will be discussed in Section 6.2), and you should indicate whether this item of evidence favors or disfavors the hypothesis that the United States imports huge quantities of oil, as previously explained.

5.8.2.2 Practice

You may now perform the actual case study to practice the procedures described in the preceding subsections and assess the hypothesis, "United States will be a global leader in wind power within the next decade." You will first browse its analysis tree to see how it is reduced to simpler hypotheses that you have to assess by searching evidence on the Internet. You will associate specific search criteria with the leaf hypotheses, invoke specific search engines with those criteria, identify relevant web information, define evidence from this information, associate evidence with the corresponding hypotheses, and evaluate its relevance and believability, with the goal of assessing the probability of the top-level hypothesis.

Start Disciple-CD, select the knowledge base "08-Evidence-Search/Scen," and proceed as indicated in the instructions from the bottom of the opened window.

5.8.2.3 Advanced Operation

This case study has illustrated the following operation:

Operation 5.14. Associate search criteria with hypotheses
• In the **Evidence** module, click on [COLLECTION GUIDANCE]. The left panel shows the leaf hypotheses and their evidential support.
• In the left panel, select a hypothesis.
• In the right panel, after **Search criterion**, click on [NEW] to define a new criterion.
• Type the search criterion and click on [SAVE].

- You may define additional criteria by repeating the two preceding steps.
- Select one of the search criteria by clicking on it.
- After **Search with**, click on one of the available search engines (i.e., [BING], [GOOGLE], [YAHOO]) to search the Internet with the selected criterion.
- Browse the documents returned by the search engine, select the relevant ones, and define items of information or evidence based on them.

5.8.3   Hands On: Justifications of Assumptions

5.8.3.1 Overview

The objective of this case study is to practice with defining and assessing a hypothesis based on previously learned patterns and synthesis functions.

This case study continues the case study from Section 5.8.2, where you analyzed the hypothesis "United States will be a global leader in wind power within the next decade." You will define a similar hypothesis, such as, "India will be a global leader in tidal power within the next decade" (by instantiating a hypothesis pattern learned in the previous case study); develop its argumentation (by reusing previously learned patterns); search evidence on the Internet (by reusing and/or updating previously defined search criteria); and assess the hypotheses based on the retrieved evidence (and previously learned synthesis functions). You will also learn how to provide a justification for an assumption. The end result of this case study should be an evidence-based assessment of the top-level hypothesis that India will be a global leader in tidal power within the next decade.

5.8.3.2 Practice

Start Disciple-CD, select the knowledge base "09-Assumption-Justification/Scen," and proceed as indicated in the instructions from the bottom of the opened window.

5.8.3.3 Advanced Operation

This case study has illustrated the following operation, which is another way to define an assumption that also allows the specification of a justification for the assumption made.

Operation 5.15. Define an assumption with justification

- Click on the **Reasoner** menu at the top of the window.
- If the right panel does not show the solutions (assessments) of the hypotheses, then click on [SHOW SOLUTIONS] at the top of the panel.
- Browse the analysis tree until the hypothesis for which you wish to define an assumption is displayed in the right panel.
- In the right panel, right-click on the hypothesis and select **New Assumption**. As a result, the agent proposes the default assessment (for example, very likely).
- If necessary, click on the default assessment and, from the displayed list, select a different value.
- Click on the **Assumption** menu at the top of the window.
- Click on [MODIFY].
- Click on the underlined space following **Justification** and write your justification in the opened editor. Then click outside the box.
- Click on [SAVE] and then on the **Reasoner** menu.

5.8.4   Hands On: Top-down and Bottom-up Argument Development

5.8.4.1 Overview

To this point in this section, we have focused on top-down development of an argument, where an initial hypothesis is successively reduced to increasingly simpler hypotheses to be assessed based on evidence. However, Disciple-CD allows the analyst to perform both top-down and bottom-up development of an argument, as will be illustrated in this practice exercise. This exercise is based on a real scenario described and analyzed in Danzig et al. (2011) and in Boicu et al. (2012). Its objectives are to learn how to:

- Develop an argument both from the bottom up and from the top down
- Insert a hypothesis above another hypothesis in an argumentation
- Move a hypothesis to the left or right of its sibling
- Update the name of an elementary hypothesis

Consider that you are an intelligence analyst and receive a tip from an informant that Aum Shinrikyo, a Japanese apocalyptic sect, has recently created a chemical company that will be able to acquire sarin. This tip arouses your curiosity because of your concern about terrorist acts in the Tokyo area. The question is, *"What hypothesis would explain this observation?"* You experience a flash of insight that Aum Shinrikyo develops sarin-based weapons. Using Disciple-CD, you first represent your abductive reasoning, as shown in the sequence of steps from Figure 5.24.

You then introduce intermediary hypotheses, from the bottom up, to develop the chain of abductive reasoning steps, as illustrated in the sequence of steps from Figure 5.25. First you right-click on the bottom hypothesis and select **New Hypothesis Above**, as in

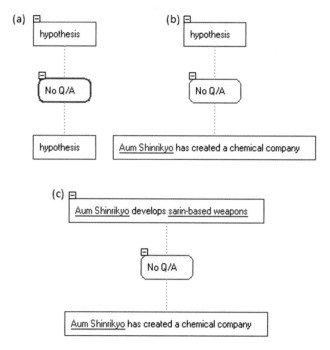

Figure 5.24. Defining the bottom and top hypotheses of the abductive reasoning chain.

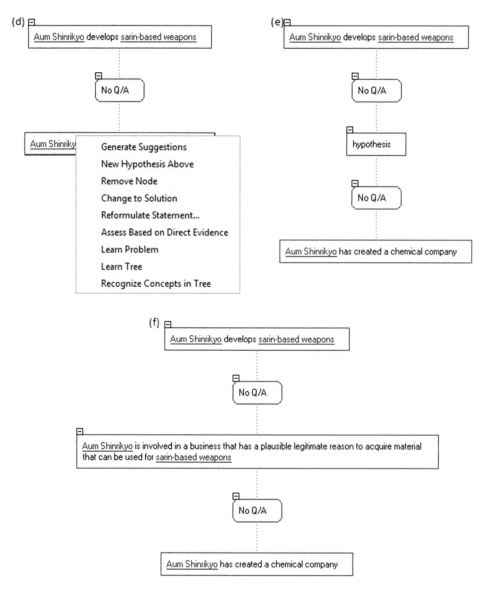

Figure 5.25. Defining an intermediary hypothesis.

Figure 5.25 (d). As a result, a new hypothesis is introduced above the bottom hypothesis, as shown in Figure 5.25 (e). Then you define this hypothesis, as shown in Figure 5.25 (f).

Finally, you complete the abductive reasoning chain by introducing another intermediary hypothesis above the middle hypothesis, as illustrated in Figure 5.26.

Next you need to analyze each hypothesis in the chain starting from the bottom up. First you need to associate the item of evidence that has led to this chain of reasoning steps (i.e., "Report that Aum Shinrikyo has created a chemical company that may acquire sarin") to the bottom hypothesis, "Aum Shinrikyo has created a chemical company." As a result, the system automatically generates the reasoning step from the bottom-right of Figure 5.27, reducing the hypothesis, "Aum Shinrikyo has created a chemical company," to an elementary hypothesis to be assessed based on evidence. This elementary hypothesis

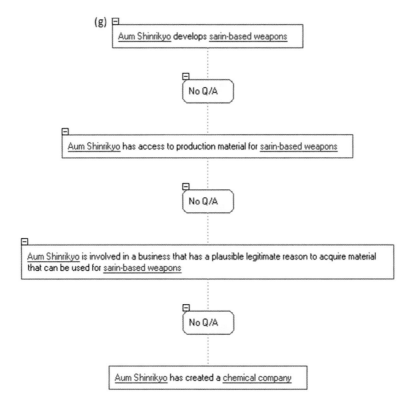

Figure 5.26. An abductive reasoning chain.

and its analysis are also introduced in the abstract tree shown in the left pane of Figure 5.27.

You may change the wording of the hypothesis, "Aum Shinrikyo has created a chemical company," by right-clicking on it in the right panel and selecting **Improve Phrasing**. You may also remove the bottom reasoning step by selecting **Remove Assessment Based on Direct Evidence** (see the bottom of Figure 5.27).

Having assessed the hypothesis "Aum Shinrikyo has created a chemical company," you continue with assessing the hypothesis above it, "Aum Shinrikyo is involved in a business that has a plausible legitimate reason to acquire material that can be used for sarin-based weapons." You do this by defining the question/answer pair, learning a pattern from the reasoning step, and selecting the composition function, as shown in the middle-left of Figure 5.28. Then you assess the next hypothesis up, "Aum Shinrikyo has access to production material for sarin-based weapons," in a similar way. In this case, the question/answer pair suggests adding one more subhypothesis, "It is relatively easy for a legitimate business to acquire production material for sarin-based weapons." Notice that this top-down analysis of each hypothesis adds a more holistic view, where you consider other aspects that may make the hypothesis true. This aspect is again illustrated with the top-down analysis of the top hypothesis shown in Figure 5.29, as discussed in the following text.

The question/answer pair ("What does it need? production material, significant funds, expertise"), which guides the analysis of the hypothesis, "Aum Shinrikyo develops sarin-based weapons," suggests considering two additional subhypotheses: "Aum Shinrikyo has significant funds," and, "Aum Shinrikyo has expertise for sarin-based-weapons"

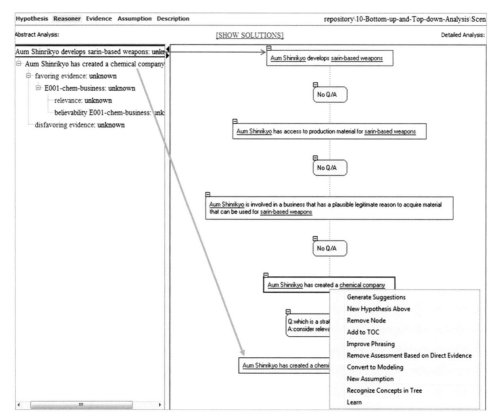

Figure 5.27. Assessing the bottom hypothesis in an abductive chain.

(see the top of Figure 5.29). Notice that you may change the order of the three subhypotheses of the top hypothesis, to correspond to the order from the answer. To do this, you right-click on the hypothesis to move and select **Move Left** or **Move Right**. You will also wish to correct the typo in the question. Because the question/answer node is in modeling (as indicated by its red border), this can be done easily by simply double-clicking on the node to open it in the editor.

5.8.4.2 Practice

In this exercise, you will practice the bottom-up and top-down development of an argument, as illustrated in the previous section. Start Disciple-CD, select the knowledge base "10-Argument-Development/Scen," and proceed as indicated in the instructions from the bottom of the opened window.

5.8.4.3 Advanced Operations

This case study has illustrated the following advanced operations:

Operation 5.16. Insert an intermediary hypothesis

- In the right panel of the **Reasoner** module, right-click on the hypothesis above which a new hypothesis is to be inserted, and select **New Hypothesis Above**.

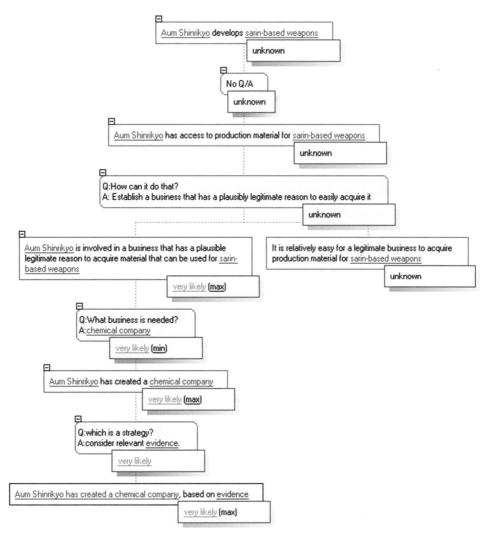

Figure 5.28. Continuing the development of the argument with the top-down analysis of intermediary hypotheses.

Operation 5.17. Move a hypothesis to the left or right

- In the right panel of the **Reasoner** module, right-click on a subhypothesis that has siblings and select **Move Left** or **Move Right**, to move it to the left of its left sibling or to the right of its right sibling.

Operation 5.18. Update the name of an elementary hypothesis

- In the right panel of the **Reasoner** module, right-click on a hypothesis that was reduced to an elementary hypothesis to be assessed based on evidence, and select **Improve Phrasing**.
- In the opened editor, update the phrasing of the hypothesis and then click outside the box.
- Notice that both this hypothesis and the corresponding elementary hypothesis have been updated accordingly.

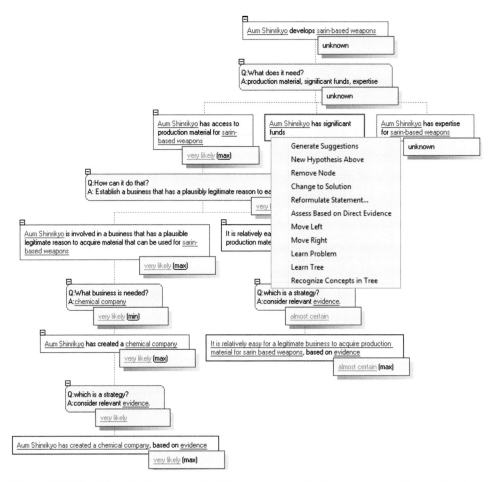

Figure 5.29. Finalizing the development of the argument with the top-down analysis of the top hypothesis.

5.9   ANALYSIS GUIDELINES

The following are several methodological guidelines for developing the analysis of a hypothesis.

Guideline 5.1. Define analysis trees in natural language using simple questions

Table 5.3 shows a recommended sequence of steps to be followed when developing the analysis tree for a specific hypothesis.

Guideline 5.2. Identify the specific instances, the generic instances, and the constants

After defining each hypothesis and question/answer pair, identify the specific instances, the generic instances, and the constants, such as "certain" or "5." The agent will automatically add all the instances in its knowledge base.

Table 5.3. The Reduction Tree Modeling Process

1. Identify the hypothesis to be assessed and express it with a clear natural language sentence.
2. Select the instances in the hypothesis.
3. Follow each hypothesis or subhypothesis with a single, concise, question relevant to assessing it. Ask small, incremental questions that are likely to have a single category of answer (but not necessarily a single answer). This usually means to ask the questions from Kipling's well-known poem, "I Keep Six Honest . . .": "What?" "Why?" "When?" "How?" "Where?" and "Who?" not complex questions such as "Who and what?" or "What and where?"
4. Follow each question with one or more answers to that question. Express answers as complete sentences, restating key elements of the question in the answer. Even well-formed, simple questions are likely to generate multiple answers. Select the answer that corresponds to the example solution being modeled and continue down that branch.
5. Select instances in the question/answer pair.
6. Evaluate the complexity of each question and its answers. When a question leads to apparently overly complex answers, especially answers that contain an "and" condition, rephrase the question in a simpler, more incremental manner leading to simpler answers.
7. For each answer, form a new subhypothesis, or several subhypotheses, or an assessment corresponding to that answer, by writing a clear natural language sentence describing the new subhypotheses or assessments. To the extent that it is practical, incorporate key relevant phrases and elements of preceding hypothesis names in subhypotheses names to portray the expert's chain of reasoning thought and the accumulation of relevant knowledge. If the answer has led to several subhypotheses, then model their solutions in a depth-first order.
8. Select instances in each subhypothesis.
9. Utilize the formalization capabilities of Disciple-CD to minimize the amount of modeling required, both for the current hypothesis and for other hypotheses.

Guideline 5.3. Learn and reuse reduction patterns

Disciple-CD will learn different patterns from reduction steps that have any differences in wording or punctuation, even though their meaning is the same, such as "with respect to" as opposed to "wrt," or "from the point of view of." To avoid the learning of semantically redundant patterns, you should reuse the previously learned patterns, as illustrated in Figure 5.30. From the reduction step in the top of Figure 5.30, the agent learns the pattern in the middle of the figure. Then, when you need to add similar reductions in your analysis you may simply instantiate this pattern (which will be proposed by the agent) by selecting appropriate values for the variables ?O1, ?O2, and ?O3, resulting in the reductions from the bottom of Figure 5.30.

Guideline 5.4. Define short hypothesis names for the abstract reasoning tree

Because you always have access to the complete description of an abstracted hypothesis, define the shortest possible abstraction, taking into account that its meaning is to be understood in the context of its upper-level hypotheses. Consider, for example, the abstract hypothesis "US Democratic Party," selected in the left-hand side of Figure 5.31. Its upper-level hypotheses indicate that this refers to one of the "major political parties," that has as a "desire" "United States global leader in wind power."

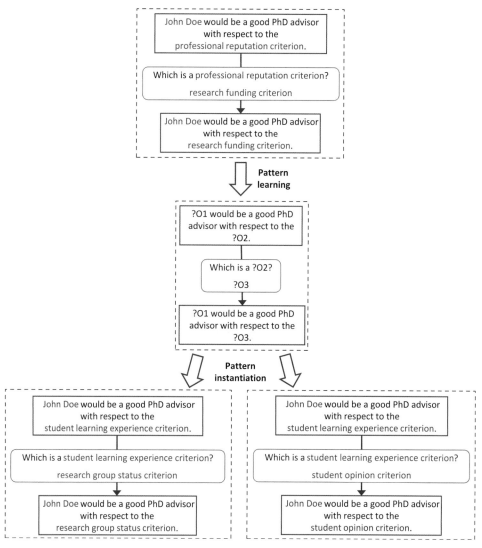

Figure 5.30. Pattern learning and reuse.

REVIEW QUESTIONS

5.1.   We began this chapter by considering problems faced by analysts who adopt entirely holistic approaches to their analyses whether they work alone or as members of a team on some complex analytic problem. In such a holistic approach, the analyst attempts to do everything in his or her head in order to reach a conclusion that the analysis requires. No attempt is made to decompose the problem into smaller elements. One very basic problem is that this holistic approach requires the analyst to try to keep many things in mind at the same time in reaching a conclusion. How does the hypothesis decomposition and structural approach in Disciple-CD help address this problem?

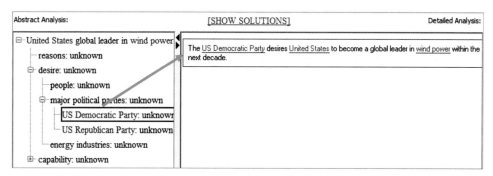

Figure 5.31. Understanding the meaning of an abstracted hypothesis in the context of its upper-level hypotheses.

5.2. We have already encountered several examples of hypothesis decompositions in Section 1.3. Review each of them and explain how they help our analysis.

5.3. Consider a hypothesis and indicate how it can be decomposed in several subhypotheses.

5.4. We mentioned that the hypothesis decomposition, or divide-and-conquer, approach to intelligence analysis raises some interesting and difficult problems. One recurrent problem involves the question, "How much decomposition is necessary? Or, at how fine a level should we attempt to divide an analytic problem?" There is another interesting and useful way to express this problem. The divide-and-conquer approach requires us to construct defensible and persuasive arguments from our evidence. These arguments, like the ones illustrated using Disciple-CD, consist of chains of reasoning. Every link in these chains involves a source of doubt or uncertainty. The question then becomes, "How many sources of doubt should analysts try to capture before reaching a conclusion in the problem at hand?" Provide some answers to this question.

5.5. In Section 5.5.1, we discussed *necessary and sufficient conditions* for inferences involving some major hypothesis **H**. Provide an illustration of the problems encountered in supplying these necessary and sufficient conditions in the field of intelligence analysis.

6 Assessing the Believability of Evidence

6.1 BELIEVABILITY: THE FOUNDATION OF ALL ARGUMENTS FROM EVIDENCE

The second major credential of evidence involves its *believability* (sometimes referred also as *credibility*). Suppose that an analyst is considering an item of information as possible relevant evidence. This credential involves the question, *"Can we believe what this item of evidence is telling us?"* Of course, this believability question involves considering the source from which this item came. The order in which we ask the relevance question, "So what?" and the believability question, "Can we believe it?" is immaterial. Which one of the relevance and believability questions we ask first will not affect our discussion of the credentials of evidence. In our view, the evidential and inferential issues surrounding believability assessment form perhaps the most difficult and interesting questions to be asked in intelligence analysis, or in any other context for that matter. One major difficulty is that we must ask different kinds of believability questions depending on the kinds of evidence we have and on the sources from which this evidence has come. In the next section, when we discuss basic substance-blind forms of evidence, we will see how various credibility questions we must ask are different for *tangible* items of evidence such as those provided by IMINT, COMINT, and MASINT than those provided by human informants or assets who provide *testimonial* evidence in the form of HUMINT. And, in the case of HUMINT, we require additional questions regarding the *competence* of HUMINT informants; one basic error often made in intelligence analyses is that the competence of a HUMINT source is often construed as evidence about this source's credibility. As we will show, competence does not entail credibility, nor does credibility entail competence; they are entirely separate matters.

Regardless of the form and source of the evidence being considered, we must distinguish between *evidence about an event* and the *event itself*. Having evidence about an event does not entail that this event actually occurred. To believe that an event did occur just because we have evidence for that invites all sorts of inferential troubles, primarily because sources of intelligence evidence of any kind have every possible gradation of believability shy of perfection. We can easily distinguish between evidence about an event and the event itself. We let E^* represent evidence that event E has occurred. Here is the basic source of doubt that will ground all of our arguments from evidence. We must infer that E occurred based on our evidence E^*. Clearly, this inference rests upon what we know about the believability of the source of E^*.

6.2   CLASSIFICATION OF EVIDENCE BASED ON BELIEVABILITY

Here is an important question we are asked to answer regarding the individual kinds of evidence we have, *"How do you, the analyst, stand in relation to this item of evidence? Can you examine it for yourself to see what events it might reveal?"* If you can, we say that the evidence is *tangible* in nature. You can examine it and apply your own senses in a determination of what the evidence may be telling you. We might say that in assessing tangible evidence, your own senses provide a direct interface with events of interest. As we will discuss momentarily, there are many forms of tangible evidence. But suppose instead you must rely upon other persons, assets, or informants to tell you about events of interest. Their reports to you, about these events, are examples of *testimonial evidence.* You yourself were not privy to the occurrence or nonoccurrence of these events, so you make inquiries of these assets who may have observed these events. It is of vital interest to know how these persons obtained the information they report. And, as we will observe, the human sources of testimonial evidence can express varying degrees of uncertainty about what they have observed.

Figure 6.1 shows the substance-blind classification of evidence that results from the preceding discussion and is further discussed in the following sections.

6.3   TANGIBLE EVIDENCE

There is an assortment of tangible items we might encounter and that could be examined by an intelligence analyst. Both IMINT and SIGINT provide various kinds of sensor records and images that can be examined. MASINT and TECHINT provide various objects, such as soil samples and weapons, that can be examined. COMINT can provide audio recordings of communications that can be overheard and translated if the communication has

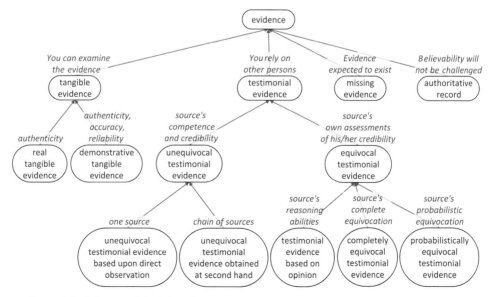

Figure 6.1. Substance-blind classification of evidence based on the believability credential.

occurred in a foreign language. We also note that documents are tangible evidence that can be examined by an analyst. These documents might have been captured or revealed by a human asset; but they also include any document obtained from open sources, whatever they may be: newspapers, books, websites, and so on. We also list as tangible items tabled measurements of any kind, including statistical records, charts showing various kinds of scientific or technological relations, and maps and diagrams or plans of various kinds. Some of these kinds of items might be included in TECHINT or MASINT sources.

One thing we are obliged to note is that the analyst observing these tangible items may need the assistance of other analysts who have expertise in explaining to the analyst what a tangible item reveals. For example, an expert in photo analysis may assist another analyst by showing what an image has revealed to us. Analysts whose assistance is required in such cases play the role of "expert witnesses," so common in both criminal and civil trials. All of this highlights the fact that intelligence analysis is so often a cooperative venture involving teams of analysts each of whom may have particular knowledge and skills.

Two different kinds of tangible evidence have been usefully discerned, at least in the field of law: *real tangible evidence* and *demonstrative tangible evidence* (Lempert et al., 2000, pp. 1146–1148).

6.3.1   Real Tangible Evidence: Authenticity

Real tangible evidence is a thing itself, and it has only one major believability attribute: *authenticity. "Is this object what it is represented as being or is claimed to be?"* There are as many ways of generating deceptive and inauthentic evidence as there are persons wishing to generate it. Documents or written communications may be faked, captured weapons may have been altered, and photographs may have been manipulated in various ways. One problem is that it usually requires considerable expertise to detect inauthentic evidence. Further, different kinds of real tangible evidence require different areas of expertise. For example, it would require quite different expertise to detect a forged document than it does to detect an altered photo or a deceptive weapon component.

6.3.2   Demonstrative Tangible Evidence: Authenticity, Accuracy, and Reliability

Demonstrative tangible evidence does not concern things themselves but only representations or illustrations of these things. Examples include diagrams; maps; scale models; statistical or other tabled measurements; and sensor images or records of various sorts, such as IMINT, SIGINT, and COMINT. Demonstrative tangible evidence has three believability attributes. The first concerns its *authenticity.* So, both real and demonstrative tangible evidence have this crucial believability attribute. For example, suppose we obtain a hand-drawn map from a captured insurgent showing the locations of various groups in his insurgency organization. Has this map been deliberately contrived to mislead our military forces, or is it a genuine representation of the location of these insurgency groups?

The second believability attribute of demonstrative tangible evidence is *accuracy* of the representation provided by the demonstrative tangible item. The accuracy question concerns the extent to which the device that produced the representation of the real tangible item had a degree of sensitivity (resolving power or accuracy) that allows us to tell what events were observed. We would be as concerned about the accuracy of the hand-drawn

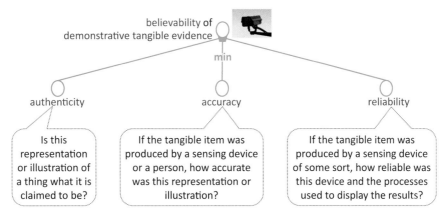

Figure 6.2. Assessing the believability of demonstrative tangible evidence.

map allegedly showing insurgent groups locations as we would about the accuracy of a sensor in detecting traces of some physical occurrence. Different sensors have different resolving power that also depends on various settings of their physical parameters (e.g., the settings of a camera). Certain settings of these parameters provide better images of objects than do other settings, given the conditions under which the image was obtained. Some sensors, such as those employed in electronic signals intelligence (ELINT), provide only approximate locations of objects, such as the error ellipses provided by ELINT records of radar emissions.

The third major attribute, *reliability*, is especially relevant to various forms of sensors that provide us with many forms of demonstrative tangible evidence. *A system, sensor, or test of any kind is reliable to the extent that the results it provides are repeatable or consistent.* You say that your car is reliable to the extent to which it will take you where you wish to go for some specified time in the future. A sensing device is reliable if it would provide the same image or report on successive occasions on which this device is used. A test is reliable to the extent that it provides the same result on repeated applications of it. Speaking of physical sensors, the reliability of any of them depends, of course, on how well they are maintained. The trouble with applying the term *reliability* to items of HUMINT reported by human sources is that what is at issue is whether or not we can believe what this source has told us; this involves his or her competence and credibility. As mentioned in the previous section and will be discussed in detail in Section 6.4, the believability of a human source requires questions that are quite different from those we would ask concerning a sensor's reliability. We could say that a reliable human source is one who will provide us with information whenever we ask for it. But whether we can believe what this source is telling us on any occasion depends on his or her competence and credibility.

Figure 6.2 expresses the assessment of the believability of demonstrative tangible evidence in the problem reduction/solution synthesis paradigm. First we reduce the believability credential to three simpler attributes. Then we combine the assessments of these attributes.

6.3.3   Examples of Tangible Evidence

Here are several examples and questions involving evidence that is tangible and that the analyst can examine personally to see what events it reveals.

Example 6.1.

Have a look at evidence item E009-MDDOTRecord in Table 5.2 on page 97. The Maryland DOT records, in the form of a tangible document, could be given to the analyst to verify that the vehicle carrying MD license plate number MDC-578 is registered in the name of the TRUXINC Company in Silver Spring, Maryland.

Example 6.2.

Now consider evidence item E008-GuardReport in Table 5.2. Here we have a document in the form of a log showing that the truck bearing license plate number MDC-578 exited the XYZ parking lot at 8:30 pm on the day in question. This tangible item could also be made available to analysts investigating this matter.

6.4   TESTIMONIAL EVIDENCE

For *testimonial evidence,* we have two basic sources of uncertainty: *competence* and *credibility.* This is one reason why it is more appropriate to talk about the *believability* of testimonial evidence, which is a broader concept that includes both competence and credibility considerations.

6.4.1   Competence

6.4.1.1 Access

The first question to ask related to competence is *whether this source actually made the observation he or she claims to have made or had access to the information that he or she reports.* In several accounts of intelligence analyses, we have observed a glaring non sequitur. These accounts all say, "We can believe what this source has reported to us because he had good access to the information he reports." This source may have had all the access in the world, but still not be credible in his report about what he observed. *The problem here is that HUMINT asset competence does not entail the asset's credibility; competence and credibility are two entirely distinct characteristics.* It is also true that a human source's credibility does not entail his or her competence. Credibility has entirely different attributes than competence.

6.4.1.2 Understandability

The second competence question concerns *whether this source understood what was being observed well enough to provide us with an intelligible account of what was observed.* Thus, besides access, competence also involves *understandability.*

There are other situations, important in intelligence analysis, in which human competence (understandability) is an issue. As you know, we rely on persons to inform us about the meaning of various forms of tangible and testimonial evidence. In addition, we rely upon many persons who process, edit, and transmit intelligence information of many kinds. Here are some examples:

- Analysts who interpret any form of information obtained from sensors
- Persons who translate documents written in foreign languages
- Persons who edit, transcribe, or summarize intelligence information
- Persons who process raw sensor records

In all of these situations, *the competence at issue concerns the skill these persons demonstrate in performing their tasks.* We might be as misled by a photo that is misinterpreted as we would be if a document written in a foreign language suffered from translation errors.

6.4.2   Credibility

HUMINT asset $\mathcal{A}$ tells us that he observed event E to have happened. Suppose, on evidence, we believe $\mathcal{A}$ to be a competent source; that is, we believe $\mathcal{A}$ made the observation he says he made. Whether we can believe that event E happened depends on three attributes of $\mathcal{A}$'s credibility: his *veracity, objectivity*, and *observational sensitivity* under the conditions of the observation. As explained in Schum (1989), these three attributes of the credibility of human sources of testimonial evidence arise in four different contexts: law, epistemology, signal detection theory, and common experience.

6.4.2.1 Veracity or Truthfulness

From experience, we learn that people do not always believe what they are telling us. We would not say that a person was being untruthful if this person believed what he or she just reported. So the first question we should ask about the source telling us that event E occurred is, *"Does this source believe that event E occurred?"* Assessing *veracity* or *truthfulness* has been a problem for centuries and some mistakes have been made in explaining what veracity means. In many old and in some newer works, it is said that a source is being truthful only if the event reported actually occurred. There is great trouble here since this explanation confounds veracity with the two other credibility attributes we need to consider. As an example, our source tells us that event E occurred and we later find out that E did not occur. Was this source being untruthful? Not necessarily, since this source might simply have been mistaken. So the veracity of sources of HUMINT who report on what they observe depends on our assessment of whether these sources actually believe what they are reporting to us.

6.4.2.2 Objectivity

From common experience, we observe that persons, including ourselves, often believe that some event has occurred because we either expect it to occur or want it to occur, regardless of what our senses are telling us. In such instances, we would say that this source lacks *objectivity*. An *objective observer* is one who bases a belief on the sensory evidence he or she received rather than on what this person expected or desired to observe. Suppose we believe that the source telling us that event E occurred is being truthful; he does believe that event E occurred. But now the question is, *"Was this belief based on the sensory evidence this source received, or was it based on what this source expected or wished to observe?"* One additional important matter concerns the role of *memory.* The reason is that our beliefs are elastic in nature; they change over time and often in response to new information we receive. If a HUMINT source made the observation some time ago, we might well question whether this source had the same belief at the time of his or her observation that this person now has while reporting to us. Is this person now telling us what he or she expected or wished to occur instead of basing this report on this person's recollection of what his or her senses recorded?

6.4.2.3 Observational Sensitivity

Suppose we believe our source to be truthful and objective in his or her report that event E occurred. This source does believe that E occurred, and this source did base this belief on sensory evidence obtained during a relevant observation. But now the question is, *"How good was the sensory evidence this source received under the conditions in which this observation was made?"* As we know, none of our senses are perfectly accurate or sensitive, particularly under a variety of ambient conditions such as reduced visibility and high noise levels. The physical condition of the source is also relevant here. We would question the adequacy of the sensory evidence this source obtained if he or she had some sensory defect or was intoxicated at the time the observation was made. Common experience tells us that human senses are not infallible and that we are all prone to make mistakes in our observations.

Figure 6.3 summarizes the believability credentials for testimonial evidence based upon direct observations and the questions we need to ask to establish such credentials. All of these credibility and competence matters are tremendously important in the task of drawing accurate conclusions from intelligence evidence. It does us no good at all to draw seemingly defensible conclusions from evidence that has any defects in terms of the credibility and competence issues we have just mentioned. There is often great complexity associated with credibility and competence assessment, as we now address.

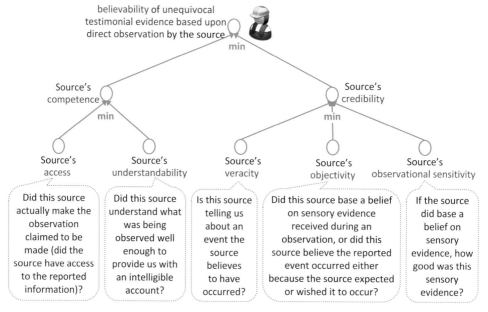

Figure 6.3. Assessing the believability of testimonial evidence.

6.4.3   Types of Testimonial Evidence

As indicated in Figure 6.1, there are several types of testimonial evidence. If the source does not hedge or equivocate about what he or she observed (i.e., the source reports that he or she is certain that the event did occur), then we have *unequivocal testimonial evidence*. If, however, the source hedges or equivocates in any way (e.g., "I'm fairly sure that E occurred") then we have *equivocal testimonial evidence*. The first question we would ask this source of unequivocal testimonial evidence is, *"How did you obtain information about what you have just reported?"* It seems that this source has three possible answers to this question. The first answer is, "I made a *direct observation* myself." In this case, we have *unequivocal testimonial evidence based upon direct observation*. The second possible answer is, *"I did not observe this event myself but heard about its occurrence (or nonoccurrence) from another person."* Here we have a case of secondhand or hearsay evidence, called *unequivocal testimonial evidence obtained at secondhand*. A third answer is possible, *"I did not observe event E myself, nor did I hear about it from another source. But I did observe events C and D and inferred from them that event E definitely occurred."* This is called *testimonial evidence based on opinion*, and it requires some very difficult questions. The first concerns the source's believability as far as his or her observation of events C and D; the second involves our examination of whether we ourselves would infer E based on events C and D. This matter involves our assessment of the source's *inferential ability*. It might well be the case that we do not question this source's credibility in observing events C and D, but we question the conclusion that the source has drawn from his or her observations that event E occurred. We would also question the certainty with which the source has reported an opinion that E occurred. Despite the source's conclusion that "event E definitely occurred," and because of many sources of uncertainty, we should consider that *testimonial evidence based on opinion* is a type of *equivocal testimonial evidence* (see Figure 6.1).

There are two other types of equivocal testimonial evidence. The first we call *completely equivocal testimonial evidence*. Asked whether event E occurred or did not, our source says, "I don't know," or, "I can't remember." This is an interesting response of the sort we so frequently observe during congressional hearings. There are two possible explanations for this complete equivocation. The first is that the source is honestly impeaching or undermining his or her own believability; he or she does not know or cannot remember. A frequent addition to this equivocation might be the further statement, "I'm not a good source here, perhaps you ought to ask X (another possible source)." Unfortunately, there is another possible explanation for this complete equivocation: The source does know or can remember, but refuses to tell us whether E occurred or not. If we had evidence that this source did know or did remember whether or not event E occurred, this would be evidence that our source is a double and has more than one employer.

But there is another way a source of HUMINT can equivocate: The source can provide *probabilistically equivocal testimonial evidence* in various ways. One way is numerical, as in the following example. Asked whether event E occurred or did not, the source might say, "I'm 60 percent sure that event E happened and 40 percent sure that it didn't happen." We could look upon this particular probabilistic equivocation as an assessment by the source of his or her own observational sensitivity. However, if we had evidence pointing to the source's underassessment of how sure he or she was that event occurred, we might be inclined to view this evidence as bearing on the source's veracity. Another way probabilistic equivocation can be expressed is in words rather than in numbers. Asked whether event E occurred, the source might say such things as, "I'm fairly sure that E occurred," "It is quite probable that E occurred," or, "It is very unlikely that E occurred." Here again we would wish to determine whether the source's stated degree of equivocation was legitimate or not.

6.4.4   Examples of Testimonial Evidence

Here are some examples and questions involving testimonial evidence from human sources that is not hedged or qualified in any away.

Example 6.3.

Evidence item E014-Grace in Table 5.2 is Grace's testimony that no one at the XYZ Company had checked out the canister for work on any project. Grace states this unequivocally. You should also note that she has given *negative evidence* saying the cesium-137 was *not* being used by the XYZ Company. This negative evidence is very important because it strengthens our inference that the cesium-137 canister was stolen.

Example 6.4.

E006-Clyde in Table 5.2 is unequivocal testimonial evidence. It represents positive evidence.

Here are some examples involving testimonial evidence given by human sources who equivocate or hedge in what they tell us.

Example 6.5.

Consider the evidence item E005-Ralph in Table 1.4. Here Ralph hedges a bit by saying that the lock on the hazardous materials storage area *appears* to have been forced. He cannot say for sure that the lock had been forced, so he hedges in what he tells us.

Example 6.6.

In new evidence regarding the dirty bomb example, suppose we have a source code-named "Yasmin." She tells us that she knew a man in Saudi Arabia named Omar al-Massari. Yasmin says she is "quite sure" that Omar spent two years "somewhere" in Afghanistan "sometime" in the years 1998 to 2000.

6.5   MISSING EVIDENCE

6.5.1   Uncertainties Associated with Missing Evidence

To say that evidence is missing entails that we must have had some basis for expecting we could obtain it. There are some important sources of uncertainty as far as missing evidence is concerned. In certain situations, missing evidence can itself be evidence. To begin with, consider some form of tangible evidence, such as a document, that we have been unable to obtain. There are several reasons for our inability to find it, some of which are more important than others. First, it is possible that this tangible item never existed in the first place; our expectation that it existed was wrong. Second, the tangible item exists but we have simply been looking in the wrong places for it. Third, the tangible item existed at one time but has been destroyed or misplaced. Fourth, the tangible item exists but someone is keeping it from us. This fourth consideration has some very important inferential implications, including denial and possibly deception. An adverse inference can be drawn from someone's failure to produce evidence. The failure to produce requested evidence may mean that producing it would not be in the best interests of the person(s) from whom the item was requested. If these interests coincide with those of an adversary, we could conclude that this failure to produce evidence is part of an attempt to deceive us, since if we did obtain this evidence, it would be in our best interests and not the best interests of the adversary.

Now consider missing testimonial evidence. Suppose we expect that a HUMINT asset A could tell us about some event of importance to us. There are several interesting possibilities here. First, A might never respond to our inquiry; put another way, A responds to our inquiry with silence. There are different rules that apply in intelligence analysis than those applying in our courts of law. In law, a defendant or a witness can claim protection under the Fifth Amendment to our Constitution. He cannot be compelled to testify, and no adverse inference is allowed by his failure to do so. But there is no such privilege in intelligence analysis. We would be entitled to draw an adverse inference about A's silence in response to our request for information to which we believe A has access. Another possibility is that A acts to impeach his own competence: A tells us that he never has made any observation of events such as those in which we are presently interested. This may sound like the complete equivocation we discussed previously. The difference in this case is that A gives a particular reason why he does not know whether this event occurred or not: A says he was never in a position to observe this event or had no access to the information requested of him. If, on evidence, we learned that A did make an observation or did have access to information about the requested event, we would certainly be entitled to draw an adverse inference concerning A's behavior and the inferential consequences of his refusing to reveal the information we are seeking from him.

In summary, there are very important uncertainties associated with missing evidence, either tangible or testimonial in nature. But there is one final matter to consider about which most analysts will already know. *We should not confuse negative evidence with missing evidence.* To adopt a common phrase, *"evidence of absence (negative evidence) is not the same as absence of evidence (missing evidence)."* Entirely different conclusions can be drawn from evidence that an event did not occur than can be drawn from our failure to find evidence. We are obliged to ask different questions in these two situations.

6.5.2 Example of Missing Evidence

Missing evidence may be either tangible or testimonial in nature.

Example 6.7.

Consider our discussion on the cesium-137 canister. Upon further investigation, we identify the person who rented the truck as Omar al-Massari, alias

Omer Riley. We tell him that we wish to see his laptop computer. We are, of course, interested in what it might reveal about the terrorists with whom he may be associating. He refuses to tell us where it is. This we refer to as the nonproduction of evidence.

6.6 AUTHORITATIVE RECORDS

There is one final category of evidence about which we would never be obliged to assess its believability. In intelligence analyses, and in many analyses in other contexts, we routinely need information whose believability we would never be expected to defend. In fact, in certain instances we could never establish the believability of this information. Tabled information of various sorts – such as tide tables, celestial tables, tables of physical or mathematical results (such as probabilities associated with statistical calculations), and many other tables of information – we would accept as being believable provided that we used these tables correctly. In some instances, of course, tabled information might contain errors. For example, tables showing the ranges or explosive power of a weapons system under various conditions might have incorrect entries that are discovered and corrected. Many other items of information are accepted facts whose believability is assumed. For example, an analyst would not be obliged to prove that temperatures in Iraq can be around 120° F in summer months, or that the population of Baghdad is greater than that of Basra.

6.7 MIXED EVIDENCE

6.7.1 Analysis of Mixed Evidence

We have just considered a categorization of individual items of evidence. But there are situations in which individual items can reveal various mixtures of the types of evidence shown in Figure 6.1. One example involves a tangible document containing a testimonial assertion based on other alleged tangible evidence. As we noted, these forms of evidence are not mutually exclusive; they can occur together in a single item of evidence. We might say that mixtures of them get crowded into the same item of evidence. Figure 6.4, for example, shows how one would need to assess the believability of a document containing the testimony of a source.

6.7.2 Examples of Mixed Evidence

Here are some examples and questions about mixtures of the forms of evidence discussed in the preceding sections.

Example 6.8.

Here is an obvious example of a mixture of two or more items of tangible evidence; it is called a *passport*. A passport is a tangible document alleging the existence of other tangible documents recording the place of birth and country of origin of the holder of the passport. In other words, a passport

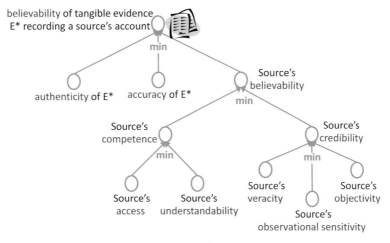

Figure 6.4. An example of assessing the believability of mixed evidence.

sets up a *paper trail* certifying the identity of the holder of the passport. In addition to the authenticity of the passport itself, we are also interested in the authenticity of all the other tangible documents on which this passport is based.

Example 6.9.

Here is another mixture of forms of evidence, this time recording a mixture of tangible and testimonial evidence. We return to our asset "Yasmin," who has given us further evidence about Omar al-Massari in our cesium-137 example. Suppose we have a tangible document recording Yasmin's account of her past experience with Omar al-Massari. This document records Yasmin's testimony about having seen a document detailing plans for constructing weapons of various sorts that was in Omar al-Massari's possession. As far as believability issues are concerned, we first have the authenticity of the transcription of her testimony to consider. Yasmin speaks only in Arabic and so we wonder how adequate the translation of her testimony has been. Also, we have concerns about Yasmin's competence and credibility to consider in her recorded testimony. Finally, we have further interest in the authenticity of the document she allegedly saw in Omar al-Massari's possession.

In this section, we have shown that we can classify all evidence, regardless of its substance or content, into just a few categories of recurrent forms and combinations of evidence. That is why this classification is called *substance-blind*. This classification of evidence is based on its inferential properties rather than upon any feature of its substance or content. Knowledge of these substance-blind forms and combinations of evidence pays great dividends. Such knowledge informs us and Disciple-CD how to evaluate the believability of evidence, based on its type. It allows us to more easily assess evidence coming from different sources and to compare the evidence and conclusions reached from it in different intelligence analyses at different times.

6.8   DEEP BELIEVABILITY ANALYSIS

In the previous sections, we have shown how to assess the believability of an item of evidence by considering various believability attributes. For example, we may assess the believability of testimonial evidence by considering the attributes of the source's competence (i.e., access and understandability) and credibility (i.e., veracity, objectivity, and observational sensitivity). Similarly, we may assess the believability of demonstrative tangible evidence by considering its authenticity, reliability, and accuracy.

If an item of evidence is really critical to our analytic conclusion, we may wish to perform an even deeper believability analysis, where we further decompose the preceding attributes. As an illustration, we present an approach to assessing the credibility of a source that relies on the rich legacy of experience gathered over the past six hundred years in the Anglo-American adversarial judicial system concerning questions to ask of witnesses who appear in trials at law.

Table 6.1 presents ten questions or tests concerning veracity of a human source. Take, for instance, the third veracity question, *"Exploitation Potential*: Is this source subject to any significant exploitation by other persons or organizations to provide us this information?" If there is evidence that this source is subject to any significant exploitation by other persons or organizations to provide us this information, then we cannot believe this source. Consider, as an example, a source whose family is detained by Al Qaeda and who has received threats from it to provide us this information.

Now let us consider the fourth veracity question, *"Any Existing Contradictory or Divergent Evidence*: Is there any existing evidence that contradicts or conflicts with what the source has reported to us?"

Table 6.1 Questions Concerning the Veracity of a Human Source

1. *Goals of this Source*: Does what this source tells us support any of his or her goals?
2. *Present Influences on this Source*: Could this source have been influenced in any way to provide us with this report?
3. *Exploitation Potential*: Is this source subject to any significant exploitation by other persons or organizations to provide us this information?
4. *Any Existing Contradictory or Divergent Evidence*: Is there any existing evidence that contradicts or conflicts with what this source has reported to us?
5. *Any Existing Corroborative or Confirming Evidence*: Is there any other evidence that corroborates or confirms this source's report?
6. *Veracity Concerning Collateral Details*: Are there any contradictions or conflicts in the collateral details provided by this source that reflect the possibility of this source's dishonesty?
7. *Source's Character*: What evidence do we have about this source's character and honesty that bears upon this source's veracity?
8. *Reporting Record*: What does the record show about the truthfulness of this source's previous reports to us?
9. *Source Expectations about Us*: Is there any evidence that this source may be reporting events this source believes we will wish to hear or see?
10. *Interview Behavior*: If this source reported these events to us, what was this source's demeanor and bearing while giving us this report?

The following is an example of contradictory evidence where a source is inconsistent, telling us different things at different times.

Example 6.10.

Here is a HUMINT source called "Rosebud." Two weeks ago, Rosebud told us she observed Amir D., running away from a car, just before a bomb in this car exploded in a crowded market in Baghdad on May 14, 2013. Now today, she tells us that it was Omar T., who was running away from this car at this time and place. We have two options here; the first concerns Rosebud's veracity. We might say that her inconsistency shows that she is not keeping her stories straight, and so we should believe she made up a story and is not being truthful. Alternatively, we might believe that Rosebud has simply forgot who she observed running away from this car just before it exploded.

Here is another case of inconsistency.

Example 6.11.

Another source named "Dingbat" tells us that it was Umar who was running away from the car just before a bomb in this car exploded in a crowded market in Baghdad on May 14, 2013. We have relied on Dingbat to keep us informed about Umar in the past. We recall that Dingbat had previously told us that he and Umar were in Karbala all day on May 14, 2013. Here again in this case, Dingbat's inconsistency may indicate his lack of veracity; but it may also mean that he was mistaken about the dates of these two events.

In assessing the veracity of a source, we should attempt to answer each of the preceding questions based on evidence. If we have evidence that the answer to each of the preceding questions supports the veracity of the source, then we can have high confidence in this source's veracity.

If, however, many of the questions in Table 6.1 are not answered by our evidence, then our confidence in our assessment has to be lower.

A very cautious approach would be to conclude that the source is not truthful if any of these tests is not passed. This approach is justified by the fact that we would do such an analysis for critical evidence for which we would need to have a high degree of confidence that it is true.

Table 6.2 presents six questions or tests concerning the objectivity of a human source. The following is a situation in which we have a HUMINT source giving us evidence about the credibility of another HUMINT source. In particular, he provides evidence relevant to answering the first two questions in Table 6.2.

Example 6.12.

Suppose we are concerned about the credibility of a source called "Mable." Mable says he observed Yaqub M., placing an IED on a road leading from Baghdad to Samarra two days ago. We have another source, "Foxtrot," who knows Mable and who has told us useful things about Mable in the past. So, we tell Foxtrot about Mable's telling us about observing Yaqub M., placing the IED on the road between Baghdad and Samarra two days ago. We ask Foxtrot whether Mable either expected, or wished, Yaqub to be the person he saw placing the IED. Foxtrot says that Mable barely knows Yaqub and has

---

Table 6.2 Questions Concerning the Objectivity of a Human Source

1. *Source's Observational Expectations*: As far as this present report is concerned, do we have any evidence concerning what this source may have expected to observe?
2. *Source's Observational Desires*: As far as this present report is concerned, do we have any evidence bearing on what this source may have wished to observe?
3. *Belief-Formation Objectives*: As far as this present report is concerned, is there any evidence that this source may have believed it risky to form certain beliefs about what was being observed?
4. *Memory Effects on Beliefs*: Suppose this source is reporting about events he or she observed some time ago. How certain can we be that this source's present beliefs are the same as this source's beliefs were at the time of the source's observation? This not only involves how good the source's memory is, but also involves possible reasons why this source may have changed a belief.
5. *Any Existing Contradictory or Divergent Evidence*: It is entirely possible that any existing contradictory or divergent evidence may bear on this source's objectivity rather than on this source's veracity. Such evidence may point to this source's only lacking objectivity and not veracity.
6. *Any Existing Corroborative Evidence*: We may have evidence that may bear corroboratively on a source's objectivity rather than on this source's veracity.

---

no grounds for expecting or wishing that Yaqub was the person he saw. Foxtrot adds, "You can be confident that Mable told you what he did see and not what he expected or what he wanted to see."

Here is an example about memory and possible changes in a source's HUMINT testimony related to the fourth question in Table 6.2.

Example 6.13.

Here is Rosebud again, who first tells us that it was Amir D., running away from a car, just before a bomb in this car exploded in a crowded market in Baghdad on May 14, 2013, and then two weeks later now tells us that it was Omar T., and not Amir D. This may simply be the result of Rosebud's changing her mind about who she saw, and not the result of her failing to keep her story straight.

Table 6.3 presents six questions or tests concerning the observational sensitivity of a human source.

The following is a situation providing evidence on the *allocation of attention*.

Example 6.14.

Here comes Mable again, who tells us that he observed Yaqub M., placing an IED on a road leading from Baghdad to Samarra two days ago. We ask Mable how sure he is that the person he saw was really Yaqub M. Mable says, "Well, I am pretty sure it was Yaqub M., who I saw as I was driving by, but I actually got only a brief look at him."

The following is a situation involving the *observational conditions*.

Example 6.15.

Here comes our source Dingbat, who tells us that it was Umar who was running away from the car just before a bomb in this car exploded in a

---

Table 6.3 Questions Concerning the Observational Sensitivity of a Human Source

1. *Relevant Sensory/Physical Capacity*: What evidence exists concerning the source's physical and sensory capacities at the time this source made the observations forming the basis for this report?
2. *Allocation of Attention*: What do we know about the allocation of attention of this source on the reported event?
3. *Observational Conditions*: What do we know about the ambient conditions existing during the time this source made the observation forming the basis for this report? Did any conditions exist that could have influenced the accuracy of these observations?
4. *Past Accuracy Record*: What does the record show about this source's observational accuracy in past reports this source has provided?
5. *Any Existing Contradictory or Divergent Evidence*: It is entirely possible that any existing contradictory or divergent evidence may bear on this source's observational accuracy rather than on this source's veracity or objectivity.
6. *Inaccuracy Concerning Collateral Details*: Are there any less important details in this source's report that we suspect are inaccurate?

---

crowded market in Baghdad on May 14, 2013. We ask Dingbat how sure he is that it was Umar who was running away from the car. Dingbat says, "I am pretty sure it was Umar, but I can't be sure since it was a foggy day and I was about half a block away from the car."

6.9 ADVANCED OPERATIONS WITH DISCIPLE-CD

6.9.1 Hands On: Believability Analysis

6.9.1.1 Overview

This case study, which continues the cesium-137 analysis with the analysis of the hypothesis "the cesium-137 canister is used in a project without being checked out from the XYZ warehouse," has two main objectives:

- Learning how to more completely represent an item of evidence
- Learning to perform a deeper believability analysis

In Section 4.4.1, we have presented how we can define an item of evidence, and Figure 4.8 (p. 74) shows the definition of E001-Willard having the type evidence.

You can provide a more specific type by clicking on the [CHANGE] button. Figure 6.5, for instance, shows the definition of E014-Grace. After you click on the [CHANGE] button, the agent displays the evidence types from the right panel. You just need to click on the [SELECT] button following the correct type, which in this case is unequivocal testimonial evidence based upon direct observation.

Once you have selected the type of E014-Grace, the agent displays it after the label **Type** and asks for its source, which is Grace (see Figure 6.6).

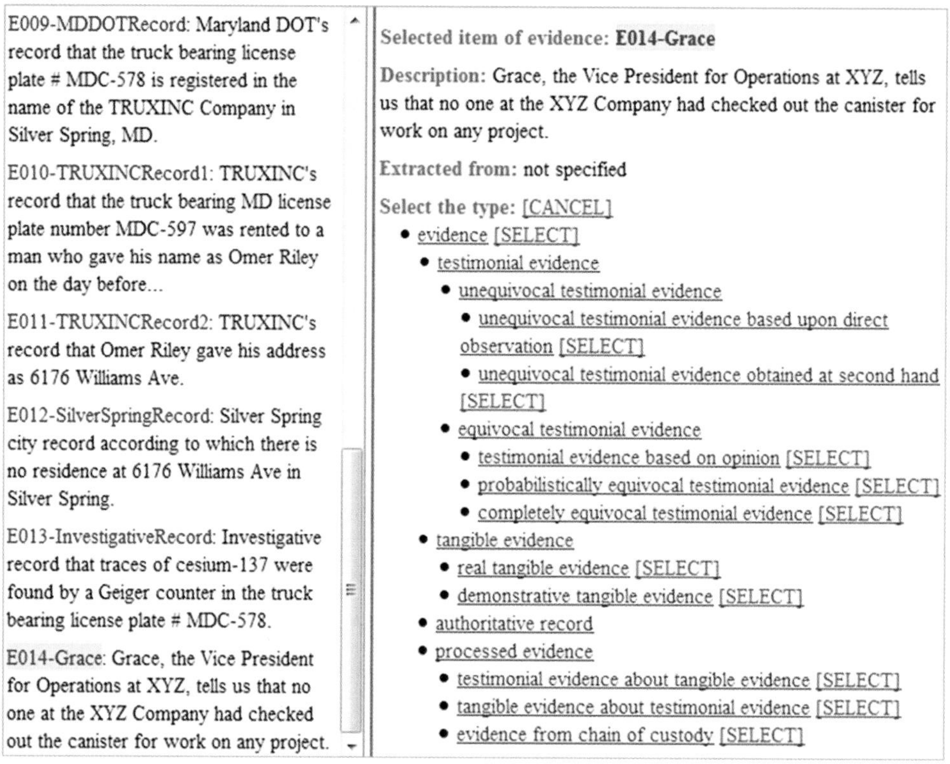

E009-MDDOTRecord: Maryland DOT's record that the truck bearing license plate # MDC-578 is registered in the name of the TRUXINC Company in Silver Spring, MD.

E010-TRUXINCRecord1: TRUXINC's record that the truck bearing MD license plate number MDC-597 was rented to a man who gave his name as Omer Riley on the day before...

E011-TRUXINCRecord2: TRUXINC's record that Omer Riley gave his address as 6176 Williams Ave.

E012-SilverSpringRecord: Silver Spring city record according to which there is no residence at 6176 Williams Ave in Silver Spring.

E013-InvestigativeRecord: Investigative record that traces of cesium-137 were found by a Geiger counter in the truck bearing license plate # MDC-578.

E014-Grace: Grace, the Vice President for Operations at XYZ, tells us that no one at the XYZ Company had checked out the canister for work on any project.

Selected item of evidence: **E014-Grace**

Description: Grace, the Vice President for Operations at XYZ, tells us that no one at the XYZ Company had checked out the canister for work on any project.

Extracted from: not specified

Select the type: [CANCEL]
- evidence [SELECT]
  - testimonial evidence
    - unequivocal testimonial evidence
      - unequivocal testimonial evidence based upon direct observation [SELECT]
      - unequivocal testimonial evidence obtained at second hand [SELECT]
    - equivocal testimonial evidence
      - testimonial evidence based on opinion [SELECT]
      - probabilistically equivocal testimonial evidence [SELECT]
      - completely equivocal testimonial evidence [SELECT]
  - tangible evidence
    - real tangible evidence [SELECT]
    - demonstrative tangible evidence [SELECT]
  - authoritative record
  - processed evidence
    - testimonial evidence about tangible evidence [SELECT]
    - tangible evidence about testimonial evidence [SELECT]
    - evidence from chain of custody [SELECT]

Figure 6.5. Selecting the type of evidence.

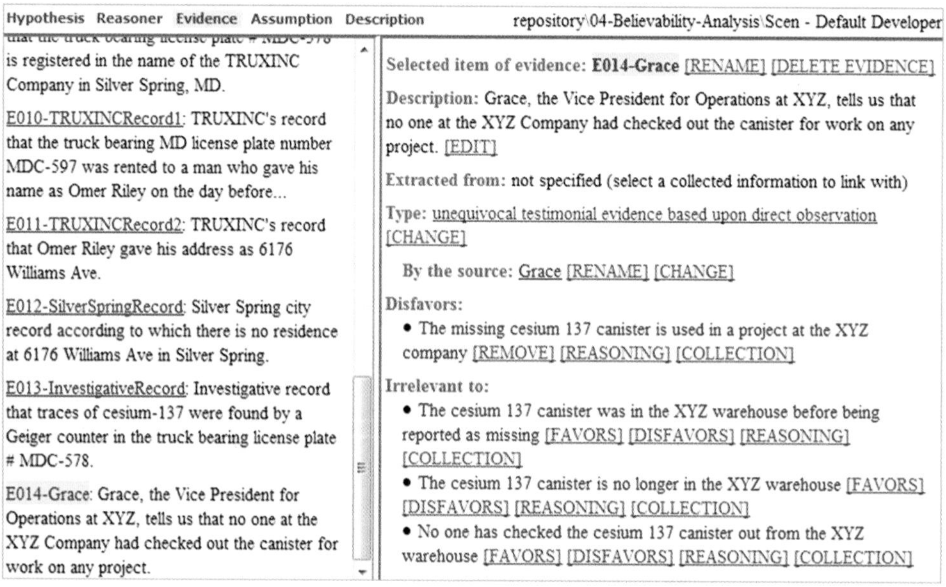

Hypothesis Reasoner **Evidence** Assumption Description   repository\04-Believability-Analysis\Scen - Default Developer

that the truck bearing license plate # MDC-578 is registered in the name of the TRUXINC Company in Silver Spring, MD.

E010-TRUXINCRecord1: TRUXINC's record that the truck bearing MD license plate number MDC-597 was rented to a man who gave his name as Omer Riley on the day before...

E011-TRUXINCRecord2: TRUXINC's record that Omer Riley gave his address as 6176 Williams Ave.

E012-SilverSpringRecord: Silver Spring city record according to which there is no residence at 6176 Williams Ave in Silver Spring.

E013-InvestigativeRecord: Investigative record that traces of cesium-137 were found by a Geiger counter in the truck bearing license plate # MDC-578.

E014-Grace: Grace, the Vice President for Operations at XYZ, tells us that no one at the XYZ Company had checked out the canister for work on any project.

Selected item of evidence: **E014-Grace** [RENAME] [DELETE EVIDENCE]

Description: Grace, the Vice President for Operations at XYZ, tells us that no one at the XYZ Company had checked out the canister for work on any project. [EDIT]

Extracted from: not specified (select a collected information to link with)

Type: unequivocal testimonial evidence based upon direct observation [CHANGE]

   By the source: Grace [RENAME] [CHANGE]

Disfavors:
- The missing cesium 137 canister is used in a project at the XYZ company [REMOVE] [REASONING] [COLLECTION]

Irrelevant to:
- The cesium 137 canister was in the XYZ warehouse before being reported as missing [FAVORS] [DISFAVORS] [REASONING] [COLLECTION]
- The cesium 137 canister is no longer in the XYZ warehouse [FAVORS] [DISFAVORS] [REASONING] [COLLECTION]
- No one has checked the cesium 137 canister out from the XYZ warehouse [FAVORS] [DISFAVORS] [REASONING] [COLLECTION]

Figure 6.6. Definition of an item of evidence.

As shown in Figure 6.6, we have also indicated that this item of evidence disfavors the hypothesis "The cesium-137 canister is used in a project at the XYZ company." As a result, the agent introduced it into the analysis tree and generated a more detailed analysis of its believability, which is shown in Figure 6.7. Notice that the believability of E014-Grace is reduced to Grace's believability, which is further reduced to her competence and credibility, and each of these credentials is further reduced to lower-level ones (access and understandability for competence, and veracity, objectivity, and observational sensitivity for credibility).

You can now perform a more detailed believability analysis, as illustrated in Figure 6.8, where you have assessed the competence, the veracity, the objectivity, and the observational sensitivity of Grace, and Disciple-CD has automatically determined her believability, and the believability of E014-Grace.

It is important to notice that, although Disciple-CD performs such a fine-grained analysis of the believability of E014-Grace, you are not required to assess the lowest-level credentials. You may assess any of the upper-level ones, and even directly the believability of E014-Grace. For example, Figure 6.8 shows that the competence of Grace was directly evaluated as being "certain" without assessing Grace's access and understandability. We can tell this because of the yellow background of "certain."

6.9.1.2 Practice

In this case study, you will practice the previous operations. You will first select the hypothesis "The cesium-137 canister is used in a project without being checked-out from the XYZ warehouse." Then you will browse its analysis to see how it is reduced to simpler hypotheses that need to be assessed based on the evidence. After that, you will represent a new item of evidence, associate it with the hypothesis to which it is relevant, assess its

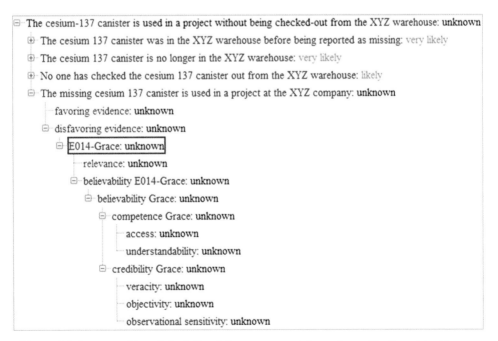

Figure 6.7. Decomposition of the believability assessment for an item of testimonial evidence.

Figure 6.8. A more detailed believability analysis.

relevance, evaluate its believability by assessing its credentials, and browse the resulting analysis tree.

Start Disciple-CD, select the case study knowledge base "11-Believability-Analysis/ Scen," and proceed as indicated in the instructions from the bottom of the opened window.

6.9.1.3 Advanced Operation

This case study has illustrated the more detailed version of the operation of defining an item of evidence, summarized as follows.

Operation 6.1. Define an item of evidence and its type

- Click on the Evidence menu at the top of the window.
- Notice the four modes of operations from the top part of the left panel. Because the selected one is [AVAILABLE EVIDENCE], the left panel shows the current evidence (if any) from the knowledge base.
- In the left panel, click on [NEW]. As a result, the right panel shows a partially defined item of evidence, such as E002-. You will complete the definition of this item of evidence.
- Complete the name E. . .- at the top of the right panel and click on [SAVE].
- Click on [EDIT] for **Description**, click inside the pane, and type the description of the item of evidence.
- Click on [SAVE].
- You may now provide additional information about the item of evidence (as indicated in the following steps) or define additional items of evidence (by repeating the preceding steps).
- After **Type:** evidence, click on [CHANGE] to specify the type of this item of evidence.
- Inspect the different evidence types and click on [SELECT] following the type corresponding to the current item of evidence.
- Provide the additional type-related information requested by the system (for example, the source in the case of a testimonial item of evidence).

6.10   REVIEW QUESTIONS

6.1.   What items of tangible evidence do you see in Table 5.2?

6.2.   The leadership in Country T has embarked upon an aggressive track regarding its relationship with neighboring countries. We are presently assessing the capability of Country T to wage war on a country with whom we have very friendly relations. We suspect that policy makers in T are considering the development of a certain tactical weapon system we will call W. If they are successful in developing system W, this would give T a decided advantage in any armed conflict they might have with this friendly country. We presently have a source S, a national of Country T, who is an engineer and an expert on the design of weapon systems such as W. Further, she meets regularly with policy makers in Country T regarding the development of tactical weapon systems. Source S has agreed to inform us about deliberations made by policy makers in T regarding the development of system W.

(a)   Does what we know so far about S bear on her *competence* or *credibility*?

Source T now reports to us the following information. She says she was just told by a ranking policy maker in Country T that all plans to develop system W have been suspended because it was thought that such development would be far too expensive.

(b)   What S has told us seems to be good news, but can we believe what she says? What general kinds of evidence should we consider about the credibility of what she has just told us?

6.3.   Indicate and justify what type of evidence is each of the following items:

(a)   A spent shell casing.
(b)   Human source X reports to us that a military coup is to be expected in Country A within the next two weeks.
(c)   A captured document.
(d)   You take your car for an oil change expecting the bill to be about $25. Instead, the bill is $350. You ask the mechanic why an oil change costs so much. The mechanic tells you that you needed a new fuel pump and a new water pump, which he changed in the interests of your safety. You ask the mechanic to let you see your two pumps, which you believed were working perfectly. The mechanic tells you how sorry he is that these two items have gone missing.
(e)   Human source Y reports to us that the morale among combat troops in Country B is at an all-time low.
(f)   A sensor image (radar, IR, photo) of some ground installations in a certain territory.
(g)   A table showing the reliability of a certain system after various numbers of hours of operation.

6.4.   Table 8.2 (p. 156) presents additional items of evidence related to the missing cesium-137 scenario. What examples of unequivocal testimonial evidence do you see in this table?

6.5.   The most important attribute of the believability of tangible evidence is its *authenticity*, "Is this evidence what it is claimed to be?" Provide some examples of real and demonstrative tangible evidence items that are not authentic.

6.6.   Why is the competence of sources of testimonial evidence so important and why is competence not the same as credibility?

6.7.   The credibility attribute, veracity or truthfulness, is widely discussed and often widely misunderstood or mistakenly attributed. It seems obvious that the veracity attribute is a property of human sources of evidence. It is very hard to imagine a mechanical or electronic sensor attempting to mislead us, willfully or not, in providing a report. Such reports can, of course, be incorrect, but for reasons not involving truthfulness. Provide some examples of the uses and misuses of the attribute veracity.

6.8.   The objectivity attribute of the credibility of a human source is widely overlooked in spite of its importance. What is odd is that lack of objectivity is much discussed in common discourse. We so often hear that we all from time to time believe things because we want to believe them in spite of having little or no evidence for them. One matter of interest concerns the possibility that objectivity is not only a property exclusive to human sensors but also relevant to sensing devices. Provide some examples of the objectivity attribute in various situations.

6.9.   It is no mystery that the sensory sensitivity of human observers is an important credibility attribute. But this sensitivity analysis must always be accompanied by evidence concerning other elements of the physical condition of the observer as well as the particular environmental situation in which a sensory observation was made. Provide some examples of the importance of these situations.

6.10.   Give some examples from your own experience when you have heard people providing information about which they hedge or equivocate.

6.11.   What inferences might we draw from Omar al-Massari's refusal to provide us with his laptop computer?

6.12.   What other items of evidence are missing so far in our discussion of the cesium-137 case?

6.13.   Do you see any example of mixtures of evidence in Table 5.2?

6.14.   Can you provide other examples of mixtures of evidence from your own experience?

6.15.   Read each of the questions from Table 6.1 and indicate why it is relevant to assessing the veracity of the source. Can you think of an example that illustrates it?

6.16.   Read each of the questions from Table 6.2 and indicate why it is relevant to assessing the objectivity of a human source. Can you think of an example that illustrates it?

6.17.   Read each of the questions from Table 6.3 and indicate why it is relevant to assessing the observational sensitivity of a source. Can you think of an example that illustrates it?

7 Chains of Custody

7.1 WHAT IS A CHAIN OF CUSTODY?

In the previous chapters, we have discussed the different types of evidence (such as testimonial or tangible) and the ingredients of their believability assessment. However, very rarely if ever does the analyst have access to the original evidence. Most often, what is being analyzed is an item of evidence that has undergone a series of transformations through a *chain of custody*. Here we have borrowed an important concept from the field of law, where a chain of custody refers to the persons or devices having access to the original source evidence, the time at which they had such access, and what they did to the original evidence when they had access to it. The original evidence may be altered in various ways at various links in chains of custody. The important point here is to consider the extent to which what the analyst finally receives is an authentic and complete account of what an original source provided. Uncertainties arising in chains of custody of intelligence evidence are not always taken into account. One result is that analysts are often misled about what the evidence is telling them.

Basically, establishing a chain of custody involves identifying the persons and devices involved in the acquisition, processing, examination, interpretation, and transfer of evidence between the time the evidence is acquired and the time it is provided to intelligence analysts. Lots of things may have been done to evidence in a chain of custody that may have altered the original item of evidence or have provided an inaccurate or incomplete account of it. In some cases, original evidence may have been tampered with in various ways. Unless these difficulties are recognized and possibly overcome, intelligence analysts are at risk of drawing quite erroneous conclusions from the evidence they receive. They are being misled, not by our original sources of evidence, but by the activities of our own persons or devices who do various things to incoming intelligence evidence.

In civilian and military courts, proponents of evidence, for either side of the matter in dispute, are required to verify the chain of custody of tangible evidence before it is admitted to trial. In many cases, evidence gathered is passed from one person to another, each of whom may examine and process the evidence in various ways. In many situations, proponents are required to select experienced and credible persons who serve as *evidence custodians*. The major task for these persons is to establish the chain of custody of evidence, keeping records of who gathered the evidence, the persons who had access to the evidence, the times at which they had access, and what these persons did with the evidence while they had access to it. A very good account of questions regarding the chains of custody of evidence in our courts is to be found in Lempert et al., 2000 (pp. 1167–1172).

Now, we are of course not privy to the actual chains of custody of various forms of intelligence evidence in any of our intelligence organizations. And we do not know whether there are any appointed evidence custodians in these organizations, as there are in our legal system. However, we can offer accounts of chains of custody of evidence that seem reasonable and necessary for different forms of evidence. In our examples of how Disciple-CD can assist analysts to establish the believability of evidence, we have established conjectural accounts of chains of custody for an item of testimonial evidence and an item of tangible evidence in order to illustrate the virtues of Disciple-CD and how it can assist the intelligence analyst to make these very difficult believability assessments.

First, suppose we have an analyst who is provided with an item of testimonial evidence by an informant who speaks only in a foreign language. We assume that this informant's original testimony is first *recorded* by one of our intelligence professionals, then *translated* into English by a paid translator. This translation is then *edited* by another intelligence professional, and then the edited version of this translation is *transmitted* to an intelligence analyst. So, there are four links in this conjectural chain of custody of this original testimonial item: recording, translation, editing, and transmission. Various things can happen at each one of these links that can prevent the analyst from having an authentic account of what our source originally provided.

Then suppose that an analyst is provided with an account of a tangible item in the form of a digital photo. This photo has been taken by one of our foreign assets. We note that the analyst may see a copy of the photo itself or just a written account of the events recorded in this photo. Suppose in this case the analyst receives only a written account of what this original photo revealed. We have supposed that this digital photo is first *transferred* to the computer of one of our intelligence professionals; it is then *transmitted* to a photo interpreter; this person *interprets* the image; and then the *written interpretation* of this photo is *transmitted* to the analyst. So, in this conjectural chain of custody, there is a transference link, an interpretation link, and two transmission links. At any of these links there are possible reasons why what the analyst receives is not an authentic account of what the asset's original photo depicted.

There are many possible chains of custody, for different types of evidence, as illustrated in Figure 7.1. However, they can all be characterized by a chain of basic evidence transformation processes (such as translation, editing, or transmission). Moreover, for each such process, one can identify the ingredients and the arguments of its believability assessment, just as for the different types of the evidence. An earlier system, Disciple-LTA (Tecuci et al., 2005a; 2007b; 2008a), employs a systematic approach to the assessment of the believability of items of evidence obtained through a chain of custody (Schum et al., 2009). The same approach may be used with Disciple-CD.

With these evidential and chain of custody ideas in mind, we can now show how Disciple-CD can assist intelligence analysts to assess the many sources of uncertainty associated with the authenticity of evidence they receive.

7.2   A CASE INVOLVING CHAINS OF CUSTODY

The cover story for this hypothetical case involves an experienced analyst named Clyde who is involved with intelligence analyses concerning matters in Iraq. Clyde's present inferential problem involves an Iraqi named Emir, a respected official of the government

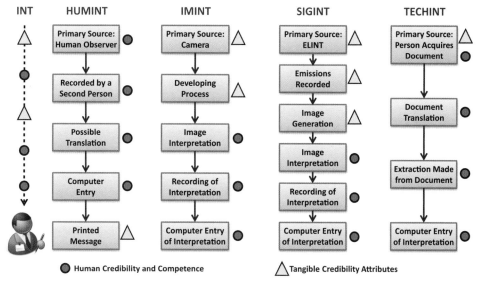

Figure 7.1. Sample chains of custody for different INTs.

in Iraq. Emir has publicly argued on many occasions about the necessity of stopping the sectarian violence that has plagued Iraq and coalition efforts to achieve stability in this country since the United States and coalition intervention in 2003. Clyde's present problem is that he wonders how respectable Emir really is. Clyde has evidence that Emir has been in contact in Iran with representatives of the Iranian Islamic Revolutionary Guard Corps (IRGC). We already have a variety of strong evidence that the IRGC has been involved in supplying weapons, training, and intelligence to various Shiite militia groups in Iraq. This has certainly not contributed to stability in Iraq. So, Clyde entertains the hypothesis H_1: "Emir is collaborating with the IRGC" (i.e., he is not the respected official we have believed him to be).

So far, Clyde has two items of evidence bearing on H_1. He first has an item of *testimonial evidence* from a source code-named "Wallflower," who reports that five days ago he saw Emir leaving a building in Ahwaz, Iran, in which the IRGC has offices. Wallflower, an Iranian national, issued his report in the Farsi language that was recorded and then translated into English by a paid interpreter. Then an edited version of this translation was recorded and transmitted to Clyde. Then Clyde received an item of *tangible evidence* in the form of a photograph taken of Emir eight days ago at an IRGC Qods Force base outside Dezful in Iran. This photo was taken by another source, code-named "Stovepipe." The identification of Emir in this photo was verified by one of the U.S. intelligence professionals who has had contact with Emir. We will assume that Clyde received this photo together with a written account of what this photo revealed. But we also allow for the possibility that Clyde received only a written account of the contents of this photo.

The following sections present the inferential problems Clyde faces as he attempts to assess how believable he imagines these two items of evidence to be.

7.3   A CHAIN OF CUSTODY FOR TESTIMONIAL EVIDENCE

We begin by examining the believability of the information Clyde has received from Wallflower. This information has passed through a chain of custody that is illustrated in Figure 7.2. The top part of Figure 7.2 shows the successive transformations suffered by

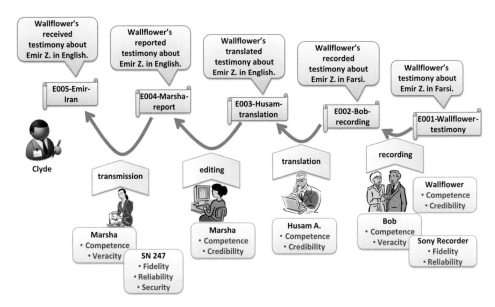

Figure 7.2. The chain of custody of Wallflower's testimony and the processes involved in this chain.

Wallflower's original testimony (E001-Wallflower-testimony) until it reaches Clyde, who actually receives the item of evidence E005-Emir-Iran. Wallflower provides testimonial evidence in the form of an assertion he made concerning Emir leaving the IRGC building in Ahwaz, Iran. Wallflower says he based this assertion on his direct observation of these events five days ago. First, Clyde has not heard Wallflower's original testimony and could not possibly have understood it unless Clyde speaks Farsi. We have identified a case officer named Bob, who may only speak limited Farsi. Bob records what Wallflower has testified on a Sony XYZ recording device. This recording is transmitted to a paid foreign national named Husam A., who speaks fluent Farsi. Husam's written translation of Wallflower's testimony about Emir is then transmitted to a reports officer named Marsha. Marsha edits Husam's translated version of Wallflower's testimony and prepares her written edited version for transmission over a (fictitious) system we will call SN 247. What Clyde receives is Marsha's edited version of Husam's translation of Bob's recording of Wallflower's original testimony. This is a tangible item that is only an account of what Wallflower originally said.

In this example, we have three identified persons involved in the chain of custody of Wallflower's report: case officer Bob, translator Husam, and reports officer Marsha. Now one thing about this fictitious example is that the analyst, Clyde, may or may not know the identities of these three persons. Obviously, in an actual situation, there may be more or different persons involved in a chain of custody.

The reader may quickly note other links in this chain of custody that we have over-looked or have different labels for the ones we have included. Not being privy to any actual chains of custody of intelligence evidence, our conjectural chains of custody may lack realism. But our claim is that they are plausible enough to illustrate the kinds of uncertainties encountered in chains of custody of intelligence evidence and also to illustrate how Disciple-CD can assist analysts in making these kinds of assessments.

The major issue here is the extent to which Clyde can believe what he is told Wallflower said. This *belief* rests not only on evidence regarding Wallflower's competence and credibility, but also on the competence and credibility issues raised by what was done to

Wallflower's original report about Emir before Clyde received a report of what Wallflower testified. The bottom part of Figure 7.2 shows the competence and credibility issues that can arise regarding the persons and the devices involved in this example.

Let's start with the original source, Wallflower, who provides *testimonial evidence* in the form of an assertion he made concerning Emir leaving the IRGC building in Ahwaz, Iran. Wallflower says he based this assertion on his direct observation of these events five days ago. In deciding whether to believe Wallflower, Clyde must first consider both Wallflower's competence and his credibility, as discussed in Section 6.4. Wallflower's competence involves his *access* and his *understanding*. The basic access question involves asking whether Wallflower was actually in a position to observe what he tells Clyde. The understanding question asks whether Wallflower knew enough about what he was observing to give Clyde an intelligible account of what he observed. His credibility involves the *veracity*, *objectivity*, and *observational sensitivity* attributes.

Then Wallflower's testimony (E001-Wallflower-testimony) was tape-recorded by the case officer, Bob, who interacts with Wallflower. So, we have natural concerns about the fidelity and reliability of this tape recording, as well as about Bob's competence and veracity. Among other things, is the recording understandable and complete? Was all of Wallflower's testimony on the recording and did no gaps appear in it? Clyde would also be interested to know whether Wallflower provided his report voluntarily or whether Bob asked him to report on Emir. This is quite important since if Wallflower gave this report voluntarily and we believe he is being untruthful, Clyde has to ask why Wallflower told Bob this particular lie in preference to any of the others he might have told. The same question will arise for Stovepipe's evidence.

As we have specified, Wallflower speaks only Farsi and not English, and Husam has translated his recorded testimony (i.e., E002-Bob-recording) into English. We have concerns here about the competence and credibility of Husam. Competence involves not only knowledge of Farsi and English, but also knowledge of the subject matter being translated. The translated account of Wallflower's original testimony (i.e., E003-Husam-translation) is then edited by Marsha. We may also have concerns about Marsha's competence and credibility.

Finally, this recorded, translated, and edited account of Wallflower's testimony (i.e., E004-Marsha-report) is transmitted through a computer network to Clyde and possibly many other interested persons. What we have here are concerns both about the competence and the veracity of the person who performed the transmission and also about the fidelity, reliability, and security of the transmission.

7.4   A CHAIN OF CUSTODY FOR DEMONSTRATIVE TANGIBLE EVIDENCE

Let us now consider the *tangible evidence* supplied by Stovepipe: a photo he says he took eight days ago of Emir at an IRGC base outside Dezful, Iran. Clyde must first consider Stovepipe's competence. What evidence does Clyde have that Stovepipe was actually in Dezful at the time he says he took the photo? In addition, what evidence does Clyde have that Stovepipe knew the person he was photographing? Clyde also has one credibility attribute for Stovepipe to consider, namely his *veracity*. Was Stovepipe truthful in telling us when, where, how, and why he took this photo? We will assume that we are treating the photo provided by Stovepipe as being *demonstrative tangible evidence*. There are several reasons why this makes sense: First, we have the believability of the photo itself to consider. Is this photo *authentic* (is it what it is represented as being, namely Emir at the IRGC base outside Dezful, Iran)? Second, has this evidence come from a *reliable* sensing device that would supply us with repeatable information? Third, is the evidence *accurate* in allowing Clyde or anyone else to tell whether it was really Emir in the photo? These three matters all concern the credibility of the photo itself.

Unfortunately, regarding the photo of Emir, allegedly taken outside of Dezful, Iran, eight days ago, we have two possibilities to consider. We have to consider whether Clyde was given a copy of this photo to examine himself or whether he was just given a written account of what this photo depicted. The major trouble, of course, is that the chains of custody will be different in these two cases. So, we will make some conjectures about what the chains of custody might look like in both of these cases. The first is where Clyde is given the photo to examine; the second is where he is just given a written account of what is in Stovepipe's photo.

7.4.1   Chain of Custody for a Photo Given Directly to the Analyst

We will begin with the case in which Clyde sees Stovepipe's photo itself or, more than likely, a copy of Stovepipe's original photo. The corresponding chain of custody involves the persons and processes shown in Figure 7.3. The top part of Figure 7.3 shows the successive transformations suffered by Stovepipe's original photo of Emir (called E006-Emir-photo-in-camera) until it reaches Clyde (as E010-Emir-Iran). First, suppose Stovepipe used an Olympus #AB1 digital camera to take the photo of Emir. We suppose that Stovepipe had some means for transferring this digital photo to case officer Bob's laptop computer. Bob then transmits this stored digital photo over a (fictitious) SN 247 system to a photo interpreter we shall name Mike. Mike examines the photo to assess its authenticity, and he also verifies that the person depicted in the photo is Emir. Mike

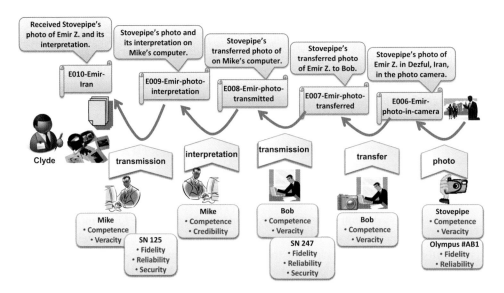

Figure 7.3. The chain of custody of the demonstrative tangible evidence sent to Clyde.

prepares a written account of his analysis of this photo. Mike then transmits his written account of this photo, and possibly a copy of the photo itself, over a (fictitious) SN 125 system. This written account of the photo, and possibly a copy of the photo, is eventually routed to Clyde for his analysis. The bottom part of Figure 7.3 shows the competence and credibility issues that can arise regarding the persons and the devices involved in this example.

In this example, we have chosen to have Stovepipe use a digital camera to eliminate the necessity of considering by whom and where the photo was developed. We will also assume that Stovepipe, who knows Emir, was instructed to follow Emir eight days ago in Dezful, to see where he went that day. Additionally, we also will assume that Stovepipe was able to visit Bob, bringing his digital camera with him. There are, of course, other means by which Stovepipe might have communicated with Bob. If Stovepipe had a laptop computer, he could have e-mailed the message to Bob, who could have been anywhere. But this would add additional risks involving the e-mail being intercepted by the Iranian IRGC. Surely, there are risks associated with Stovepipe's meeting personally with Bob. It took Stovepipe eight days between the time he took the photo and the time he delivered it to Bob. How Stovepipe actually got the photo to Bob is interesting and will eventually bear on Stovepipe's competence and the authenticity of the photo. Maybe the procedures necessary for Stovepipe to communicate directly with Bob are very complex and have been designed to reduce the risks associated with this direct communication. For example, suppose Bob is in Baghdad, Iraq, but meets with Stovepipe in Al Amara, Iraq. Both cities are near the Iraq–Iran border, about eighty miles from each other. Perhaps it takes several days for Stovepipe to communicate with Bob and then arrange the cover necessary to go into Iraq. These are all matters that bear upon Stovepipe's competence and may also concern the authenticity of the photo.

But the major assumption underlying this scenario concerns whether or not we can say that Clyde was provided with the original photo that Stovepipe allegedly took. This involves the assumption that the image Bob uploaded on his computer and then transmitted to Mike was not altered in any way, nor was the image that Mike transmitted to Clyde altered. If the image that Clyde received had exactly the same pixels as the one on Bob's computer, we could probably say that Clyde received the same original photo that Bob received from Stovepipe.

7.4.2 Chain of Custody for a Written Description of a Photo Given to the Analyst

This second case is interesting for the following reason: We are treating the photo as being demonstrative tangible evidence since it is just a possible representation of Emir being outside of Dezful eight days ago. Then, if Clyde is only given a written account of this photo, this is only demonstrative evidence of Stovepipe's original demonstrative evidence. So, in cases such as this, we have a chain of demonstrative evidence involving two or more sources.

The preceding discussion shows how complex the processes of analyzing the probability of the hypothesis "H_1: Emir is collaborating with the IRGC" are, even when we have just a small amount of evidence. However, for a good analysis, one would have to consider many more items of evidence, and to consider both favoring and disfavoring evidence. Unfortunately, the complexity of the analytic process grows so much with the addition of new items of evidence that all the involved probabilities cannot be assessed. There is simply not enough time for the analyst to assess them, or evidence necessary to support these assessments is not available.

7.5   ANALYZING A CHAIN OF CUSTODY

We now describe how our cognitive assistant, Disciple-CD, allows the analyst Clyde to perform the complex analysis involved in chains of custody of evidence. Clyde will be allowed to drill down as much as he wishes; he can make assumptions concerning various verbal assessments of uncertainty and revise these assumptions in light of new evidence.

Let us consider again the chain of custody illustrated in Figure 7.2. One may use Disciple-CD to assess the believability of the evidence received by Clyde about Emir, that is, E005-Emir-Iran, as shown in Figure 7.4. The believability of E005-Emir-Iran is the minimum between the believability of E004-Marsha-report and the believability of the transmission process; the believability of E004-Marsha-report is the minimum between the believability of E003-Husam-translation and the believability of the editing process; the believability of E003-Husam-translation is the minimum between the believability of E002-Bob-recording and the believability of the translation process; and, finally, the believability of E002-Bob-recording is the minimum between the believability of E001-Wallflower-testimony (the original testimony) and the believability of the recording process. Thus, the believability of the evidence received by Clyde is a function of the believability of Wallflower's original testimony and the believability of the recording, translation, editing, and transmission processes.

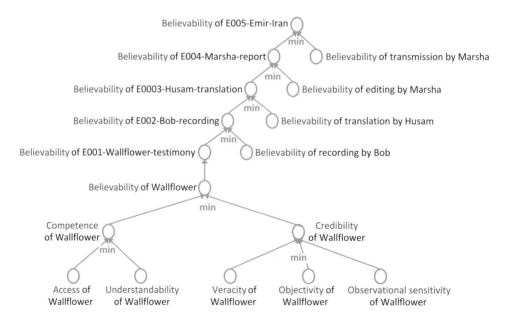

Figure 7.4. Assessing the believability of E005-Emir-Iran.

7.6   DRILL-DOWN ANALYSIS OF CHAINS OF CUSTODY

As indicated previously, the analyst may not have the time or the evidence to assess all the factors involved. In such a case, Disciple-CD allows him or her to make assumptions with respect to the solutions of the unsolved problems. For example, the analyst may assume that the believability of most of the processes involved in the chain of custody is almost certain and concentrate his or her analysis on assessing the believability of Wallflower. The analyst may further make some assumptions about Wallflower's competence, veracity, objectivity, and observational sensitivity, and then Disciple-CD will automatically estimate the overall believability of E005-Emir-Iran.

But the analyst can also drill down to analyze each of the processes from the chain of custody. For example, based on the general fidelity and reliability of a Sony XYZ recorder, the recording made by Bob may be assessed as "certain." Disciple-CD also allows the analyst to investigate all sorts of "what-if" scenarios. For example, Clyde may consider alternative values for the veracity of Husam A., the translator of Wallflower's testimony.

7.7   REVIEW QUESTIONS

7.1.   Figure 7.4 shows how to assess the believability of the evidence received by Clyde from Wallflower through the chain of custody shown in Figure 7.2. Draw a similar figure showing how to assess the believability of evidence received by Clyde from Stovepipe through the chain of custody shown in Figure 7.3.

7.2.   Human source Y reports to us that the morale among combat troops in Country B is at an all-time low. We ask Y to give us some specifics. He then reports seeing a classified document at a military installation in B that describes the increasing rate of defections and soldiers being absent without official leave (AWOL) over the past year. What kind of evidence is this and how should it be analyzed?

7.3.   It has been noted for years, and by many persons, that intelligence analysts are hampered by not being the persons who assess the believability or credibility of much of their evidence; this is particularly true of HUMINT evidence. In many cases, sources of HUMINT are under deep cover and their identities are not revealed to analysts. In addition, evidence bearing on the competence and credibility of these HUMINT sources is not always made available to intelligence analysts who will use this HUMINT evidence. Show how this competence and credibility burden on intelligence analysts is made so much heavier when we consider the chains of custody discussed in this chapter. You may refer to the examples from Figures 7.2 and 7.3.

7.4.   Intelligence analysts may choose to ignore the heavy burden mentioned in Question 7.3. Analysts might prefer to accept versions of HUMINT reports they receive without questioning anything about chains of custody of these reports. Show some of the consequences of failure to assess possible sources of doubt that may lurk in a chain of custody.

7.5.   One thing analysts are trained to do is to assess the consistency of one item of evidence with other items of evidence they may also have. Show how even this consistency assessment is affected by ignoring chains of custody.

8 Recurrent Substance-Blind Combinations of Evidence

We have considered a categorization of individual items of evidence but have also mentioned situations in which individual items can reveal various mixtures of the types of evidence shown in Figure 6.1 (p. 119). We now consider combinations of two or more individual items of evidence. These combinations are also recurrent and do not involve the substance or content of the evidence.

There are three main classes of evidence combinations – harmonious, dissonant, and redundant – all of which we may encounter in a mass of evidence being considered in an intelligence analysis or an analysis in any other context.

8.1 HARMONIOUS EVIDENCE

8.1.1 Basic Forms of Harmonious Evidence

Two or more items of evidence are harmonious if they are directionally consistent in the sense that they all point toward, or favor, the same hypothesis or possible conclusion.

There are two basic forms of harmonious evidence. The first is called *corroborative evidence*. In this combination of evidence, we first have two or more sources telling us that the same event has occurred. Suppose both of these sources report that event E has occurred. Directional consistency is apparent here since E is consistent with itself. The sources of corroborative evidence may be any combination of the "INTs" we have mentioned. For example, we may have both IMINT and HUMINT telling us that a certain event has occurred at a location at a certain time. Or, we may have IMINT and COMINT both saying that a certain event occurred. This form of corroboration often, but not always, allows us to have greater confidence that the event in question did occur. In such cases, we would say that one source has verified what the other source has told us. The exception involves instances in which we have other evidence suggesting that two or more HUMINT sources collaborated in deciding what to tell us, or that one source influenced or coerced another source to report the same event. As we know, HUMINT sources are frequently not independent; they can interact in ways designed to deceive us.

But there is another way evidence can be corroborative in nature involving items of directly relevant and ancillary evidence. Suppose HUMINT asset $\mathcal{A}$ reports an event we take to be directly relevant in an analysis. Suppose that in assessing $\mathcal{A}$'s believability, we have ancillary evidence that we believe supports an attribute of $\mathcal{A}$'s believability. Such evidence would be corroborative in the sense that we gain further confidence that the event $\mathcal{A}$ reports did in fact occur. An example would involve information about $\mathcal{A}$'s track record in his previous reports (if he made any). Such ancillary evidence would support $\mathcal{A}$'s veracity or observational sensitivity as far as his present report is concerned. But ancillary evidence can bear upon a human source's competence as well. In assessing asset $\mathcal{A}$'s competence, we may have evidence from another asset $\mathcal{B}$, who says that $\mathcal{A}$ could in fact have made the observation that $\mathcal{A}$ says he made. We could also verify $\mathcal{A}$'s competence by IMINT showing that $\mathcal{A}$ was at the place where he says he made his observation.

There is another combination of harmonious evidence that differs from corroborative evidence of the same event; it is called *convergent evidence*. This combination of evidence involves two or more evidence items that concern *different events that point toward or favor the same hypothesis*. Convergent evidence can involve any of the "INTs." Suppose we have the following situation. We have IMINT evidence that event E occurred, and we have MASINT evidence that event F occurred. But we believe that both of the events E and F would point to or favor the same hypothesis H. In other words, these two events are directionally consistent; they both point us in the same inferential direction.

But convergent evidence can have an additional and most important property that we will now explain. Convergent evidence can exhibit what is called *evidential synergism*. In many situations, *two or more evidence items, considered jointly, have greater inferential force or weight than they would have if considered separately or independently*. Another equivalent way to characterize evidential synergism is to say that one item of evidence can have greater force if we consider it in light of other evidence we have. Suppose again that we have evidence about events E and F that converge in favoring hypothesis H. But when taken together, or considered jointly, these two events have additional force favoring hypothesis H. Additionally, we might observe that evidence about event F seems to have more force or weight when we consider it in light of evidence about event E. As we have mentioned before, one tragic example of our failure to exploit evidential synergism involves events that occurred before September 11, 2001. The FBI had evidence of persons from the Middle East who arrived at flying schools here in the United States paying in cash for their flying lessons. But these students wished only to learn how to steer and navigate heavy aircraft, and not how to make takeoffs and landings in these aircraft. At the same time, our intelligence services had evidence that new attacks would be made on the World Trade Center in New York, this time using airliners. Unfortunately, for various reasons, these items were never considered jointly, and hypotheses suggested by these joint events were never considered.

What it comes to is that important evidential synergisms will never be recognized unless intelligence evidence is shared among all agencies involved in its collection and analysis. We have written more on the probabilistic underpinnings of evidential synergism (Schum, 1994 [2001a], pp. 401–409; Anderson et al., 2005, pp. 46–50).

8.1.2 Patterns of Evidential Harmony

Recall our saying the harmonious evidence is *directionally consistent* because all of it points to the same conclusion. Here are some examples.

Example 8.1.

In the cesium-137 scenario, we have examples of both forms of evidential harmony. The first involves what we called *corroborative evidence*, in which two or more sources report the same event. Have a look at evidence E001-Willard and E004-Ralph in Table 1.4. Here we have both Willard and Ralph telling us that the cesium-137 canister was missing from the XYZ Company warehouse. Ralph's report corroborates Willard's initial report.

Example 8.2

Convergent evidence involves evidence about different events, all of which point to the same conclusion. Look at evidence items E009-MDDOTRecord, E010-TRUXINCRecord1, TRUXINCRecord2, and E012-SilverSpringRecord from Table 5.2, all of which point toward the conclusion that Omar al-Massari was the person who rented the truck from the TRUXINC Company in Silver Spring, Maryland.

Evidential synergism was illustrated in Example 5.2. Person Y has been under surveillance in connection with terrorist activities. We suspect that Y will attempt to leave the country in a short while. Three days ago, we received information that Y sold his car. Today, we received information that he closed his account at his bank. Either item of evidence does not tell us much. He could be planning to buy a new car. He could also be dissatisfied with his bank. But, taken together, these two items of evidence are suggestive that Y is planning to leave the country.

8.2 DISSONANT EVIDENCE

8.2.1 Basic Forms of Dissonant Evidence

Dissonant evidence involves combinations of two or more items that are directionally inconsistent; they can point us in different inferential directions or toward different hypotheses.

There are two basic forms of evidential dissonance. The first involves *contradictory evidence.* Contradictory evidence always involves events that are mutually *exclusive* (they cannot have occurred jointly). From one source, we learn that event E occurred; but from another source we learn that this same event did not occur. The dissonance seems obvious in this case since event E cannot have both occurred and not have occurred. Contradictory evidence can involve any sources of intelligence evidence and any number of sources. For example, we may have some five sources, three telling us that event E occurred and two telling us that event E did not occur. We must first be a bit careful in discussing the directional inconsistency of contradictory evidence. Suppose we are considering whether hypothesis H is true; an obvious alternative is the hypothesis not-H (H is not true). We further believe that event E, if it occurred, would favor hypothesis H. With some views of probability, which we discuss in Chapter 10, this means that hypothesis not-H would be favored by event E not occurring. However, with another view of probability we will consider, we may not always believe it necessary to say that the nonoccurrence of E favors the nonoccurrence of H. On other occasions, we may not even be sure what the nonoccurrence of E is telling us.

In any case, evidential contradictions are always resolved on believability grounds. There is quite an interesting history concerning how we have come to rely on this form of resolution. As an example, suppose we have three HUMINT sources who tell us that event

E occurred, and one HUMINT source who tells us that event E did not occur. In the not-so-distant past, it was believed that we should always resolve the contradiction by counting heads – that is, majority rules. So, on this basis we would side with the three sources who tell us that event E did occur. This reliance on the number of witnesses on either side of a contradiction has a biblical origin. As the Bible records (Deuteronomy, 19:15): "... for any iniquity, at the mouth of two witnesses, or at the mouth of three witnesses shall the matter be decided." This numerical strategy lasted at least till the time of Napoleon. As Wigmore records (Wigmore, 1940, p. 256), Napoleon was disturbed by the strategy, saying, "Thus one honorable man by his testimony could not prove a single rascal guilty, though two rascals by their testimony could always prove an honorable man guilty." The trouble here is that counting heads assumes that all of the four sources involved in this episode of contradictory evidence have equal believability. This may be a very bad assumption since, on ancillary evidence about these four sources, we may well believe that the one source telling us that E did not occur has greater believability than does the aggregate believability of the three sources who tell us that event E did occur. As Wigmore also observed, our courts do not accept a majority rule interpretation. What matters is the aggregate believability of the witnesses on either side. This happens to be entirely consistent with what a Bayesian analysis tells us (Schum, 1994 [2001a], pp. 409–412). *So, what matters in resolving evidential contradictions is the aggregate believability of the sources on either side of this contradiction.*

In some accounts we have read, dissonant evidence is described as being necessarily contradictory in nature; but this is quite erroneous. There is another quite different form of dissonant evidence called *divergent evidence.* Contradictory evidence involves whether one event occurred or did not occur. But divergent evidence involves entirely different events. The directional inconsistency here means that these events point us toward different hypotheses. In one case, suppose believable evidence about event E would favor hypothesis H, but believable evidence about event F would favor hypothesis not-H. In a more general case, suppose an analyst is considering four hypotheses $\{H_1, H_2, H_3,$ and $H_4\}$. One body of evidence is consistent in pointing most strongly to hypothesis H_1, while another body of evidence is consistent in pointing most strongly toward H_3.

Resolving evidential divergences, or *evidential conflicts* as they are sometimes called, is a more difficult matter than resolving evidential contradictions. Believability assessment does play an important role in both cases, but there is an additional difficulty with divergent or conflicting evidence. Suppose we return to the simple situation in which we have believable evidence items regarding events E and F. Two analysts agree that evidence of E favors hypothesis H but the evidence of F favors hypothesis not-H. A third analyst observes the two analysts who have just agreed that these two evidence items are divergent or conflicting. This third analyst says, "I don't agree with your assessment of this evidence. The trouble is that you are considering these two evidence items separately. If you consider them together, the apparent conflict disappears. The reason is that the occurrence of event E would effectively swamp the occurrence of event F and so there is no conflict here. These two items of evidence taken together make their dissonance disappear." So, dissonance involving divergent evidence always calls for an analyst's judgments on the directionality of evidence about different events. It is often the case that if we knew more about the situation in which different events have occurred, we might be able to explain away divergences or conflicts that seem to appear.

8.2.2   Patterns of Evidential Dissonance

We discussed two forms of dissonant, or *directionally inconsistent*, evidence that point us toward different hypotheses or possible conclusions. Such evidence can be either *contradictory* or *divergent*. As we mentioned, one of the unrealistic features about our cesium-137 example is that all the evidence we have so far is harmonious in pointing toward the hypothesis that a dirty bomb containing cesium-137 will be set off somewhere in Washington, D.C. In short, we have no contradictory or divergent evidence so far. So, we will have to imagine what some items of dissonant evidence might be.

Example 8.3.

Consider E014-Grace from Table 5.2 (p. 96), Grace's evidence that no one at the XYZ Company was using cesium-137 on a current project. We might have a source who contradicts Grace.

Example 8.4.

We might have evidence that the XYZ Company has had radioactive materials stolen in the past by persons working for competitors; this would be divergent evidence on E014-Grace because it would point to a different hypothesis.

8.3   REDUNDANT EVIDENCE

8.3.1   Basic Forms of Redundant Evidence

Redundant evidence involves combinations of two or more items that either say the same thing over again or do not add anything to what we already have.

This final recurrent and substance-blind combination of evidence is in effect the opposite of the possible evidential synergism mentioned previously for convergent evidence. We often encounter two or more items of evidence in which the first item acts to reduce the force of subsequent items of evidence. Stated another way, the first item acts to make subsequent items *redundant* to some degree. There are two ways this can happen, as we will see.

The first form of evidential redundance involves the corroborative evidence we discussed in Section 8.1. In this case, we have repeated evidence of the same events. Although having corroborative evidence does add to our confidence that an event of interest did occur, each additional item adds less and less to our confidence. At some point we will surely say, "We already believe that this event occurred; we don't need any further evidence about this event." We refer to this situation as *corroborative redundance*. The believability of our sources plays a crucial role in determining how redundant successive reports of the same event will be. To illustrate, suppose event E favors hypothesis H and we have successive items of evidence E^*_1, E^*_2, and E^*_3, all telling us that event E occurred. First, suppose we believe that our first source of evidence, the one who provided E^*_1, is perfectly credible. In short, we know for sure that event E occurred. In this case, having evidence E^*_2 and E^*_3 would tell us nothing we do not already know, so they are perfectly redundant. But now suppose that the first source is not perfectly credible. In this case, E^*_2 can add to the verification that event E occurred, depending on how credible we believe the second source to be. To the extent that the second source is not perfectly credible, the third source can add some additional verification.

The second form of redundancy involves different events in which evidence about one event, if credible, takes something away from the inferential force of evidence about another event. We have called this *cumulative redundance*. The word *cumulative* is an expression used in law to refer to evidence that does not add anything to what we already know. The following is an example of cumulative redundance.

Example 8.5.

Suppose asset $\mathcal{A}$ tells us that it was Omar, the terrorist, who he saw two days ago planting the shaped explosive device that killed two American soldiers outside of Tikrit. Then asset $\mathcal{B}$ tells us that he saw someone who looked like Omar planting this device two days ago at this same location outside of Tikrit. We have two different events here: The first source says it was Omar, but the second source only says it was someone who looked like Omar. Suppose we believe that the first source is perfectly credible. Then the report from the second source is completely redundant. If Omar was there, it follows necessarily that someone who *looked like* Omar was there. The report of the second source springs to life only if the first source is not credible.

The importance of considering these two forms of evidential redundancy cannot be overstated. In the case of corroborative redundancy, we risk *double-counting* evidence about the same event and ascribing additional weight to the evidence that it does not have. In the case of cumulative redundancy, we risk getting more inferential mileage out of the evidence than can be justified.

8.3.2   Patterns of Evidential Redundance

We mentioned two forms or redundant evidence, which we called *corroborative* and *cumulative* redundance. Corroborative redundance involves repeated evidence of the same event; cumulative redundance involves evidence about different events. In either case, we have instances in which some evidence can reduce the inferential force of other evidence. Here are some examples concerning redundance:

Example 8.6.

Look again at Willard's and Ralph's reports in evidence items E001-Willard and E004-Ralph (see Table 1.4). If we believed that Willard was completely believable in his report that the cesium-137 canister was missing, then Ralph's report would tell us nothing we do not already know for sure. This would make Ralph's report completely redundant. Ralph's report has value to the extent that Willard is not completely believable. But we could have asked other persons if they believed the cesium-137 canister to be missing. Here comes Joe and then Frank, who each tell us that the canister was missing. Each new report of the same event tells us less and less depending on the believability of earlier reports of the same event. This is what *corroborative redundance* is all about.

Example 8.7.

If we obtain the same reports from two or more sources, these reports will be corroboratively redundant to some degree. Cumulative redundance involves evidence about different events. We already have evidence of minute cesium-137 traces on the hair and skin of Omar al-Massari, but if we now get evidence of traces of cesium-137 on his clothes we would be inclined to say, "So what?" Finding such traces on his body makes finding traces on his clothes pretty likely and would tell us little we don't already believe, namely, that Omar al-Massari was exposed to cesium-137.

8.4   WHY CONSIDERING EVIDENCE COMBINATIONS IS IMPORTANT

There may be very few, if any, situations in which the conclusion of an intelligence analysis problem is based on just a single item of evidence. Intelligence analysts usually draw conclusions based on masses of evidence of different kinds and coming from a variety of different sources. What is obvious is that careful assessment of the joint impact or force of masses of evidence is crucial in drawing conclusions about what is happening or what will happen in a situation of interest. Determining the joint impact or force of a mass of evidence is no easy matter. The basic reason is that individual evidence items can have a variety of different effects on each other. Another way of expressing this is to say that our items of evidence can interact in different ways; this is what makes assessments of joint impact or force so complex. It also means that we must consider *combinations of evidence* to see how they might interact. We have presented several basic patterns of interactions among evidence items when we consider possible combinations of evidence items. They are summarized in Figure 8.1.

One reason for carefully considering these combinations of evidence is that they are often confused or incorrectly identified, leading to mistakes in how the evidence is described in an analysis. But perhaps the most important reason is that *there are very important sources of uncertainty lurking in these evidential combinations.*

But we have one more task to perform regarding uncertainty and evidence. There are five characteristics of evidence that make conclusions drawn from it necessarily probabilistic. They are described in detail later in Chapter 9.

8.5   BASIC OPERATIONS WITH DISCIPLE-CD

8.5.1   Hands On: Who Has Stolen the Cesium Canister?

8.5.1.1 Overview

This case study has two main objectives:

- Improving your understanding of the evidence-based hypothesis analysis process by analyzing a more complex hypothesis
- Providing an example for illustrating various types of evidence combinations

> **Table 8.1 Information on the Presumed Stealing of the Cesium-137 Canister**
>
> **INFO-010-Santa:** An asset code-named "Santa" tells us that the name Omer Riley is one of the aliases used by a person named Omar al-Massari, who came to the USA in 2000, apparently from Saudi Arabia, on an extended work permit. Omar al-Massari is a physicist employed for the past two years by the Ultratech Company in Silver Spring. He lives with two other males at 403 Winston Road in Silver Spring. Santa also tells us that Omar al-Massari (alias Omer Riley) is intimately associated with an unnamed jihadist organization in the Washington, DC, area.
>
> **INFO-011-Test:** Omar al-Massari (alias Omer Riley) was apprehended at his place of work at the Ultratech Company in Silver Spring. During his questioning, he was given a test called "whole body counting" with a Geiger counter that can detect the gamma radiation emitted by cesium-137. This test indicated the presence of traces of cesium-137 on his skin and hair.
>
> **INFO-012-Walsh:** The president of Ultratech Company, Mr. John Walsh, reported that Omar al-Massari's (alias Omer Riley) work at Ultratech does not involve his handling any radioactive substances.

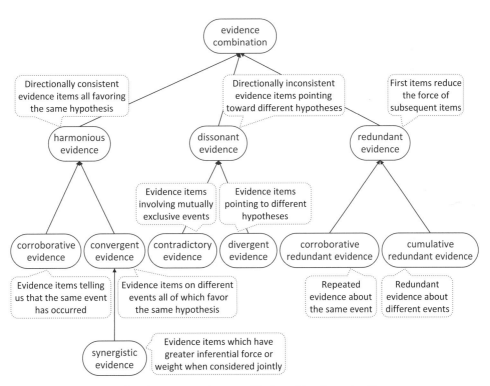

Figure 8.1. Recurrent substance-blind combinations of evidence.

The case study continues our dirty bomb analysis from earlier chapters. Having been established that the available evidence favors the hypothesis that the cesium-137 canister was stolen from the XYZ warehouse with the MDC-578 truck, the next step is to identify who has actually stolen it. A natural suspect is Omer Riley, who has rented the MDC-578 truck. As indicated by INFO-010-Santa in Table 8.1, our asset, Santa, has given us significant leads for getting additional information about our suspect. This has led to our

Table 8.2 Dots from Table 8.1

E015-SantaAlias: Santa's testimony that Omer Riley is an alias used by Omar al-Massari.

E016-SantaWork: Santa's testimony that Omar al-Massari is a physicist employed for the past two years by the Ultratech Company in Silver Spring.

E017-SantaAdr: Santa's testimony that Omer Riley lives with two other males at 403 Winston Road in Silver Spring.

E018-SantaTerOrg: Santa's testimony that Omar al-Massari (alias Omer Riley) is intimately associated with an unnamed jihadist organization in the Washington, DC, area.

E019-OmarTest: "Whole body counting" test result on Omar al-Massari (alias Omer Riley) with a Geiger counter indicating traces of cesium-137 on his skin and hair.

E020-Walsh: Walsh's testimony that Omar al-Massari's work does not involve handling of radioactive substances.

obtaining of INFO-011-Test and INFO-012-Walsh. The information from Table 8.1 and the corresponding dots in Table 8.2 suggest the following scenario: Omar al-Massari rented the MDC-578 truck, giving his alias, Omer Riley, and a false address, and then used the truck to steal the cesium-137 canister, which in turn caused it to become contaminated because cesium-137 is a radioactive material. This leads to the development of the hypothesis analysis tree from Figure 8.2.

8.5.1.2 Practice

Start Disciple-CD, select the knowledge base "12-Who-Stole-Cesium/Scen," and proceed as indicated in the instructions from the bottom of the opened window.

8.6   REVIEW QUESTIONS

8.1. Can you make up some examples of evidence that corroborates other evidence in our dirty bomb scenario? Ask yourself what items of evidence we now have that you would like to see corroborated.

8.2. Consider the evidence provided by John Walsh, President of the Ultratech Company in Silver Spring, Maryland, in which Omar al-Massari (alias Omer Riley) works (i.e., E020-Walsh in Table 8.2). Walsh tells us that Omer Riley's job does not require him to handle any radioactive materials such as cesium-137. But suppose we interview another executive at the Ultratech Company, Dan Moore, who is more directly familiar with the work Omer Riley actually performs. This person tells us that Omer Riley has worked recently on devices for measuring soil dampness gradients, and this work does involve the use of radioactive materials. What kind of evidence combination do we have here?

8.3. Recall the evidence item E017-SantaAdr in Table 8.2, where Santa is telling us that Omar al-Massari lives with two other males at 403 Winston Road in Silver Spring, Maryland. We interview a person named Martha, who says she saw a person she knows as Omer Riley (the alias Omar al-Massari uses) park a panel

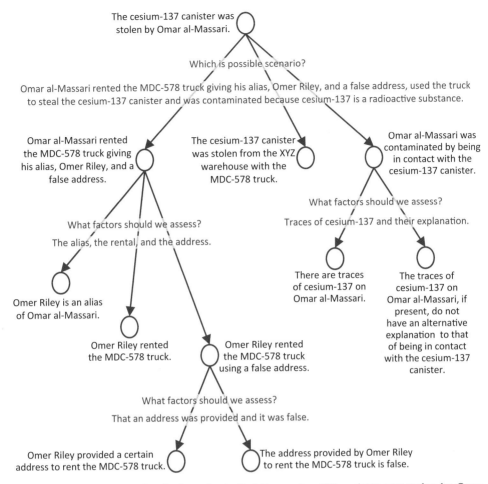

Figure 8.2. Analysis tree for the hypothesis that the cesium-137 canister was stolen by Omar al-Massari.

truck in the driveway of the house Omer shares with two other males. Then we have another neighbor, Paul, who tells us that he saw someone, who looked like Omer Riley, park a panel truck in the driveway of the house at 403 Winston Road in Silver Spring, Maryland. What kind of evidence combination do we have in this case?

8.4. You have two sources reporting the current location of a certain tank column. One source says it is five miles away to the north; the other says it is three miles away to the east. How would you characterize these two items of evidence?

8.5. Two human sources each report observing Person X in company yesterday with a known distributor of narcotics. Is this evidence corroborative or convergent?

8.6. You have an aerial photograph you believe shows three surface-to-surface missiles of a certain sort at map coordinates (x, y); this photograph was taken one week ago. You also have HUMINT from a source who reports observing three missiles of this sort one week ago at nearly the same coordinates. Is this redundant evidence?

8.7.   One source tells us that T, a known terrorist, was observed at location X at 10:00 PM last Friday. Then another source tells us that T was at location Y (one hundred miles away from X) at this same time. What kind of evidence is this?

8.8.   From one source we receive information that Country A is moving military forces in the direction of Country B; we believe this favors hostile action between countries A and B. But another source tells us of recent secret negotiations between representatives of countries A and B that were successful in resolving major differences between countries A and B. This evidence you believe favors the possibility that there will be no hostile action involving A and B. What kind of evidence is this?

8.9.   In assessing these three forms of evidence combinations (i.e., harmonious, dissonant, and redundant), show why it is so necessary to consider carefully the believability of sources of the evidence being considered.

8.10.   We naturally encounter instances of harmonious, dissonant, and redundant combinations of evidence in our daily lives. Provide some examples.

8.11.   Here is a problem that involves resolving dissonant patterns of contradictory evidence. Suppose you have six persons who say that event E occurred, and only two persons who say that E did not occur. Can you resolve this contradiction by simply counting heads and siding with the majority?

9 Major Sources of Uncertainty in Masses of Evidence

There are five major reasons why conclusions reached in intelligence analysis based on evidence will be necessarily probabilistic in nature: Our evidence is always *incomplete*, usually *inconclusive*, frequently *ambiguous*, commonly *dissonant*, and with various degrees of *believability*. Any one of these reasons can lead to uncertain conclusions, but an analyst drawing conclusions based on masses of different forms and combinations of evidence will likely encounter all five of these reasons at the same time. Intelligence analysts who report conclusions with varying degrees of uncertainty are often unjustly criticized for doing so. Persons providing such criticisms are doubtless unaware of many or most of the reasons why it is necessary to hedge conclusions in probabilistic terms. *One main reason we have for providing a careful account of these five reasons is that no single view of probability we know about captures all five of these sources of uncertainty.* Each view of probability we will mention provides useful insights about some of these sources of uncertainty, but no single view says all there is to be said.

9.1 INCOMPLETENESS

9.1.1 What Is Incompleteness of Evidence?

We may have all heard someone say, "I am going to wait until I have *all the evidence* before I draw a conclusion or make a decision." This person faces an infinitely long wait because there is no situation in which we can say we have all the possible evidence. The first way of showing that this statement is true is to consider the distinction we have made between directly relevant and ancillary evidence. In doing so, we also referred to ancillary evidence as being meta-evidence, or evidence about evidence. The trouble here is that we face an infinite regression in which we have evidence, ancillary evidence about this evidence, ancillary evidence about this ancillary evidence, and so on, ad infinitum. Suppose we have an HUMINT asset who provides us with some interesting evidence; call this asset our primary source. But then we have a secondary source who provides us with ancillary evidence about the believability of our primary source. But then we have a tertiary source who provides ancillary evidence about the believability of our secondary source. This process could go on and on indefinitely. This fact was noted years ago by the CIA's James J. Angleton, who encountered situations in which chains of HUMINT sources provided contradictory and divergent evidence about each other's believability. He described this situation as similar to being in a "wilderness of mirrors" (Martin, 1980).

There are many other situations in which we could have endless chains of evidence, and evidence about evidence, even in empirical statistical situations. It is often said that the conclusions reached by statisticians are always misleading to some extent and that they must choose ways of reporting conclusions that are minimally misleading. Consider an intelligence analyst who reports the results of a statistical analysis of the capabilities of a weapon system of some sort. Her conclusions are challenged by another analyst. In turn, the comments made by this challenger are then challenged by a third analyst. This process could go on forever until someone decides to call a halt to this evidence-about-evidence situation. This fact is noted in our procedures for trials at law that limit the extent to which we can follow this chain. If this were not the case, a trial might go on for years without any verdict ever being reached.

But there is another even more important reason for our evidence always being incomplete. In how many intelligence analyses could it ever be said that every one of the relevant questions that could have been asked was in fact answered by the evidence that was gathered and analyzed? There probably has never been an intelligence analysis in which there were no lingering unanswered questions at the time a conclusion was required. In the absence of clairvoyance, there may be considerable uncertainty about what questions should be asked in an intelligence analysis. In Section 6.5, we discussed missing evidence as a possible category of evidence. In such cases, we attempted to answer certain questions but were unable to do so. But there will be many questions lingering that we have never even attempted to answer as well as many questions that we may not even recognize as being relevant. In Section 10.7, we will discuss a view of probability, called the *Baconian* view, which uniquely places special emphasis on the extent to which our evidence in an analysis is complete in its coverage of all the questions we recognize as being relevant to the conclusions we must reach. This view requires us to consider the force of evidence we do have, but it also says that this force depends on questions that are unanswered by the present evidence we are considering. This issue of completeness is bound to be of interest to intelligence analysts engaged in *current intelligence* in which conclusions are often required in a very short time. An issue here concerns the extent to which any analyst could have the time to cover all the questions that might occur to this person as being relevant to the conclusion being requested.

9.1.2   Examples of Incompleteness

Example 9.1.

On various matters concerning events in the past, it might be argued that we have complete evidence. For example, we believe we have evidence that allows us *now* to conclude, *beyond all shadow of doubt*, that The Twin Towers of the World Trade Center in New York City were destroyed on September 11, 2001, and that the then-President of the United States, John F. Kennedy, was assassinated in Dallas, Texas, on November 22, 1963. We can go to New York and see for ourselves where the World Trade Center used to be and then view television images of the two aircraft that slammed into the buildings, and the horror of the subsequent collapse of the buildings. Or, we can view the monument to John F. Kennedy in Arlington National Cemetery in Virginia that records the place and time of his death. We can also watch the so-called Zapruder film that shows President Kennedy being struck in the head and then collapsing into his wife Jacqueline's arms after he was struck. In each of these cases, we have what can be regarding as *conclusive evidence* (more on conclusive evidence in a moment).

There are two points to be made about the two examples we have just provided. First, it does appear that the occurrence of these two events is no longer a topic of analytic interest, since we are certain that they occurred. But there are very many other questions concerning these two events that are now of great interest and will continue to be of interest in future analyses. Concerning the tragedy in New York, we are asking such questions as, "Who were all the persons involved in the planning of this action?" and, "Why did these persons take this action at this particular time?" As far as the Kennedy assassination is concerned, it is still being asked, "Did Lee Harvey Oswald act by himself or was he part of a conspiracy to kill President Kennedy?" The evidence on these questions will never be complete. The second point concerns the stability over time of the conclusions we have now reached with certainty. Five hundred years from now, will these two conclusions about the destruction of the World Trade Center and the assassination of President Kennedy still be regarded as certain (if they are, indeed, matters of concern at all)? Perhaps the evidence we now regard as conclusive will have vanished long before the year 2516.

Example 9.2.

Intelligence analysts will not normally be concerned about what will be inferred five hundred years from now about events of interest today. In many cases, they are asked to reach conclusions concerning past events based on evidence that is far from complete. For example, new evidence is coming to light as we write these words on whether Lee Harvey Oswald acted alone in the assassination of President Kennedy. New accounts of the identities and motivations of the nineteen terrorists who destroyed the World Trade Center appear regularly as well. Even more evidence about these events will certainly emerge in the future. Now, consider an intelligence analysis that involves the prediction of some future event, such as whether countries such as Iran, Iraq, Saudi Arabia, Syria, Egypt, and Turkey will engage in all-out war if we remove all of our forces from countries in the Middle East. Unless we have a person who is certifiably clairvoyant and can see into the future, we will never know for certain. The only thing certain is that we can only draw inferences about events such as these based on evidence about events in the past and the ever-fleeing present. This evidence will obviously be incomplete, if only because we may not be asking the right questions. In addition, and of the greatest importance, there will always be questions unanswered by the evidence we do have. There is only one view of probabilistic reasoning, the Baconian view, that asks how complete is our coverage of evidence and how many questions remain unanswered by the evidence we have considered.

Example 9.3.

This is one final example concerning evidential incompleteness; it involves what we have said about ancillary evidence, or evidence about evidence. We are always facing an infinite regression involving evidence, evidence about the evidence, evidence about the evidence about the evidence, and so on, ad infinitum. Consider our source Santa in the dirty bomb example. Santa has given us two very important items of evidence: (1) that Omer Riley is an alias used by Omar al-Massari (E015-SantaAlias in Table 8.2) and (2) that Omar al-Massari is a member of an unnamed jihadist organization in Washington, D.C. (E018-SantaTerOrg). The question is, "What do we really know about Santa's competence and credibility as far as these two items of evidence are concerned?" By the way, it should be obvious that Santa is an informant about terrorist activities in this general area. One question we would ask concerns Santa's competence in these reports, "Has he had any actual contact with Omar al-Massari and any knowledge of with whom Omar al-Massari associates?" To answer such questions, we rely upon another asset code-named "Raindrop." Raindrop tells us that he is sure that Santa knows Omar al-Massari and also knows about possible terrorist organizations with which Santa has contact. The same questions now arise concerning Raindrop's competence and credibility concerning what he tells us about Santa's competence and credibility. To answer these questions, we could query yet another source and even another source about this source. There is no end to it.

We leave the issue of incompleteness with two thoughts we ask you to keep in mind. With the exception of situations like the ones given in Example 9.1 concerning past events and conclusive evidence, in any other case we have two reasons why our evidence is never complete:

- We will always have some unanswered questions.
- We will always encounter the need for meta-evidence or evidence about evidence, there being no end to this need.

9.2 **INCONCLUSIVENESS**

9.2.1   What Is Inconclusiveness of Evidence?

The evidence encountered in intelligence analysis is commonly inconclusive in nature. This means that evidence is consistent with more than one possibility, hypothesis, or explanation. Conclusions reached from such evidence can only be probabilistic in nature. Another term we might use here is to say that intelligence analysis usually involves *circumstantial evidence*. Circumstantial evidence, even if credible, supplies only some but not complete grounds for a conclusion. Conclusive evidence, that which is consistent with only one possibility or hypothesis, is usually in very short supply. Conclusive evidence would supply complete grounds for, or make necessary or certain, some hypothesis or possible conclusion.

There is an expression used by intelligence analysts with reference to conclusive evidence on some major hypothesis that comes from a completely credible source; the term *nugget* is used with reference to such evidence. Here is an example of such a nugget using our dirty bomb (cesium-137) example. Suppose we have a trusted source who reports the following events. This source tells us, "Persons associated with the North

American Jihadist Organization (NAJO) in Silver Spring, MD, did acquire the cesium-137 that was stolen from the XYZ warehouse in Baltimore. They are now constructing a dirty bomb in the garage of a residence at 221 Colesville Rd. in Silver Spring, MD, which they intend to set off on the grounds of the capitol building in Washington, DC, next Thursday at 12:00PM." If we had such a nugget, we could easily prevent this disaster from occurring. Barring the acquisition of such a nugget, we must, as the phrase goes, "mine lots of lower grade ore" in the form of inconclusive and circumstantial evidence.

9.2.2 Examples of Inconclusiveness

Example 9.4.

The five evidence items E001-Willard, E004-Ralph, E005-Ralph, E006-Clyde, and E014-Grace (from Table 1.4 and Table 5.2) do not conclusively show, taken separately or together, that the proposition, "The canister containing cesium-137 was stolen," is true. This evidence does not entitle us to believe with certainty that the cesium-137 canister was stolen from the XYZ warehouse. We may obtain later evidence that Grace was wrong, and that someone at the XYZ Company did in fact remove the cesium-137 canister for work on a project for one of XYZ's customers.

Example 9.5.

Consider our dirty bomb analysis and E018-SantaTerOrg in Table 8.2 (Santa's report that Omar al-Massari is intimately associated with an unnamed jihadist organization in the Washington, D.C., area). Even if Omar al-Massari is a member of a jihadist organization in Washington, D.C., this does not mean that a dirty bomb will be set off somewhere in Washington, D.C. Our source Santa might not be credible; Santa might be lying to us or simply be mistaken. In short, his report is just inconclusive evidence that the event he reports is true.

9.3 AMBIGUITY

9.3.1 What Is Ambiguity of Evidence?

Evidence is ambiguous to the extent to which we cannot determine what it is telling us. We might also describe ambiguous evidence as being imprecisely stated. Ambiguity is different from inconclusiveness. We may have precisely stated, nonambiguous, evidence that is still circumstantial or consistent with more than one hypothesis or possible conclusion. As an example of ambiguity, we will discuss a conversation we have intercepted between two persons of interest who are involved in known terrorist activities. In this conversation, they make use of words used to describe persons and their activities that are designed to conceal their intentions or to mislead others who may be listening. It is well known, for example, that terrorist organizations in the Middle East spend a great amount of time training their operatives to be skillful in disguising their identities, capabilities, and intentions. Even our best efforts to disambiguate evidence we receive are not always successful. A person listening to such a conversation may be perfectly fluent in the language and dialect used by the two persons overheard, but still be unable to tell us exactly what these two persons were saying.

9.3.2   Examples of Ambiguity

Example 9.6.

In many cases, we may encounter information that would seem relevant if we could decide what it is telling us; in other words, it is ambiguous, imprecise, or vague. We may, for example, be provided with a document concerning apparently current plans of a certain terrorist organization. This document, on careful examination, is reckoned to be authentic. The document says, "Our destiny is now approaching. We will meet at the usual place at the agreed-upon time and proceed to the Crusader site. If Allah is willing, we will kill many of them." This message is certainly vague with respect to the time and place of what seems to be an intended terrorist operation. With any luck, we might have other evidence about this group that might allow us to remove at least some of the ambiguity apparent in this document. The basic trouble with ambiguous evidence is that it certainly generates uncertainty, but we are often at a loss about how to remove at least some of this uncertainty.

Example 9.7.

In many cases involving intelligence reports you receive, you cannot tell exactly what information is being conveyed in these reports. Very good examples are provided by the equivocal testimonial evidence. Here is a source of HUMINT who hedges when asked if event E occurred. The source says, "I am not sure, but I believe it is about 60 percent likely that event E happened." The trouble is that "60 percent" for this source might not be the same as what you believe "60 percent" means. Evidence is frequently encountered that is imprecise in some way, with the result that you cannot tell exactly what event is being reported. If you can't be sure what your evidence says, you can hardly avoid hedging your conclusions.

Example 9.8.

In so many instances of HUMINT reports, the sources of it provide *ambiguous* accounts of observed events. Here is a source who reports seeing,"a *large number* of Taliban fighters assembling, *a short time ago*, near *location X* in Afghanistan." This is an imprecise or fuzzy account of this situation. Hearing this account, we do not know exactly how many, when, and where this assemblage of Taliban fighters occurred. Was the exact number twenty, fifty, one hundred, five hundred, or larger? Was the time twelve hours ago, three hours, thirty minutes, or shorter? Was the location ten, five, or two kilometers or only five hundred meters from location X? Why do such ambiguous reports so often occur? The reason is quite simple: Human observers cannot make precise judgments under many conditions and are trying to do their best in honestly reporting what they observed. Suppose instead this source had given the following report: "At exactly 2 hours and 17 minutes ago, I observed exactly 257 Taliban fighters assembling exactly 0.76 kilometers from location X." We might be quite suspicious of a source who provided such a precise account, especially when we hear about the conditions under which the source said he made this observation.

Example 9.9.

Often analysts are criticized for providing ambiguous conclusions in their analyses. For example, here is an intelligence analyst who says her analysis shows that it is *quite probable* that the Russians are increasing the number of their air defense forces in Damascus, Syria. She is criticized for not providing a precise probability to go along with her conclusion. She says, "OK, you want me to give you a precise numerical probability here and so I will say that the probability is exactly 0.75 that the Russians are increasing the number of their air defense forces in Damascus, Syria." After she provides this number, she tells a colleague: "I have just responded to a stupid request. I was asked to give a precise probability to the Russians increasing the number of their air defense forces in Damascus, Syria. I said this probability was 0.75. But I certainly did not base this number on one hundred past occasions on which the Russians increased the number of their air defense forces seventy-five times. No one has such a record. The number I gave is just a good guess about what, for me, 'quite probable' means. But this number might actually be any number between 0.65 and 0.85."

9.4   DISSONANCE

9.4.1   What Is the Dissonance of Evidence?

We devoted Section 8.2 to a discussion of dissonant evidence as being a recurrent combination of intelligence evidence. We described dissonant evidence as being directionally inconsistent in the sense that it points us toward more than one hypotheses or possible conclusions. We described the two forms of dissonance as involving contradictory and divergent evidence. Suppose we have an analysis in which it is stated that *all* of the evidence analyzed was harmonious or directionally consistent in favoring the conclusion reported in the analysis. The first question someone should ask is, "Are you sure you did not gather and analyze just the evidence you believe would favor the conclusion you reported?" In some situations, this is called "cherry picking." At least some pattern of dissonance may be expected in any intelligence analysis, especially one that involves any degree of complexity. To be sure, some of the evidence may be harmonious in pointing in one direction, but on balance we will have other harmonious evidence pointing in another direction. In short, some dissonance will be expected in every intelligence analysis having any degree of complexity. Failure to report this dissonance will arouse justified suspicions of the intentions and the competence of the persons performing the analysis.

9.4.2   Examples of Dissonance

Examples 8.3 and 8.4 (p. 152) in Section 8.2 are both examples of dissonant evidence. Here is another example:

Example 9.10.

Suppose that, in our dirty bomb scenario, we obtain evidence from an asset code-named "Wonderboy," who knows Omar al-Massari very well. Wonderboy tells us that Omar al-Massari has recently put a down payment of $25,000 on a house at 2321 23rd Street in the Georgetown area of Washington, D.C. This might be dissonant evidence suggesting that our main hypothesis (that a dirty bomb containing cesium-137 will be set off somewhere in Washington, D.C.) is not true after all. Why would Omar al-Massari invest in a house in a city where a dirty bomb is to be set off? We would obviously be interested in the believability of the evidence Wonderboy has given us. Did he rely only on what Omar al-Massari told him, or did Wonderboy see a contract for the sale of this house? It is very possible, of course, that Omar al-Massari is attempting to mislead Wonderboy, whom Omar may suspect has infiltrated a terrorist organization to which Omar belongs.

9.5   IMPERFECT BELIEVABILITY

9.5.1   What Is Imperfect Believability of Evidence?

Sources of evidence of any kind (i.e., all of the possible "INTs") have any possible degree of believability. No mechanical or electronic sensor is perfectly *accurate*; and on occasion sensor records of various sorts can even be *faked*. As we all know, no human observer is always perfectly *credible*. In some cases, a person may not even be a *competent* source of information. Here are some examples of these distinctions. Radar and other sources of sensory images are not always sensitive enough to discriminate between events of interest to us. On occasion, we can obtain estimates of a sensor's hit rate and false-positive rate. It is certainly not unheard of in the intelligence business for documents, photographs, and other similar items of evidence to be faked or forged. At least some items of evidence you may encounter will not be *authentic*; they are not what they seem to be. Human sources are not always truthful, objective, or accurate as observers. Further, a person may be truthful, objective, or accurate about some matters but not about others. Just because a human source has given us what we take to be believable evidence in the past is no guarantee that he or she will continue to do so in future. Failure to recognize this simple fact has produced more than one intelligence-related catastrophe.

9.5.2   Examples of Imperfect Believability

Example 9.11.

In Chapter 7, we considered a human source code-named Wallflower, who gave us the report concerning the Iraqi Emir Z., coming out of a building in

Ahwaz, Iran, that houses offices of the Iranian IRGC Qods Forces. We considered the major attributes of Wallflower's credibility: veracity, objectivity, and observational sensitivity.

But we also must be concerned about the believability of any *tangible evidence* we obtain. These attributes concern the authenticity, reliability, and accuracy of such evidence. In Table 8.2, we have several items of tangible evidence. Here are some examples of believability-related questions we should ask about this evidence.

Example 9.12.

E013-InvestigativeRecord in Table 5.2 (p. 96) concerns the traces of cesium-137 that were found in the truck we believe to have been driven by Omar al-Massari. We have examined the chain of custody through which the tangible record of measurements taken of these traces was made. Suppose we are convinced that this record is authentic. But we must also consider the reliability and accuracy of the device used to obtain these measurements. The first question we should ask is, "How reliable are these measurements we have? Were repeated measures taken using the same measuring device and did they give the same readings on each measure?" The second question involves the accuracy of the device. In particular, "What is its hit rate and false-positive rate for detecting cesium-137 traces?"

An experienced analyst reading the account of uncertainty in intelligence evidence just provided may easily recognize all five of these characteristics, and will have encountered most of them at one time or another. Any critic of intelligence analysts for expressing their uncertainty in reporting conclusions should be made aware of the five reasons we have mentioned that require intelligence analysts to acknowledge the extent of their uncertainty, which will always be present. But there are additional reasons why uncertainty is evident in all complex activities such as intelligence analysis.

We suspect that one reason for the current interest in uncertainty in intelligence analysis is that analysts have encountered sources of uncertainty that are not captured by conventional views of probability. This is the main reason we have for presenting alternative systems of probabilistic reasoning in the next chapter.

9.6   BASIC OPERATIONS WITH DISCIPLE-CD

9.6.1   Hands On: Does a Terrorist Organization Have the Cesium Canister?

9.6.1.1 Overview

This case study, which continues our dirty bomb analysis, has the following objectives:

- Improving your understanding of how to extract evidence from the collected information
- Improving your understanding of evidence-based hypothesis analysis by analyzing a more complex hypothesis
- Providing an example for discussing the sources of uncertainty in intelligence analysis

We have established that the cesium-137 canister was stolen by Omar al-Massari. Now the question is, "Who is Omar al-Massari? Is he someone working for a competitor, someone hoping to sell this valuable material, or someone having terrorist connections?"

Figure 9.1 shows the indicators that guide us in collecting evidence to prove that Omar al-Massari has ties to terrorist organizations. As a result, we collect the information in Table 9.1.

9.6.1.2 Extracting Evidence from Information

Up to now, most of the case studies included both the items of information collected and the items of evidence extracted from them. In this case study, you will have to extract the items of evidence from the collected information yourself, as you did in Section 4.5.1. As discussed before, this involves the necessity of parsing incoming information to see what evidential dots or trifles this information reveals. Testimonial information or descriptions of tangible items might contain very many details, dots, or trifles. Some of the details might be interesting and relevant evidence, and others not. What we always have to do is to parse the incoming information to extract the information that we believe is relevant in the inference task at hand.

In so many instances, we have seen persons taking a lump of information containing many details, some interesting and some not, and treating it as a single item of potential evidence. There are two problems here. The first is that the relevant individual details in this lump might bear on different inferential issues; they will rarely all bear on the same issue. The second is that the irrelevant details only act to confuse the inferential bearings of the relevant details. Now, the problem is that determining what the relevant and irrelevant details are is a subjective matter. We might not all agree that a particular detail is relevant or irrelevant.

Here comes an example involving INFO-014-Clark from Table 9.1. In this case, Clark tells us a variety of things, some of which seem potentially relevant and others not. Looking carefully at this testimony from Clark, we can first identify details that seem irrelevant as far as al-Massari's terrorist activities are concerned. Here are some of them:

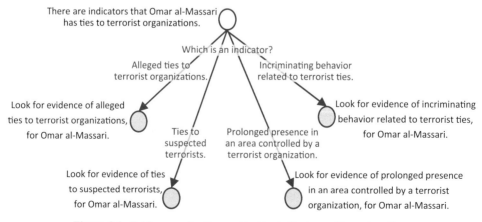

Figure 9.1. Evidence collection guided by indicators of terrorism ties.

Table 9.1 Information on the Presumed Terrorism Ties of Omar al-Massari

INFO-013-Laptop: In further investigation of Omar al-Massari, we tell him that we wish to see his laptop computer. We are, of course, interested in what it might reveal about the terrorists with whom he may be associating. He refuses to tell us where the computer is. We referred to this as the nonproduction of evidence.

INFO-014-Clark: As we have learned, Omar al-Massari lives with two other males, Richard Clark and Fahd al-Quso, at 403 Winston Road in Silver Spring. We were only able to interview Richard Clark. Clark is an American citizen of Anglo-Saxon origin who was born in 1973 in Lanham, MD, and is the owner of the residence at 403 Winston Road in Silver Spring. He has lived there since 2005, when he purchased the house. He says he had trouble making his house payments and was forced to take in renters who could contribute to his house payment. Clark went on to say that he rented rooms to al-Massari and al-Quso (who came together to look at the rooms) because they were professionals who could pay their rents on time, which Clark says they always did. We told Clark about al-Massari's detention and asked for further information about him and al-Quso. Clark responded that Fahd al-Quso had suddenly moved out two days ago and that he had not seen al-Massari for the past two days. However, Clark says that al-Massari had driven up two days ago in a U-Haul panel truck, but had stayed for only a minute before he left. Clark says he wondered why al-Massari was driving around in a U-Haul truck. Finally, Clark says that his two renters kept to themselves most of the time they were home and that he never looked inside their rooms (which would have been an invasion of their privacy), but that he frequently overheard their conversations concerning a place called Allied Import, that Clark guessed was a business of some kind.

INFO-015-Quso: The other housemate (besides Richard Clark) of Omar al-Massari is Fahd al-Quso, a Yemeni who, like Omar al-Massari, has been here on an extended work permit. Fahd al-Quso is also a physicist who has been employed for the past three years by a company called Physicom in Laurel, MD. We have not been able to interview him. Just yesterday, Fahd al-Quso boarded Emirates Flight #207 bound for Dubai. He purchased a one-way ticket using a credit card. He was not on any no-fly lists. We have just learned from a trusted source that Fahd al-Quso has been detained by United Arab Emirate (UAE) authorities for questioning about his association with terrorist incidents in the UAE.

INFO-016-FBI: Allied Import is a business at 2121 M Street East in Washington, D.C., that deals with a variety of items from various places in the Middle East. FBI contacts tell us that Allied Import has been under surveillance for several months in connection with possible narcotics trafficking. We asked the FBI for any surveillance records they might have about trucks entering and leaving Allied Import. We were shown a surveillance video of a single man arriving two days ago in a U-Haul panel truck with MD license number MDC-578. The driver was positively identified as Omar al-Massari. The video shows al-Massari handing off a single canisterlike container to a man. So, Allied Import may be in the terrorist business in addition to being in the narcotics business, since we know from experience that these two activities often go hand in hand. The man in the video accepting the container from al-Massari was identified by the FBI as a Maryland resident named Kenny Derwish. Derwish lists his residence as 113 4th St. in Oxon Hill, MD. Derwish has been with Allied Import for four years.

INFO-017-Yasmin: A source code-named "Yasmin" tells us that she knew a man in Saudi Arabia named Omar al-Massari. Yasmin says she is "quite sure" that Omar spent two years "somewhere" in Afghanistan "sometime" in the years 1998 to 2000. Yasmin also tells us that she once met Omar al-Massari at a large gathering last August in Bethesda, MD, held (allegedly) to support charities in the Middle East. She said that Omar al-Massari attended this gathering with a person he identified as his roommate and that they were both physicists. Yasmin says that funds collected at this gathering were never intended to be used for charitable purposes, but to support terrorist activities both here and around the globe. Additionally, Yasmin tells us that Kenny

> Derwish is an alias used by Saeed al-Nami. She says that Saeed was associated with a now-disbanded Islamic Jihad cell in Herndon, VA. She further tells us that Saeed is now a principal member of an active terrorist cell in Washington, D.C., called Jihad Bis Sayf (Striving through the Sword).

- *Clark had trouble making payments on the house he purchased in 2005. So he had to take in renters.*
- *The renters, al-Massari and al-Quso, always paid their rent on time.*
- *The renters, al-Massari and al-Quso, kept to themselves most of the time when they were home.*

But here are some apparently relevant details, dots, or trifles that bear on different matters:

- *Clark is of Anglo-Saxon origin and was born in 1973 in Lanham, Maryland.* These details are potentially relevant concerning Clark's credibility and competence. That he is of Anglo-Saxon origin says that he is probably a kufr, a Muslim word for an infidel. That he was born in 1973 might arise in assessments of his competence.
- *Al-Massari and al-Quso roomed together.* This bears on al-Massari's association with a suspected terrorist.
- *Al-Massari and al-Quso frequently discussed the Allied Import Company.* This bears on *where* al-Massari might have taken the cesium-137.
- *Two days ago, al-Massari drove up to their residence in a U-Haul truck.* This also bears on *where* al-Massari might have taken the cesium-137.
- *Al-Massari stayed for only a minute two days ago when he drove up in the U-Haul truck.* This may be relevant to *when* al-Massari took the cesium to Allied Import.
- *Al-Quso suddenly moved out two days ago.* This bears on al-Quso's behavior as a possible terrorist.

This analysis is an example of the necessity for parsing lumps of information to identify what different specific details, dots, or trifles are relevant, and how they are relevant to different issues in an analysis.

9.6.1.3 Practice

The information from Table 9.1 suggests a scenario where Omar al-Massari, who has ties with terrorist organizations, has stolen the cesium-137 canister and has given it to Saeed al-Nami, alias Kenny Derwish, who is a member of Jihad Bis Sayf. Consequently, we develop the analysis tree in Figure 9.2 to assess the hypothesis that the terrorist organization Jihad Bis Sayf has the cesium-137 canister. First you will define evidence based on the available information. Then you will associate it with elementary hypotheses and evaluate them. As a result, you will assess the probability of the top-level hypothesis. This analysis will be used in the next case study.

Start Disciple-CD, select the knowledge base "13-Terrorist-Organization," and proceed as indicated in the instructions from the bottom of the opened window.

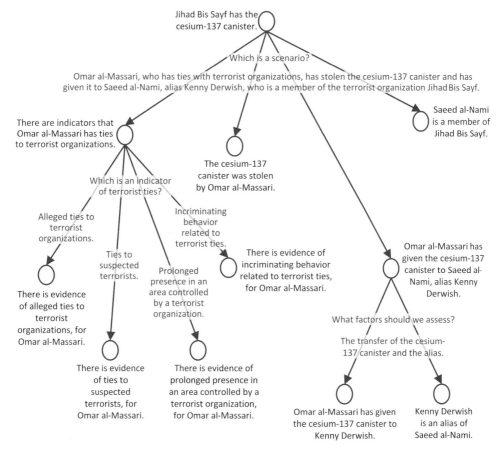

Figure 9.2. Analysis of the hypothesis that a terrorist organization has the stolen cesium-137.

REVIEW QUESTIONS

9.1. We suspect that Person P is a double agent and is presently passing classified information to a certain potential adversary. We thought he worked only for us, but now have some grounds for a belief that he is also employed by this adversary. What would constitute absolutely complete evidence that P is in fact a double agent?

9.2. For what other evidence items in Table 8.2 (p. 156) would you wish to have other sources available that could help in deciding whether or not to believe what the items tell us?

9.3. Show why all the evidence in Table 1.4 (p. 22) and Table 5.2 (p. 96) is inconclusive.

9.4. One of our military transport aircraft made a stop at a civilian airfield in Country C, with whom we have had friendly relations over the years. Two days ago, this aircraft was destroyed on the ground by an explosive device. There are identified groups in Country C that do not favor C's continued friendly associations with us; one of these groups is called the "Purples." Person Q, believed to be associated with the Purples, was observed, by a usually believable source, in an aircraft parking area of this airfield just one hour before our aircraft was destroyed. Why is this just inconclusive evidence that the Purples were involved in this incident?

9.5.   Look again at INFO-017-Yasmin in Table 9.1, in which we have Yasmin telling us that she knew a man in Saudi Arabia named Omar al-Massari. Yasmin says she is "quite sure" that Omar spent two years "somewhere" in Afghanistan "sometime" in the years 1998 to 2000. Why is this information ambiguous?

9.6.   We believe the person shown in a photograph is P. However, the figure is blurred. Why is this evidence ambiguous?

9.7.   A radar image shows the possibility of *one or more* aircraft at a certain location. Why is this evidence ambiguous?

9.8.   An observer tells us that he saw a tall man with very dark hair driving away in an old car from the sight of a terrorist incident shortly after it occurred. Why is this evidence ambiguous?

9.9.   From your own experience, can you recall other items of ambiguous evidence you have received?

9.10.   However credible you believe a person might be, you also must give consideration to this person's competence. Provide an example of a credible source which is not believable.

9.11.   How does intelligence analysis differ from evidential analyses in law trials as far as the completeness of evidence is concerned?

9.12.   Can you think of instances in which you might say you have conclusive evidence when this is actually not correct?

9.13.   What are some causes that make evidence ambiguous, and how does ambiguity differ from inconclusiveness?

9.14.   Show how evidential dissonance and selectivity are related in ways that can be inferentially hazardous.

9.15.   It can be argued that of all the inferential issues involved in intelligence analysis, the most important and interesting ones involve the *believability* of evidence and its sources. Give some reasons why this is so.

9.16.   The veracity, objectivity, and observational sensitivity need to be considered for all of the human sources in our dirty bomb example. Pick a human source in this example and state what kinds of questions you would ask about the veracity, objectivity, and observational sensitivity of the person you have chosen.

9.17.   Consider E008-GuardReport and other items of tangible evidence in Table 5.2 (p. 96). What kind of questions would you ask about these tangible items?

10 Assessing and Reporting Uncertainty: Some Alternative Methods

10.1 INTRODUCTION

We have now considered the major sources of uncertainty related to evidence and have shown how uncertainty arises in chains of reasoning linking evidence to hypotheses we entertain. A major credential of evidence we have only mentioned briefly is its *inferential force or weight*. As we noted, this credential is always expressed in probabilistic terms but is a source of great controversy. In Figure 4.6 (p. 73), we showed how the force or weight of evidence concerns the strength of all the believability and relevance links in our chains of reasoning. But this illustration concerns the chains of reasoning from just few items of evidence. In any intelligence analysis, there will be many items of evidence to consider and very many sources of uncertainty or doubt that will be associated with complex arguments linking this mass of evidence to hypotheses at issue in the analysis. It would not be uncommon to be able to identify hundreds or even thousands of sources of doubt arising from masses of evidence being considered.

There are other matters apart from assessing the force or weight of evidence in which uncertainty arises. One way of describing evidence-based reasoning is to say that it involves the *revision* of probabilistic beliefs about hypotheses based on the evidence we have obtained. To say that we are revising these beliefs suggests that they must have had some initial state in order for them to be revised. The term *prior probability* is used to indicate the initial conditions of our uncertainty before we consider evidence that begins to emerge. In truth, there has been considerable controversy about prior probabilities and how they can be assessed. When we consider our evidence and its force or weight, we can begin the process of revising these prior beliefs based upon evidence. In the process, we revise our prior beliefs to form what are usually termed *posterior beliefs*, those assessed after we receive and incorporate the evidence we have. But we must take a bit of care concerning the process of belief revision just described.

In the process of discovery or investigation in intelligence analysis and elsewhere, we may have evidence in search of hypotheses and hypotheses in search of evidence all going on at the same time, as discussed in Section 1.3. In other words, it would be quite wrong to suggest that an intelligence analysis always begins with a complete set of hypotheses having been identified. The generation of hypotheses rests on potential evidence we begin to accumulate. Further evidence may suggest new hypotheses or revisions in ones we have generated. In short, evidence not only causes revisions in our probabilistic beliefs about a collection of hypotheses, but it also causes mutations or changes in this collection itself. How this probabilistic belief-revision process proceeds and what its major ingredients are depend vitally upon our view of probability and uncertainty. In the following sections, we consider different probability systems.

10.2   GENERAL CLASSES OF PROBABILITY AND UNCERTAINTY

A major trouble we all face in thinking about probability and uncertainty concerns the fact that the necessity for probability calculations, estimations, or judgments arises in different situations. In addition, there are many different attributes of our judgments that we would like to capture in assessments of uncertainty we are obliged to make. As we will see, there are some forms of intelligence analyses, or at least parts of them, in which you can estimate probabilities of interest by counting things. But there are many other situations in which analysts have uncertainty but will have nothing to count. These situations involve events that are singular, unique, or one-of-a-kind. We start with Table 10.1, which categorizes the alternative views of probability we will discuss as we proceed.

We begin by discussing two views of probability that involve processes in which we can obtain probabilities or estimates of them by enumerative or counting processes.

10.3   ENUMERATIVE PROBABILITIES: OBTAINED BY COUNTING

There are two conceptions of probability that involve counting operations. The first is termed *aleatory probability*. This term has its roots in the Latin term *alea,* meaning chance, game of chance, or devices such as dice involved in games of chance. Games of chance have two important ground rules:

- There is a finite number n(S) of possible outcomes.
- All outcomes in S are assumed to have equal probability.

For example, in a game involving a pair of fair six-sided dice, where we roll and add the two numbers showing up, there are thirty-six ways in which the numbers showing up will have sums between 2 and 12, inclusive. So, in this case, n(S) = 36. Suppose you wish to determine the probability that you will roll a 7 on a single throw of these dice. There are exactly six ways in which this can happen. If E = "the sum of the numbers is 7," then n(E) = 6. The probability of E, P(E), is simply determined by dividing n(E) by n(S), which in this example is P(E) = 6/36 = 1/6. So, aleatory probabilities are always determined by dividing n(E) by n(S), whatever E and S are, as long as E is a subset of S.

Table 10.1 Some Alternative Views of Probability

Enumerative	Nonenumerative
Aleatory (Chances)	Epistemic (1): Subjective Bayesian
Relative Frequency and Statistics	Epistemic (2): Belief Functions
Bayesian Statistics (under debate)	Baconian: Eliminative and Variative Inference
	Imprecision and Fuzzy Probability

We can dismiss aleatory probability as not being interesting in intelligence analysis since there seem to be no instances in which the two aleatory ground rules will apply. However, we should note that there are frequent instances in which analysts may use the term "chance" when it may not be appropriate. For example, suppose that an analyst says, "The *chances* are nine in ten (probability equals 0.9) that country Green is supplying arms to insurgents in country Orange." This judgment cannot have arisen by any counting operation in which the two ground rules for aleatory probabilities apply. One rather unfortunate occurrence is that most people are initially introduced to probability theory by use of games of chance to illustrate various concepts. People then often believe that these concepts occur and retain the same meaning when they are used in entirely different contexts in which uncertainty assessments are required.

The second way of assessing probabilities involves the many situations in which aleatory ground rules will not apply but where we do have empirical methods at hand to estimate probabilities. These situations arise when we have *replicable* or *repeatable* processes in which we can count the number of times events have occurred in the past. Suppose that, employing a defensible method for gathering information about the number of times event E has occurred, we determine the *relative frequency* of an occurrence of E by counting the number of times E has occurred, $n(E)$ and then dividing this number by N, where N is the number of observations we have made, or the sample size we have taken. In this case, the relative frequency of E, $f(E)$, equals $n(E)/N$. You recognize that this is a *statistical process* that can be performed in many situations, provided that we assume processes that are replicable or repeatable. It is true, of course, that a relative frequency $f(E)$ is just an estimate of the true probability of E, $P(E)$. The reason, of course, is that the number N of observations we have made is always less than the total number of observations that could be made. In some cases, there may be an infinite number of possible observations. If you have had a course in probability theory, you will remember that there are several formal statements, called the *laws of large numbers*, for showing how $f(E)$ approaches $P(E)$ when N is made larger and larger.

Probability theory presents an interesting paradox. It has a very long history, but a very short past. There is abundant evidence that people as far back as Paleolithic times used objects resembling dice either for gambling or, more likely, to foretell the future (David, 1962). But attempts to calculate probabilities date back only to the 1600s, and the first attempt to develop a theory of mathematical probability dates back only to 1933 in the work of Russian A. N. Kolmogorov (1956). Kolmogorov was the first to put probability on an axiomatic basis. The three basic axioms he proposed are the following:

Axiom 1: *For any event E, $P(E) \geq 0$.*
Axiom 2: *If an event is sure or certain to occur, which we label S, $P(S) = 1.0$.*
Axiom 3: *If two events, E and F, cannot occur together, or are mutually exclusive, the probability that one or the other of these events occurring is the sum of their separate probabilities. In symbols, $P(E \text{ or } F) = P(E) + P(F)$.*

All Axiom 1 says is that probabilities are never negative. Axioms 1 and 2, taken together, mean that probabilities are numbers between 0 and 1. An event having 0 probability is commonly called an "impossible event." Axiom 3 is called the *additivity* axiom, and it holds for any number of mutually exclusive events.

Certain transformations of Kolmogorov's probabilities are entirely permissible and are often used. One common form involves *odds*. The odds of event E occurring to its not occurring (written as E^C), which we label Odds(E, E^C), is determined by Odds(E, E^C) = $P(E)/P(E^C)$ = P(E)/(1 - P(E)). For any two mutually exclusive events E and F, the odds of E to F, Odds(E, F), are given by Odds(E, F) = P(E)/P(F). Numerical odds scales range from zero to an unlimited upper value. The person who said the chances that country Green is supplying weapons to insurgents in country Orange is nine in ten might better have said that the odds favoring Green supplying the weapons, to their not supplying weapons, are nine to one.

What is very interesting, but not always recognized, is that Kolmogorov had only enumerative probability in mind when he settled on the preceding three axioms. He makes this clear in his 1933 book and in his later writings (Kolmogorov, 1969). It is easily shown that both aleatory probabilities and relative frequencies obey these three axioms. But Kolmogorov went an important step further in defining conditional probabilities that are necessary to show how the probability of an event may change as we learn new information. He defined the probability of event E, given or conditional upon some other event F, as P(E given F) = P(E and F)/P(F), assuming that P(F) is not zero. P(E given F) is also written as P(E|F). He chose this particular definition since conditional probabilities, so defined, will also obey the three axioms just mentioned. In other words, we do not need any new axioms for conditional probabilities.

Now comes a very important concept you may have heard about. It is called *Bayes' rule* and results directly from applying the definition of the conditional probability. From P(E* and H) = P(H and E*), you obtain the following:

P(E*|H) P(H) = P(H|E*)P(E*)

This can then be written as shown in Figure 10.1.

This rule is named after the English clergyman, the Reverend Thomas Bayes (1702–1761), who first saw the essentials of a rule for revising probabilities of hypotheses, based on new evidence (Dale, 2003). He had written a paper describing his derivation and use of this rule, but he never published it; this paper was found in his desk after he died in 1761 by Richard Price, the executor of Bayes' will. Price realized the importance of Bayes' paper and recommended it for publication in the *Transactions of the Royal Society*, in which it appeared in 1763. He rightly viewed Bayes' rule as the first canon or rule for inductive or probabilistic reasoning. Bayes' rule follows directly from Kolmogorov's three axioms and his definition of a conditional probability, and is entirely uncontroversial as far as its derivation is concerned. But this rule has always been a source of controversy on other grounds. The reason is that it requires us to say how probable a hypothesis is before we have gathered evidence that will possibly allow us to revise this probability. In short, we

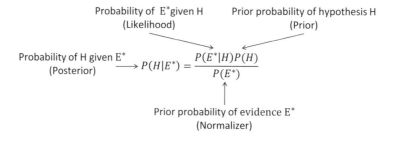

Figure 10.1. The Bayes' rule.

need *prior probabilities* on hypotheses in order to revise them, when they become *posterior probabilities*. Persons wedded to enumerative conceptions of probability say we can never have prior probabilities of hypotheses since, in advance of data collection, we have nothing to count. Statisticians are still divided today about whether it makes sense to use Bayes' rule in statistical inferences. This is why we have put "under debate" after "Bayesian Statistics" in Table 10.1. Some statisticians argue that initial prior probabilities could only be assessed subjectively and that any subjective assessments have no place in any area that calls itself scientific. Bayes' rule says that if we are to talk about probability *revisions* in our beliefs, based on evidence, we have to say where these beliefs were *before* we obtained the evidence.

It is time for us to consider views of probability in situations where we will have nothing to count, either a priori or anywhere else.

10.4   NONENUMERATIVE PROBABILITIES: NOTHING TO COUNT

Intelligence analysts will encounter works by some individuals who will argue that the term *probability* is applicable only to the enumerative situations just described in the preceding section. In short, we are always out of luck applying Bayes' rule because of its requirement for subjective prior probabilities; and we are especially out of luck applying probabilities in situations in which the events of concern are singular, unique, or one-of-a-kind, and so we have nothing to count. However, some probabilists argue that subjective judgments are always necessary and that we can assess numerical probabilities provided that they obey the Kolmogorov axioms just described. We will also mention the views of probabilists, who argue that not all of the Kolmogorov axioms make sense for subjective judgments of singular or unique events. They can point to the basic sources of uncertainty we listed in Chapter 9 and argue that probabilities enumerated or judged in accordance with the Kolmogorov axioms cannot capture all of these sources of uncertainty. There are alternative methods for expressing uncertainty that do capture some of these sources but do not rest on the Kolmogorov axioms or his definition of a conditional probability. What follows is a brief account of the essentials for four quite different views of uncertainty assessments: the *subjective Bayesian* view, *Belief functions*, *Baconian probabilities*, and *Fuzzy probabilities*. We can provide a look at only the essentials of these four views. More extensive comparisons of these four views appear in Schum (1994 [2001a], pp. 200–269). In restricting our presentation to only the essentials, we have chosen to focus on what each one has to tell us about what the force or weight of evidence means. Remember that it is in the process of assessing the force or weight of evidence that uncertainties concerning evidence are first expressed.

10.5   EPISTEMIC PROBABILITY (1): THE SUBJECTIVE BAYESIAN VIEW

We refer to our first non-enumerative view as an *epistemic view*, since it assumes that probabilities in any case are based on some kind of knowledge, *whatever form it may take*. In short, probabilities are the result of informed judgments.

10.5.1   Likelihood Ratios

10.5.1.1 Analysis Using Likelihood Ratios

Many statisticians now favor the use of Bayes' rule in enumerative or frequentistic situations and have no objection to subjective assessments of prior probabilities. Bayes' rule requires the assessment of two basic probabilistic ingredients: *prior probabilities* on hypotheses, and *likelihoods or their ratios*. As we will illustrate, it is these likelihoods and their ratios that are the ingredients of Bayes' rule that concern the inferential force of evidence. Furthermore, many persons favor the use of Bayes' rule for combining subjective assessments of all the prior and likelihood ingredients of Bayes' rule. *But what these persons require is that these assessments be entirely consistent with Kolmogorov's three axioms and his definition of conditional probabilities we noted previously.* Since Bayes' rule rests on these axioms and definition, we must adhere to them in order to say that our assessment process is coherent or consistent.

Here is a simple explanation of how ratios of likelihoods express the force of evidence in Bayes' rule. Suppose we have two hypotheses, H and H^c (the complement of H, i.e., *notH*), and a single item of evidence E^* saying that event E occurred. What we are interested in determining are the posterior probabilities: $P(H|E^*)$ and $P(H^c|E^*)$. Using the Bayes' rule from Figure 10.1, we can express these posterior probabilities as:

$$P(H|E^*) = \frac{P(E^*|H)P(H)}{P(E^*)}$$

$$P(H^c|E^*) = \frac{P(E^*|H^c)P(H^c)}{P(E^*)}$$

The next step is to divide $P(H|E^*)$ by $P(H^c|E^*)$, which produces three ratios; in the process, the term $P(E^*)$ will drop out. Here are the three ratios that result:

$$\frac{P(H|E^*)}{P(H^c|E^*)} = \frac{P(H)}{P(H^c)}\frac{P(E^*|H)}{P(E^*|H^c)}$$

The left-hand ratio $\frac{P(H|E^*)}{P(H^c|E^*)}$ is called the *posterior odds* of H to H^c, given evidence E^*. In symbols, we can express this ratio as: $Odds(H : H^c|E^*)$. The first ratio on the right, $\frac{P(H)}{P(H^c)}$, is called the *prior odds* of H to H^c. In symbols, we can express this ratio as: $Odds(H : H^c)$. The remaining ratio on the right, $\frac{P(E^*|H)}{P(E^*|H^c)}$, is called the *likelihood ratio* for evidence E^*; we give this ratio the symbol L_{E^*}. In terms of these three ratios, Bayes' rule applied to this situation can be written simply as:

$$Odds(H : H^c|E^*) = Odds(H : H^c)L_{E^*}$$

This simple version of Bayes' rule is called the *odds-likelihood ratio* form. It is also called, somewhat unkindly, "idiots" Bayes. If we divide both sides of this equation by the prior odds, $Odds(H : H^c)$, we observe that the likelihood ratio L_{E^*} is simply the ratio of posterior odds to prior odds of H to H^c. This likelihood ratio shows us how much, and in what direction (toward H or H^c), our evidence E^* has caused us to change our beliefs toward H or toward H^c from what they were before we obtained evidence E^*. In short, likelihood ratios grade the force of evidence in Bayesian analyses. But this is the simplest case possible. Likelihood ratios become much more complex when we attempt to show how relevant E^* is to H and H^c and to capture the believability of the source of evidence E^*.

10.5.1.2 Examples

Example 10.1.

Here is an example of how likelihoods and their ratios provide a method for grading the Bayesian force of an item of evidence. This is an example of a situation involving a singular evidence item where we have nothing to count. Suppose you are an analyst whose interest concerns whether or not the Greens are supplying parts necessary for the construction of shaped explosive devices to a certain insurgent militia group in the neighboring country Orange. Thus you are entertaining the following binary hypotheses:

- H: The Greens are supplying parts necessary for the construction of shaped explosive devices.
- H^c: The Greens are not supplying parts necessary for the construction of shaped explosive devices.

Suppose you believe, before you have any evidence, that the prior probability of H is $P(H) = 0.20$. Because you must obey the rules for enumerative probabilities, you must also say that $P(H^c) = 0.80$. This follows from the third axiom we discussed in Section 10.3. So, your prior odds on H relative to H^c have a value of $Odds_0 = \frac{P(H)}{P(H^c)} = \frac{0.20}{0.80} = \frac{1}{4}$.

Your first item of evidence, E_1^*, is a report that a member of the Green's military was captured less than one kilometer away from a location in Orange at which parts necessary for the construction of these shaped explosives were found. You ask yourself how likely is this evidence E_1^* if H were true, and how likely is this evidence E_1^* if H were not true. Suppose you say that $P(E_1^*|H) = 0.80$ and $P(E_1^*|H^c) = 0.10$. You are saying that this evidence is eight times more likely if H were true than if H were not true. So, your likelihood ratio $L_{E_1^*} = \frac{P(E_1^*|H)}{P(E_1^*|H^c)} = \frac{0.8}{0.1} = 8$. You now have all the ingredients necessary in Bayes' rule to determine the posterior odds $Odds_1 = \frac{P(E_1^*|H)}{P(E_1^*|H^c)}$ and the posterior probability of hypothesis H, $P(H|E_1^*)$. In this case:

$$Odds_1 = Odds_0 \times L_{E_1^*} = \frac{1}{4} \times 8 = 2.$$

This means that you now believe the posterior odds favoring H over H^c are two to one. But you started by believing that the prior odds of H to H^c were one in four, so the evidence E_1^* changed your belief by a factor of eight, which is just what $L_{E_1^*}$ says. As we have noted, the ingredient in Bayes' rule that indicates the force or weight of evidence is represented by likelihood ratios.

When we have just one hypothesis together with its complement, we can easily convert odds to probabilities using the familiar rule: $Probability = \frac{Odds}{1+Odds}$. This rule follows from the fact that we have defined $Odds$ to be $\frac{P(H)}{P(H^c)} = \frac{P(H)}{1-P(H)}$.

Suppose we wish to determine the posterior probability $P(H|E_1^*)$ from $Odds_1$. In this case, we have $(H|E_1^*) = \frac{Odds_1}{1+Odds_1} = \frac{2}{1+2} = \frac{2}{3} = 0.67$. So, in terms of probabilities, evidence E_1^* caused you to increase the probability of H by 0.47 (from 0.2 to 0.67).

There are various difficulties associated with grading the Bayesian force of evidence in terms of the difference between prior and posterior probabilities. The next example shows what the difficulties are.

Example 10.2.

Suppose a critic argues that your assessment of the prior probability of H was foolishly low; she argues that the prior probability of H is more like $P(H) = 0.75$. So her prior odds are $Odds_0 = \frac{0.75}{0.25} = 3$. But she agrees entirely with your assessment of the likelihood ratio of E_1^* being $L_{E_1^*} = 8$. From Bayes rule we now have:

$$Odds_1 = Odds_0 \times L_{E_1^*} = 3 \times 8 = 24$$

Notice first that the ratio of posterior to prior odds is still 8:1. But now consider the posterior probability of H; it is $P(H|E_1^*) = \frac{24}{1+24} = 0.96$. So the difference between her posterior and prior probabilities is now just $0.96 - 0.75 = 0.21$, a much smaller difference than it was using your prior probabilities. But the ratio of posterior odds to prior odds remains the same in her case and in yours, that is, her posterior to prior odds ratio is $\frac{24}{3} = 8$. The likelihood ratio indicates the same force in both situations when the problem is construed in odds. This is the major reason why the odds-likelihood ratio form of Bayes' rule is so helpful and informative about what the force or weight of evidence means in Bayesian terms.

But you have only one item of evidence so far; what happens when you have additional items of evidence? Suppose you now have a new item of evidence that we label E_2^*. How do you combine this new evidence to revise or update your posterior $Odds_1$, based on this new item of evidence? Suppose this new item of evidence E_2^* is a report that a fragment of a shaped explosive device was found on a road leading to the Sand City, Orange. This fragment carries a serial number that we learn identifies this device as having been made in a munitions factory outside the capital of Green. To illustrate how Bayes' rule allows us to combine our uncertainties based on new evidence, we must take a short detour to illustrate a most important concept in the Bayesian view of evidence-based reasoning: *conditional dependence* or *conditional nonindependence*. This concept allows us to capture an amazing array of complexities or subtleties in evidence. Here is a brief account of conditional dependence.

The probabilistic independence of two events A and B means that P(A|B) = P(A), or equivalently that P(B|A) = P(B). That is, the occurrence of B has no influence on the probability of A, and vice versa. Events A and B are then nonindependent if these equations do not apply. But there are many situations in which the independence of two events depends on some other event, say event C. It might be the case that events A and B are independent only if C is true, in which case we can say that P(A|BC) = P(A|C). This equality implies a product rule for conditional probabilities. If P(A|BC) = P(A|C), this also means that P(AB|C) = P(A|C)P(B|C). Either expression says that A and B are independent, given event C. Now, what is of interest are situations in which A and B are *not independent*, given event C. In this case, we have P(AB|C) ≠ P(A|C)P(B|C). This is a probabilistic expression of the fact that considering two events jointly in light of event C, as we do in considering P(AB|C), means something different than they would mean if we considered them independently or separately as we do in considering P(A|C) and P(B|C).

We now give an example of the importance of conditional dependence. Suppose we have evidence for events A and B. In symbols, we have evidence items A* and B*. These two items are *synergistic* in nature, given event C, if P(A*B*|C) > P(A*|C)P(B*|C). This means that these two items have greater probability, given C and when taken together, than they would have if we considered them separately or independently, given event C. What is interesting is that when P(A*B*|C) > P(A*|C)P(B*|C), this also means that P(B*|A*C) > P(B*|C). What this means is that B* has greater probability, given C, when we also consider A*, than it would have if we did not consider A*.

We now turn again to your inference concerning whether the Greens are supplying shaped explosive devices to insurgent groups in Orange. So far, you have determined the posterior odds

$$Odds_1 = Odds_0 \times L_{E_1^*} = \frac{1}{4} \times 8 = 2.$$

But now you have the new evidence E_2^* saying that a fragment of a shaped explosive device found on a road near the Sand City in Orange carried a serial number that identifies this device having been made in a munitions factory outside the capital of Green. The question is, how do you combine evidence items E_1^* and E_2^* together in Bayes' rule?

What we must now do is to describe the *recursive* nature of Bayes' rule. What this says is that our new posterior odds, $Odds_2$, depends on our old posterior odds, $Odds_1$. One way of saying this is to say that yesterday's posterior odds become today's prior odds in light of today's new evidence. In short, we never begin from scratch with each new item of evidence but incorporate old evidence with new evidence. The first thing we must do is to carefully define our new posterior odds, $Odds_2$. We now have two items of evidence, so $Odds_2 = \frac{P(H|E_1^*E_2^*)}{P(H^c|E_1^*E_2^*)}$. When we decompose these two conditional probabilities using the rules provided previously, we obtain:

$$Odds_2 = \frac{P(H|E_1^*E_2^*)}{P(H^c|E_1^*E_2^*)} = \frac{P(H)}{P(H^c)} \frac{P(E_1^*|H)}{P(E_1^*|H^c)} \frac{P(E_2^*|E_1^*H)}{P(E_2^*|E_1^*H^c)}$$

The first thing to notice is that the first two ratios on the right-hand side of this equation form the old posterior odds, $Odds_1$ that just concerns E_1^*, our first item of evidence. This illustrates the recursive nature of Bayes' rule. The posterior odds for the first item of evidence become the prior odds in determining the posterior odds for the combined evidence E_1^* and E_2^*.

But now we come to the most interesting ingredient of Bayes' rule, it concerns the likelihood ratio $\frac{P(E_2^*|E_1^*H)}{P(E_2^*|E_1^*H^c)}$. Here is where our discussion of conditional independence and dependence becomes so important. What Bayes' rule requires us to answer is whether E_1^* and E_2^* are independent, given H and given H^c. Another way of posing this question is to ask, "Does the force of evidence E_2^* on H and H^c depend on our first item of evidence, E_1^*?" Suppose that E_1^* acts to increase the probability of E_2^*, given H, and also acts to decrease the probability of E_2^*, given H^c. In this case, our two evidence items would be synergistic in their effects; taken together, they point more strongly toward H than they would do if they were considered separately or independently. If they were independent under both H and H^c, then we would have $\frac{P(E_2^*|E_1^*H)}{P(E_2^*|E_1^*H^c)} = \frac{P(E_2^*|H)}{P(E_2^*|H^c)}$.

Here are two examples illustrating matters we just discussed concerning what Bayes' rule requires concerning the combination of evidence.

Example 10.3.

Suppose in the example involving whether the Greens are supplying shaped explosive devices to the insurgents in Orange, our analyst first decides that there's no connection between E_1^* and E_2^*, as defined previously. He says to himself, "I don't see the connection between a Green being found a kilometer away from a shaped explosive device and a fragment of another such device bearing a number showing that the device was made in some factory no one ever heard of in Green. So, I am going to judge $P(E_2^*|H) = 0.6$ and $P(E_2^*|H^c) = 0.2$. My reasoning here is that the Oranges could have purchased the parts for this device from some other country that had purchased these parts from Green. So, the Oranges made this device themselves." So now we can use these likelihood assessments for evidence E_2^* and determine

$$Odds_2 = Odds_0 \times L_{E_1^*} \times L_{E_2^*} = \frac{1}{4} \times 8 \times 3 = 6.$$

In this case, the analyst is saying that the posterior probability of H, given E_1^* and E_2^*, is $\frac{6}{1+6} = 0.86$.

Example 10.4.

Our critic appears again, and this time she argues strongly that E_1^* and E_2^* are not at all independent given either H or H^c. She says, "I can't believe you don't see any connection between E_2^* and E_1^*. If there was a member of the Green military just a short distance from where a shaped explosive device was found, does this not suggest to you that we will eventually find some of these devices that can be identified as having been made in Green, which we have just discovered in E_2^*? I'm going to judge $P(E_2^*|E_1^*H) = 0.90$ and $P(E_2^*|E_1^*H^c) = 0.05$. Now, let's see what Bayes' rule says your posterior odds and probability should be using my assessments." So we calculate:

$$Odds_2 = Odds_0 \times L_{E_1^*} \times L_{E_2^*} = \frac{1}{4} \times 8 \times 18 = 36.$$

In this case, the posterior probability of H, given E_1^* and E_2^*, is $\frac{36}{37} = 0.97$. What the critic has done is to say that because of the conditional dependence of E_1^* and E_2^*, given H and given H^c, E_2^* has six times as much force or weight when we consider E_1^* than it would have if we did not consider E_1^*.

Whose view of the weight of evidence in the preceding two examples makes the most sense to you? Only you can answer this question.

These examples using "idiots" Bayes are simple because we have not constructed any arguments showing the believability of E_1^* and E_2^* and showing their relevance on our hypotheses H and H^c. This is where matters become very complex indeed. The next section discusses the use of Bayesian networks to perform such analyses.

10.5.2 Bayesian Networks

A variety of software systems, referred to as Bayesian networks systems, have been designed to perform probabilistic analyses in complex inference networks, such as those discussed in the previous sections of this book. To illustrate the use of Bayesian networks for evidence-based hypothesis analysis, let us consider the hypothesis, "The cesium-137 canister is missing from the XYZ warehouse," analyzed with Disciple-CD in Section 3.5. We are going to analyze this hypothesis using a Bayesian network.

10.5.2.1 Constructing the Argument Structure

Bayesian network analysis goes from the top down, from hypotheses to evidence. Following are the steps necessary in constructing a Bayesian network analysis.

> **Step 1**: Construct the chain of questions or the argument structure to be analyzed. In this case, we are using the argumentation from Figure 1.10 (p. 21), resulting in the Bayesian network from Figure 10.2.

10.5.2.2 Forming the Key List

> **Step 2:** Form the key list for the chart in Figure 10.2 to identify its ingredients, as shown in Table 10.2. Notice that we designate the items of evidence by D*, E*, F*, G*, and the events described by these items of evidence as D, E, F, G, respectively. But just because evidence D*, for example, says that the event D has happened, that does not mean that D has actually happened. At issues here is the believability of the source of that item of evidence. Therefore, we have to consider both the event D and its negation or complement D^c. Notice that we must describe an event (e.g., A) and its complement (i.e., A^c) at all stages above the evidence. This is necessary for probabilistic analyses.

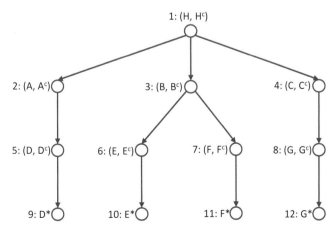

Figure 10.2. Bayesian network for the hypothesis H: "The cesium-137 canister is missing from the XYZ warehouse."

Table 10.2 Key List for Figure 10.2

1: H = The cesium-137 canister is missing from the XYZ warehouse.

H^C = The cesium-137 canister is not missing from the XYZ warehouse.

2: A = The cesium-137 canister was in the XYZ warehouse before being reported as missing.

A^C = The cesium-137 canister was not in the XYZ warehouse before being reported as missing.

3: B = The cesium-137 canister is no longer in the XYZ warehouse.

B^C = The cesium-137 canister is still in the XYZ warehouse.

4: C = No one has checked out the cesium-137 canister from the XYZ warehouse.

C^C = Someone has checked out the cesium-137 canister from the XYZ warehouse.

5: D = The cesium-137 canister is registered as being in the XYZ warehouse.

D^C = The cesium-137 canister is not registered as being in the XYZ warehouse.

6: E = A canister containing cesium-137 was missing from the XYZ warehouse in Baltimore, MD.

E^C = A canister containing cesium-137 was not missing from the XYZ warehouse in Baltimore, MD.

7: F = The cesium-137 canister is not located anywhere in the hazardous materials locker.

F^C = The cesium-137 canister is located somewhere in the hazardous materials locker.

8: G = No one at the XYZ Company had checked out the cesium-137 canister.

G^C = Someone at the XYZ Company had checked out the cesium-137 canister.

9: D* = E002-Ralph testimony to D in 5.

10: E* = E001-Willard testimony to E in 6.

11: F* = E004-Ralph testimony to F in 7.

12: G* = E003-Ralph testimony to G in 8.

Finally, notice that the construction of our network chart and its accompanying key list proceeds concurrently. In other words, we must say what all the ingredients of our chart mean when we are constructing it. Our inference network contains various lines of argument linking our evidence to hypotheses we are considering. This task involves imaginative reasoning as we have discussed in Section 1.2. Our Bayesian network system cannot perform this imaginative reasoning as we will note in a minute.

10.5.2.3 Identifying the Likelihoods and Prior Probabilities

Step 3. The next step is to identify the probabilities that Bayes' rule says are required in the network as constructed. These are listed in Table 10.3 and explained in the following.

The first thing to note here is that Bayes' rule requires two basic forms of probabilistic ingredients: *priors* and *likelihoods*. The ones listed in Table 10.3 are particular to the inference network shown in Figure 10.2. Look again at this network and first observe that

Table 10.3 Required Probabilities for the Bayesian Network in Figure 10.2 (Assuming No Conditional Dependencies)

1: $P(H)$, $P(H^C)$. Priors

2: $P(A|H)$, $P(A|H^C)$. Likelihoods.

3: $P(B|H)$, $P(B|H^C)$. Likelihoods.

4: $P(C|H)$, $P(C|H^C)$. Likelihoods.

5: $P(D|A)$, $P(D|A^C)$. Likelihoods.

6: $P(E|B)$, $P(E|B^C)$. Likelihoods.

7: $P(F|B)$, $P(F|B^C)$. Likelihoods.

8: $P(G|C)$, $P(G|C^C)$. Likelihoods.

9: $P(D^*|D)$ = Ralph's *Hit* probability in reporting D (also likelihood, but related to Ralph's believability).

   $P(D^*|D^C)$ = Ralph's *False Positive* probability in reporting D(also likelihood, but related to Ralph's believability).

10: $P(E^*|E)$ = Willard's *Hit* probability in reporting E (also likelihood, but related to Willard's believability).

   $P(E^*|E^C)$ = Willard's *False Positive* probability in reporting E (also likelihood, but related to Willard's believability).

11: $P(F^*|F)$ = Ralph's *Hit* probability in reporting F (also likelihood, but related to Ralph's believability).

   $P(F^*|F^C)$ = Ralph's *False Positive* probability in reporting F (also likelihood, but related to Ralph's believability).

12: $P(G^*|G)$ = Ralph's *Hit* probability in reporting G (also likelihood, but related to Ralph's believability).

   $P(G^*|G^C)$ = Ralph's *False Positive* probability in reporting G (also likelihood, but related to Ralph's believability).

the top-level node 1 contains our major question in the form of hypotheses: H and H^C. The question is, "Is the cesium-137 canister missing from the XYZ warehouse?" The two possible answers are yes (H) and no (H^C). Then notice that this node contains no parents above it. What this means is that, in our network as shown, there are no questions or sources of influence on our basic hypotheses. Actually, there are, but we have not included them to make this example simple. There being no sources of influence on H and H^C means that we must assign prior probabilities to the hypotheses at this node, indicating the strength of our beliefs in them before we consider any evidence relevant to them.

All the other ingredients, called likelihoods, allow us to assess the strength of our arguments on these questions or hypotheses based on the evidence we have. What we are trying to determine are the *posterior probabilities* of H and H^C, based on the four items of evidence we have. The bottom four pairs of likelihoods shown in Table 10.3 concern the believability of the sources (Ralph and Willard) of the four items of evidence we have. In any inference network, believability considerations always form the basic foundations of our arguments. What Bayes' rule shows us is how to combine all these prior and likelihood ingredients in order to determine the posterior probabilities of H an H^C, based on the evidence we have.

Here's a problem associated with computer-assisted Bayesian network analyses regardless of the software system you are using. We cannot show you the exact equations the computer is using to calculate posterior probabilities for H and H^C, under various conditions. The reason is that the equations are always buried below the surface and the computer does not reveal them to us. So we have to be confident that the computer knows which equations to use under various conditions that we specify. Being unable to see the exact equations being used often causes difficulties for us as we try to explain the results of our Bayesian network calculations.

Given an inference network structure such as the one we are considering, our Bayesian network system will tell us what probabilities we need in order for us to determine posterior probabilities for major questions or hypotheses on this network, based on the evidence we have. No Bayesian network system will tell us how to ask these questions or construct this network. Remember that the construction of an inference network is an imaginative reasoning task followed by critical reasoning in which we evaluate the logical consistency of the arguments we have constructed on this network. The network we have constructed has a hierarchical structure. The top-level question at node 1 suggests three questions at the next lower level. Then these three second-tier questions suggest one or more questions at the third tier that can be answered by the four items of evidence at the bottom.

Notice that we could have made the network in Figure 10.2 more complex by adding additional links having the following very general meaning. Basically, we have to ask whether the answers we could get to one question influence the probability of getting answers to a different question. Here's an example. Suppose the answer to the question at node 2 is A: "The cesium-137 canister was in the XYZ warehouse before being reported as missing." If so, then we also ought to ask whether the occurrence of this event would influence the probability of answers, B and B^C, at node 3. Specifically, if the answer is A ("The cesium-137 canister was in the XYZ warehouse before being reported as missing"), does this make the answer to B, "The cesium-137 canister is no longer in the XYZ warehouse," more or less likely? In other words, are the questions we are asking dependent in various ways?

What we have not done in constructing this network is to include what are termed *conditional dependencies* (also called *conditional nonindependencies*). The existence of conditional dependencies allows us to capture a wide assortment of evidential and inferential subtleties or complexities in a probabilistic analysis. Here is a very brief description of what conditional dependence involves. First, at a very basic level, two or more events taken together may mean something quite different from what they would if considered separately or independently. Second, if the first is true, there is an equivalent statement we could make. The second of two events means something different if we took the first event into account than it would if we failed to take the first event into account. Following is an example illustrating conditional dependence of the events we have just considered.

Here is our basic question or hypothesis: H = "The cesium-137 canister is missing from the XYZ warehouse." Two events relevant to inferences about H are: A = "The cesium-137 canister was in the XYZ warehouse before being reported as missing"; and B = "The cesium-137 canister is no longer in the XYZ warehouse." Here's the issue we could address, "Are events A and B more or less forceful in inferences about H if we took them together or jointly than they would be if we considered them separately or independently?" If A and B mean more in inferring H if we took A and B together, we would say that A and B are dependent, conditional on H. To capture this dependence involving A and B, we would draw an arc or arrow linking nodes 2 and 3 in the network from Figure 10.2.

If we did so, our Bayesian network system would recognize this and inform us about the new and additional probabilistic assessments we must make. As you see, there are other such dependence linkages we might consider, such as the ones between nodes 3 and 4 and between 6 and 7. The topic of conditional dependence is complex but very important in Bayesian analyses of any sort and requires careful study by anyone contemplating such analyses. This is one of the high points about Bayesian analyses: They can capture a wide assortment of evidential complexities or subtleties, more than any other probabilistic system. For more on conditional dependencies, see Chapter 7 in Schum (1994 [2001a]).

10.5.2.4 Using the Bayesian Network

Step 4. This fourth step involves putting a Bayesian network analysis to work in the probabilistic hedging of conclusions regarding inferences about our major hypotheses. As we have discussed, given an inference network structure such as the one for Figure 10.2, a Bayesian network system will show us what probabilities we must assess in order to calculate posterior probabilities for hypotheses of interest. We might say first that the network structure defines the major plot of stories we can tell about the inference of concern to us. When we assess the probabilities that Bayes' rule says are required, we breathe life into our story plot and consider the "actors" in this story and their roles in it. By "actors," we mean the events of concern in our inference task. Of course, we can give the actors different identities depending on the probabilities we assign to them. This can be done in an unlimited number of ways and so we can tell an unlimited number of different stories about the same inference network. But, once we have decided upon a specific set of probabilities for the actors in a story, a calculation involving Bayes' rule tells us how this story ends in terms of the posterior probabilities for hypotheses of interest. In the following, we will tell five different stories about the Figure 10.2 network and offer an explanation of them. In doing so, we are essentially performing what is called a *sensitivity analysis*.

Given the Bayesian network analyses here, an infinite number of stories might be told, one for each possible combination of probabilistic ingredients (see Table 10.4). We started in Story 1 by supposing that H and H^C are equally likely a priori. Then we assessed the first eight likelihood pairs with values that seemed to make sense. We next assessed hits and false-positive likelihoods for Ralph in his testimony of D*, F*, and G*. We picture Ralph as being a very credible source of evidence; his hits/false-positive (h/f) ratio is 95: 1. But we have pictured Willard as being less credible than Ralph; Willard's h/f ratio is only 7:1. The row labeled H Posterior (all evidence) is how Bayes' rule says Story 1 should end if we considered all four items of evidence we have. The ERGO Bayesian Networks System (developed by Noetic Systems Inc.) calculated posterior probabilities: P(H|all evidence) = 0.92, and P(H^C|all evidence) = 0.08. But then we asked, "How would this story end if we only had Willard's testimony?" The ERGO system lets us determine posterior probabilities of major hypotheses for various combinations of evidence. The next row shows P(H|Only Willard) = 0.73; and P(H^C|Only Willard) = 0.27. The last row shows what happens when we leave out Willard's evidence; the posterior probability of H would be 0.90.

As you see, Story 2 has the same ingredients as Story 1 with the exception of Willard's hits and false positives for his testimony E*. We wondered what would happen if we made Willard at least as credible as Ralph. What happens here is that only very small increases occur in the posterior of H when we consider all the evidence or when we ignore Willard's evidence. These increases don't show up in our table since we are only carrying these

Table 10.4 Network Stories

Probabilities	Story 1	Story 2	Story 3	Story 4	Story 5
$P(H)$; $P(H^C)$	0.5; 0.5	0.5; 0.5	0.5; 0.5	**0.25; 0.75**	**0.25; 0.75**
$P(A\|H)$; $P(A\|H^C)$	0.6; 0.15	0.6; 0.15	0.6; 0.15	0.6; 0.15	0.6; 0.15
$P(B\|H)$; $P(B\|H^C)$	0.8; 0.1	0.8; 0.1	0.8; 0.1	0.8; 0.1	0.8; 0.1
$P(C\|H)$; $P(C\|H^C)$	0.05; 0.8	0.05; 0.8	0.05; 0.8	0.05; 0.8	0.05; 0.8
$P(D\|A)$; $P(D\|A^C)$	0.95; 0.1	0.95; 0.1	0.95; 0.1	0.95; 0.1	0.95; 0.1
$P(E\|B)$; $P(E\|B^C)$	0.95; 0.1	0.95; 0.1	0.95; 0.1	0.95; 0.1	0.95; 0.1
$P(F\|B)$; $P(F\|B^C)$	0.98; 0.03	0.98; 0.03	0.98; 0.03	0.98; 0.03	0.98; 0.03
$P(G\|C)$; $P(G\|C^C)$	0.8; 0.4	0.8; 0.4	0.8; 0.4	0.8; 0.4	0.8; 0.4
$P(D^*\|D)$; $P(D^*\|D^C)$	0.95; 0.01	0.95; 0.01	0.95; 0.01	0.95; 0.01	0.95; 0.01
$P(E^*\|E)$; $P(E^*\|E^C)$	0.7; 0.1	**0.98; 0.01**	**0.10; 0.80**	**0.10; 0.80**	**0.01; 0.99**
$P(F^*\|F)$; $P(F^*\|F^C)$	0.95; 0.01	0.95; 0.01	0.95; 0.01	0.95; 0.01	0.95; 0.01
$P(G^*\|G)$; $P(G^*\|G^C)$	0.95; 0.01	0.95; 0.01	0.95; 0.01	0.95; 0.01	0.95; 0.01
H Posterior(all evd)	0.92; 0.08	0.92; 0.08	0.82; 0.18	0.60; 0.40	0.42; 0.58
Only Willard	0.73; 0.27	0.80; 0.20	0.27; 0.73	0.11; 0.89	0.08; 0.91
No Willard	0.90; 0.10	0.90; 0.10	0.90; 0.10	0.75; 0.25	0.42; 0.58

numbers to two places. The only noticeable change occurs when we consider only Willard's evidence. The posterior of H increases over what it was in Story 1.

Now, in Story 3, the only ingredient change involves Willard again. But this time we have supposed that Willard may not be truthful. Notice that his false-positive probability is eight times larger than his hit probability. This results in decreases in the posterior probability of H when we consider all the evidence. When we consider only Willard's evidence, the posterior on H^C is 0.73 and on H it is only 0.27. What this says is that, if Willard is lying, we can come to believe the opposite of what he tells us. Finally, if we ignore Willard, our beliefs about the posterior probability of H don't change over what they were in Story 2.

Now, the only change we have made in Story 4 over Story 3 is to decrease the prior probability of hypothesis H from 0.5 to 0.25. As you see, the posterior on H is noticeably reduced when we consider all the evidence, only Willard's evidence, or without Willard's evidence. Finally, in Story 5 we have just made Willard much more probably untruthful. This causes the posterior on H to be noticeably smaller in all three of the evidence cases: all evidence, only Willard, or no Willard.

A good question is, "Why did we choose to tell these five particular stories in preference to others we might have told?" The answer is that changes in only credibility-related values or prior probabilities allow us quite easily to explain what happens to the endings of stories. We could have told stories involving changes in the other likelihood ingredients, but we would have had a much more difficult time accounting for the endings of stories. As we noted, the mathematics in Bayesian network systems are always buried below the surface and never revealed to the user. We could have told stories that were much more interesting, and in many cases counterintuitive, by incorporating the aforementioned conditional dependencies. The five stories we have told simply illustrate one of the virtues of Bayesian analyses. We can show how different stories might end if we use different conventional probability values in telling these stories.

10.5.2.5 Utility and Feasibility of Bayesian Network Analyses

As we noted, Bayesian network analyses are quite well-known among many analysts, and there are persons who stoutly advocate this form of analysis for inferences in intelligence analysis and in other contexts. We have also mentioned that Bayesian network analyses are unexcelled in their ability to capture and exploit an array of evidential and inferential complexities or subtleties, provided that we recognize them and adjust our networks to allow us to capture them.

The feasibility of Bayesian network analyses raises many questions we must consider. The most obvious matter concerns the time and effort it can take to perform such an analysis when we drill down to levels at which we try to capture as many sources of doubt or uncertainty as we believe to be important. The example we have used in this account has been part of a very complex inference involving the major question or hypothesis concerning a dirty bomb being set off in the Washington, D.C., area, discussed in the previous chapters, to be finalized in the case study from Section 10.10. As you know by now, such a network is very large and complex. Our Bayesian network example in Figure 10.2 involves only one very small sector or fragment of this very large and complex network. As you see in Table 10.3, even this small sector requires twenty-four probability assessments. If we linked together a large number of such sectors or fragments, some of which would be much more complex than the Figure 10.2 network, the number of assessments would almost certainly be many times more than any analyst, or group of analysts, might have the time or inclination to make.

But Bayesian network advocates might argue that there are many ways in which we can drill down to shallower levels of detail in order to simplify our structural analysis and reduce the number of required probability assessments. But doing so would require us to ignore or suppress valuable sources of uncertainty of great importance that may influence our final inferences about the major hypotheses in the complex inference just described.

10.6   EPISTEMIC PROBABILITY (2): BELIEF FUNCTIONS

10.6.1   Belief Functions and Evidential Support

Both the enumerative and the subjective Bayesian interpretations of probability conform to Kolmogorov's three axioms. We asserted that these axioms rest on the investigation of replicable or repeatable processes such as statistical analysis of the results obtained in a sample of observations. But there are many reasons for wondering whether these three axioms remain self-evident concerning subjective probability judgments we all make from time to time involving unique events for which no enumerative process can be involved. In a very influential work, the probabilist Professor Glenn Shafer pointed to an array of difficulties associated with Axiom 3 concerning the additivity of enumerative probabilities for mutually exclusive events (Shafer, 1976). In particular, Shafer asserts that this axiom places various constraints on our judgments or beliefs about uncertainty that we may not be willing to accept. Here it is necessary to mention only two of the difficulties Shafer mentions:

- Indecisions we routinely face concerning ambiguities in our evidence
- Instances in which we encounter what historically has been called "pure" evidence

In so many instances, we may not be sure what evidence is telling us, and so we wish to be able to *withhold* a portion of our beliefs and not commit it to any particular hypothesis or possible conclusion. A very important element in what Shafer terms *Belief Functions* is that the *weight of evidence means the degree of support* that evidence provides to hypotheses we are considering. Shafer allows that we can grade degree of support **s** on a 0–1 scale similar to the scale for Kolmogorov probabilities; but we can do things with support assignment **s** that the Kolmogorov additivity Axiom 3 does not allow. To illustrate, suppose we revisit the analyst concerned about whether or not the Greens are supplying parts necessary for the construction of shaped explosive devices. Her hypotheses are the following:

H: "The Greens are supplying parts necessary for the construction of shaped explosive devices."

H^C: "The Greens are not supplying parts necessary for the construction of shaped explosive devices."

At some stage this analyst is required to state her beliefs about the extent to which the evidence supports H or H^C. Here is her assessment:

	{H}	{H^C}	{H or H^C}
s	0.5	0.3	0.2

What does this support assignment mean? She is saying that she believes the evidence supports H exactly to degree **s** = 0.5, and that this evidence also supports H^C exactly to degree **s** = 0.3. But there is something about this evidence that makes her unsure about whether it supports H or H^C. So, she has left the balance of her **s** assignment, **s** = 0.2, *uncommitted among H or H^C*. In other words, she is telling us that she has withheld a portion of her beliefs because she is not sure what some element of her evidence is telling her.

If she were required to obey Kolmogorov's Axiom 3, she would not be allowed to be indecisive in any way in stating her beliefs. Here is what her support assignment would have to look like:

	{H}	{H^C}
s	a	1-a

In this case, she would be required to say that the evidence supports H to degree **s** = a, and supports H^C to degree **s** = (1 – a) in agreement with Axiom 3 since H and H^C are mutually exclusive and exhaustive. In short, Kolmogorov Axiom 3 does not permit the analyst any indecision in stating her beliefs; she must commit all of it to H and to H^C. This, she believes, would not be a faithful or accurate account of her beliefs.

But Shafer's Belief Functions approach allows us to cope with another difficulty associated with Kolmogorov's axioms. For centuries, it has been recognized that a distinction is necessary between what has been termed *mixed* and *pure evidence*. Mixed evidence has some degree of probability under every hypothesis we are considering. But pure evidence may support one hypothesis but say nothing at all about other hypotheses. In other words, we may encounter evidence that we believe offers zero support for some hypothesis. Here is another example involving our Green–Orange situation. Suppose our analyst encounters an item of evidence she believes supports H to a degree, but she believes offers no support at all for H^C. Here is her support assignment **s** for this evidence:

	{H}	{ H^C}	{H or H^C}
s	0.5	0	0.5

In this situation, the analyst is saying that the evidence supports H to degree **s** = 0.5, but offers no support at all to H^C. The rest of her support she leaves uncommitted between H and H^C. But now we have to examine what **s** = 0 for H^C means; does it mean that H^C could not be supported by further evidence? The answer is no, and the reason why it is no allows us to compare what ordinary probabilities mean in comparison with what support **s** means. This comparison is shown in Figure 10.3.

The (a) scale in Figure 10.3, for conventional or Kolmogorov probabilities, has a lower boundary with a meaning quite different from the meaning of this lower boundary on Shafer's support scale, shown in (b). The value 0 in conventional probability refers to an event judged to be impossible and that you completely disbelieve. We will refer to this scale again in Section 10.7 when discussing Baconian probability. But all 0 means on Shafer's **s** scale is *lack of support or belief*, not disbelief. This is very important, since we can go from lack of belief to some belief as we gather more evidence. But we cannot go from disbelief to some belief. On a conventional probability scale, a hypothesis once assigned the probability value 0 can never be resuscitated by further evidence, regardless of how strong it may be. But some hypothesis, assigned the value **s** = 0, can be revised upward since we can go from lack of belief to some belief in this hypothesis when and if we have some further evidence to support it. Thus, **s** allows us to account for pure evidence in ways that ordinary probabilities cannot do.

Consider the evidence in our dirty bomb example introduced in Section 1.3 and other evidence we introduced in later examples. We begin by listing the hypotheses we are considering at the moment:

H_1:   A dirty bomb will be set off somewhere in the Washington, D.C., area.
H_1^C: A dirty bomb will not be set off in the Washington, D.C., area (it might be set off somewhere else or not at all).

In the Belief Functions approach, we have just specified what is called a *frame of discernment* – in shorthand, a *frame* F. What this frame F = {H_1, H_1^C} says is how we are

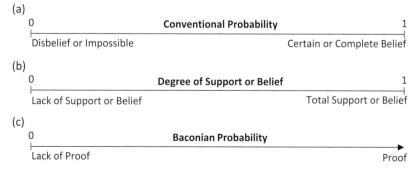

Figure 10.3. Different probability scales.

viewing our hypotheses just now. We might, on further evidence, wish to revise our frame in any one of a variety of ways.

For example, we might have evidence suggesting other specific places where a dirty bomb might be set off, such as in Annapolis, Maryland, or in Tysons Corner, Virginia. So our frame F' in this case might be:

H_1:   A dirty bomb will be set off somewhere in Washington, D.C.
H_2:   A dirty bomb will be set off in Annapolis, Maryland.
H_3:   A dirty bomb will be set off in Tysons Corner, Virginia.

All that is required in the Belief Functions approach is that the hypotheses in a frame be mutually exclusive. They might or might not be exhaustive. However, they are required to be exhaustive in a Bayesian approach. So this revised frame F' = $\{H_1, H_2, H_3\}$, as stated, is not exhaustive. But we are assuming, for the moment at least, that these three hypotheses are mutually exclusive: The dirty bomb will be set off at exactly one of these three locations. But, on further evidence, we might come to believe that dirty bombs will be set off in both Washington, D.C., and in Tysons Corner, Virginia. We know that the terrorists we are facing have a preference for simultaneous and coordinated attacks. So, our revised frame F'' might be:

H_1:   A dirty bomb will be set off in Washington, D.C., and in Tysons Corner, Virginia.
H_2:   A dirty bomb will be set off in Annapolis, Maryland.

The point of all this so far is that the Belief Functions approach allows for the fact that our hypotheses may mutate or change as a result of new evidence we obtain. This is a major virtue of this approach to evidential reasoning.

The next thing we have to consider is the *power set* of the hypotheses in a frame. This power set is simply the list of all possible combinations of the hypotheses in this frame. When we have **n** hypotheses in F, there are 2^n possible combinations of our hypotheses, including all of them and none of them. For example, when F = $\{H_1, H_1^C\}$, the power set consists of $\{H_1\}$, $\{H_1^C\}$, $\{H_1, H_1^C\}$, and Ø, where Ø = the empty set (i.e., none of the hypotheses). For F' = $\{H_1, H_2, H_3\}$, as defined previously, there are $2^3 = 8$ possible combinations: $\{H_1\}$, $\{H_2\}$, $\{H_3\}$, $\{H_1, H_2\}$, $\{H_1, H_3\}$, $\{H_2, H_3\}$, $\{H_1, H_2, H_3\}$, and Ø. Now, here comes an important point about support function **s**: The assigned values of **s** for any item or body of evidence must sum to 1.0 across the power set of hypotheses in a frame. The only restriction is that we must set **s**$\{Ø\} = 0$. We cannot give any support to the set of none of the hypotheses we are considering.

10.6.2   Examples of Assigning Evidential Support

We are now ready to consider some specific examples of the assignment of evidential support **s** in our dirty bomb example. We will suppose that in all of these examples, we have frame F = $\{H_1, H_1^C\}$, where:

H_1:   A dirty bomb will be set off somewhere in the Washington, D.C., area.
H_1^C: A dirty bomb will not be set off in the Washington, D.C., area (it might be set off somewhere else, or not at all).

So, our power set here is $\{H_1\}$, $\{H_1^C\}$, $\{H_1, H_1^C\}$, and Ø. Let's first see how an analyst could assign support to some patently ambiguous evidence.

Example 10.5.

Our analyst may have considered other evidence concerning Omar al-Massari, who we believe to be associated with the theft of the cesium-137 canister and the construction of a dirty bomb. But we now just consider how the analyst assigns support to the evidence she has received from "Yasmin" (see Example 6.6, p. 126), who tells us that she knew a man in Saudi Arabia named Omar al-Massari who she is "quite sure" spent two years "somewhere" in Afghanistan "sometime" in the years 1998 to 2000. Because of the vagueness of this report, the analyst decides not to commit her support **s** for this evidence, just to the hypotheses $\{H_1\}$ and $\{H_1^C\}$; she decides to hold some of it back. Here is the support she assigns on the power set of the frame F:

	$\{H_1\}$	$\{H_1^C\}$	$\{H_1, H_1^C\}$	Ø
Yasmin's evidence **s**	0.5	0.2	0.3	0

What our analyst has done here is to indicate her indecision about what Yasmin's report is telling us about Omar al-Massari. The analyst does not commit all of her belief or support specifically to H_1 or to H_1^C, but she decides to hold some of it back by assigning some of her support (**s** = 0.3) to the set $\{H_1, H_1^C\}$. You should read the comma between H_1 and H_1^C in $\{H_1, H_1^C\}$ as the word "or." What this assignment says is that she is withholding 0.3 of support for Yasmin's evidence by assigning it to either H_1 or H_1^C, but in no settled proportion. She is saying, "This amount of support could go to either H_1 or H_1^C, but I can't now decide."

Example 10.6.

Now consider what our analyst does with the evidence we have from our asset code-named "Wonderboy" (see Example 9.10, p. 166). Wonderboy tells us that Omar al-Massari has recently put a down payment of $25,000 on a house at 2321 23rd Street in the Georgetown area of Washington, D.C. As we noted, this evidence, if credible, seems to argue against H_1, "Why would Omar al-Massari put a down payment of $25,000 on a house in a city that is to be the target of a dirty bomb?" Our analyst decides that this evidence offers zero support to H_1 and some support to H_1^C. In other words, she is saying that Wonderboy's evidence is *pure evidence* since it says nothing at all about H_1. Here is what her assignment of **s** looks like for Wonderboy's evidence:

	$\{H_1\}$	$\{H_1^C\}$	$\{H_1, H_1^C\}$	Ø
Wonderboy's evidence **s**	0	0.7	0.3	0

There are two reasons our analyst has been indecisive here. First, she may not be convinced that Wonderboy is a completely credible asset. Second, she does allow the possibility that an elegant cover for the action proposed in H_1 would be to have Omar al-Massari put down $25,000 on a house in the Washington, D.C., area to throw us off the track. This is why she has assigned $\mathbf{s}\{H_1, H_1^C\} = 0.3$.

10.6.3 Dempster's Rule for Combining Partial Beliefs

Now that we have two items of evidence, the question is, "What is the rule for combining their support?" Since one of the Kolmogorov axioms is violated in Shafer's system, we should not expect to see Bayes' rule as being the device that allows us to combine support assignments across multiple items of evidence. There is indeed a different rule, called *Dempster's rule*, for combining support assignments **s** across different items or bodies of evidence, which will be introduced in the following example. Dempster's rule allows us to determine the *orthogonal sum* of support assignments **s**. We will use the symbol $\oplus$ to indicate the support assignments we are combining. For instance, $\mathbf{s_1} \oplus \mathbf{s_2}$ = the orthogonal sum of support assignments $\mathbf{s_1}$ and $\mathbf{s_2}$. The two support assignments whose orthogonal sum we will determine using Dempster's rule are the support assignments we have just discussed for Yasmin's and Wonderboy's evidence. The following example allows us to say some very interesting things about Belief Functions and Dempster's rule.

Example 10.7.

Table 10.5 shows how we determine orthogonal sums of support assignments $\mathbf{s_1}$ and $\mathbf{s_2}$ according to Dempster's rule. The steps we must follow are presented in the following.

Step 1. As shown in Table 10.5, we first list on the axes what are called the *focal elements* of our support assignments. Focal elements are those sets of hypotheses that are assigned nonzero values of **s**. As you see, $\mathbf{s_1}$ has three focal elements whose values of $\mathbf{s_1}$ are recorded. But $\mathbf{s_2}$ has only two focal elements whose values of $\mathbf{s_2}$ are recorded.

Step 2. We next find all possible intersections of the focal elements for our two support functions $\mathbf{s_1}$ and $\mathbf{s_2}$. These intersections are recorded in the table. An example is the intersection [∩] of $\{H_1\}$ and $\{H_1, H_1^C\}$, in symbols: $\{H_1\} \cap \{H_1, H_1^C\} = \{H_1\}$. Another example is the intersection $\{H_1, H_1^C\} \cap \{H_1, H_1^C\} = \{H_1, H_1^C\}$. But notice that the intersection $\{H_1\} \cap \{H_1^C\} = \emptyset$ is empty. We will have much more to say about this empty intersection in just a moment.

Step 3. Here comes the "orthogonal part" of the orthogonal sums we are determining. *Orthogonality* essentially means *independence*, and it is assumed in Dempster's rule that the support assignments, $\mathbf{s_1}$ and $\mathbf{s_2}$ in the present case, are independent, and so a product rule holds. What we do is to multiply together the separate support assignments for each of the intersections we have determined. For example, in the upper-left intersection we have $\{H_1\} \cap \{H_1, H_1^C\} = \{H_1\}$. We find the probability of this intersection by multiplying $\mathbf{s_1}\{H_1\} \times \mathbf{s_2}\{H_1, H_1^C\} = 0.5 \times 0.3 = 0.15$. We do the same thing for all the other intersections in Table 10.5.

Step 4. Here comes the "sums part" of the orthogonal sums we are determining. Here we find the sum of the support that is provided for each one of the intersections in the table. For example, the total support provided for $\{H_1^C\}$ is $0.06 + 0.14 + 0.21 = 0.41$. For $\{H_1\}$, the sum is 0.15; for $\{H_1, H_1^C\}$, the sum is 0.09; and for $\emptyset$, the sum is 0.35. We now list these initial orthogonal sums as follows, observing that we have some difficulties that must be overcome.

	$\{H_1\}$	$\{H_1^C\}$	$\{H_1, H_1^C\}$	$\emptyset$
Initial $\mathbf{s_1} \oplus \mathbf{s_2}$	0.15	0.41	0.09	0.35

Table 10.5 An Application of Dempster's Rule

s_2 for Wonderboy's evidence			
$\{H_1, H_1{}^C\}$ 0.3	$\{H_1\}$ 0.15	$\{H_1{}^C\}$ 0.06	$\{H_1, H_1{}^C\}$ 0.09
$\{H_1{}^C\}$ 0.7	∅ 0.35	$\{H_1{}^C\}$ 0.14	$\{H_1{}^C\}$ 0.21
	$\{H_1\}$ 0.5	$\{H_1{}^C\}$ 0.2	$\{H_1, H_1{}^C\}$ 0.3

s_1 for Yasmin's evidence

What we see immediately is that, applying Dempster's rule, we have violated a restriction in Belief Functions that says that $\mathbf{s}\{\emptyset\}$ must always be zero. What has happened here? Going back to Table 10.5, we determined an intersection support of 0.35 for two nonintersecting events, $\{H_1\}$ and $\{H_1{}^C\}$. What we would be saying in this assignment of evidential support is that we have a simultaneous belief in two contradictory events, since by definition, $\{H_1\}$ and $\{H_1{}^C\}$ are mutually exclusive. What we could do to avoid this extreme cognitive dissonance is simply to pretend that this dissonance did not occur. So, we could just eliminate the orthogonal sum of 0.35 for ∅ and say the following:

	$\{H_1\}$	$\{H_1{}^C\}$	$\{H_1, H_1{}^C\}$	∅
Initial $\mathbf{s_1} \oplus \mathbf{s_2}$	0.15	0.41	0.09	0

But doing this presents another problem since our orthogonal sum $\mathbf{s_1} \oplus \mathbf{s_2}$ does not sum to 1.0 across the focal elements of this combined support assignment; observe that this sum is only 0.65.

Step 5. We can make the support assignments across the nonempty subsets of F sum to 1.0 simply by normalizing them. Any set of positive numbers can be made to sum to one by dividing each one by the sum of the numbers; this is called *normalization* in this case. If we divide each of the values of $\mathbf{s_1} \oplus \mathbf{s_2}$ by 0.65, they will sum to 1.0, as shown in the following result. Notice here that this sum $0.65 = 1 - \mathbf{s_1} \oplus \mathbf{s_2}(\emptyset) = 1 - 0.35$. Our final result is:

	$\{H_1\}$	$\{H_1{}^C\}$	$\{H_1, H_1{}^C\}$	∅
Normalized $\mathbf{s_1} \oplus \mathbf{s_2}$	0.23	0.63	0.14	0

What we have done is to show the steps necessary in calculating the orthogonal sum of any subset of the hypotheses that result when we combine two support assignments like s_1 and s_2. We have applied Dempster's rule, which can be stated in the general case as follows:

$$s(C) = \frac{\displaystyle\sum_{A_i \cap B_k = C} s_1(A_i) s_2(B_k)}{1 - \displaystyle\sum_{A_i \cap B_k = \phi} s_1(A_i) s_2(B_k)}.$$

This complicated formula is quite easy to decipher based on Table 10.5. To illustrate, let C = $\{H_1{}^C\}$. The numerator of this equation says the following: Add together all the products of the intersections of the focal elements of our support assignments whose intersection is C = $\{H_1{}^C\}$. This sum will be 0.06 + 0.14 + 0.21 = 0.41. The denominator says divide this number (0.41) by one minus the sum of support assigned to any intersection of focal elements that is empty. In the example shown in Table 10.5, the total support given to $\{H_1\} \cap \{H_1{}^C\}$ = Ø is 0.35. So we have divided 0.41 by (1 – 0.35) = 0.65 to determine $s_1 \oplus s_2$ for $\{H_1{}^C\}$ to be 0.63. In short, the denominator prescribes the normalizing constant we have determined in this case.

There was some initial dissatisfaction with the manner in which Dempster's rule removes the cognitive dissonance we described. However, this dissatisfaction has dissipated for various reasons. Here are some of the important results of applying Belief Functions and Dempster's rule in situations in which we have unique or singular events and must assess the weight of evidence judgmentally or subjectively. First, our analyst was allowed to be indecisive about how she allocated evidential support to power sets of her hypotheses for both items of evidence she was considering. Bayes' rule would not allow her to be indecisive in such matters. Second, she has judged one of the items of evidence to be pure evidence, saying that Wonderboy's evidence offers zero support to $\{H_1\}$. However, as Dempster's rule shows, this does not mean that $\{H_1\}$ is dead forever, as would be the case if she assigned a Bayesian likelihood of zero for this evidence under $\{H_1\}$. Notice that the normalized $s_1 \oplus s_2$ for $\{H_1\}$ = 0.23. This is a fine illustration of how in Belief Functions zero indicates *lack of belief* and not *disbelief*. We illustrated this in Figure 10.3. Our analyst had a lack of belief in $\{H_1\}$ just based on Wonderboy's evidence, but she did have some basis for believing $\{H_1\}$ when she combined Wonderboy's evidence with Yasmin's evidence according to Dempster's rule.

Our final word on Belief Functions is that Dempster's rule can of course be used over and over again for any number of evidence items and is recursive, as is Bayes' rule, but in its own way. For example, suppose our analyst has a third item of evidence and the same frame F she has been considering for her first two items of evidence. She wishes to determine the orthogonal support normalized $s_1 \oplus s_2 \oplus s_3$ based on her support s_3 for this new evidence. Suppose she believes this new item of evidence provides the following support: $s_3\{H_1\}$ = 0.6, $s_3\{H_1{}^C\}$ = 0.1, and $s_3\{H_1, H_1{}^C\}$ = 0.3. She would apply Dempster's rule to combine the following support assignments:

	$\{H_1\}$	$\{H_1{}^C\}$	$\{H_1, H_1{}^C\}$	Ø
Normalized $s_1 \oplus s_2$	0.23	0.63	0.14	0
s_3	0.6	0.1	0.3	0

Further discussion of the Shaferian and Bayesian views of the weight of evidence are given elsewhere (Schum, 1994 [2001a], pp. 222–243).

10.7 BACONIAN PROBABILITY AND THE IMPORTANCE OF EVIDENTIAL COMPLETENESS

10.7.1 Variative and Eliminative Inferences

Here is a view of probabilistic reasoning that puts particular emphasis on a very important matter not specifically addressed in any other view of probability. In this view, the *weight of evidence* depends on *how much* relevant and believable evidence we have and upon *how complete* is our coverage of existing evidence on matters we ourselves have recognized as being relevant in the analysis at hand. This Baconian view of probability and the weight of evidence is perhaps the least well known of any current views of probability, but it deserves much wider recognition. This Baconian view rests on the work of Professor L. Jonathan Cohen from Queens College, Oxford (Cohen, 1977, 1989).

The label "Baconian" on this system of probability acknowledges the work of Sir Francis Bacon (1561–1626), who revolutionized the process of inference in science. Bacon argued that attempting to prove some hypothesis by gathering instances favorable to it is mistaken, since all it would take to refute the generality of this hypothesis was one unfavorable instance of it. What Bacon argued was that we ought to design research with the objective of *eliminating* hypotheses. The hypothesis that best resists our eliminative efforts is the one in which we should have the greatest confidence. As this eliminative process proceeds, it is obvious that we should not keep performing the same test over and over again. What we need is an array of *different* tests of our hypotheses. The hypothesis that holds up under the most varied set of tests is the one having the greatest probability of being correct. So, Baconian inferences are *eliminative and variative* in nature.

Several attempts were made in the past, without success, to relate conventional probability to eliminative and variative inferences. Jonathan Cohen was the first person to generate a system of probabilities expressly congenial to this. His Baconian system of probabilities has properties unlike the two we have examined so far. Baconian probabilities have only ordinal properties and cannot be combined algebraically in any way. The Baconian probability scale is shown as (c) in Figure 10.3, to be compared with the conventional probability scale shown as (a) in Figure 10.3. On the conventional probability scale, 0 means *disproof*; but on the Baconian scale, 0 simply means *lack of proof*. A hypothesis now having zero Baconian probability can be revised upward in probability as soon as we have some evidence for it. As noted, we cannot revise upward in probability any hypothesis disproved or having zero conventional probability.

10.7.2 Importance of Evidential Completeness

Figure 10.4 shows the major point of interest for intelligence analysts in this Baconian system that we illustrate with an example.

Professor Cohen argues that in any evidential reasoning situation, we are always out on an inferential limb that might be longer and weaker than we may believe it to be. Suppose an analyst has generated three hypotheses: H_1, H_2, and H_3. A body of evidence has been examined and Bayes' rule is used to combine the likelihoods for this evidence together with stated prior probabilities. The result is that Bayes' rule shows the posterior probability of H_3, in light of the evidence, to be 0.998, very close to certainty on the Kolmogorov

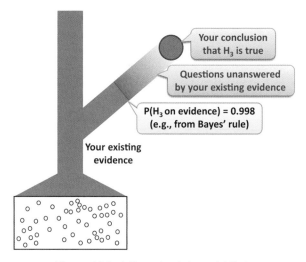

Figure 10.4. A Baconian inferential limb.

probability scale. Therefore, the analyst confidently reports his conclusion that H_3 is true to an important "customer," together with its very large posterior probability he has determined. A short time passes and the analyst hears the depressing news that H_3 is not true, a fact about which his customer will surely let him know. What could have gone wrong? After all, the analyst performed an analysis that is highly respected by many persons.

A person having knowledge of Cohen's Baconian probability arrives on the scene of the analyst's distress and makes the following comments:

> You gathered some evidence, fair enough, quite a bit of it, in fact. But, how many relevant questions you can think of that were not answered by the evidence you had? Depending upon the number of these unanswered questions, you were out on an inferential limb that was longer and weaker than you imagined it to be (see Figure 10.4). If you believed that these unanswered questions would supply evidence that also favored H_3, you were misleading yourself, since you did not obtain any answers to them. The posterior probability you determined by itself is not a good indicator of the weight of evidence. What makes better sense is to say the weight of evidence depends on the amount of favorable evidence you have and how completely it covers matters you said were relevant. In your analysis, you completely overlooked the inferential importance of questions your existing evidence did not answer.

Apart from the Baconian system, no other view of evidential reasoning focuses on evidential completeness and the importance of taking into account questions recognized as being relevant that remain unanswered by the evidence we do have. This is why Jonathan Cohen's Baconian system is so important in intelligence analysis. What we do not take account of in intelligence analyses can hurt us very badly.

As we all know, intelligence analysts frequently have to make inferences about matters for which they often have scant evidence, or no evidence at all. In other instances in which there may be available evidence, analysts may have no time to search for it or consider it carefully. In such cases, analysts say they are forced to make *assumptions* that may be vigorously challenged. Analysts, and those they serve, usually employ the term "assumption" when there is another term that could be used. There are reasons for arguing that the word "generalization" is preferable to the word "assumption." All inferences, made by intelligence analysts or anyone else, require generalizations that license inferential steps, and also require ancillary evidence to support the applicability of the generalization in the particular case in which it is being invoked. This is why we have said that generalizations and ancillary evidence form the "glue" that holds our arguments together. On some occasions, of course, this glue will fail to hold an argument together. The Baconian view being discussed offers much guidance in such matters.

But there is another important consequence of lack of time and evidence. This involves failure to decompose complex arguments into logically consistent or defensible stages. All arguments from evidence to hypotheses, or matters to be proved or disproved, involve chains of reasoning. Each link in such chains involves a source of doubt or uncertainty. Under the pressures of time or lack of evidence, an analyst may not even articulate in any way what these interposed sources of doubt may be. This results in a suppression of uncertainties and can lead to inferential miscarriages of many sorts. In our Disciple-CD system, we have used the term "drilling down" to indicate how much detail will be captured by an analyst in the construction of arguments from evidence. Disciple-CD allows an analyst to drill down to various levels depending upon the time and evidential resources available to an intelligence analyst. In many cases, this drilling down will be only very slight or nonexistent, in which cases the analysts will say that they must make assumptions. But this amounts to giving an assumption or a generalization the *benefit of the doubt* (without supporting it in any way), to believing *as if* some conclusion were true (absent any evidential support for it), or to *taking something for granted* without testing it in any way. All of these situations involve the suppression of uncertainties.

It happens that only the Baconian probability system provides any guidance about how to proceed when we must give benefit of doubt, believe as if, or take things for granted. The major reason is that it acknowledges what almost every logician says about the necessity for asserting generalizations and supplying tests of them in evidential reasoning. Search the Bayesian or Belief Functions literature and you will find almost no discussion of generalizations (assumptions) and ancillary tests of them. Suppose we are interested in inferring F from E. Bayes' rule grinds to a halt when we have no basis for assessing the likelihoods $P(E|F)$ and $P(E|F^C)$. Bayesians counter by saying that we will always have some evidence on which to base these judgments. But they never say what this evidence is in particular cases and how believable or credible it might or might not be. The Belief Functions approach comes closer by saying that we can assess the evidential support for a *body* of evidence that may include both directly relevant and at least some ancillary evidence. Following is an account of the Baconian license for giving an assumption or generalization benefit of doubt, believing as if it were true, or taking it for granted, provided that we are willing to mention all of the uncertainties we are suppressing when we do so. Stated another way, we must try to account for all of the questions we can think of that remain unanswered by the absence, or very scant amount, of evidence. This will be crucial in assisting an analyst to defend the assumption this analyst says is being made.

Here are the essentials of Cohen's Baconian approach to reasoning based on little or no ancillary evidence either to support or undermine a generalization. The first step, of course, is to make sure that the generalization is not a non sequitur, that is, that it makes logical sense. In the simplest possible case, suppose we are interested in inferring proposition or event F from proposition or event E. The generalization G in doing so might read,

"If E has occurred, then probably F has occurred." We recognize this if-then statement as an *inductive generalization* since it is hedged. Generalization G might also be stated in the future tense: "If E has occurred, then F will probably occur." Second, we consider various tests of this generalization using relevant ancillary evidence. Third, we consider how many evidential tests of this generalization there might be. Suppose we identify N such tests. The best case would be when we perform all N of these tests and they all produce results favorable to generalization G. But we must not overlook generalization G itself; we do so by assigning it the value 1; so we have $N + 1$ things to consider. Now we are in a position to show what happens in any possible case.

First, suppose we perform *none* of these N evidential tests. We could still proceed by giving generalization G the *benefit of the doubt* and detach a belief that F occurred (or will occur) just by invoking this generalization G regarding the linkage between events E and F. To do this, we assign G the value 1 so that we are considering $N + 1$ things: the N evidential tests and our generalization G. So, when no evidential tests are performed, we are saying: "Let's believe *as if* F occurred based on E and generalization G." This would amount to saying that the Baconian probability of event F is $B(F) = 1/(N + 1)$. This expression is never a ratio; all it says is that we considered just one thing in our inference about F from E, namely just the generalization G. We could also say, "Let's take event F *for granted* and believe that F occurred (or will occur) because E occurred as our generalization G asserts." However, note that in doing so, we have left all N ancillary evidential questions unanswered. This we represent by saying that our inference of F from E has involved only one of the $N + 1$ considerations, and so we have $(N + 1 - 1) = N$, the number of questions we have left unanswered. As far as evidential completeness is concerned, this is when the evidence we have is totally incomplete. But the Baconian system allows us to proceed anyway based on giving a generalization benefit of doubt. But our confidence in this result should be very low.

Now suppose we have performed some number k of the N possible ancillary evidential tests of generalization G, as asserted in the preceding, and they were all passed. The Baconian probability of F in this situation is given by $B(F) = (k + 1)/(N + 1)$. The difference between the denominator and numerator in such an expression will always equal the number of unanswered questions as far as the testing of G is concerned. In this case, we have $(N + 1) - (k + 1) = N - k$ questions that were unanswered in a test of generalization G. How high our confidence is that F is true depends on how high $k + 1$ is as compared to $N + 1$.

But now suppose that not all answers to these k questions are favorable to generalization G. Under what conditions are we entitled to detach a belief that event F occurred, based on evidence E, generalization G, and the k tests of G? The answer requires a subjective judgment by the analyst about whether the tests, *on balance*, favor or disfavor G. When the number of the k tests disfavoring G exceeds the number of tests favoring G, we might suppose that we would always detach a belief that event F did not occur, since G has failed more tests than it survived. But this will not always be such an easy judgment if the number of tests G passed were judged to be more important than the tests it failed to pass. In any case, there are $N - k$ tests that remain unanswered. Suppose that k is quite large but the number of tests favorable to G is only slightly larger than the number of tests unfavorable to G. In such cases, the analyst might still give event F the *benefit of the doubt,* or believe, at least tentatively, *as if* F occurred pending the possible acquisition of further favorable tests of G. And in this case, the confidence of the analyst in this conclusion should also be very low.

Whatever the basis for an assumption or a benefit of doubt judgment there is, one of the most important things about the Baconian approach is that the analyst must be prepared to give an account of the questions that remain unanswered in evidential tests of possible conclusions. This will be especially important when analysts make assumptions or, more appropriately, give generalizations benefit of doubt, draw as-if conclusions, or take certain events for granted. These are situations in which analysts are most vulnerable and in which Baconian ideas are most helpful.

10.7.3   Baconian Probability of Boolean Expressions

Some of the most important properties of Baconian probabilities concern their application to Boolean combinations of propositions such as hypotheses. Because the probabilities in the Baconian system have only *ordinal properties*, we can say only that hypothesis H_1 is more likely than H_2, but we cannot say how much more likely H_1 is than H_2. Also, in the Baconian system, it is never necessary to assess subjective probabilities. In our saying that H_1 is more probable than H_2, all we are saying is that there is more favorably relevant evidence on H_1 than there is on H_2. What counts most in the Baconian system is the *completeness of our evidence* and the extent to which we have questions that remain unanswered by the evidence we have. Here are the three most important Baconian properties of interest to us concerning intersections, unions, and negation.

Baconian Intersections: Suppose we have some events of interest such as events F, G, and H. Suppose we have some favorably relevant evidence about each one of these events and have also considered how complete the evidence is for these events. So we determine that the Baconian probabilities (B) for these three events are $B(F) \geq B(G) \geq B(H)$. Here's what these probabilities say: We have more favorably relevant and complete evidence for event F than we do for event G, and more favorably relevant and complete evidence for event G than we have for event H. So, asked what the Baconian probability is for their intersection (F and G and H), we must say that $B(F$ and G and $H) = B(H)$. What this says is that the Baconian probability of the intersection of these three events is equal to the Baconian probability of the event with the least favorably relevant and complete evidence. This is an example of the MIN rule for Baconian intersections. We might compare this with the conventional probability of the intersection of these three events. Suppose that events F, G, and H are independent events where $P(F) = 0.8$, $P(G) = 0.6$, and $P(H) = 0.4$. In this case, $P(F$ and G and $H) = 0.8 \times 0.6 \times 0.4 = 0.192 < P(H) = 0.4$. In the Baconian system, the probability of a conjunction of events or propositions can never be less than that of the event having the smallest Baconian probability.

Baconian Unions: Now consider the same case involving events F, G, and H. Again, suppose that $B(F) \geq B(G) \geq B(H)$. Now what we wish to determine is the Baconian probability $B(F$ or G or $H)$. In this case, $B(F$ or G or $H) \geq B(F)$, where $B(F)$ is the largest of the Baconian probability for the events we are considering. This is the MAX rule for Baconian probability, and what it says is that the probability of a disjunction of events is at least as large as the largest Baconian probability of any of the individual events.

Baconian Negation: Baconian negation is not complementary. The Baconian rule is quite complex. Here's what it says: If we have A and A^C, if $B(A) > 0$, then $B(A^C) = 0$. What this means essentially is that we cannot commit beliefs simultaneously to two events that cannot both occur.

What is quite interesting is that the Baconian treatment of conjunctions and disjunctions is the same as in Zadeh's Fuzzy probability system (Zadeh, 1963), namely they both make use of MIN-MAX rules for these connectives.

Example 10.8.

To illustrate the use of Baconian probabilities, let us consider Wallflower's report of Emir Z.'s leaving the building at 221 Dezab Street in Ahwaz, Iran, which was discussed in Chapter 7 (see Figure 7.2, p. 142). Clyde, the analyst, brings together the ancillary evidence he has about Wallflower's veracity, objectivity, and observational sensitivity. He uses this evidence to perform the ten veracity tests in Table 6.1 (p. 130), the six objectivity tests from Table 6.2 (p. 132), and the six observational sensitivity tests from Table 6.3 (p. 133). For each test (question) considered, Clyde has four possible results: the test *favors* the corresponding credibility attribute (e.g., the answer of the question, "Is Wallflower subject to any significant exploitation by other persons or organizations to provide us this information?" is, "No," supporting his veracity), the test *disfavors* it, Clyde *cannot decide* (because the favoring and disfavoring evidence balance each other), and Clyde *cannot answer* (because there is no evidence relevant to that question).

Let us assume that, with respect to the ten veracity questions, one favors it, four disfavor it, two are undecided, and three are unanswered. Here, using an on-balance judgment, we conclude that there is a lack of proof for Wallflower's veracity. We could also have moderate confidence in this result because we have been able to answer five of the ten questions.

Since we can regard credibility as the conjunction of veracity, objectivity, and observational sensitivity, we can also conclude that there is a lack of proof for Wallflower's credibility. Similarly, there is a lack of proof for Wallflower's believability (regarded as the intersection of credibility and competence).

Again, the Baconian system is the only system we know about that is concerned about the completeness of evidence and the importance of considering how many questions remain unanswered by the evidence we have.

10.8   IMPRECISION AND FUZZY PROBABILITY

10.8.1   Fuzzy Force of Evidence

The final way an analyst can express uncertainty about a conclusion reached is to use words rather than numbers. The analyst might say, "I am very certain that ..."; "What probably will happen is ..."; "It is unlikely that ..."; and so on. Years ago, Sherman Kent tried his best to relate intelligence analysts' verbal expressions of uncertainty such as these to specific ranges of numbers on a conventional probability scale (Kent, 1994). One instance we have all heard about involving words was use of the term "slam dunk" to indicate virtual certainty. This illustrates how no less care must be taken in verbal assessments of uncertainty than in the numerical methods just discussed.

Verbal expressions of uncertainty are certainly not confined to intelligence analysis. In the field of law, for example, forensic standards of proof are always employed using words instead of numbers. We all know about standards such as: "beyond reasonable doubt" (in criminal cases); "preponderance of evidence" (in civil cases); "clear and convincing evidence" (in many Senate and congressional hearings); and "probable cause" (employed by magistrates to determine whether a person should be held in custody pending further hearings).

All the verbal examples just cited have a current name; they can be called *Fuzzy probabilities*. Words are less precise than numbers. There is now extensive study of fuzzy inference involving what has been termed *approximate reasoning*, which involves verbal statements about things that are imprecisely stated. Here is an example of approximate reasoning: "Since John believes he is *overworked* and *underpaid*, then he is *probably not very satisfied* with his job." All the italicized ingredients of this statement are imprecise or fuzzy. We are indebted to Professor Lofti Zadeh (University of California, Berkeley), and his many colleagues, for developing logics for dealing with fuzzy statements, including Fuzzy probabilities (Zadeh, 1983; Negoita and Ralescu, 1975). It is, of course, entirely reasonable to grade the force of evidence in fuzzy terms, such as "strong force," "weak force," "very strong force," and so on.

We have mentioned that Sherman Kent was concerned with Fuzzy probabilities long before Lofti Zadeh began to study them carefully (Kent, 1994). But an American jurist named John H. Wigmore was well ahead of Sherman Kent as far as using words to grade uncertainty in evidential reasoning (Wigmore, 1913; 1937). Wigmore understood that the linkages between propositions in chains of reasoning reveal the sources of doubt or uncertainty we mentioned in connection with Figures 1.11 and 1.12. What Wigmore was concerned about was the inferential force of one proposition on another in these chains of reasoning. But Wigmore was no probabilist and did not consider any numerical methods for grading evidential force. Instead, he used words such as "strong force," "weak force," and "provisional force" to indicate the strength of linkages in chains of reasoning. The point here is that verbal assessments of uncertainty in intelligence analysis have a long and very respectable lineage.

Zadeh went a bit further than Kent did in his methods for relating verbal assessments of uncertainty with numerical equivalents. Zadeh employed what he termed a *possibility function*, μ, to indicate ranges of numerical probabilities a person might associate with a verbal expression of uncertainty. Zadeh reasoned that a person might not be able to identify a single precise number he or she would always associate with a verbal statement or Fuzzy probability. Here is an example of a possibility function for the Fuzzy probability "very probable."

Asked to grade what numerical probabilities might be associated with an analyst's Fuzzy probability "very probable," the analyst might respond as follows:

For me, "very probable" means a numerical probability of at least 0.75 and at most 0.95. If it were any value greater than 0.95, I might use a stronger term such as "very, very probable." I would further say that I would not use the term "very probable" if I thought the probability was less than 0.75. In such cases, I would weaken my verbal assessment. Finally, I think it is most possible ($\mu = 1.0$) that my use of the verbal assessment "very probable" means something that has about 0.85 probability of occurring.

If the analyst decides that "very probable" declines linearly on either side of $\mu = 1.0$, we would have the possibility function shown in Figure 10.5.

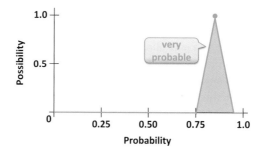

Figure 10.5. Possibilities and Fuzzy probabilities.

As an example of using Fuzzy probabilities, suppose we have three events or propositions A, B, and C. We consider the following Fuzzy probabilities (F) for these events, and we say the following:

- Event A is very likely.
- Event B is likely.
- Event C is very unlikely.

We express this by saying that F(A) > F(B) > F(C).

10.8.2　Fuzzy Probability of Boolean Expressions

Fuzzy Intersections: In the situation just described, the fuzzy conjunction of these three events F(A and B and C) = F(C), which is the *minimum* Fuzzy probability of the three events.

Fuzzy Unions: In the situation just described, the fuzzy disjunction of these three events F(A or B or C) = F(A), which is the *maximum* Fuzzy probability of these three events.

So, both in the Baconian system and in the Fuzzy system, we have MIN/MAX rules for combining probabilities for complex events. These systems give us formal license to use the MIN and MAX rules in Disciple-CD.

Fuzzy Negation: Fuzzy negation is complementary. It is here that the Baconian and Fuzzy views depart. If we have some event and its complement, such as A and A^C, then $F(A) = 1 - F(A^C)$.

10.8.3　On Verbal Assessments of Probabilities

Let us also consider the critics who sneer at *verbal assessments of probabilities*, saying that *numerical assessments*, conforming to the Kolmogorov axioms, are the only ones acceptable. As a top-ranking analyst, you are asked by an equally high-ranking customer for the probability of a crucial hypothesis H_K. All the evidence in this case is for one-of-a-kind event, so your assessment is necessarily subjective. You tell the customer, "Sir, the probability of H_K, on our analysis is 78 percent." The customer asks, "This is a very precise number; how did you arrive at it, given the subjective nature of your assessment?" You reply, "Yes, sir, what I really should have said was that my probability is between 73 percent and 83 percent, and 78 percent seemed like a good figure to quote." The customer then says, "But the limits to the probability interval you quoted are also precise; how did you arrive at them?" You might say, "Well, my lower limit is really between 70 percent and 76 percent, and my upper limit is between 80 percent and 86 percent." Your customer says,

"But these are also precise numbers." There is, as you see, an infinite regress of similar questions regarding the basis for subjective numerical assessments.

There are many places to begin a defense of verbal or *Fuzzy probability statements*. The most obvious one is law. All of the forensic standards of proof are given verbally: "beyond reasonable doubt," "clear and convincing evidence," "balance of probabilities," "sufficient evidence," and "probable cause." Over the centuries, attempts have been made to supply numerical probability values and ranges for each of these standards, but none of them has been successful. The reason, of course, is that every case is unique and rests upon many subjective and imprecise judgments. Wigmore (1913) understood completely that the catenated inferences in his Wigmorean networks were probabilistic in nature. Each of the arrows in the chain of reasoning describes the force of one hypothesis on the next one, such as E → F. Wigmore graded the force of such linkages verbally using such terms as "strong force," "weak force," "provisional force," and so on. Toulmin (1963) also used Fuzzy qualifiers in the probability statements of his system, which grounds Rationale (Van Gelder, 2007). There are many other examples of situations in which it is difficult or impossible for people to find numerical equivalents for verbal probabilities they assess. Intelligence analysis so often supplies very good examples in spite of what Sherman Kent said some years ago. Indeed, using words is quite often necessary in analyses based on masses of evidence that are so complex that they resist even the most devoted attention to the construction of inference networks. Couple this with the fact that different analysts might disagree substantially about what specific probability should be assigned to a conclusion. In addition, an analyst might assign a different probability to the same conclusion, based on the same evidence, on different occasions. What this says is that there will be interanalyst and intra-analyst variation in the assessment of probabilities. Words are less precise than numbers, so there will often be less disagreement about a verbal or a Fuzzy probability.

We conclude this discussion by recalling what the well-known probabilist Professor Glenn Shafer said years ago (Shafer, 1988): "Probability is more about structuring arguments than it is about numbers. All probabilities rest upon arguments. If the arguments are faulty, the probabilities, however determined, will make no sense."

10.9 A SUMMARY OF UNCERTAINTY METHODS AND WHAT THEY BEST CAPTURE

We regard the alternative views we have discussed for assessing and reporting uncertainty as being not only interesting but also *necessary*. Each view captures important elements of probabilistic reasoning, but no single view best captures all of them. Table 10.6 presents a summary of things analysts might consider when they contemplate how to assess and report uncertainty that will be associated with their conclusions. We include in this table just the four views we have discussed concerning nonenumerative situations. Analysts can easily find many works on statistics, frequentistic or Bayesian, in enumerative situations in which they can estimate probabilities from observed relative frequencies. Further explanations of the entries in this table follow.

The first entry in Table 10.6 lists a major strength that is exclusive to the Baconian system, its concern about how much favorable evidence was taken into account in an analysis and how completely this evidence covered matters judged relevant to conclusions that could be reached. A major question this form of analysis allows us to address is the extent to which questions that have not been answered by existing evidence could have

Table 10.6 A Summary of Nonenumerative Uncertainty Methods and What They Best Capture

Major Strength	Subjective Bayes	Belief Functions	Baconian	Fuzzy
Accounting for *incompleteness* of coverage of evidence			☑	
Coping with *inconclusiveness* in evidence	☑	☑	☑	☑
Coping with **ambiguities** or **imprecision** in evidence, and judgmental indecision.		☑		☑
Coping with *dissonance* in evidence	☑	☑	☑	☑
Coping with *source believability* issues	☑		☑	
Capturing a wide variety of evidential **subtleties** or **complexities**	☑			
Applications in current **inference network** technologies	☑	☑		
Most **familiar** ways of expressing uncertainty	☑			☑

altered the conclusion being reached. It would be quite inappropriate to assume that answers to the remaining unanswered questions would, if they were obtained, all favor the conclusion that was being considered. This, of course, requires analysts to consider carefully matters relevant to any conclusion that are not addressed by available evidence. We acknowledge that completeness matters are difficult to manage in current intelligence in which analysts are asked to provide conclusions on very short order. The shorter the time available for the assessment of evidence, the more unanswered questions there will be. We hope customers requiring quick analyses appreciate this fact.

The second entry in Table 10.6 notes that all four of the uncertainty methods have very good ways for dealing with the inconclusive nature of most evidence, but they do so in different ways. The subjective Bayesian does so by assessing nonzero likelihoods for the evidence under every hypothesis being considered. Their relative sizes indicate the force the evidence is judged to have on each hypothesis. But the Belief Functions advocate assigns numbers indicating the *support* evidence provides for hypotheses or subsets of them. We should be quick to notice that Bayesian likelihoods do not grade evidential support, since in Belief Functions an analyst can say that an item of evidence provides no support at all to some hypothesis. But a Bayesian likelihood of zero under a particular hypothesis would mean that this hypothesis is impossible and should be eliminated. Offering no support in Belief Functions does not entail that this hypothesis is impossible, since some support for this hypothesis may be provided by further evidence. The

Baconian acknowledges the inconclusive nature of evidence by assessing how completely, as well as how strongly, the evidence favors one hypothesis over others. In Fuzzy probabilities, it would be quite appropriate to use words in judging how an item or body of evidence bears on several hypotheses. For example, an analyst might say, "This evidence is indeed consistent with H_1 and H_2, but I believe it *strongly favors* H_1 over H_2."

The third entry in the table first acknowledges the Belief Functions and Fuzzy concerns about ambiguities and imprecision in evidence. In the Belief Functions approach, an analyst is entitled to *withhold belief* for some hypotheses in the face of ambiguous evidence. In such cases, the analyst may not be able to decide upon the extent to which the evidence may support any hypothesis being considered, or even if the evidence supports any of them. Judgmental indecision is not allowed in the Bayesian system since it assumes the analyst can say precisely how strongly evidence that has been judged relevant favors every hypothesis being considered. Judgmental indecision, as allowed in the Belief Functions system, seems a natural attribute of many evidential matters encountered by intelligence analysts. Ambiguities in evidence may be commonly encountered. The Fuzzy advocate will argue that ambiguities or imprecision in evidence hardly justifies precise numerical judgments. In the face of fuzzy evidence, we can only make fuzzy judgments of uncertainty.

The fourth entry in Table 10.6 shows that all four probability systems have very good mechanisms for coping with dissonant evidence in which there are patterns of contradictory and divergent evidence. Recall that dissonant evidence is directionally inconsistent; some of it will favor certain hypotheses, and some of it will favor others. In resolving such inconsistencies, both the Bayesian and Belief Functions approaches will side with the evidence having the strongest believability, though the mechanisms for doing so differ in Bayes' rule and Dempster's rule. The Bayesian approach to resolving contradictions is especially interesting since it shows how "counting heads" is not the appropriate method for resolving contradictions. In times past, "majority rule" was the governing principle. Bayes' rule shows that what matters is the aggregate believability on either side of a contradiction. The Baconian approach also rests on the strength and aggregate believability in matters of dissonance, but it also rests on how much evidence is available on either side and upon the questions that remain unanswered. In Fuzzy terms, evidential dissonance, and how it might be resolved, can be indicated in verbal assessments of uncertainty. In such instances, an analyst might say, "We have dissonant evidence favoring both H_1 and H_2, but I believe the evidence favoring H_1 predominates because of its very strong believability."

Row five in Table 10.6 concerns the vital matter of assessing the believability of intelligence evidence. From considerable experience, we find that the Bayesian and Baconian systems are especially important when they are combined. In many cases, these two radically different schemes for assessing uncertainty are not at all antagonistic but are entirely complementary. Let us consider a body of evidence about a HUMINT asset or informant. Ideas from the Baconian system allow us to ask, *"How much evidence do we have about this asset, and how many questions about his asset remain unanswered?"* Ideas from the Bayesian system allow us to ask, *"How strong is the evidence we do have about this asset"* (Schum, 1991)?

Row six in Table 10.6 has just one entry that involves the Bayesian system. The mathematical underpinnings of this system lead to a very rich system for capturing a very wide array of evidential and inferential subtleties or complexities. Many of these complexities are described and analyzed in another work (Schum, 1994 [2001a], chapters 6, 7, and 8 in both editions). Some of them can involve single items of evidence, while others involve many items in a mass of evidence. In virtually all cases, many or most of the probabilistic ingredients of these situations will involve nonenumerative probabilities. The Bayesian system incorporates a concept called *conditional dependence* that provides the primary means for capturing evidential and inferential complexities for study and analysis. One distinct virtue of Bayesian analyses of evidence is that it prompts us to ask questions of our evidence that we might never have thought of asking if we had not performed this kind of analysis. There are so many important subtleties in evidence that do not meet the eye on casual examinations of evidence.

The seventh row in Table 10.6 concerns the rapidly emerging technology for the analysis of complex arguments based on many items of evidence; they are referred to as *inference networks*. Both Bayesian and Belief Functions networks have been developed, but it seems fair to say that Bayesian networks have received the most attention in intelligence-related work. Although all inference networks have common properties, there are quite different purposes to which inference networks can be put. In some situations, an inference network is constructed in order to make sense out of an emerging mass of evidence. In other instances, an inference network is constructed in order to provide a model of some complex process involving many linked probabilistic variables. These models provide a basis for predictions that a model allows when we have various combinations of evidence for some of its probabilistic variables. Regardless of the purpose for which an inference network is being constructed, the basic methodology can be described as "divide and conquer" or "task decomposition." A complex evidence-based inference task is broken down into bits and pieces that are allegedly easier to manage than a "holistic" assessment in which the analyst tries to assess and combine all necessary probabilistic ingredients in his or her head. One should keep in mind that this divide-and-conquer approach makes necessary the judgment of often huge numbers of probabilities, not all of which may be easy to assess.

The final row in Table 10.6 simply acknowledges the fact that the subjective Bayesian and the Fuzzy systems make use of uncertainty responses that are the most familiar. We have all been tutored in conventional probabilities and can easily express uncertainty in terms of numbers between zero and one, as percentages when they are appropriate, or in terms of odds. But these same responses, with the exception of percentages, are appropriate for the subjective Bayesian. And, we certainly all know how to use words in the form of Fuzzy probabilities to indicate the extent of our uncertainty; we do it all the time. The responses required in the Belief Functions and Baconian probability systems are certainly less familiar. But in order to take full advantage of what these systems allow in uncertainty assessment, analysts should become more familiar with the works of professors Jonathan Cohen and Glenn Shafer that we cited earlier in this chapter.

10.10   BASIC OPERATIONS WITH DISCIPLE-CD

10.10.1   Hands On: Will a Bomb Be Set Off in Washington, D.C.?

10.10.1.1 Overview

This case study, which completes our analysis of the cesium situation, has the following objectives:

- Practicing with extracting evidence from the collected information
- Improving your understanding of the evidence-based hypothesis analysis process

---

Table 10.7 New Information Related to Saeed al-Nami

INFO-018-Miller: A loading dock worker at Allied Import named Rocky Miller says that Derwish put the object he received from the U-Haul guy in the trunk of his car.

INFO-019-Garcia: To learn more about al-Nami (alias Derwish), we interview the management of the Allied Import Company. The first thing we are told by Jose Garcia, a Vice President of Allied Import, was that he knew Kenny Derwish only by this name; Garcia says he was very surprised to learn that this name was an alias. Garcia also said that Derwish had worked for Allied Import for five years and is an expert in the evaluation of firearms and explosives that Allied Import purchases from foreign suppliers. Garcia said that Derwish knew more about these items than anyone he had ever known. We asked Garcia what kind of explosives the company imports. He said that the company imports only plastic explosives such as Semtex, RDX, and C-4 that are very stable and can be shipped safely by ground and sea transport. Many American demolition companies use these explosives but can get them cheaper from China and some European companies. We asked Garcia whether any of Allied Imports' imported explosives had gone missing. He said that this has rarely happened, but about two weeks ago, a small amount of RDX, about two pounds, went missing from a storage facility to which al-Nami (Derwish) had access. We then asked Garcia whether we could talk with Derwish; Garcia said that Derwish had gone on vacation two days ago.

NFO-020-Yasmin: We contacted our source, Yasmin, again. All she has told us so far was that Saeed al-Nami used an alias (Kenny Derwish) and that he was associated with the militant jihadist group Jihad Bis Sayf. We now asked her for more information about al-Nami. She said that the name Derwish was a Yemeni name but al-Nami was a Saudi name. Yasmin said that he took this alias, Derwish, for two reasons: first, because it would sound a much less Muslim name to Americans, and second, because he admired the Yemenis and had spent a year in 2003 in an al Qaeda training camp in Yemen, where he received training in the use and construction of explosive devices. We asked Yasmin if any of this training might have included the assembly of dirty bombs. She says she would not rule this out because al Qaeda for many years wished to have these weapons and had assembled some stocks of radiological materials.

We have concluded that the terrorist organization Jihad Bis Sayf, through its member Saeed al-Nami, has taken possession of the cesium-137 canister. The next hypothesis to evaluate is whether this organization is capable of constructing a dirty bomb. We direct our intelligence collection efforts on Saeed al-Nami and obtain the items of information from Table 10.7, which will be used to assess this hypothesis, as indicated in Figure 10.6.

Finally, we investigate the top-level hypothesis, that Jihad Bis Sayf will set off a dirty bomb in the Washington, D.C., area. This reduces to assessing its reasons, desires, and capabilities, as shown in Figure 10.7. The case study in the next section allows you to assess this top-level hypothesis.

10.10.1.2 Practice

In this case study, you will analyze the hypothesis that Jihad Bis Sayf will set off a dirty bomb in the Washington, D.C., area. First you will define evidence based on the available

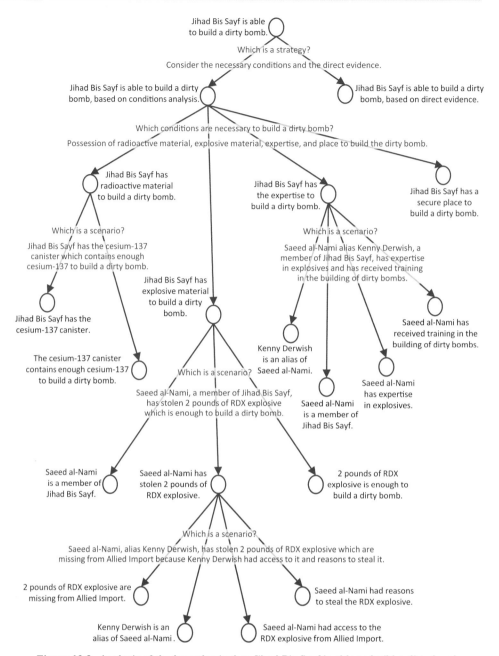

Figure 10.6. Analysis of the hypothesis that Jihad Bis Sayf is able to build a dirty bomb.

information. Then you will associate it with elementary hypotheses and evaluate them. Finally, you will define assumptions for the hypotheses that lack evidence. As a result, you will assess the probability of the top-level hypothesis.

Start Disciple-CD, select the knowledge base "14-Bomb-Set-Off," and proceed as indicated in the instructions from the bottom of the opened window.

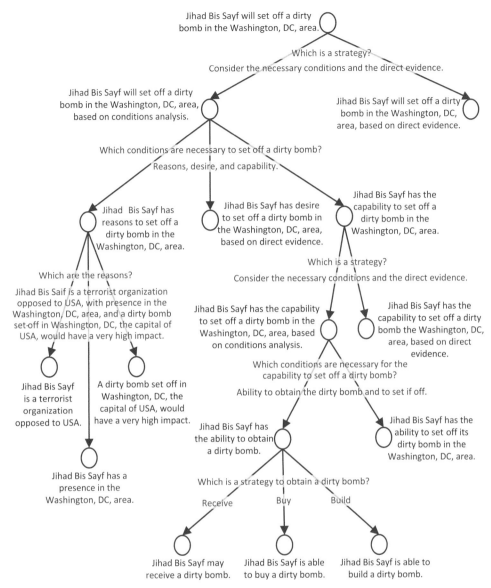

Figure 10.7. Analysis of the hypothesis that Jihad Bis Sayf will set off a dirty bomb in the Washington, D.C., area.

10.11 REVIEW QUESTIONS

10.1. Suppose in Example 10.2 (p. 180) you said that the prior probability of H is P(H) = 0.30, and the posterior probability is P(H|E*$_1$) = 0.95. What would be the force of evidence E*$_1$ that is implied by these assessments you have made?

10.2. Consider the following support assignments discussed in Section 10.6.3 (p. 196):

	{H$_1$}	{H$_1$^{C}}	{H$_1$, H$_1$^{C}}	Ø
Normalized s$_1$ ⊕ s$_2$	0.23	0.63	0.14	0
s$_3$	0.6	0.1	0.3	0

Apply the Dempster's rule and determine what our analyst's support for the new orthogonal sum $s_1 \oplus s_2 \oplus s_3$ should be.

10.3. Think back to the very first time you were ever tutored about probability, what it means, and how it is determined. What were you told about these matters? What are your present views about these probability matters?

10.4. As we noted, the subjective Bayesian view of probability lets us assess probabilities for singular, unique, or one-of-a-kind events, provided that our assessed probabilities obey the three Kolmogorov axioms we discussed previously regarding enumerative probabilities. First, is there any way of showing that these axioms for enumerative probabilities also form the basis for ideal or optimal probability assessments in the nonenumerative case? Second, can this really be the rational basis for all probability assessments based on evidence?

10.5. Show how Bayes' rule supplies no method for incorporating "pure evidence" as does the Belief Functions system.

10.6. Provide an example showing how an analyst's numerical assessment of a probability applied to a conclusion can invite criticism.

11 Analytic Bias

The topic of *bias* comes up repeatedly in works on intelligence analysis. Much of the discussion is based on research performed by psychologists decades ago. As a result of this research, psychologists have made some depressing and quite unreasonable claims about the extent of our inferential rationality. Conclusions reached and reported in this research have formed an important basis for the very influential work of R. J. Heuer (1999).

In this chapter, we will discuss different biases that have been identified in intelligence analysis and how Disciple-CD can help recognize and partially counter them. We will begin by examining various meanings attached to the term *bias* and to its various origins and possible species and relations. Also important are possible value-related consequences for the persons whose views are labeled as being biased in various ways. Reading other existing works on bias in intelligence analysis, many persons are likely to conclude that the only origins of bias are the intelligence analysts themselves. But there are other important origins of possible bias, including the *sources* of intelligence evidence (i.e., HUMINT), *persons in chains of custody of intelligence evidence*, and the policy-making *customers* of intelligence analyses. These additional classes of sources have their own species of bias.

11.1 BASIC INTERPRETATIONS OF THE TERM *BIAS*

The term *bias* arises in a variety of different contexts, some of which do not concern us, such as in dressmaking and in the game of bowls. A dressmaker is said to make cuts along the bias, meaning that he or she makes oblique cuts across the warp of a fabric. In the game of bowls, the swerving course of a bowl when thrown or lagged is termed *bias*. *Bias* does, of course, have some technical uses such as in statistics, machine learning, and engineering. In statistics and machine learning, we speak of a biased result if it is distorted in some way and arises from a neglected factor or an approximate model learned. In electrical engineering, one form of *bias* refers to steady voltages applied to an electronic device to stabilize its operation or to minimize distortions in recordings. *But our interests concern the use of the term* bias *with reference to people's views, beliefs, opinions, and related behaviors*; this use began in the midsixteenth century (Chantrell, 2004, p. 52). The term *bias* comes from the French *biais*. This word has its origin in the Greek *epikarsios*, meaning "oblique."

The question of interest to us is, *What is meant by the term* bias *when it is applied to peoples' views, beliefs, opinions, and related behaviors?* One place to begin answering this question is by considering words that have been used as synonyms for the word *bias*. First, some meanings that have been commonly associated with the term *bias* are prejudice, partiality, partisanship, favoritism, unfairness, one-sidedness, bigotry, intolerance, discrimination, leaning tendency, inclination, and predilection (Lindberg, 2004, p. 82).

The term *bias* often occurs in the field of law. As happens on so many other occasions, the interpretations of evidential and inferential concepts in legal contexts are very useful in intelligence analysis. *Black's Law Dictionary* provides several interpretations of the term bias (Black, 1968, p. 205): inclination, bent, preconceived opinion, a predisposition to decide a cause or an issue in a certain way that does not leave the mind perfectly open to conviction, and the inability to judge a matter impartially in a particular case. As we expect, all parties in some legal dispute – the parties in the dispute and their advocates, judges, and fact-finders – have their own particular biases.

The most well-known description of biases in intelligence analysis is that of Heuer (1999, pp. 111–171), who defines them as consistent and predictable mental errors caused by our simplified information processing strategies (Heuer, 1999, p. 111). "Cognitive biases are similar to optical illusions in that the error remains compelling even when one is fully aware of its nature. Awareness of the bias, by itself, does not produce a more accurate perception. Cognitive biases, therefore, are, exceedingly difficult to overcome" (Heuer, 1999, p. 112).

So, what can we do to reduce or eliminate recognized biases? We think that the best protection against biases in an intelligence analysis comes from the collaborative effort of teams of analysts, who become skilled in the evidential and argumentational elements of their tasks, who are willing to share their insights with colleagues, and who are also willing to listen. Employing a systematic approach to intelligence analysis that is based on scientific reasoning with evidence, which makes explicit all the reasoning steps, probabilistic assessments, and assumptions, so that they can be critically analyzed and debated, is the best protection against biases. That is why the use of an analytic tool such as Disciple-CD, which helps the analyst perform such an analysis, is one way to recognize and counter biases, as discussed in the rest of this chapter.

In the next section, we will review the analysts' biases discussed by Heuer: evaluation of evidence, perception of cause and effect, estimation of probabilities, and retrospective evaluation of intelligence reports. After that, we will present three other origins of bias that are rarely discussed, even though they may be at least as important on occasion as any analyst's biases. As we review various types of biases, we also discuss how the use of Disciple-CD helps identify and mitigate them. But before we proceed, let us mention that it would be quite impossible for anyone to list all the biases that can occur since people will always find new ways to be prejudiced, one-sided, and partisan. In any case, the biases of interest to us concern the views, beliefs, opinions, and related behaviors of people, intelligence analysts in particular. These are all subjective phenomena that occur intermittently in situations that are nearly impossible to predict. Further, biases in one situation may not be so in another. Finally, as we noted, it is one thing to recognize a possible relevant bias in intelligence analysis, and quite another thing to do something about it.

11.2   BIASES OF THE ANALYST

Heuer discusses analysts' biases that affect the evaluation of evidence, perception of cause and effect, estimation of probabilities, and retrospective evaluation of intelligence reports.

11.2.1   Biases in the Evaluation of Evidence

Heuer first mentions *vividness of evidence* as a necessary criterion for establishing its force. Analysts, like other persons, have preferences for certain kinds of evidence, and these preferences can induce biases. In particular, analysts can have a distinct preference for vivid or concrete evidence when less vivid or concrete evidence may be more inferentially valuable. In addition, their personal observations may be overvalued.

First, the hypothesis in search of evidence phase of the analysis helps identify a wide range of evidentiary needs. Consider, for example, the argumentation from the right side of Figure 11.1. It shows that we need evidence relevant to **L**, evidence relevant to **G**, evidence relevant to **H**, evidence relevant to **I**, and so on. It is unlikely that we would have vivid evidence for each leaf hypothesis. So we would be forced to use less vivid evidence as well.

Second, as discussed in Section 4.3, Disciple-CD guides us to assess a simple hypothesis **H** by performing a uniform, detailed, and systematic evaluation of the relevance and believability of each item of evidence, *regardless of its "vividness,"* helping us be more objective in the evaluation of the force of evidence.

Heuer also mentions the *absence of evidence* as another origin of bias. The bias here concerns a failure to consider the degree of completeness of available evidence. Consider again the argumentation from Figure 11.1, which decomposes complex hypotheses into simpler subhypotheses that are assessed based on evidence. This argumentation structure makes very clear that **I** is not supported by any evidence. Thus the analyst should lower his or her confidence in the final conclusion, countering the *absence of evidence* bias.

The next source of bias mentioned by Heuer is a related one: *oversensitivity to evidence consistency, and not enough concern about the amount of evidence we have.* This kind of bias can easily manifest when using an analytic tool such as Heuer's analysis of competing hypotheses (ACH) (Heuer, 2008), where the analyst judges alternative hypotheses based on evidence, without building any argumentation. With Disciple-CD, the argumentation will reveal whether most of the evidence is relevant only to a small fraction of subhypotheses, while many other subhypotheses have no evidentiary support. For example, the argumentation from Figure 11.1 shows that most of the evidence is related to hypothesis **H**.

According to Heuer (1999, pp. 121–122), "When working with a small but consistent body of evidence, analysts need to consider how representative that evidence is of the total body of potentially available information." The argumentation from Figure 11.1 makes

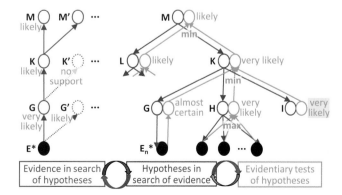

Figure 11.1. Scientific method framework of Disciple-CD.

very clear that the available evidence is not representative of all the potentially available information. We have no evidence relevant to **I**. If we would later find such evidence that would indicate "no support" for **I**, then the considered argumentation would provide "no support" for the top-level hypothesis **M**. When faced with subhypotheses for which there is no evidence (e.g., **I** in Figure 11.1), Disciple-CD allows the analyst to consider various what-if scenarios, making alternative assumptions with respect to the probability of **I**, and determining their influence on the probability of **M**. This should inform the analyst on how to adjust his or her confidence in the analytic conclusion, to counter the oversensitivity to evidence consistency bias.

Finally, Heuer lists the *persistence of impressions based on discredited evidence* as an origin of bias. If Heuer had written his book in 2003, he might have used the case of Curveball as a very good example (Drogin, 2007). In this case, Curveball's evidence was discredited on a number of grounds but was still believed and taken seriously by some analysts as well as many others.

Disciple-CD helps countering this bias by incorporating in the argumentation an explicit analysis of the believability of evidence, especially for key evidence that has a direct influence on the analytic conclusion. When such an evidence item is discredited, specific elements of its analysis are updated, and this leads to the automatic updating of the probability of each hypothesis to which it is relevant. For example, as shown in the Figure 6.3 (p. 124), the believability of the observations performed by a source (such as Curveball) depends on source's competence and credibility. Moreover, competence depends on access and understandability. Credibility depends on veracity, objectivity, and observational sensitivity under the conditions of observation. Thus, the bias that would result from the persistence of impressions based on discredited evidence is countered in Disciple-CD with a rigorous, detailed, and explicit believability analysis.

But there are additional biases in the evaluation of evidence that Heuer does not mention, particularly with respect to establishing the credentials of evidence: relevance, believability, and inferential force or weight. An analyst may confuse the competence of a HUMINT source with the source's credibility. Or, the analyst may focus on the veracity of the source and ignore the source's objectivity and observational sensitivity. Analysts may fail to recognize possible synergisms in convergent evidence, as happened in the September 11, 2001, disaster. Analysts may even overlook evidence having significant inferential force.

11.2.2 Biases in the Perception of Cause and Effect

As noted by Heuer, analysts seek explanations for the occurrence of events and phenomena. These explanations involve assessments of causes and effects. But biases arise when analysts assign causal relations to those that are actually accidental or random in nature. One related consequence is that analysts often overestimate their ability to predict future events from past events because there is no causal association between them. One major reason for these biases is that analysts may not have the requisite level of understanding of the kinds and amount of information necessary to infer a dependable causal relationship.

According to Heuer, when feasible, the "increased use of scientific procedures in political, economic, and strategic research is much to be encouraged," to counter these biases (Heuer, 1999, p. 128). Because Disciple-CD makes all the judgments explicit, they can be examined by other analysts to determine whether they contain any mistakes or are incomplete. Because different people have different biases, comparing and debating analyses of the same hypothesis made by different analysts can also help identify individual biases. Finally, as a learning system, Disciple-CD can acquire from expert analysts correct reasoning patterns that can then be used to analyze similar hypotheses.

Now, here is something that can occur in any analysis concerning chains of reasoning. It is always possible that an analyst's judgment will be termed biased or fallacious on structural grounds if it is observed that this analyst frequently leaves out important links in his or her chains of reasoning. This is actually a common occurrence, since in fact there is no such thing as a uniquely correct or perfect argument. Someone can always find alternative arguments to the same hypothesis; what this says is that there may be entirely different inferential routes to the same hypothesis. Another possibility is that someone may find arguments based on the same evidence that lead to different hypotheses. This is precisely why there are trials at law; the prosecution and defense will find different arguments, and tell different stories, from the same body of evidence.

11.2.3 Biases in Estimating Probabilities

As discussed in Chapter 10, there are different views among probabilists on how to assess the force of evidence (Schum, 1994 [2001a]). The view of probability that Heuer assumes is the conventional or Kolmogorov view of probability discussed in Section 10.3. This is also the only view of probability considered by Heuer's sources of inspiration on biases: Daniel Kahneman, Amos Tversky, and their many colleagues in psychology (Kahneman and Tversky, 1974; Kahneman et al., 1982). In his writings, Kolmogorov makes it abundantly clear that his axioms apply only to instances in which we can determine probabilities by counting. So, also clearly, Kolmogorov probabilities apply only to replicable, repeatable, or enumerative phenomena, those we can observe over and over again.

But Heuer also notes that intelligence analysis usually deals with one-of-a-kind situations for which there are never any statistics. In such cases, analysts resort to subjective or personal numerical probability expressions. He discusses several reasons why verbal assessments of probability are frequently criticized for their ambiguity and misunderstanding. In his discussion, he recalls Sherman Kent's advice that verbal assessments should always be accompanied by numerical probabilities (Kent, 1994). Heuer obviously agrees with Kent's advice.

Since Heuer considers only numerical probabilities conforming to the Kolmogorov axioms, any biases associated with them (e.g., using the availability rule, the anchoring strategy, expressions of uncertainty, assessing the probability of a scenario) are either irrelevant or not directly applicable to a type of analysis that is based on different probability systems, such as the one performed with Disciple-CD, which is based on the Baconian and Fuzzy probability systems. Indeed, analysts using Disciple-CD never assess any numerical probabilities.

Heuer (1999, p. 122) mentions *coping with evidence of uncertain accuracy* as an origin of bias:

> The human mind has difficulty coping with complicated probabilistic relationships, so people tend to employ simple rules of thumb that reduce the burden of processing such information. In processing information of uncertain accuracy or reliability, analysts tend to make a simple yes or no decision.

If they reject the evidence, they tend to reject it fully, so it plays no further role in their mental calculations. If they accept the evidence, they tend to accept it wholly, ignoring the probabilistic nature of the accuracy or reliability judgment. This is called a "best guess" strategy. Such a strategy simplifies the integration of probabilistic information, but at the expense of ignoring some of the uncertainty. If analysts have information about which they are 70- or 80-percent certain but treat this information as though it were 100-percent certain, judgments based on that information will be overconfident.

Then further Heuer (1999, p. 123) notes:

Analysts must consider many items of evidence with different degrees of accuracy and reliability that are related in complex ways with varying degrees of probability to several potential outcomes. Clearly, one cannot make neat mathematical calculations that take all of these probabilistic relationships into account. In making intuitive judgments, we unconsciously seek shortcuts for sorting through this maze, and these shortcuts involve some degree of ignoring the uncertainty inherent in less-than-perfectly-reliable information. There seems to be little an analyst can do about this, short of breaking the analytical problem down in a way that permits assigning probabilities to individual items of information, and then using a mathematical formula to integrate these separate probability judgments.

First, as discussed in the previous section, concerning the believability of evidence, there is more than just its accuracy to consider. Second, as discussed previously, Heuer considers only the *conventional view of probability,* which, indeed, involves complex probability computations.

With Disciple-CD, the analyst does precisely what Heuer imagined that could be done for countering this bias. It breaks a hypothesis into simpler hypotheses (see Figure 11.1) and assesses the simpler hypotheses based on evidence (see Figure 4.6, p. 73). Also, Disciple-CD allows the analyst to express probabilities in words rather than numbers and to employ simple min/max strategies for assessing the probability of interim and final hypotheses that do not involve any full-scale and precise Bayesian or other methods that would require very large numbers of probability assessments.

11.2.4   Hindsight Biases in Evaluating Intelligence Reporting

As Heuer notes, analysts often overestimate the accuracy of their past judgments; customers often underestimate how much they have learned from an intelligence report; and persons who conduct postmortem analysis of an intelligence failure will judge that events were more readily foreseeable than was in fact the case:

The analyst, consumer, and overseer evaluating analytical performance all have one thing in common. They are exercising hindsight. They take their current state of knowledge and compare it with what they or others did or could or should have known before the current knowledge was received. This is in sharp contrast with intelligence estimation, which is an exercise in foresight, and it is the difference between these two modes of thought – hindsight and foresight – that seems to be a source of bias. . . . After a view has been restructured to assimilate the new information, there is virtually no way to accurately reconstruct the pre-existing mental set (Heuer, 1999, p. 162).

Apparently Heuer did not envision the use of a system such as Disciple-CD that keeps track of the performed analysis, what evidence we had, what assumptions we made and what were their justifications, and what was the actual logic of our analytic conclusion. We can now add additional evidence and use our hindsight knowledge to restructure the argumentation and reevaluate our hypotheses, and we can compare the hindsight analysis with the foresight one. But we will not confuse them. As indicated by Heuer (1999, pp. 166–167): "A fundamental question posed in any postmortem investigation of intelligence failure is this: Given the information that was available at the time, should analysts have been able to foresee what was going to happen? Unbiased evaluation of intelligence performance depends upon the ability to provide an unbiased answer to this question." We suggest that this may be accomplished with a system such as Disciple-CD.

11.3 SOME FREQUENTLY OVERLOOKED ORIGINS OF BIAS

So much of the discussion of bias in intelligence analysis is directed at intelligence analysts themselves. But we have identified three other origins of bias that are rarely discussed, even though they may be at least as important on occasion as any analyst's alleged biases. The three other origins of bias we will consider are the following:

- Persons who provide testimonial evidence about events of interest (i.e., HUMINT sources)
- Other intelligence professionals having varying capabilities who serve as links in what we term "chains of custody" linking the evidence itself, as well as its sources, with the users of evidence (i.e., the analysts)
- The "consumers" of intelligence analyses (government and military officials who make policy and decisions regarding national security)

11.3.1 HUMINT Sources

Our concern here is with persons who supply us with testimonial evidence consisting of reports of events about matters of interest to us. Heuer (1999, p. 122) does mention the "bias on the part of the ultimate source," but he does not analyze it. In our work on evidence in a variety of contexts, we have always been concerned about establishing the believability of its sources, particularly when they are human witnesses, sources, or informants (Schum, 1994 [2001a]). In doing so, we have made use of the six-hundred-year-old legacy of experience and scholarship in the Anglo-American adversarial trial system concerning witness believability assessments. As discussed in Section 6.4, we have identified the three major attributes of the credibility of ordinary witnesses: veracity, objectivity, and observational sensitivity (see Figure 6.3, p. 124). We will show how there are distinct and important possible biases associated with each such believability attribute.

As discussed previously, assessing the credibility of a human source S involves assessing S's veracity, objectivity, and observational sensitivity. We have to consider that source

S can be biased concerning any of these attributes. On *veracity*, S might prefer to tell us that event **E** occurred, whether S believed **E** occurred or not. As an example, an analyst evaluating S's evidence **E*** might have evidence about S suggesting that S would tell us that **E** occurred because S wishes to be the bearer of what S believes we will regard as good news that event **E** occurred. On *objectivity*, S might choose to believe that **E** occurred because it would somehow be in S's best interests if **E** did occur. On *observational sensitivity*, there are various ways that S's senses could be biased in favor of recording event **E**; clever forms of deception supply examples.

These three species of bias possible for HUMINT sources must be considered by analysts attempting to assess the credibility of source S and how much weight or force S's evidence **E*** should have in the analyst's inference about whether or not event **E** did happen. The existence of any of these three biases would have an effect on an analyst's assessment of the weight or force of S's report **E***. As we know, all assessments of the credibility of evidence rest upon available evidence about its sources. In the case of HUMINT, we need ancillary evidence about the veracity, objectivity, and observational sensitivity of its sources. In the process, we have to see whether any such evidence reveals any of the three biases just considered. Disciple-CD supports the analyst in this determination by guiding him or her to answer specific questions based on ancillary evidence. The veracity questions to be considered are shown in Table 6.1 (p. 130), the objectivity questions are shown in Table 6.2 (p. 132), and the observational sensitivity questions are shown in Table 6.3 (p. 133).

11.3.2 Persons in Chains of Custody of Evidence

Unfortunately, there are other persons, apart from HUMINT sources, whose possible biases need to be carefully considered. We know that analysts make use of an enormous variety of evidence that is not testimonial or HUMINT, but is tangible in nature. Examples include objects, images, sensor records of various sorts, documents, maps, diagrams, charts, and tabled information of various kinds.

But the intelligence analysts only rarely have immediate and first access to HUMINT assets or informants. They may only rarely be the first ones to encounter an item of tangible evidence. What happens is that there are several persons who have access to evidence between the times the evidence is first acquired and when the analysts first receive it. These persons may do a variety of different things to the initial evidence during the time they have access to it. In law, these persons constitute what is termed a "chain of custody" for evidence.

Heuer (1999, p. 122) mentions the "distortion in the reporting chain from subsource through source, case officer, reports officer, to analyst," but he does not analyze it. In criminal cases in law, there are persons identified as "evidence custodians" who keep careful track of who discovered an item of evidence, who then had access to it and for how long, and what if anything they did to the evidence when they had access to it.

These chains of custody add three major additional sources of uncertainty for intelligence analysts to consider that are associated with the persons in chains of custody whose competence and credibility need to be considered. The first and most important question involves *authenticity*, "*Is the evidence received by an analyst exactly what the initial evidence said, and is it complete?* " The other questions involve assessing the *reliability* and *accuracy* of the processes used to produce the evidence if it is tangible in nature, or also used to take various actions on the evidence in a chain of custody, whether the evidence is tangible or testimonial. As an illustration, consider the chain of custody from Figure 7.2 (p. 142), concerning an item of testimonial HUMINT coming from a foreign national whose code name is "Wallflower" and who does not speak English. Wallflower gives his report to *case officer* Bob. This report is *recorded* by Bob and then *translated* by Husam. Then, Wallflower's translated report is *transmitted* to a *report's officer* Marsha, who *edits* it and *transmits* it to the analyst Clyde, who evaluates it and assesses its weight or force.

Now, here is where forms of bias can enter that can be associated with the persons involved in these chains of custody. The case officer, Bob, might have intentionally overlooked details in his recording of Wallflower's report. The translator, Husam, may have intentionally altered or deleted parts of this report. The report's officer, Marsha, might have altered or deleted parts of the translated report of Wallflower's testimony in her editing of it. The result of these actions is that Clyde, the analyst receiving this evidence, almost certainly did not receive an authentic and complete account of it, nor did he receive a good account of its reliability and accuracy. What he received was the transmitted, edited, translated, recorded testimony of Wallflower. Figure 7.4 shows how Disciple-CD may determine the believability of the evidence received by the analyst. Although the information to make such an analysis may not be available, the analyst should adjust the confidence in his or her conclusion, in recognition of these biases.

11.3.3   Consumers of Intelligence Analyses

The policy-making consumers or customers of intelligence analysts are also subject to a variety of inferential and decisional biases that may influence the reported analytic conclusions. As is well known, the relationships between intelligence analysts and governmental policy makers are much discussed and involve considerable controversy (Johnston, 2005; George and Bruce, 2008). On the one hand, we hear intelligence professionals say that they do not make policies but only try to help policy makers be as informed as they can be when they do form policies and make decisions in the nation's best interests. But we also learn facts about the intelligence process that complicate matters. An intelligence analysis is usually a hierarchical process involving many intelligence officers, at various grade levels, who become involved in producing an intelligence "product." At the most basic level of this hierarchy are the "desk analysts" who are known and respected experts in the specific subject matter of the analysis at hand. An analysis produced by one or more desk analysts is then passed "upward" through many administrative levels, at each of which persons at these higher levels can comment on the desk analysts' report. It is often recognized that the higher an editor is in this hierarchy, the more political his or her views and actions become that may affect the content and conclusions of the analysis at hand. As this "upward" process continues, the analysis that results may be quite different from the one produced by the desk analysts, reflecting the biases of those who have successively edited it. In some cases, these editing biases are the direct result of the biases of the consumer, who may wish to receive a certain analytic conclusion. Using a system such as Disciple-CD that shows very clearly how the analytic conclusion is rooted in evidence would significantly help in reducing the aforementioned biases.

11.4   BIASES AND THE EVALUATION OF ANALYSTS

We must also be concerned about the consequences to a person, such as an intelligence analyst, of being identified as displaying a bias of some sort. In the previous sections, we considered an array of biases identified by psychologists as being ones to which none of us are allegedly immune to having on occasion. For example, some of these biases are said to involve the numerical probabilities we might use to hedge conclusions about the hypotheses we assert as a result of an analysis of evidence. Here comes analyst A, whose assigned probability to hypothesis H_K is very high, say $P(H_K) = 0.95$. A is now labeled biased by critics since they provide good arguments that A has been one-sided or narrow-minded in his present analysis of evidence concerning the hypotheses of interest. A's probabilistic assessment is not taken seriously and may even be the object of scorn among colleagues whose considerably smaller assigned probabilities to H_K are the ones reported to an interested customer who concludes that hypothesis H_K is not true. But time passes and it is discovered that hypothesis H_K is true, much to the distress of the customer. This raises some interesting and difficult issues concerning the relation between bias and error.

The question is, *"Are all demonstrably biased judgments necessarily erroneous?"* In our example, analyst A's biased judgment initially invited criticism. But because it was more correct than the judgments of other analysts, should it now invite praise? The issues raised in such instances are value-related. Suppose it is argued that, since A's judgments are frequently the result of one-sided or narrow-minded analyses, A was only lucky in the case of A's inferences regarding hypothesis H_K, and therefore A deserves no praise. So, the answer to the preceding question seems to be that a biased judgment does not entail that it is necessarily erroneous. Whether a biased judgment that happens to be correct deserves praise involves some difficult choices.

There are some facts about the world that add great complexity to intelligence analysis and bear on the relations between bias and error. First, the world is not stationary, and new things happen all the time. As a result, discovery in intelligence analysis is continuous and never ceases. We learn new things all the time. Beliefs about some hypothesis regarded as being very likely or unlikely a short time ago are overtaken by events that occurred just today. This means that intelligence analysis is a seamless process involving mixtures of three basic forms of reasoning: abductive (imaginative or insightful), deductive, and inductive. These mixtures of reasoning form one of the basic features of Disciple-CD. Here is an example of how continuing discovery bears on bias and error.

There is a reason why analyst A's high probability for H_K was criticized as being biased because A's analysis was one-sided or narrow-minded. Critics noted that A ignored even considering events E, F, and G, which, if they occurred, would be evidence against hypothesis H_K. Perhaps A preferred not to take into account events that would make A's favored hypothesis less likely. These same critics either assumed or had evidence for some or all of events E, F, and G; this is why their assessments of the numerical probability of H_K were so much smaller than A's $P(H_K) = 0.95$. But we have recently discovered evidence that events E, F, and G definitely did not occur; evidence of their occurrence was not credible for various reasons. And we also learned that H_K is true after all.

So, in light of these new discoveries, A's being one-sided or narrow-minded apparently worked to A's advantage in this instance. However, if these biases are routinely characteristic of A's analyses, we would be entitled to be skeptical of A's probabilistic judgments. The critics' beliefs that A was simply lucky in the present analysis seem to have merit. Here is a view, quite reasonable but controversial, concerning how an intelligence analysis should be graded. *On this view, an analysis should be graded in terms of how well it was done and not whether it was correct or not.* This is precisely the view often taken in much of contemporary decision analysis (Clemen, 1995, pp. 3–4). According to this criterion, $\mathcal{A}$ should not be praised for the high probability $\mathcal{A}$ assigned to a true hypothesis, but criticized for the manner in which $\mathcal{A}$ inferred this high probability.

11.5   RECOGNIZING AND COUNTERING BIASES WITH DISCIPLE-CD

A wide variety of biases affect the correctness of intelligence analyses. In the previous sections, we have shown how the use of Disciple-CD helps analysts recognize and counter many of them. There are two complementary ways by which Disciple-CD helps mitigate biases. First, as a cognitive assistant, it helps automate many parts of the analysis process, making this task much easier for the analyst. Thus it alleviates one of the main causes of cognitive biases, which is the employment of simplified information-processing strategies on the part of the analyst. Second, Disciple-CD performs a rigorous evidence-based hypothesis analysis that makes explicit all the reasoning steps, evidence, probabilistic assessments, and assumptions, so that they can be critically analyzed and debated. Indeed, the best protection against biases comes from the collaborative effort of teams of analysts, who become skilled in solving their analytic tasks through the development of sound evidence-based arguments, who are willing to share their insights with colleagues, and who are also willing to listen. Disciple-CD and its predecessor (TIACRITIS) make all these possible (Tecuci et al., 2013a).

Finally, in the debate on how to improve intelligence analysis significantly, this discussion adds a strong argument in favor of using structured analytic methods (Marrin and Clemente, 2005; Marrin, 2011).

11.6   REVIEW QUESTIONS

11.1. An intelligence analysis has miscarried on an important matter concerning national security, and a postmortem hearing is now in progress to determine what went wrong. Attention is focused on the work of analyst A, who provided key judgments during the analysis process. At the hearing a critic notes, "Our main trouble was that we paid too much attention to analyst A, who gave us a *biased* assessment of the force of evidence E*. A said this evidence very strongly favored hypothesis H_2, which we now know did not occur. H_4 really happened and we have all been embarrassed since we reported that H_2 was true." What could have happened that led this critic to say that A was biased? Who or what determines analytic bias? And, can analytic bias be prevented?

11.2. Are there sources of bias that cannot be linked to individual analysts or teams of analysts?

11.3. An episode of intelligence analysis can go wrong for many reasons. On many accounts we have read, assorted alleged analytic biases are the major reasons why an analysis has gone wrong. In some cases, it seems that it is argued that analytic bias is the only reason why an intelligence analysis can go wrong. However, an analysis may go wrong for other reasons not involving *bias* but rather for an assortment of analytic *errors* that might be made. What is the distinction between *bias* and *error* in intelligence analysis, and why is this distinction so important to recognize and discuss?

11.4.   In discussions of bias, so much attention has been based on numerical assessments of the probability of hypotheses considered in intelligence analysis. What other properties of intelligence analysis represent a much more important emphasis in assessing the quality of an analysis?

11.5.   Some intelligence analysts may look upon Heuer's ACH methods, as well as other methods, as being ways of simplifying intelligence analyses. There are some problems associated with such views; can you think of some of these problems?

11.6.   What approaches can be taken if there are no ways of simplifying the requirements for the analyses intelligence professionals face in an ever-changing world?

11.7.   Can analysts ever be criticized for having drawn incorrect conclusions? Or, are some alleged "intelligence failures" actually failures after all?

12 Learning and Reusing Analytic Expertise: Beyond Disciple-CD

12.1 INTRODUCTION

The Disciple-CD system provided with this book is a very general cognitive assistant for an end-user analyst who has no knowledge engineering experience and no access to or support from a knowledge engineer. However, Disciple-CD was created as a limited customized version of a more powerful system, called Disciple-EBR, a learning agent shell for evidence-based reasoning (Tecuci et al., 2013b; 2016). With Disciple-CD, the end-user can only access those modules of Disciple-EBR that can be used without any assistance from a knowledge engineer.

If, however, an organization can (occasionally) provide some knowledge engineering support to its analysts, then it can use Disciple-EBR, which has much more powerful reasoning and learning capabilities. Disciple-EBR has been trained with general knowledge for evidence-based reasoning, which is also used by Disciple-CD. But Disciple-EBR can be further trained by an expert analyst (with limited knowledge engineering support) on how to analyze complex hypotheses in a given intelligence analysis domain. The resulting cognitive assistant can then be used by a typical analyst to analyze hypotheses rapidly from this intelligence analysis domain. During its use, the system continues to learn from its user.

A trained Disciple-EBR system will significantly reduce the time required to perform an analysis, which will also have an improved quality. Indeed, developing an argumentation to assess a hypothesis will be much faster because the system will automatically retrieve and apply previously learned argumentation fragments. Moreover, the resulting argumentation will be more complete and more correct because it will incorporate vetted analytic fragments learned from expert analysts.

The development of cognitive assistants for evidence-based reasoning with a tool such as Disciple-EBR is presented in detail in Tecuci et al. (2016). In this chapter, we will provide only a general description of this process that could result in significantly more powerful cognitive assistants than Disciple-CD, for a wide variety of evidence-based reasoning domains besides intelligence analysis, such as forensics, cybersecurity, medicine, law, and any branch of science (physics, chemistry, etc.).

12.2 LEARNING AGENT SHELL

For many years (Tecuci, 1988; 1998; Tecuci et al., 2016), we have researched a theory, methodology, and tools for the development of knowledge-based cognitive assistants that:

- Learn complex problem solving expertise directly from subject matter experts
- Support experts and nonexperts in problem solving and decision making
- Teach their problem-solving expertise to students

The investigated approach relies on developing a powerful learning agent shell that can be taught by a subject matter expert how to solve problems in the expert's area (Tecuci et al., 1999; Boicu et al., 2000; Tecuci et al., 2005b). Because the resulting agent learns to replicate the problem-solving behavior of its human expert, we have called it a Disciple agent.

The overall architecture of a learning agent shell is shown in Figure 12.1. It contains a general problem-solving engine, a learning engine, and a general knowledge base.

The problem-solving engine implements a general method of solving (assessing) the input problems (hypotheses) based on the knowledge from the knowledge base. An example of such a general method is problem reduction and solution synthesis, which was presented in Chapter 5 and used throughout this book, in the context of intelligence analysis. As illustrated in the right side of Figure 12.2, this method consists in solving a problem, such as P_1, by successively reducing it, from the top down, to simpler and simpler problems; finding the solutions of the simplest problems; and successively combining these solutions, from the bottom up, into the solution of the initial problem (i.e., S_1).

Knowledge of the actual problems to solve and how they can be reduced to simpler problems depends on the expertise domain. This knowledge is represented in the knowledge base of the system by using different representation formalisms. The left and middle parts of Figure 12.2 illustrate the representation of this knowledge by using an ontology of

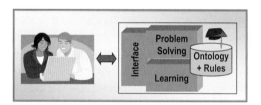

Figure 12.1. The overall architecture of a learning agent shell.

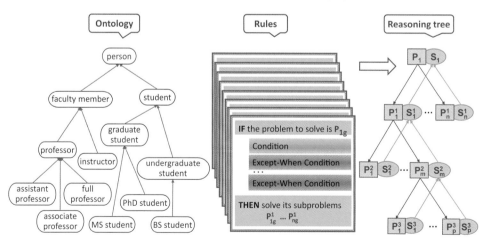

Figure 12.2. Knowledge and reasoning.

concepts and a set of rules expressed with these concepts. The ontology describes the types of objects in the application domain, as well as the relationships between them. Some of the rules are if-then structures that indicate the conditions under which a general problem (such as P_{1g}) can be reduced to simpler problems. Other rules indicate how the solutions of simpler problems can be combined into the solution of the more complex problem. These reduction and composition (synthesis) rules are applied to generate the reasoning tree from the right part of Figure 12.2.

Building an agent for a specific application consists in customizing the learning agent shell for that application and in developing the knowledge base. The learning engine facilitates the building of the knowledge base by subject matter experts and knowledge engineers. In essence, the subject matter expert teaches the Disciple agent shell how to solve problems in ways that are similar to how the expert would teach a student or a collaborator (Tecuci et al., 2001; 2002b; 2005b). For example, the expert will show the agent examples of how to solve specific problems, helping it to understand the solutions, and will supervise and correct the problem-solving behavior of the agent. The agent will learn from the expert by generalizing the examples and building its knowledge base. This approach is based on the synergism between the expert who has the knowledge to be formalized and the agent that knows how to formalize knowledge. It is based on methods for *mixed-initiative problem solving* (Tecuci et al., 2007a), where the expert solves the more creative parts of the problem and the agent solves the more routine ones; *integrated teaching and learning* (Tecuci and Kodratoff, 1995), where, for example, the agent helps the expert to teach it by asking relevant questions, and the expert helps the agent to learn, by providing examples, hints, and explanations; and *multistrategy learning* (Tecuci and Michalski, 1991; Tecuci 1993; Michalski and Tecuci, 1994), where the agent integrates multiple learning strategies, such as learning from examples, learning from explanations, and learning by analogy, to learn from the expert how to solve problems.

Disciple agents have been developed for many domains besides intelligence analysis; for example, they have been used to model the behavior of violent extremists, to determine strategic centers of gravity in military conflicts (Tecuci et al., 2002a; 2002b; 2008b), to critique military courses of action with respect to the principles of war and the tenets of Army operations (Boicu et al., 2000; Tecuci et al, 2001), to plan how to work around infrastructure damage (Tecuci et al., 2000) or how to respond to emergencies (Tecuci et al., 2008c), to perform financial services, and to teach students (Tecuci and Keeling, 1999).

The long-term goal of the Disciple approach is to contribute to a new revolution in the use of computers by enabling typical computer users to develop their own cognitive assistants. Thus, non–computer scientists will no longer be only users of generic programs developed by others (such as word processors or Internet browsers), as they are today, but also agent developers themselves. They will be able to train their personal Disciple assistants to help them with their increasingly complex tasks in the knowledge society, which should have a significant beneficial impact on their work and life. This goal is consistent with the Semantic Web vision of enabling typical users to author web content that can be understood by automated agents (Allemang and Hendler, 2011; W3C, 2015). Bill Gates has also stressed the great potential and importance of software assistants (Simonite, 2013).

12.3   LEARNING AGENT SHELL FOR EVIDENCE-BASED REASONING

12.3.1   Disciple-EBR

Tasks in many domains, such as intelligence analysis, cybersecurity, law, forensics, medicine, physics, chemistry, history, or archaeology, involve evidence-based reasoning. While expressed in various forms, many tasks in all these domains use similar concepts and problem-solving methods or rules. We have abstracted this knowledge in a domain-independent way and have taught a learning agent shell with general evidence-based reasoning knowledge from the science of evidence (Schum, 2011), transforming it into a learning agent shell for evidence-based reasoning, called Disciple-EBR (Tecuci et al., 2013b). An abstract architecture of Disciple-EBR is shown in Figure 12.3. It includes multiple modules for reasoning and learning, as well as a hierarchically organized knowledge base (KB) with domain-independent knowledge for evidence-based reasoning at the top of the knowledge hierarchy (called Shared EBR KB in Figure 12.3).

The Shared EBR KB contains both a general ontology and a set of general reasoning rules that are applicable in an evidence-based reasoning domain, such as intelligence analysis. For example, the Shared EBR KB contains a general ontology of evidence that includes the ontology fragment from Figure 6.1 (p. 119) that defines the various types of tangible and testimonial evidence. It also includes the ontology fragment from Figure 8.1 (p. 155) that defines the recurrent substance-blind combinations of evidence. Additionally, it defines other evidence-based concepts that have been discussed in this book, such as relevance, believability, inferential force, competence, credibility, authenticity, accuracy, reliability, veracity, objectivity, observational sensitivity, favoring evidence, and disfavoring evidence.

Learned general rules include those for directly assessing a hypothesis based on evidence. As shown in Figure 4.6 (p. 73), these rules automatically reduce the assessment of any elementary hypothesis H to assessments based on favoring and disfavoring evidence and, further down, to the assessment of the *relevance* and the *believability* of each item of evidence with respect to H. Once these assessments are made, they are combined,

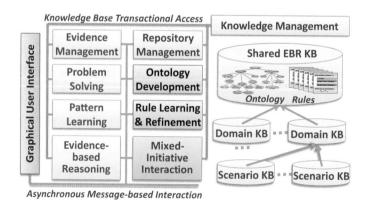

Figure 12.3. The architecture of Disciple-EBR.

from the bottom up, to obtain the *inferential force* of all the items of evidence on H, which results in the probability of H.

Learned general rules also include those for assessing the believability of different types of evidence. These rules are automatically applied to generate reasoning trees such as those shown in Figure 6.3 (p. 124), Figure 6.7 (p. 135), and Figure 6.8 (p. 136). Other learned believability rules correspond to mixed evidence, such as tangible evidence about testimonial evidence (see Figure 6.4, p. 129) or evidence obtained through a chain of custody, such as when a person describes the observation performed by another person (see Figure 7.4, p. 146).

The important point here is that the Disciple learning agent shell has been taught a significant amount of general evidence-based reasoning knowledge, transforming it into a customized learning agent shell for evidence-based reasoning tasks. Thus, when a subject matter expert starts teaching Disciple-EBR for a specific evidence-based reasoning domain (e.g., predictive analysis related to energy sources or assessments related to the current production of weapons of mass destruction by various actors), the system already has a significant amount of evidence-based reasoning knowledge. What it will learn from the subject matter expert is domain-specific knowledge that will populate a domain knowledge base (Domain KB), shown just under the Shared EBR KB (see Figure 12.3). The Domain KB will contain domain-specific concepts (e.g., state, power source) and reasoning rules (e.g., reduction rules to analyze hypotheses from that domain). Under each Domain KB there are several Scenario KBs, each corresponding to an instance of a problem from that domain, such as assessing the hypothesis that the United States will be a global leader in wind power within the next decade. This Scenario KB will contain specific knowledge about the United States, as well as items of evidence to make the corresponding assessment. The actual analysis will be done by using this knowledge as well as more general knowledge inherited from the corresponding Domain KB and from the Shared EBR KB.

Once Disciple-EBR has been trained by a subject matter expert to analyze hypotheses in a given domain, such as energy sources, it becomes an expert assistant in that domain. At that point, it can be used by a typical analyst to analyze hypotheses rapidly from the agent's area of expertise. During its use, the agent continues to learn from its user.

12.3.2 Disciple-CD

Disciple-CD (Tecuci et al., 2014), which was extensively used in this book, is a reduced version of Disciple-EBR. This version was created for the end-user who has no knowledge engineering experience and receives no support from a knowledge engineer. Therefore, the user does not have access to any Disciple-EBR module that may require any kind of knowledge engineering support, such as Ontology Development, Rule Learning, or Rule Refinement (see Figure 12.3).

Because Disciple-CD contains the general evidence-based reasoning knowledge, it is applicable to any evidence-based reasoning domain. But its learning capabilities are limited to the learning of context-independent reasoning patterns, as was presented in Sections 5.7.2 and 5.7.3.

Figure 12.4 contrasts pattern learning from a reduction example with rule learning from the same example. A pattern is a context-independent generalization of the example where each entity (such as US Democratic Party) is replaced with a variable (i.e., ?O3). This means that, from the system's perspective, the variable ?O3 can be replaced with any instances, even those for which the resulting hypothesis or reduction will make no sense. It is the user's responsibility to define the correct value for such a variable, which may be a challenging task. When developing an argumentation, the agent will suggest to the user all the reduction patterns that match the current hypothesis, and the user has to select the appropriate one (if any) and provide the values for some of the variables (such as ?O3). As the number of learned patterns increases, browsing them and selecting the appropriate one becomes increasingly difficult.

As opposed to a pattern, a rule is a context-dependent generalization of the example that expresses semantics of the example in the form of an applicability condition. In particular, the rule from the right-hand side of Figure 12.4 states that the learned reduction pattern is applicable if ?O1 is a state, ?O2 is a power source, ?O3 is a political party, and ?O1 has ?O3 as a major political party.

Notice in the representation of a learned rule the same principle as in the Semantic Web (Allemang and Hendler, 2011; W3C, 2015): We have two representations of the rule's applicability condition, a natural language expression for human use (represented by the question/answer pair), and a formal representation for automatic reasoning by the agent (represented by the MAIN CONDITION).

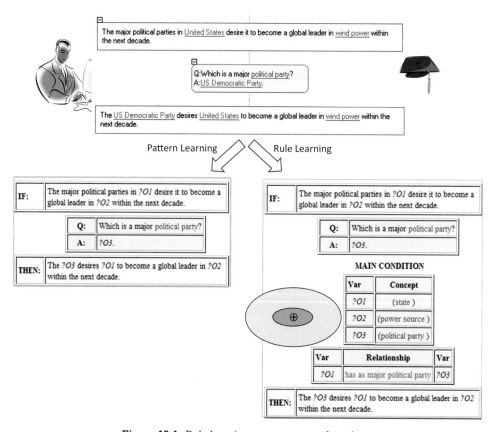

Figure 12.4. Rule learning versus pattern learning.

When the system encounters a hypothesis that matches the pattern "The major political parties in ?O1 desire it to become a global leader in ?O2 within the next decade," such as, "The major political parties in United Kingdom desire it to become a global leader in wind power within the next decade," it uses the knowledge from its ontology to check whether the applicability condition of the rule is satisfied. That is, it checks whether the United Kingdom (which corresponds to ?O1) is a state, whether wind power (which corresponds to ?O2) is a power source, and whether the United Kingdom (?O1) has some major political party (which corresponds to ?O3). It finds that all these conditions are satisfied, where ?O3 can be the UK Conservative Party, the UK Labor Party, or the UK Liberal Democrats. As a result, the system automatically reduces the hypothesis as shown in Figure 12.5.

Pattern learning has the advantage that it could be employed by a typical analyst, while rule learning relies on the existence of an ontology that has to be developed by a knowledge engineer before rule learning can be employed.

However, with the increase in the number of learned patterns it becomes more and more difficult for the analyst to reuse them. This is because the patterns do not have applicability conditions, and a large number of them are proposed to the analyst, who has to select the correct one and properly instantiate it. Moreover, a pattern can extend the reasoning with only one step, and therefore the process needs to be repeated for each step of the reasoning. In contrast, rules are automatically applied in sequence, automatically generating entire reasoning trees such as that in Figure 6.7 (p. 135).

As compared to the patterns, the rules (through their applicability conditions) encode more of the subject matter expertise and are much easier for other analysts to reuse.

12.4   DEVELOPMENT OF A COGNITIVE ASSISTANT

Figure 12.6 shows the main stages of the learning-based methodology of evolving the Disciple-EBR learning agent shell into a cognitive assistant for a particular evidence-based reasoning domain, such as predictive analysis on energy sources.

The first phase is *agent specification,* during which a knowledge engineer and an expert analyst define the desired expertise domain of the agent, or the types of hypotheses to be assessed with the agent. For example, the domain might be predictive analysis of what

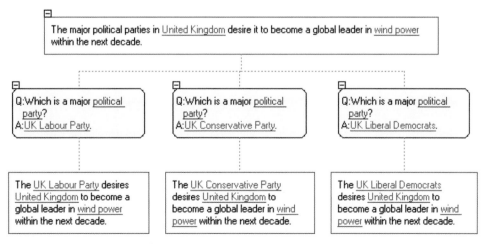

Figure 12.5. Reduction of a hypothesis through the automatic application of a learned rule.

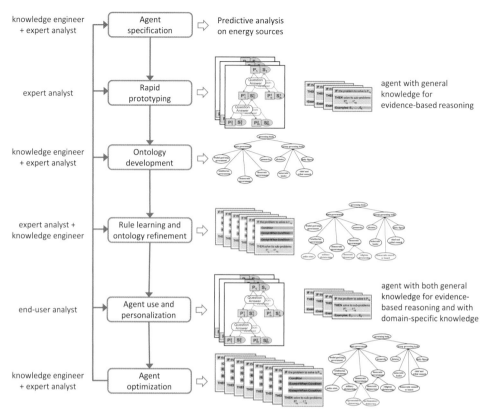

Figure 12.6. Main stages of the agent development methodology.

actors will be the world leaders in developing different types of energy sources within a certain period of time. Another domain might be to assess whether a certain actor is currently pursuing a certain type of weapons of mass destruction.

The second phase is *rapid prototyping*, where the expert analyst develops argumentation structures for specific but representative hypotheses. Such an argumentation is shown in Figure 12.7. Notice in Figure 12.7 that the reduction of each hypothesis is guided by an introspective question/answer pair. Consider the hypothesis "United States has the desire to be a global leader in wind power within the next decade." The expert asks himself or herself, "Which are the main stakeholders who determine the desire of United States?" The answer, "The people, the major political parties, and the energy industries because United States has a democratic government," guides the expert to reduce the hypothesis to three simpler hypotheses, as shown in the middle of Figure 12.7. Notice that the question/answer pair also includes the explanation of the reduction ("because United States has a democratic government"), which will greatly facilitate the learning of a general reduction rule from this step alone, as will be discussed later in this section.

The next phase is that of *ontology development*. The guiding question is, "What are the domain concepts, relationships, and instances that would enable the agent to automatically generate the reasoning trees developed during rapid prototyping?"

From each reasoning step, the knowledge engineer, with support from the expert analyst, identifies the ontology elements mentioned in it and their necessary relationships. For example, the reasoning step from the top of Figure 12.8 suggests that the Domain KB

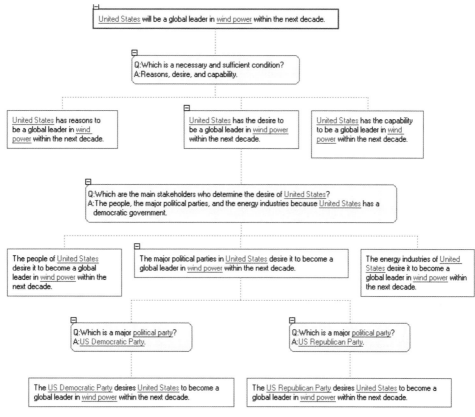

Figure 12.7. Inquiry-driven hypothesis analysis.

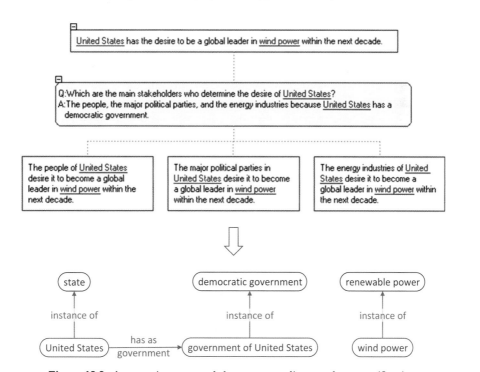

Figure 12.8. A reasoning step and the corresponding ontology specification.

should include the objects and the relationships from the bottom of Figure 12.8, which also represent an explanation of why the reduction step is correct.

Such ontology (semantic network) fragments represent a specification of the needed ontology. In particular, the ontology fragment from the bottom-left side of Figure 12.8 suggests the need for an ontology of government types, such as that in Figure 12.9. Also, the ontology fragment from the bottom-right side of Figure 12.8 suggests the need for an ontology of power types (wind power, solar power, wave power, etc.). Based on such specifications, and using the ontology development tools of the Disciple-EBR shell, the knowledge engineer develops a domain ontology. As part of ontology development, the knowledge engineer may reuse concepts and relationships from previously developed ontologies, including those on the Semantic Web (Allemang and Hendler, 2011; W3C, 2015).

The next stage in agent development is that of *rule learning and ontology refinement*. The expert analyst guides the agent to learn a general reduction rule from each reduction step of the reasoning trees developed during rapid prototyping. To illustrate, the IF-THEN reduction rule learned from the middle reduction in Figure 12.7 is shown in Figure 12.10. The rule pattern is obtained by generalizing each instance and constant in the reduction step to a variable (e.g., United States is generalized to ?O1). The rule's condition (MAIN CONDITION) is partially learned, consisting of a lower bound and an upper bound. The lower bound is obtained as the minimal generalization of the ontology (semantic network) fragments from Figure 12.8, while the upper bound is obtained as the maximal generalization, with both generalizations being based on the entire agent's ontology, which is used as a generalization hierarchy (Tecuci et al., 2005b; 2008c). During rule refinement (discussed in the following paragraphs), the two bounds will converge toward one another and toward the exact applicability condition. This exact condition will ensure that the rule will generate only correct reductions. A completely learned rule, with an exact applicability condition, is shown in Figure 12.4

Next the expert analyst teaches the agent how to assess similar hypotheses, such as "China will be a global leader in solar power within the next decade," and the agent automatically generates the reasoning tree by applying the learned rules. The analyst critiques the agent's reasoning, and the agent refines the rules accordingly (Tecuci et al., 2005b). Incorrect reductions lead to the specialization of the upper bound conditions, while correct reductions lead to the generalization of the lower bound conditions, the bounds converging toward one another and toward exact applicability conditions.

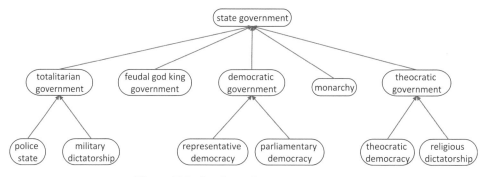

Figure 12.9. Ontology of government types.

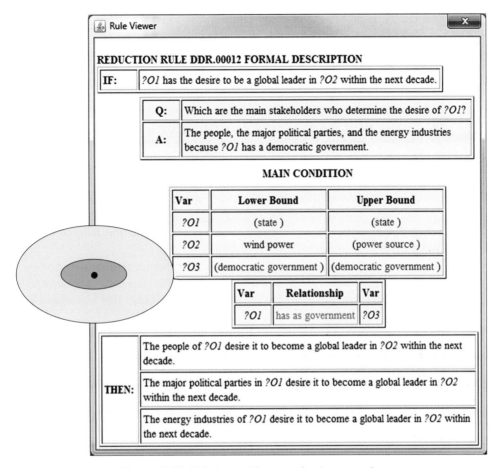

Figure 12.10. Rule learned from a reduction example.

The ontology may also be refined during this phase, for example by adding new concepts and relationships that explain why a reduction step is incorrect.

Now the assistant is ready to be used by typical analysts as part of the next phase, *agent use and personalization.* Typically, the analyst will specify the hypothesis to analyze (e.g., "United Kingdom will be a global leader in wave power within the next decade") by simply instantiating the corresponding pattern. Then the agent will automatically generate a reduction tree like the one in Figure 12.7 by applying the learned reduction rules. This tree reduces the top-level hypothesis to elementary hypotheses to be directly assessed based on evidence. The analyst will then have to search the Internet and other repositories for evidence and attach each item of evidence to the hypothesis to which it is relevant. As a result, the agent will automatically reduce the elementary hypotheses based on evidence credentials, as indicated in the previous chapters. Next the analyst has to assess the relevance and the believability of each item of evidence, and, based on them, the agent automatically computes the inferential force of evidence by applying the corresponding synthesis functions. This will eventually result in the probability of the top-level hypothesis.

So when does the additional learning take place? It may be the case that the agent does not know how to reduce a specific hypothesis. Then the end-user analyst needs to indicate its reduction. As a result, the agent will learn a reduction pattern like the one from the left-hand side of Figure 12.4.

Periodically the agent can undergo an *optimization phase,* which is the last phase in Figure 12.6. During this phase, a knowledge engineer and an expert analyst will review the patterns learned from the typical analyst, will learn corresponding rules from them, and will correspondingly refine the ontology.

12.5   EVIDENCE-BASED REASONING EVERYWHERE

As illustrated in Figure 12.11, evidence-based reasoning is at the core of many problem-solving and decision-making tasks in a wide variety of domains, including physics, chemistry, history, archaeology, medicine, law, forensics, intelligence analysis, cybersecurity, and many others. This is not surprising because, as Jeremy Betham stated over two centuries ago, "The field of evidence is no other than the field of knowledge" (Betham, 1810).

As discussed in this book, an intelligence analyst formulates alternative hypotheses that would explain the evidence about an event. Then he or she puts each of the hypotheses to work to guide him or her in the collection of additional evidence that is used to assess the probability of each hypothesis.

Scientists from various domains, such as physics, chemistry, or biology, may recognize this as a formulation of the scientific method.

In medicine, a doctor makes observations with respect to a patient's complaints and attempts to generate possible diagnoses (hypotheses) that would explain them. He or she then performs various medical tests that provide further evidence for or against the various hypothesized illnesses. After that, the doctor uses the obtained evidence to determine the most likely illness.

In law, an attorney makes observations in a criminal case and seeks to generate hypotheses in the form of charges that seem possible in explaining these observations. Then, assuming that a charge is justified, attempts are made to deduce further evidence bearing on it. Finally, the obtained evidence is used to prove the charge.

In forensics, observations made at the site of an explosion in a power plant lead to the formulation of several possible causes. Analysis of each possible cause leads to the discovery of new evidence that eliminates or refines some of the causes, and may even suggest new ones. This cycle continues until enough evidence is found to determine the most likely cause.

In cybersecurity, a suspicious connection to our computer from an external computer triggers the automatic generation of alternative threat and nonthreat hypotheses. Each generated hypothesis is used to guide the collection of additional evidence, which is used to assess the probability of each hypothesis (Meckl et al., 2015).

The following, for instance, are examples of different hypotheses one may be interested in assessing based on evidence:

- University U would be a good university for the student S.
- Professor P would be a good Ph.D. Advisor for the student S.
- The house H would be a good house to be bought by the person P.
- Country C will be a world leader in nonconventional energy sources within the next decade.
- Country C has nuclear weapons.

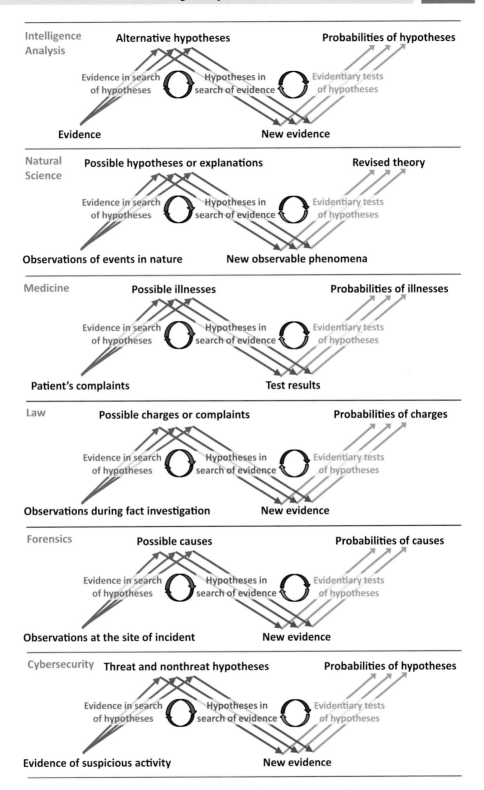

Figure 12.11. Evidence-based reasoning everywhere.

- Person P was murdered by the suspect S.
- Patient P has illness I.
- Building B has collapsed because of the use of low-quality materials.
- Connection C is part of APT1 intrusion using the malware M.

Thus, there are very many applications of agents developed with Disciple-EBR. To explore the development of cognitive assistants for evidence-based reasoning tasks further, we refer the reader to Tecuci et al. (2016).

Glossary of Terms

Abductive reasoning (imaginative, creative, or insightful reasoning).
A form of reasoning that makes some conclusion possibly true, used to generate hypotheses from data.

Access.
An attribute of the competence of a human source characterizing the extent to which that source actually made the observation he or she claims to have made or had access to the information that he or she reports.

Accuracy.
Also termed *sensitivity*. An attribute of the credibility of certain kinds of tangible evidence such as those provided by sensing devices and tabled information.

Ambiguous evidence.
Evidence that is imprecisely stated and does not enable people to determine exactly what it is telling.

Analysis.
A reasoning operation by which we break down a hypothesis into components to better assess it. This operation is complementary to synthesis.

Ancillary evidence.
Evidence about other evidence and its inferential force probative strength; also termed *indirectly relevant evidence* and *meta-evidence.*

Anomaly.
Evidence that seems unexplainable or out of place.

Argument.
A chain of reasoning connecting observed evidence with a hypothesis of interest; the links in such chains represent ordered sequences of sources of doubt that the analyst believes to be interposed between evidence and hypothesis.

Argument magnet.
Magnet that attracts trifles that will form relevant evidence on major arguments for some hypothesis being entertained.

Assumption.
An inference made in the absence or deficits of evidence.

Authenticity.	An attribute of the credibility of tangible evidence referring to whether a tangible item is what it is claimed to be.
Auxiliary evidence.	Another term for ancillary evidence.
Baconian probability system.	A probability system based on Sir Francis Bacon's eliminative and variative views on evidential reasoning. This is the only system that captures how completely our evidence covers matters that should be covered in an inference problem.
Balance of probability.	A probability standard used in law to refer to cases in which the evidence favors one hypothesis over another even by the smallest amount.
Bayesian probability system.	A probability system based on the conventional axioms of probability that concern games of chance and statistics, both of which involve repeatable phenomena. This system has deficits when applied to cases involving nonrepeatable events and situations.
Belief Functions.	A probability system very useful for nonrepeatable events and situations. In this system, beliefs are associated with any combination of the considered hypotheses.
Believability.	Credential of evidence indicating the degree to which we can believe what the evidence is telling us.
Believability magnet.	Magnet that attracts trifles we have concerning the competence and credibility of our sources of intelligence information.
Beyond reasonable doubt.	A probability standard used in law to refer to the highest grade of support evidence can provide some hypothesis of interest.
Bias.	A tendency to reach conclusions on the basis of personal preference rather than on a careful consideration of the evidence.
Big data.	Data sets that are too large or too complex for traditional data-processing applications.
Chain of custody.	The sequence of the persons or devices that had access to the original source evidence, the time at which they had such access, and what they did to the original evidence when they had access to it.
Chronology magnet.	Magnet that attracts inferred times at which reported events have occurred and allows

inferences about the temporal ordering of these events.

Circumstantial evidence.

Evidence that makes the existence of a hypothesis in an argument more or less probable "indirectly," in that at least one further inferential step is involved.

Clear and convincing evidence.

A standard of proof required in congressional hearings and other tribunals.

Competence.

Believability credential of human sources of evidence. A source of evidence is competent if she or he had access to what was reported and was able to understand it. Competence also refers to any skills a person might have to do some required job.

Composition.

Another term for *Synthesis*.

Conclusive evidence.

Evidence that, if believable, would make some conclusion certain.

Conjunction.

The combination of judgments about the probability of individual hypotheses into a single hypothesis as a whole, where *all* the individual hypotheses need to be true to make the single hypothesis true. See also *Disjunction*.

Connecting the dots.

Marshaling thoughts and evidence in the generation or discovery of productive hypotheses and new evidence, and in the construction of defensible and persuasive arguments on hypotheses we believe to be most favored by the evidence we have gathered and evaluated.

Contradictory evidence.

Type of dissonant evidence involving events that are mutually exclusive, that is, which cannot occur jointly. For example, one evidence item says that event E occurred while another evidence item says that event E did not occur.

Convergent evidence.

Two or more evidence items that concern different events that point toward or favor the same hypothesis.

Corroborative evidence.

Evidence that reports the same event.

Corroborative redundant evidence.

Repeated evidence about the same event.

Credential of evidence.

A property of evidence that needs to be established or justified. Three major credentials of evidence are relevance, believability or credibility, and inferential force or weight.

Credibility.	The extent to which an item of evidence or a source of evidence may be believed. On occasion, this term is wrongly equated with the term *reliability* which has a more restricted definition. As a credential of evidence, credibility has several different attributes that depend upon the form of evidence, whether it is tangible or testimonial.
Credibility attributes.	For tangible evidence, these attributes are authenticity, accuracy, and reliability. For testimonial evidence, these attributes are veracity, objectivity, and observational sensitivity.
Critical reasoning.	Reasoning represented by an argument that is logically coherent, free of disconnects and non sequiturs.
Cumulative redundant evidence.	Redundant evidence about different events.
Current intelligence.	Intelligence for cases in which an analyst's customer requires a conclusion in a very short time.
Data.	Uninterpreted signals, raw observations, or measurements, such as such as the number 6 or the color red. See also *Evidence and data or item of information.*
Deductive reasoning.	A form of reasoning that makes some conclusion necessarily true or certain.
Defensible and persuasive argument.	An argument that is both free from logical disconnects (defensible) and compelling (persuasive). The trouble is that not all persuasive arguments are defensible and not all defensible arguments persuasive.
Demonstrative tangible evidence.	Evidence not of a thing itself but of a representation or image of this thing.
Direction.	The hypothesis we believe our evidence favors most.
Directly relevant evidence.	Evidence for which a defensible chain of reasoning can be constructed that links this evidence with a hypothesis whose proof is at issue.
Discovery.	The process of generating new hypotheses or new lines of inquiry and new evidence.
Disjunction.	The combination of judgments about the probability of individual hypotheses into a single hypothesis as a whole, where *only one* of the individual hypotheses needs to be true to make the single hypothesis true.

Disfavoring evidence.	Evidence that argues against the truth of some hypothesis.
Dissonant evidence.	Directionally inconsistent items of evidence pointing toward different hypotheses.
Divergent evidence.	Type of dissonant evidence where the evidence points to different hypotheses, as opposed to contradictory evidence, which involves events that are mutually exclusive.
Divide and conquer.	The act of decomposing a complex reasoning task into its simpler ingredients and of combining their conclusions. See *Analysis* and *Synthesis*.
Dots.	Details in the observable information or data about an intelligence situation, as well as potential links in chains of reasoning or arguments we may construct to link dots to hypotheses we are trying to prove or disprove.
Eliminative induction.	A method of proof in which a variety of evidential tests are employed in an effort to eliminate alternative hypotheses being considered. The hypothesis that best resists our eliminative attempts is the one that can be taken most seriously.
Eliminative magnet.	Magnet that attracts trifles representing evidence relevant in showing why some hypothesis can be safely eliminated.
Epistemology.	A branch of philosophy concerning the acquisition and validity of knowledge.
Evidence.	Any observable sign, indicator, or datum we believe is relevant in deciding upon the extent to which we infer any hypotheses we have entertained as being correct or incorrect.
Evidence and data or items of information.	Evidence differs from data or items of information. Data or items of information become evidence only when their relevance is established regarding some matter to be proved or disproved.
Evidence and event.	There is an important distinction to be made between evidence of some event and the event itself. Having evidence that an event occurred does not entail that this event did occur. What is at issue is the believability of the evidence and its source(s).
Evidence-based hypothesis assessment.	The process of determining the probability of a hypothesis based on the available evidence.

Evidence custodian.

Person designated to keep careful records of every person who had access to an evidence item from the time it was received, what each person did with this item, how long that person held the item, and who next received the item before it was finally introduced at trial.

Evidence in search of hypotheses.

The "bottom-up" generation of a new hypothesis from evidence.

Evidential dots.

One of two forms of dots that must be connected. The other form of dots concerns ideas about the meaning of an evidential dot.

Evidentiary testing of hypothesis.

See *Evidence-based hypothesis assessment.*

Fact.

Any event or act or condition of things, assumed (for the moment) as having happened or having existed.

Favoring evidence.

Evidence that is directionally consistent in favoring the same hypothesis.

Force.

See *Inferential force or weight.*

Fuzzy probability system.

A probability system where the uncertainty about a conclusion reached is expressed in words (such as "likely" or "almost certain"), each "fuzzy" word being related to a range of numerical probabilities by a possibility function.

Generalization.

A general proposition claimed to be true that is used implicitly or explicitly to argue that a conclusion has been established.

Harmonious evidence.

Two or more items of evidence that are directionally consistent in the sense that they all point toward, or favor, the same hypothesis or possible conclusion.

Heuristic.

A rule of thumb that aids you in any discovery, inference, learning, or decision problem.

Holistic approach to analysis.

Work on an analysis problem where you do all the analysis in your own head without decomposing it in any way or seeking the assistance of others.

HUMINT.

Testimonial evidence given by a human source about some matter of intelligence interest.

Hypotheses magnet.

Magnet that uses generated hypotheses to attract information items that could become relevant evidence in favor of or against the hypotheses.

Hypothesis.	A general proposition put forward as a possible explanation for known facts from which additional investigations can be planned to generate evidential data that will tend to strengthen or weaken the basis for accepting the proposition as the best or strongest explanation of the available data. The term commonly refers to possible alternative conclusions we could entertain about matters of interest in an analysis.
Hypothesis in search of evidence.	The "top-down" discovery of evidence believed to be consistent with the hypothesis and therefore useful in testing this hypothesis.
Idea dots.	One of two types of dots that must be connected, having the form of links in chains of reasoning or arguments we construct to link evidential dots to hypotheses. The other type of dots are the evidential dots.
Imaginative reasoning.	See *Abductive reasoning.*
IMINT.	Tangible evidence gathered from satellite, aerial photography, or mapping/terrain data.
Inconclusive evidence.	Evidence that is consistent with the truth of more than one hypothesis or possible explanation.
Indirectly relevant evidence.	See *Ancillary evidence.*
Inductive reasoning.	A form of reasoning that makes some conclusion probably true, used to test hypotheses based on evidence.
Inference.	The process of deriving logical conclusions from premises.
Inference network.	Network consisting of multiple lines of argument that connect many different kinds of evidence to the hypothesis under consideration.
Inferential force or weight.	Credential of evidence indicating how strong the evidence is in favoring or disfavoring hypotheses we are considering.
Information.	Data equipped with meaning provided by a certain context, such as "6 A.M." or "$6." See also *Evidence and data or item of information.*
Knowledge.	Justified true belief. We say that Person A knows that event B occurred if the event B did occur (true), then Person A got nondefective evidence that B occurred (justified), and A believed this evidence (belief).

Likelihood.	Probability of evidence E* given some hypothesis H, written P(E*|H).
Likeliness.	Probability of hypothesis H given some evidence E*, written P(H|E*).
Marshaling.	Bringing together thoughts and evidence during hypotheses generation and argument construction. Having useful strategies for marshaling thus helps advance the processes of hypotheses generation and analysis.
Marshaling magnet.	A metaphoric description of an evidence marshaling operation that serves to attract particular combinations of evidence from some collection of data or trifles and that can assist in generating new hypotheses or that can open up new lines of inquiry and evidence.
MASINT.	Measures and signatures intelligence. Evidence of the traces left behind by objects and processes.
Meta-evidence.	See *Ancillary evidence.*
Nugget.	A term used by intelligence agencies with reference to believable or credible evidence that would make some conclusion certain.
Objectivity.	An attribute of the credibility of a human source characterizing the extent to which that source based his or her belief that the reported event occurred on his or her sensory evidence rather than on what this source expected or desired to observe.
Observational sensitivity.	An attribute of the credibility of a human source characterizing how good was the sensory evidence this source received under the conditions in which his or her observation was made.
Posterior belief.	Belief assessed after we receive and incorporate the evidence we have.
Posterior probability.	Probability of hypothesis after we receive and incorporate the evidence we have. See *Likeliness.*
Prior probability.	Probability used to indicate the initial conditions of our uncertainty before we consider evidence that begins to emerge.
Probability.	Measure of the uncertainty about a given event, statement, hypothesis, or conclusion. Differing conceptions of probability are a matter of considerable controversy and debate within statistics and the logic of proof.

Proposition.	A statement that is true or false, that can be affirmed or denied.
Question magnet.	Magnet that attracts trifles representing possible answers to any question that comes to mind as an intelligence analysis proceeds.
Real tangible evidence.	Evidence of the thing itself that can be directly examined.
Reduction.	See *Analysis*.
Redundant evidence.	Two or more evidence items that either say the same thing over again or do not add anything to what we already have.
Relevance.	Credential of evidence indicating how a datum or information item is linked to something we are trying to prove or disprove.
Relevant evidence.	Evidence having any tendency to make the existence of any fact that is of consequence to the determination of the action more probable or less probable than it would have been without the evidence (Federal Rule of Evidence 401).
Reliability.	The extent to which a system, sensor, or test of any kind provides results that are repeatable or consistent. Reliability is especially relevant to various forms of sensors that provide us with many forms of demonstrative tangible evidence. This term is often used incorrectly as a synonym for the term *credibility* or *believability,* which involves other attributes.
Scenario magnet.	Magnet that attracts a temporally ordered sequence of dots or trifles forming relevant evidence about events that will form the basis for a story or scenario about what has happened in some situation of interest.
SIGINT.	Signals intelligence used with reference to evidence obtained with sensors and recording devices.
Standard of proof.	The degree of persuasion required to establish a particular fact. The standard of proof in civil cases is typically "the preponderance of evidence" or "the balance of probabilities." In criminal cases, the prosecution has to satisfy the standard of "beyond reasonable doubt" in order to succeed. In some noncriminal cases, the standard of proof is said to be "clear and convincing."

Substance-blind.	A particular way of categorizing forms and combinations of evidence without regard to its substance or content. Such a categorization is based on the inferential properties of evidence and not on its content.
Synergistic evidence.	Two or more evidence items that have greater inferential force or weight than they would have if considered separately or independently.
Synthesis.	A reasoning operation by which we combine the assessments of the subhypotheses of a hypothesis in order to obtain an assessment of the hypothesis. This operation is complementary to analysis.
Tangible evidence.	Evidence that can be directly examined by persons drawing conclusions to see what event(s) this evidence reveals. Examples include objects, documents, images, measurements, and charts.
Task decomposition.	See *Analysis*.
Testimonial evidence.	Evidence provided by a human source. Testimonial evidence about some event can be based on direct observations, on secondhand reports from another source, or on opinion or inferences based on information about the occurrence of other events.
Trifles.	A term used by Sherlock Holmes to refer to the many details (dots) he observed that formed the basis for his investigations.
Understandability.	An attribute of the competence of a human source characterizing the extent to which that source understood what was being observed well enough to provide us with an intelligible account.
Veracity.	An attribute of the credibility of a human source characterizing the extent to which that source believes that the reported event occurred.
Weight of evidence.	See *Inferential force or weight*.

References

Allemang, D., and Hendler, J. (2011). *Semantic Web for the Working Ontologist: Effective Modeling in RDFS and Owl*, Morgan Kaufmann, Burlington, MA.

Anderson, T., Schum, D., and Twining, W. (2005). *Analysis of Evidence*, Cambridge University Press, New York, NY.

Baring-Gould, W. S. (1967). *The Annotated Sherlock Holmes*, vols. I and II, Clarkson N. Potter, New York, NY.

Betham, J. (1810). *An Introductory View of the Rationale of the Law of Evidence for Use by Non-Lawyers as Well as Lawyers* (vi works 1–187 [Bowring edition, 1837–43] originally edited by James Mill circa 1810).

Black, H. C. (1968). *Black's Law Dictionary*, 4th ed. West Publishing Co., St. Paul, MN.

Boicu, M., Tecuci, G., Marcu, D. (2012). Rapid Argumentation Capture from Analysis Reports: The Case Study of Aum Shinrikyo, in *Proceedings of the Seventh International Conference on Semantic Technologies for Intelligence, Defense, and Security – STIDS 2012*, Fairfax, VA, October 23–26. ceur-ws.org/Vol-966/STIDS2012_T05_BoicuEtAl_RapidArgumentation.pdf (accessed November 25, 2015)

Boicu, M., Tecuci, G., Marcu, D., Bowman, M., Shyr, P., Ciucu, F., and Levcovici, C. (2000). Disciple-COA: From Agent Programming to Agent Teaching, in *Proceedings of the Seventeenth International Conference on Machine Learning* (ICML), Stanford, CA, June 29–July 2, Morgan Kaufman, Stanford, CA. lac.gmu.edu/publications/data/2000/2000_il-final.pdf (accessed November 25, 2015)

Bruce, J. B. (2008). Making Analysis More Reliable: Why Epistemology Matters to Intelligence, in George, R. Z., and Bruce, J. B., eds., *Analyzing Intelligence: Origins, Obstacles, and Innovations*, Georgetown University Press, Washington, DC, pp. 184–185.

Chantrell, G., ed. (2004). *Oxford Dictionary of Word Histories*, Oxford University Press, Oxford, UK.

Clemen, R. T. (1995). *Making Hard Decisions*, Duxbury Press, Belmont, CA.

Cohen, L. J. (1977). *The Probable and the Provable*, Clarendon Press, Oxford, UK.

Cohen, L. J. (1989). *An Introduction to the Philosophy of Induction and Probability*, Clarendon Press, Oxford, UK.

Dale, A. (2003). *Most Honourable Remembrance: The Life and Work of Thomas Bayes*, Springer-Verlag, New York, NY.

Danzig, R., Sageman, M., Leighton, T., Hough, L., Yuki, H., Kotani, R., and Hosford Z. M. (2011). *Aum Shinrikyo: Insights into How Terrorists Develop Biological and Chemical Weapons*, Center for a New American Security, Washington, DC.

David, F. N. (1962). *Gods, Games and Gambling*, Griffin, London, UK.

Drogin, B. (2007). *CURVEBALL: Spies, Lies, and the Con Man Who Caused a War*, Random House, New York, NY.

George, R., and Bruce, J. B., eds. (2008). *Analyzing Intelligence: Origins, Obstacles, and Innovations*, Georgetown University Press, Washington, DC.

Heuer, R. J. (1999). *Psychology of Intelligence Analysis, Center for the Study of Intelligence*, Central Intelligence Agency, Washington, DC.

Heuer, R. J. (2008). Computer-Aided Analysis of Competing Hypotheses, in George, R. Z., and Bruce, J. B., eds., *Analyzing Intelligence: Origins, Obstacles, and Innovations*, Georgetown University Press, Washington, DC, pp. 251–265.

Hintikka, J. (1983). Sherlock Holmes Formalized, in Eco, U., and Sebeok, T., eds., *The Sign of Three: Dupin, Holmes, Peirce*, Indiana University Press, Bloomington, pp. 170–178.

Howe, M. (1999). *Genius Explained*, Cambridge University Press, Cambridge, UK.

Johnston, R. (2005). *Analytic Culture in the U. S. Intelligence Community*, Central Intelligence Agency, Washington, DC.

Kahneman, D., Slovic, P., and Tversky, A. (1982). *Judgment under Uncertainty: Heuristics and Biases*, Cambridge University Press, New York, NY.

Kahneman, D., and Tversky, A. (1974). Judgment under Uncertainty: Heuristics and Biases. *Science*, vol. 185 (September 27), pp. 1124–1131.

Kent, S. (1994). Words of Estimated Probability, in Steury, D. P., ed., *Sherman Kent and the Board of National Estimates: Collected Essays, Center for the Study of Intelligence*, Central Intelligence Agency, Washington, DC, pp. 151–166.

Kolmogorov, A. N. (1956). *Foundations of a Theory of Probability*, 2nd English ed. (1933), Chelsea, New York, NY, pp. 3–4.

Kolmogorov, A. N. (1969). The Theory of Probability, in Aleksandrov, A. D., Kolmogorov, A. N., and Lavrentiev, M. A., eds., *Mathematics: Its Content, Methods, and Meaning*, vol. 2, ch. XI, MIT Press, Cambridge, MA, pp. 231–264.

Lempert, R. O., Gross, S. R., and Liebman, J. S. (2000). *A Modern Approach to Evidence*, 3rd ed., West, St. Paul, MN, pp. 1146–1148.

Lindberg, C. A., ed. (2004). *The Oxford American Writer's Thesaurus*, Oxford University Press, Oxford, UK.

Marrin, S. (2011). *Improving Intelligence Analysis: Bridging the Gap between Scholarship and Practice*. Routlege, London, UK, and New York, NY.

Marrin, S., and Clemente, J. D. (2005). Improving Intelligence Analysis by Looking to the Medical Profession. *International Journal of Intelligence and CounterIntelligence*, vol. 18, no. 4, pp. 707–729.

Martin, D. C. (1980). *Wilderness of Mirrors*, Ballantine, New York, NY.

Meckl, S., Tecuci, G., Boicu, M., and Marcu, D. (2015). Towards an Operational Semantic Theory of Cyber Defense against Advanced Persistent Threats, in Laskey, K. B., Emmons, I., Costa, P. C. G., and Oltramari, A., eds., *Proceedings of the Tenth International Conference on Semantic Technologies for Intelligence, Defense, and Security - STIDS 2015*, pp. 58–65, Fairfax, VA, November 18–20. lac.gmu.edu/publications/2015/APT-LAC.pdf (accessed January 12, 2016)

Michalski, R. S., and Tecuci, G., eds. (1994). *Machine Learning: A Multistrategy Approach*, vol. IV, Morgan Kaufmann, San Mateo, CA.

Mueller, C. B., and Kirkpatrick, L. C. (2009). *Federal Rules of Evidence*, 2009 ed., West, St. Paul, MN.

Murphy, P. (2003). *Evidence, Proof, and Facts: A Book of Sources*, Oxford University Press, Oxford, UK, p. 1.

Negoita, C. V., and Ralescu, D. A. (1975). *Applications of Fuzzy Sets to Systems Analysis*, Wiley, New York.

Nilsson, N. J. (1971). *Problem Solving Methods in Artificial Intelligence*, McGraw-Hill, New York, NY.

Peirce, C. S. (1992 [1898]). *Reasoning and the Logic of Things. The Cambridge Conferences Lectures of 1898*, Ketner, K., ed., Harvard University Press, Cambridge, MA.

Peirce, C. S. (1955 [1901]). Abduction and Induction, 1901, in *Philosophical Writings of Peirce*, Buchler, J., ed., Dover, New York, NY, pp. 150–156.

Schum D. A. (1987). *Evidence and Inference for the Intelligence Analyst* (2 volumes), University Press of America, Lanham, MD.

Schum, D. A. (1989). Knowledge, Probability, and Credibility, *Journal of Behavioral Decision Making*, vol. 2, pp. 39–62.

Schum, D. A. (1991). Jonathan Cohen and Thomas Bayes on the Analysis of Chains of Reasoning, in Eells, E., and Maruszewski, T., eds., *Probability and Rationality: Studies on L. Jonathan Cohen's Philosophy of Science*, Editions Rodopi, Amsterdam, Netherlands, pp. 99–145.

Schum, D. A. (1999). Marshaling Thoughts and Evidence during Fact Investigation. *South Texas Law Review*, vol. 40, no. 2 (Summer), pp. 401–454.

Schum, D. A. (1994 [2001a]). *The Evidential Foundations of Probabilistic Reasoning*, Northwestern University Press, Evanston, IL.

Schum, D. A. (2001b). Species of Abductive Reasoning in Fact Investigation in Law. *Cardozo Law Review*, vol. 22, nos. 5–6, pp. 1645–1681.

Schum, D. A. (2011). Classifying Forms and Combinations of Evidence: Necessary in a Science of Evidence, in Dawid, P., Twining, W., and Vasilaki, eds., *Evidence, Inference and Enquiry*, British Academy, Oxford University Press, Oxford, UK, pp. 11–36.

Schum, D. A., and Morris, J. (2007). Assessing the Competence and Credibility of Human Sources of Evidence: Contributions from Law and Probability, *Law, Probability and Risk*, vol. 6, pp. 247–274.

Schum, D. A., Tecuci, G., and Boicu, M. (2009). Analyzing Evidence and Its Chain of Custody: A Mixed-Initiative Computational Approach, *International Journal of Intelligence and Counterintelligence*, vol. 22, pp. 298–319. lac.gmu.edu/publications/2009/Schum et al - Chain of Custody .pdf (accessed November 25, 2015)

Shafer, G. (1976). *A Mathematical Theory of Evidence*, Princeton University Press, Princeton, NJ.

Shafer, G. (1988). Combining AI and OR. *University of Kansas School of Business Working Paper No. 195*, April.

Simonite, T. (2013). Bill Gates: Software Assistants Could Help Solve Global Problems, *MIT Technology Review*, July 16. technologyreview.com/news/517171/bill-gates-software-assistants-could-help-solve-global-problems/ (accessed November 25, 2015)

Tecuci, G. (1988). Disciple: A Theory, Methodology and System for Learning Expert Knowledge, *Thèse de Docteur en Science*, University of Paris-South. lac.gmu.edu/publications/1988/TecuciG_PhD_Thesis.pdf (accessed November 25, 2015)

Tecuci, G. (1993). Plausible Justification Trees: A Framework for the Deep and Dynamic Integration of Learning Strategies. *Machine Learning Journal*, vol. 11, pp. 237–261. lac.gmu.edu/publications/1993/TecuciG_Plausible_Justification_Trees.pdf (accessed November 25, 2015)

Tecuci, G. (1998). *Building Intelligent Agents: An Apprenticeship Multistrategy Learning Theory, Methodology, Tool and Case Studies*. Academic Press, London, UK. lac.gmu.edu/publications/1998/TecuciG_Building_Intelligent_Agents/default.htm (accessed November 25, 2015)

Tecuci, G., and Keeling, H. (1999). Developing an Intelligent Educational Agent with Disciple. *International Journal of Artificial Intelligence in Education*, vol. 10, no. 3–4. lac.gmu.edu/publications/1999/TecuciG_Intelliget_Educational_Agent.pdf (accessed November 25, 2015)

Tecuci, G., and Kodratoff, Y., eds. (1995). *Machine Learning and Knowledge Acquisition: Integrated Approaches*, Academic Press, London, UK. lac.gmu.edu/publications/1995/TecuciG_MLKA_Integrated_Approaches.pdf (accessed November 25, 2015)

Tecuci, G., and Michalski, R. S. (1991). A Method for Multistrategy Task-adaptive Learning Based on Plausible Justifications, in Birnbaum, L., and Collins, G., eds., *Machine Learning: Proceedings of the Eighth International Conference*, pp. 549–553, Chicago, IL, June, Morgan Kaufmann, San Mateo, CA. lac.gmu.edu/publications/1991/TecuciG_Multistrategy_Learning_Method.pdf (accessed November 25, 2015)

Tecuci, G., Boicu, M., Wright, K., Lee, S. W., Marcu, D., and Bowman, M. (1999). An Integrated Shell and Methodology for Rapid Development of Knowledge-Based Agents, in *Proceedings of the Sixteenth National Conference on Artificial Intelligence* (AAAI-99), Orlando, FL, July 18–22, AAAI Press, Menlo Park, CA. lac.gmu.edu/publications/data/1999/ismrdkba.pdf (accessed November 25, 2015).

Tecuci, G., Boicu, M., Wright, K., Lee, S. W., Marcu, D., and Bowman, M. (2000). A Tutoring Based Approach to the Development of Intelligent Agents, in Teodorescu, H. N., Mlynek, D., Kandel, A., and Zimmermann, H. J., eds., *Intelligent Systems and Interfaces*, Kluwer Academic Press, Boston, MA. lac.gmu.edu/publications/data/2000/2000_Disciple-Planning.pdf (accessed November 25, 2015)

Tecuci, G., Boicu, M., Bowman, M., and Marcu, D., with commentary by Burke, M. (2001). An Innovative Application from the DARPA Knowledge Bases Programs: Rapid Development of a Course of Action Critiquer, *AI Magazine*, vol. 22, no. 2, pp. 43–61. lac.gmu.edu/publications/2001/TecuciG_Disciple_COA_IAAI.pdf (accessed November 25, 2015)

Tecuci, G., Boicu, M., Marcu, D., Stanescu, B., Boicu, C., Comello, J., Lopez, A., Donlon, J., and Cleckner, W. (2002a) Development and Deployment of a Disciple Agent for Center of Gravity Analysis, in *Proceedings of the Eighteenth National Conference of Artificial Intelligence and the Fourteenth Conference on Innovative Applications of Artificial Intelligence*, AAAI-02/IAAI-02, pp. 853–860, Edmonton, Alberta, Canada, AAAI Press, Menlo Park, CA/MIT Press, Boston, MA. lac.gmu.edu/publications/data/2002/dddacga.pdf (accessed November 25, 2015)

Tecuci, G., Boicu, M., Marcu, D., Stanescu, B., Boicu, C., Comello, J. (2002b). Training and Using Disciple Agents: A Case Study in the Military Center of Gravity Analysis Domain, *AI Magazine*, vol. 24, no. 4, pp. 51–68, AAAI Press, Menlo Park, CA. lac.gmu.edu/publications/2002/TecuciG_Disciple_COG_IAAI.pdf (accessed November 25, 2015)

Tecuci G., Boicu M., Ayers C., and Cammons D. (2005a). Personal Cognitive Assistants for Military Intelligence Analysis: Mixed-Initiative Learning, Tutoring, and Problem Solving, *in Proceedings of the First International Conference on Intelligence Analysis*, McLean, VA, May 2–6. lac.gmu.edu/publications/data/2005/Tecuci-Disciple-LTA.pdf (accessed November 25, 2015)

Tecuci, G., Boicu, M., Boicu, C., Marcu, D., Stanescu, B., and Barbulescu, M. (2005b). The Disciple-RKF Learning and Reasoning Agent. *Computational Intelligence*, vol. 21, no. 4, pp. 462–479. lac.gmu.edu/publications/2005/TecuciG_Disciple_RKF_CI.pdf (accessed November 25, 2015)

Tecuci, G., Boicu, M., and Comello, J. (2008b). *Agent-Assisted Center of Gravity Analysis*, CD with Disciple-COG and Lecture Notes used in courses at the U.S. Army War College and Air War College, George Mason University Press, Fairfax, VA. lac.gmu.edu/cog-book/ (accessed November 25, 2015)

Tecuci, G., Boicu, M., and Cox, M. T. (2007a). Seven Aspects of Mixed-Initiative Reasoning: An Introduction to the Special Issue on Mixed-Initiative Assistants. *AI Magazine*, vol. 28, no. 2, pp. 11–18. www.aaai.org/ojs/index.php/aimagazine/issue/view/174/showToc (accessed May 29, 2015)

Tecuci, G., Boicu, M., Marcu, D., Boicu, C., Barbulescu, M., Ayers, C., and Cammons, D. (2007b). Cognitive Assistants for Analysts. *Journal of Intelligence Community Research and Development (JICRD)*. Also published in Auger, John, and Wimbish, William, eds., (2007) *Proteus Futures Digest: A Compilation of Selected Works Derived from the 2006 Proteus Workshop*, Joint publication of the National Intelligence University, Office of the Director of National Intelligence, Tysons Corner, VA, and U.S. Army War College Center for Strategic Leadership, Carlisle, PA, pp. 303–329. lac.gmu.edu/publications/2007/TecuciG_Cognitive_Assistants.pdf (accessed November 25, 2015)

Tecuci, G., Boicu, M., Marcu, D., Boicu, C., and Barbulescu, M. (2008a). Disciple-LTA: Learning, Tutoring and Analytic Assistance, *Journal of Intelligence Community Research and Development (JICRD)*, July. lac.gmu.edu/publications/2008/Disciple-LTA08.pdf (accessed November 25, 2015)

Tecuci, G., Boicu, M., Marcu, D., and Schum, D. (2013b). How Learning Enables Intelligence Analysts to Rapidly Develop Practical Cognitive Assistants, in *Proceedings of the 12th International Conference on Machine Learning and Applications* (ICMLA'13), Miami, FL, December 4–7. lac.gmu.edu/publications/2013/LAC-ICMLA-13.pdf (accessed November 25, 2015)

Tecuci, G., Marcu, D., Boicu, M., Schum, D. A., and Russell K. (2011a). Computational Theory and Cognitive Assistant for Intelligence Analysis, in Costa, P. C. G., and Laskey, K., eds., *Proceedings of the Sixth International Conference on Semantic Technologies for Intelligence, Defense, and Security – STIDS* 2011, pp. 68–75, Fairfax, VA, November 16–18. CEUR Workshop Proceedings, Fairfax, VA. ceur-ws.org/Vol-808/STIDS2011_CR_T9_TecuciEtAl.pdf (accessed May 29, 2015)

Tecuci, G., Marcu, D., Boicu, M., and Schum, D. A. (2016). *Knowledge Engineering: Building Cognitive Assistants for Evidence-based Reasoning*, Cambridge University Press, New York, NY.

Tecuci, G., Boicu, M., Marcu, D., Barbulescu, M., Boicu, C., Le, V., and Hajduk, T. (2008c). Teaching Virtual Experts for Multi-Domain Collaborative Planning. *Journal of Software*, vol. 3, no. 3 (March), pp. 38–59. lac.gmu.edu/publications/2008/TecuciG_Disciple_VE_JS.pdf (accessed November 25, 2015)

Tecuci, G., Schum, D. A., Boicu, M., Marcu, D., Hamilton, B., and Wible, B. (2010). Teaching Intelligence Analysis with TIACRITIS, *American Intelligence Journal*, vol. 28, no. 2 (December), pp. 50–65. lac.gmu.edu/publications/2010/Tiacritis-AIJ.pdf (accessed November 25, 2015)

Tecuci, G., Schum, D. A., Boicu, M., and Marcu, D. (2011b). *Introduction to Intelligence Analysis: A Hands-on Approach with TIACRITIS*, 2nd ed. Learning Agents Center, George Mason University, Fairfax, VA. lac.gmu.edu/publications/2011/TecuciG_Introduction_Intelligence_Analysis.pdf (accessed November 25, 2015)

Tecuci, G., Schum, D. A., Marcu, D., and Boicu, M. (2013a). Recognizing and Countering Biases in Intelligence Analysis with TIACRITIS, in Laskey, K. B., Emmons, I., and Costa, P. C. G., eds., *Proceedings of the Eighth International Conference on Semantic Technologies for Intelligence,*

Defense, and Security – STIDS 2013, Fairfax, VA, November 13–14. CEUR Workshop Proceedings, Fairfax, VA. ceur-ws.org/Vol-1097/STIDS2013_T04_TecuciEtAl.pdf (accessed May 29, 2015)

Tecuci, G., Schum, D. A., Marcu, D., and Boicu, M. (2014). Computational Approach and Cognitive Assistant for Evidence-based Reasoning in Intelligence Analysis. *International Journal of Intelligent Defence Support Systems*, vol. 5, no. 2, pp. 146–172. lac.gmu.edu/publications/2014/Disciple-CD-IJIDSS.pdf (accessed November 25, 2015)

Toulmin, S. E. (1963). *The Uses of Argument*, Cambridge University Press, Cambridge, UK.

Van Gelder, T. J. (2007). The Rationale for Rationale, *Law, Probability and Risk*, vol. 6, pp. 23–42. https://sites.google.com/site/timvangelder/publications-1/therationaleforrationale (accessed February 11, 2016)

Wigmore, J. H. (1913). The Problem of Proof, *Illinois Law Review*, vol. 8, no. 2, pp. 77–103.

Wigmore, J. H. (1937). *The Science of Judicial Proof: As Given by Logic, Psychology, and General Experience and Illustrated in Judicial Trials*, 3rd ed., Little, Brown, Boston, MA.

Wigmore, J. H. (1940). *Treatise on the Anglo-American System of Evidence in Trials at Common Law* (usually referred to as *Wigmore on Evidence*), vol. 7, 3rd ed., Little, Brown, Boston, MA..

W3C (2015). Semantic Web. www.w3.org/standards/semanticweb/ (accessed November 25, 2015)

Zadeh, L. (1983). The Role of Fuzzy Logic in the Management of Uncertainty in Expert Systems, *Fuzzy Sets and Systems*, vol. 11, pp. 199–227.

Appendixes

3   OPERATIONS WITH DISCIPLE-CD

Index